WORKS of
ST. BONAVENTURE X

WRITINGS

ON THE SPIRITUAL LIFE

Bonaventure
Texts in Translation
Series

General Editor
Robert J. Karris, O.F.M.

Volume X

Writings on the Spiritual Life

WORKS of
ST. BONAVENTURE

WRITINGS ON THE SPIRITUAL LIFE

Introductions and Notes
by F. Edward Coughlin, O.F.M.

Franciscan Institute Publications
The Franciscan Institute
Saint Bonaventure University
Saint Bonaventure, NY 14778
2006

Library of Congress Cataloging-in-Publication Data

Bonaventure, Saint, Cardinal, ca. 1217-1274.
  [Selections. English. 2006]
  Writings on the spiritual life / introductions and annotated
    notes [by] F. Edward Coughlin. p. cm. -- (Works of St.
    Bonaventure)
Includes bibliographical references and indexes.
ISBN: 1-57659-162-X (alk. paper)
1. Spirituality--Catholic Church.. 2. Catholic Church--
Doctrines. 3. Spiritual life--Catholic Church. I. Coughlin, F.
Edward. II. title.

BX2179.B47E5 2006

248.4'82--dc22

2006032361

Printed in the United States of America
Bookmasters, Inc.
Ashland, Ohio

CONTENTS

PREFACE

This volume contains selected spiritual and theological texts by St. Bonaventure. The texts included are: *The Threefold Way, On the Perfection of Life, On Governing the Soul, The Soliloquium: A Dialogue on the Four Spiritual Exercises.* An appendix includes four additional texts that provide some important and helpful clarifications on aspects of the Seraphic Doctor's theology of the spiritual life found in this volume. It includes: the prologue to the *Commentary on Book II of the Sentences* of Peter Lombard and three short sermons: "On the Way of Life," "On Holy Saturday," and "On the Monday after Palm Sunday."

In keeping with the original intention of the series, this volume makes available important Bonaventurian texts in English-language translations. The general introduction to this volume limits itself to providing a summary overview of the theology of the spiritual life as articulated by St. Bonaventure. In addition, each text is preceded by a brief introduction. Notes that explain or define some of Bonaventure's key concepts as well as cross-references to related passages in other Bonaventurian texts are provided. Presuming that many of those who would be most interested in these texts may not have facility with a variety of languages, English-language sources and scholarship have been used wherever possible.

Bonaventure: The Soul's Journey into God, The Tree of Life, and The Life of St. Francis was published in 1978 in the Classics of Western Spirituality Series. Translated and edited by Dr. Ewert Cousins, the volume included an introduction to the life of St. Bonaventure and the works of Bonaventure in general as well as the three texts. The goals and size limits imposed by the Classics of Western Spirituality Series forced Cousins to select a limited number of texts that "clearly qualified as classics both because of their content and because they have been acknowledged as such by their acceptance and influence."[1] Cousins presented the volume with the expressed hope that the three texts selected would "together present an integral picture of Franciscan Spirituality as Bonaventure perceived it."[2] In realizing his goal, Dr. Cousins made an invaluable contribution to the retrieval of important texts from the Franciscan-Bonaventurian spiritual tradition.

In a sense, this present volume continues the work begun by Ewert Cousins. It begins with a translation of *The Threefold Way,* the one addition Cousins would have liked to include in the *Bonaventure* volume.[3] As Cousins put it: *"The Threefold Way* qualifies as a classic since it contains one of the most significant studies of the three stages of spiritual development ... which have become accepted in Western spirituality as the classical way of formulating the dynamics of spiritual growth."[4]

Within the Franciscan tradition in particular, other texts of Bonaventure have long been recognized as classics. They have been afforded a certain normative status in that they "disclose a compelling truth" about the human spirit and the journey into God within the tradition inspired by St. Francis.[5]

Each of these texts invites the reader to a deeper understanding of Bonaventure's thought. Addressed to

---

[1] Ewert Cousins, *Bonaventure: The Soul's Journey into God, The Tree of Life and The Life of St. Francis,* CWS (Mahwah, NJ: Paulist Press, 1978), 12.

[2] Cousins, 12.

[3] Cousins, 16.

[4] Cousins, 16.

[5] David Tracy, *The Analogical Imagination* (New York: Crossroad, 1981), 108, 68, 14, and the whole of Chapter 5: "The Religious Classic," 193-229. This topic will be treated at greater length in section IV of this introduction.

individuals in differing contexts – a professed friar-priest, a community of Poor Clares, a laywoman, or individuals who had no theological training – all the texts reflect his theology of the spiritual life in different but interrelated ways. Read in the light of each other, the different texts clarify and demonstrate the depth as well as the breadth of his thought. They also reflect Bonaventure's desire to encourage every man and woman, friar or lay person, to respond personally to the gift of grace and make the spiritual journey into God. Considered as a whole, the texts demonstrate Bonaventure's creative capacity to invite others to strive for the perfection of love.

In conjunction with Cousins's *Bonaventure* volume, all of Bonaventure's primary works addressing his theology of the spiritual life are now available in English-language translations. Readers who are unfamiliar with Bonaventure's theology of the spiritual life are encouraged to read Zachary Hayes' essay entitled "Bonaventure" in *The History of Franciscan Theology* and Dominic Monti's introduction to the *Writings Concerning the Franciscan Order*. A more extensive, helpful, and in-depth treatment of Bonaventure's Christology and many of the interrelated dimensions of the Seraphic Doctor's theology of the spiritual life may be found in *The Hidden Center: Spirituality and Speculative Christology in St. Bonaventure* by Zachary Hayes. *Bonaventure: Mystical Writings* by Zachary Hayes is also highly recommended.

The publication of this volume affords members of the Franciscan family a unique opportunity to express a word of thanks to Kevin Lynch, CSP, former President and Publisher of the Paulist Press, as well as to the Editorial Board of the Classics of Western Spirituality Series. In addition to the *Bonaventure* volume, the Series has included *Francis and Clare: The Complete Works* (1982), *Jacopone da Todi* (1982), *Francisco de Osuna: The Third Spiritual Alphabet* (1981), and *Angela of Foligno: The*

Complete Works (1993). While the series as a whole has contributed a great deal toward a better understanding of a wide variety of sources, Franciscans are deeply grateful for the gift this series has been toward the ready availability of a rich variety of sources from their own spiritual tradition. In the English-speaking world, these volumes have served as the primary door though which many, at long last, have access to these texts.

Zachary Hayes, OFM
2005

FOREWORD

I would like to thank Dr. Girard (Jerry) Etzkorn for his "labor of love" in completing these translations. After many years of dedicated work as a member of the Franciscan Institute's research team that completed the critical edition of Ockham's theological and philosophical works as well as began work on the critical edition of Scotus's philosophical works, he responded graciously to my request to undertake this translation project as the first of the many projects he had waited patiently to pursue through the "gift of his freedom" in retirement. It is but one of the many projects he has completed as he continues his, as yet, elusive search for a hole in one!

In the preparation of these texts for publication Jerry and I frequently turned to Zachary Hayes, OFM, for his advice and suggestions in an effort to find a better or more adequate way to express Bonaventure's thought in English to individuals in significantly different times. As always, Zachary responded with great generosity and patience. He made many helpful suggestions with gracious good humor. I acknowledge gratefully the assistance of Giles Bello, OFM, Michael Blastic, OFM, and Dr. Timothy J. Johnson in particular for reviewing and making helpful suggestions as this work progressed and evolved. I want to thank Dr. Oleg Bychkov for his translation of one of the sermons included in the Appendix. I want also to acknowledge gratefully Robert Karris, OFM, for his very generous assistance in translating Bonaventure's quotations of Sacred Scripture from the Latin Vulgate text, in locating innumerable references, and for his translation of two of the sermons included in the Appendix. The knowledge, experience, generosity, and insightful critiques of these and other individuals contributed much to this volume. For any of the volume's inadequacies or limitations, I take full responsibility.

In Bonaventure's Franciscan vision of Gospel life, I have found inspiration, guidance, consolation, many challenges both academic and personal, as well as the encouragement to continue my personal search for wisdom, to better understand the demands of Gospel love, and to hope joyfully for those things for which my heart yearns.

I pursued this project with the sincere hope that many in the English-speaking world would have more ready access to the Seraphic Doctor's theology of the spiritual life. Along the way, I found great encouragement and assistance, for which I am deeply grateful, from three friends in particular, Kathleen Moffatt, OSF, Elise Saggau, OSF, and Noel Riggs. I also hope that, despite the challenges of completing this work, a variety of men and women, Franciscan brothers and sisters in particular, will have an opportunity to learn more of the enduring wisdom in the works of St. Bonaventure found in this volume.

F. Edward Coughlin, OFM
July 15, 2006

ABBREVIATIONS

ACW	Ancient Christian Writers
CA:ED	*The Lady Clare of Assisi: Early Documents*. Revised Edition and Translation by Regis Armstrong. New York: New City Press, 2006.
CCSL	*Corpus Christianorum*. Series Latina.
CCSL xiv	*Sancti Ambrosii Mediolanensis Opera Pars IV Expositio Evangelii secundum Lucam. Fragamenta in Esaiam*. Edited by M. Adriaen. Turnhout: Brepols, 1957.
CCSL lxxii	*S. Hieronymi Presbyteri Opera Pars I Opera Exegetica 1: Hebraicae Quaestiones in Libro Geneseos, Liber Interpretationis Hebraicorum Nominum, Commentarioli in Psalmos, Commentarius in Ecclesiasten*. Edited by P. Antin. Turnhout: Brepols, 1955.
CCSL cxx	*Bedae Venerabilis Opera Pars* II *Opera Exegetica 3: In Lucae Evangelium Expositio. In Marci Evangelium Expositio*. Edited by D. Hurst. Turnhout: Brepols, 1955.
CSEL	*Corpus Scriptorum Ecclesiasticorum Latinorum*.
CFS	Cistercian Fathers Series
CSS	Cistercian Studies Series
FA:ED	*Francis of Assisi, Early Documents*. Volume I: The Saint. Edited by Regis Armstrong, J.A. Wayne Hellmann, William Short. New York: New City Press, 1999.

FC	Fathers of the Church
GGHG	Gregory the Great's Homilies on the Gospel.
Glossa Ordinaria	*Sacrorum Bibliorum cum Glossa Ordinaria…. Tomus Quintus*. Lugduni: 1590.
Hurst	*Gregory the Great: Forty Gospel Homilies*. Translated from the Latin by Dom David Hurst. CSS 123; Kalamazoo: Cistercian Publications, 1990.
LChC	Library of Christian Classics
Morals	*Morals on the Book of Job*. Library of the Fathers of the Holy Catholic Church. Oxford: J.H. Parker, 1844-1850. Volumes I-VI.
NAB	New American Bible
NPNF 1 / 2	Nicene and Post-Nicene Fathers, First or Second Series. Edited by Philip Schaff. Peabody, MA: Hendrickson, 1994-1995. Reprint of 1888/93 editions.
Opera Omnia	*S. Bonaventurae Opera Omnia*. Edited by PP. Collegii a S. Bonaventura. Ad Claras Aquas (Quaracchi): Collegium S. Bonaventurae, 1882-1902. There are nine volumes of text in the series and one volume of indices. The volume number is followed by the page number, e.g., V: 24.
On Consideration	*Pope Eugene, Five Books on Consideration, Advice to a Pope*. CFS, 13. Kalamazoo: Cistercian Publications, 1976.

PL	*Patrologiae Cursus Completus.* Series Latina. Ed. J. P. Minge.
QuarEd	The editors who produced the text and the notes for Bonaventure's Opera Omnia.
SBOp	*Sancti Bernardi Opera* I-VIII. Edited by J. Leclercq and H. M. Rochais with the assistance of C. H. Talbot for Volumes I-II. Rome: Editiones Cisterciensis, 1957-1977.
SBSermons	*St. Bernard's Sermons for the Seasons and Principal Festivals of the Year.* Volumes 1-3. Translated from the original Latin by a Priest of Mount Melleray. Westminster, MD: Carroll Press, 1950.
Vulgate	*Biblia Sacra iuxta Vulgatum Versionem.* Adiuvantibus B. Fisher, I. Gribmont (†), H.F.D. Sparks, W. Thiele recensit et brevi apparatus critico instruxit Robertus Weber editionem quartam emendatam cum sociis B. Fisher, H. I. Frede, H. F. D. Sparks, W. Thiele praeparavit Roger Gryson. Stuttgart: Deutsche Bibelgesellschatt, 1969, 4th ed. 1994.
WBC	Works of St. Bernard of Clairvaux
WSA	Works of St. Augustine
WSB	Works of St. Bonaventure

Introduction

The Journey of the Heart
into Wisdom

In her memoir *Ordinary Time*, Nancy Mairs describes herself as a "wanton Gospeller."[1] She asserts that her essays are a "search into the ways one woman deals with God's presence day after day." Throughout her slim book, Mairs focuses her attention on a few practical questions: "What does it mean to live in the presence of God? Present to God? What responsibilities do I bear for the creation of my life? What choices must I make to sustain it?" While she sets out to write a kind of spiritual-autobiography, she also flatly states that, among other things, her book is not a "cookbook for conversion." After all, she says, "in describing life's ambiguities, each of us is bound to get at least one point wrong." One can assume that Mairs' book will never achieve anything near the perennial significance of Augustine's *Confessions* or the contemporary popularity of Thomas Merton's *Seven Storey Mountain*. Rather, the significance of her work lies in her willingness to explore honestly the central questions of every woman or man's spiritual life – the journey of the heart into God. While some have written insightfully of their personal struggles and experience, others have written to encourage, instruct, and assist those who were wrestling with those questions.

In the person of St. Bonaventure, the Franciscan spiritual tradition has been blessed with a gifted guide

---

[1] Nancy Mairs, *Ordinary Time*: *Cycles of Marriage, Faith and Renewal* (Boston: Beacon Press, 1993), see pages 7-12 in particular.

toward understanding what it means to live in the presence of God day after day. Each of his works, whether they are categorized as works of theology, asceticism, spirituality, or mysticism invite the reader to make the spiritual journey into the wisdom that comes through true experience as envisioned by the Seraphic Doctor. Despite the diversity of these works, the variety of forms they take, and the different audiences to which they were first addressed – friars, sisters, laity – the Seraphic Doctor seems always to be urging everyone to believe, to understand, to contemplate, and to become enflamed with the love of the triune God.

The introduction to this volume of Bonaventurian texts in translation will seek to provide: (I) a brief introduction to the person of St. Bonaventure, (II) a sense of his understanding of how the human person is made in the image of God and is empowered to become a greater likeness to Christ, (III) an overview of Bonaventure's understanding of the threefold journey of the heart into wisdom, (IV) comments on the challenges of interpreting spiritual classics as well as information on the methodology used in the preparation of this volume of texts in translation, and (V) summary comments on the implications of Bonaventure's theology of the spiritual life as a resource for spiritual pilgrims in different ages.

Parts II and III of this introduction were written with the intention of providing some basic information and foundational orientations for readers who may be unfamiliar with Bonaventure's theology of the spiritual life. A deliberate effort has also been made to use the words of the Seraphic Doctor himself to acquaint the reader with his language and style as an aid to reading the texts and better grasping his intended meaning.

Bonaventure's conceptual categories and classical world-view are steeped in the richness of the Christian tradition. It is a tradition to which he made a significant and creative contribution. Later generations of scholars and spiritual pilgrims would subsequently find in the Seraphic Doctor "a significant theologian of the past to be a partner in conversation; a partner whose efforts may help shed light on our present situation."[2]

I: Bonaventure: Disciple, Teacher, Mystical Theologian

Bonaventure played a significant role in the early development of the Franciscan theological tradition. Given the more extensive treatments of his life, work, and significance within the Order and the Church that are available elsewhere, a few summary observations will suffice here.

First, he entered the Franciscan Order in Paris sometime between 1238 and 1243.[3] He was quickly recognized as one of the most intellectually outstanding followers of the poor man from Assisi. In a rare personal reference, he indicated that what "made me love St. Francis' way of life" was the belief that, as in the early Church, the Order grew and "proved to be God's doing" when wise men – illustrious and learned doctors – joined the company of "simple folk."[4]

---

[2] Zachary Hayes, *The Hidden Center: Spirituality and Speculative Christology in St. Bonaventure* (NY: The Franciscan Institute, 1993, 1981), 2.

[3] It is difficult to reconstruct the chronology of St. Bonaventure due to a lack of reliable information. See Jacques Guy Bougerol, *Introduction to the Works of Bonaventure*, trans. José de Vinck (Paterson, NJ: St. Anthony's Guild, 1964), 171-77; Theodore Crowley, "St. Bonaventure Chronology Reappraisal," *Franziskanische Studien* (1974): 310-22.

[4] Bonaventure, "Letter in Response to Three Questions of an Unknown Master," n. 13, in *Writings Concerning the Franciscan Order*, trans. Dominic Monti, *Works of St. Bonaventure* V (St. Bonaventure,

Second, Bonaventure was an outstanding teacher and preacher. Following in the footsteps of some of the Franciscan Order's earliest masters that included among others Alexander of Hales and John of La Rochelle, Bonaventure began lecturing on the Bible in 1248 and later on the *Sentences* of Peter Lombard. Although the dates are difficult to determine precisely, it is probable that Bonaventure received the license to teach in 1254/55 and served as regent master at the Franciscan house in Paris from 1254 until the time of his election as Minister General.[5] In his capacity as *magister*, Bonaventure would have been charged with the threefold responsibility of "'reading' Sacred Scripture, 'disputing' theological questions, and 'preaching' before the university body."[6] His formal teaching career abruptly ended in 1257, however, when he was elected the seventh minister general of the Order.

Third, Bonaventure was a creative pastoral leader. He put the depths of his own faith experience and the theology of the schools in the service of the pastoral needs of the rapidly growing Franciscan movement. For example, as Minister General, he played a significant role in the organization and subsequent chapter approval of the

NY: The Franciscan Institute, 1994), 54. See also Bonaventure's *The Major Legend of St. Francis*, (pro. 3), in *Francis of Assisi: Early Documents* II, ed. Regis Armstrong, J.A. Wayne Hellmann, and William Short (NY; New City Press, 2000), 528. Hereafter, this series will be referred to as FA:ED, with appropriate volume number and page. In *The Major Legend* Bonaventure makes reference to his personal devotion to Francis, having been "snatched from the jaws of death by his invocation and merits" during a boyhood illness.

[5] Due to controversies at the university, Bonaventure was not formally awarded the doctoral degree and given full recognition as a master until October 23, 1257, a few months after his election as Minister General.

[6] Ignatius Brady, "St. Bonaventure's Doctrine of Illumination: Reactions Medieval and Modern," in *Bonaventure and Aquinas: Enduring Philosophers,* R. Shahan and F. Kovach eds. (Norman, OK: University of Oklahoma Press, 1976), 59.

Constitutions of Narbonne (1260). As Dominic Monti notes, he organized the *Constitutions* "around topical quotations from the Rule." It was a practical way of encouraging the friars to "approach their constitutions not simply as a random bunch of laws, but as the systematic application of the Order's foundational document in concrete terms for their current situation."[7] These constitutions and his Major Life of St. Francis (1263) would, in fact, according to Monti, shape the "ideals and life of the brotherhood for generations to come."[8]

From another perspective, the *Disputed Questions on Evangelical Perfection* (1257) and the *Defense of the Mendicants* (1269) are two examples of Bonaventure's ability and readiness to address those external critics who questioned openly the Order's Mendicant-Franciscan identity and even its existence. In a similar way, works like *The Collations on the Seven Gifts of the Holy Spirit* (1268) and the unfinished *Collations on the Six Days of Creation* (1273) demonstrate his willingness to involve himself in some of the most significant theological-philosophical questions of his time with clarity and theological insight.

Bonaventure's creative pastoral leadership is perhaps most evident in his works of spiritual, ascetical, and mystical theology. As the texts found in this volume demonstrate, he seemed eager to take advantage of different opportunities to instruct and encourage a friar, the sisters, a lay woman, and others to open themselves to God's graced-filled presence in their lives, to know through experience God's Wisdom, and to strive to live in the love which is God as best they could. Many of these texts were afforded normative status as classic texts toward which

---

[7] "Constitutions of Narbonne," *Writings Concerning the Franciscan Order*, 73-74.

[8] *Writings Concerning the Franciscan Order*, 71.

successive generations of Franciscans and others turned
in search of understanding and wisdom.

II: The Human Person
Made in the image of God ...
Called to become a greater likeness to Christ

In his fifth admonition, Francis of Assisi challenges everyone to "Consider ... in what excellence the Lord God has placed you for [God] created you and formed you to the image of [God's] beloved Son according to the body, and to [God's] likeness according to the Spirit." He concludes the admonition by inviting all women and men to "glory in our infirmities and in bearing daily the holy cross of our Lord Jesus Christ."[10]

The ancient wisdom at the heart of this admonition became a central theme in the Franciscan theological tradition. It played a prominent role in the theology of Alexander of Hales, Bonaventure, John Duns Scotus, and others. Through the ongoing theological reflection of these and other early theologians within the tradition, this doctrine acquired some distinctively Franciscan characteristics. In Bonaventure's theology of the spiritual life, for example, a correct understanding of the noble dignity of the person "made in the image of God" is a key to understanding how "God is so present to [the soul] that it actually grasps God and potentially 'has the capacity for God and the ability to participate in God.'"[11]

In this section, attention will be focused on Bonaventure's medieval-Franciscan understanding of what it means to be "made in the image of God" – an embodied and rational soul. A measure of familiarity with

---

[10] Francis of Assisi, *The Fifth Admonition* (FA:ED I, 131). Paul's letter to the Corinthians (2 Corinthians 12:5) provides the key scriptural reference for interpreting Francis's understanding of human infirmity (*infirmitas*), physical weakness.

[11] *Itinerarium Mentis in Deum*, ch. III, n. 2, in Works of St. Bonaventure II, trans. Zachary Hayes, Introduction and Commentary by Philotheus Boehner (St. Bonaventure, NY: Franciscan Institute Publications, 2002), 83. Hereafter, *Itinerarium*.

some of his conceptual categories and distinctions will provide the basis for better grasping his understanding of the dynamic and ongoing processes through which the person as an image of God, in cooperation with grace, is invited and empowered to become a greater likeness to Christ through knowledge, love, and free choice.[12] To put it another way, a measure of familiarity with some of his conceptual categories and distinctions will provide the necessary foundation for better understanding how the rational soul, "of its own accord," is made to "*praise God, serve God, find delight* in God, and be at rest in God."[13] This section is divided into three parts to offer a working knowledge of key aspects of the Seraphic Doctor's understanding of (A) the nature of the embodied and rational creature, (B) the reality of sin, and (C) the gift of grace.

The Human Person: Formed Right and Upright

The human person – rational creature – was fashioned by God from "two natures that were the maximum distance from each other," that is, a body (*caro*) that is a corporal substance and a soul (*mens*) that is a spiritual and immaterial substance.[14] Formed right and upright,

---

[12] *On the Reduction of the Arts to Theology*, n. 12, in *Works of Saint Bonaventure* I, trans. Zachary Hayes (St. Bonaventure, NY: The Franciscan Institute, 1996), 51.

[13] *On the Reduction of the Arts to Theology*, n. 14 (Hayes, 52-53). See also Francis of Assisi, *The Earlier Rule*, 22:25-27 (FA:ED I, 80) and *The Canticle of Brother Sun*, 14 (FA:ED I, 114).

[14] *Breviloquium*, pt. II, ch. 10, n. 3, in *Works of St. Bonaventure,* vol. IX, trans. Dominic V. Monti (St. Bonaventure, NY: Franciscan Institute Publications, 2005), 90. A more complete discussion of Bonaventure's understanding of the human person can be found in chapters 9 and 12. In this instance, *mens* refers to the whole "rational soul" in its threefold powers of memory, understanding, and will. Bonaventure uses a variety of terms and phrases to describe the nature of the human

the human person "stands midway" between those things that are "most distant" from God (traces and vestiges – that which is corporal/temporal) and those that are "closest" to God (angelic natures – those which are incorporeal and spiritual).[15]

The body was endowed with existence, life, intelligence, and freedom of choice.[16] It was both "proportioned" and "subject" to the soul. The body was understood to be "proportioned" to the soul in that it possessed a "well-balanced physical constitution, a beautiful and highly complex structure, and upright posture."[17] The physical "uprightness of the body's carriage" was "to bespeak the rectitude of its mind."[18] The body was "united with the soul as its perfective principle, so that it might move toward and attain" the blessedness for which it was made.[19]

The soul (*anima* / *mens* / *homo interior*), the spiritual dimension of the human person, was created "in the image of the Trinity" in its trinity of powers – memory (*memoria*), understanding (*intelligentia*), and will (*voluntas*). Bonaventure understood these three powers to be "consubstantial, coequal and coeval, and mutually interpenetrating."[20] Thus, Bonaventure can assert that when "one considers the order, origin, and relation of

---

person: *intellectualibus seu spiritibus rationalibus* (*Breviloquium*, II, ch. 12); *anima rationalis* (*Breviloquium*, II, ch. 9).

[15] See *Breviloquium*, pt. II, ch. 12, n. 4 and ch. 6 (Monti, 77-79); and *Commentary on Book II of the Sentences*, Prologue, found in the Appendix of this volume.

[16] *Breviloquium*, pt. II, ch. 9, n. 1 and n. 5 (Monti, 84 and 87).

[17] *Breviloquium*, pt. II, ch. 10, n. 1 (Monti, 89). It may be helpful to recall that, according to Bonaventure, "the judgment that a thing is beautiful or pleasant or wholesome ... lies in the proportion of harmony" (*proportio aequalitatis*); see *Itinerarium*, ch. II, n. 6 (Hayes, 69). It refers to his whole understanding of aesthetics.

[18] *Breviloquium*, pt. II, ch. 10, n. 4 (Monti, 91) .

[19] *Breviloquium*, pt. II, ch. 10, n. 4 (Monti, 91).

[20] *Itinerarium*, ch. III, n. 5 (Hayes, 91).

these faculties (*potentia*) to one another, one is led to the most blessed Trinity itself."[21]

As the "most noble form of the body," the soul was designed to serve as the principle through which the rational spirit was made capable of being "led back, as if in an intelligible circle, to its beginning in which it is perfected and beatified."[22] The body was, therefore, created "subject," that is, "to be obedient to the soul...."[23]

In the initial state of creation, the embodied and intelligent creature was "granted the possibility of blessedness" (*beatitudo*), the fullness of life conformed by grace to God in glory.[24] The creature so made was gifted with an inner orientation of spirit (*anima*) to strive for an always greater measure of its perfection in the state of human pilgrimage through the "two-fold rectitude" of its nature, that is, the "rectitude of conscience" for

---

[21] *Itinerarium*, ch. III, n. 5 (Hayes, 91).

[22] *Breviloquium*, pt. II, ch. 4, n. 3 (Monti, 70-71).

[23] *Breviloquium*, pt. II, ch. 10, n. 1 (Monti, 89). In the state of original innocence, the human person was "free from misery and guilt" [p. II, ch. 9, n. 1 (Monti, 84); see also ch. 10, n. 5 (Monti, 91-92)]. He also states that the "body was to conform to the soul as the principle of its ascension toward heaven" (n. 4). He assumed that God created a human "body so completely obedient that it was free from all hostility and rebellion, all propensity to lust ... enfeeblement ... moral dissolution ... yet liable to fall into suffering" (n. 5).

In his description of the embodied soul "in the initial state of creation," Bonaventure develops a positive, even overly idealized, understanding of human nature that serves as an important counterpoint to his description of the state of fallen humanity. For a contrasting and very negative but nonetheless influential and popular description of the human person in 1195, see Lothario Dei Segni (Pope Innocent III), *The Misery of the Human Condition: De Miseria Humane Conditionis*, Donald Howard, ed. (Indianapolis: The Bobbs-Merrill Co. Inc., 1969).

[24] *Breviloquium*, pt. II, ch. 9, n. 2 (Monti, 85). In the state of glory, he assumed that grace stabilized the rational soul's free will in right choice and fully enlightened its intellect. See his discussion of the "confirmation of the good angels" in *Breviloquium*, pt. II, ch. 8 (Monti, 81-84).

"judging correctly" and the "rectitude of right willing, which is synderesis, warning against evil and prompting toward good." In addition to the twofold assistance of humankind's created nature, the supremely bountiful God also provided the twofold assistance of actual grace and sanctifying grace.[25]

Bonaventure acknowledges readily, however, that the human person, "because of its precarious nature, formed from nothing and not yet confirmed by glory" was "liable to fall."[26] He also believed that, as a consequence of the failure to use freedom rightly, the first human turned away from higher/spiritual goods and turned toward the self through disordered desire (*concupiscentia*)[27] and the desire for temporal goods (*cupiditas*), that is, sinned. Therefore, as the Seraphic Doctor imaged it, the human person became bent over (*incurvatus*) as opposed to being right and upright (*rectus*) as created originally. All human nature was described consequently as being "infected" with ignorance in the mind (*ignorantia mentis*) and with disordered desire in the flesh (*concupiscentia carnis*) as a consequence of the original sin of the first human.[28] The right order found in the original state of creation became disordered. Humankind's lower faculties were no longer subject, that is, obedient to the higher faculties – the sense appetites did not submit to reason, the desires of the flesh opposed reason, the powers of the soul disobeyed the law of love.[29] Rectitude was lost but "not the tendency to

---

[25] *Breviloquium*, pt. II, ch. 10, n. 6 (Monti, 96).

[26] *Breviloquium*, pt. II, ch. 10, n. 6 (Monti, 95).

[27] The meaning of concupiscence can be somewhat ambiguous in that it sometimes refers to the concupiscible appetite's orientation to desire the good naturally. More typically, it is understood negatively as disordered desire which arises from the inordinate desire for carnal pleasure, curiosity, or vanity. See *Threefold Way*, ch. I, n. 5.

[28] *Itinerarium*, ch. I, n. 7 (Hayes, 51).

[29] See The Evening Sermon on St. Francis, 1262 (FA:ED II, 725).

rectitude."[30] Rectitude and uprightness serve, therefore, as appropriate metaphors for imaging the challenge each individual faces in the struggle to be conformed to Christ "in as far as possible in this pilgrim state" through the imitation of Christ.[31]

The Rational Spirit (*anima rationalis*): An Image of the Triune God

Created in the image of the triune God, the nature of the human person is perhaps best grasped both in terms of the meaning of "rationality" and/or in terms of the soul's three powers.

"Rationality" provides a twofold philosophical framework through which the Seraphic Doctor describes the cognitive power's orientation to infinite truth and the affective power's orientation to infinite goodness. One should also be mindful of his assumption that if

> the intellectual and affective powers of the rational soul are never brought to rest except in God and in the infinite good, this is not because the soul comprehends God, but because nothing is sufficient for the soul unless it exceeds the soul's capacity. Therefore, it is true that the intellect and affectivity of the rational soul are directed to the infinite good and truth.[32]

---

[30] Cf. *Commentary on Book II of the Sentences*, prol. 13, in the Appendix of this volume.

[31] *Itinerarium*, ch. VII, n. 1 (Hayes, 133). In *The Earlier Rule*, ch. 22, n. 26, Francis of Assisi begs his brothers "in the holy love which is God" to overcome "every impediment and putting aside every care and anxiety, to serve, love, honor and adore the Lord God with a clean heart and a pure mind in whatever way they are best able to do, for this is what He wants above all else." (FA:ED I, 80).

[32] Bonaventure, q. IV, conclusion, in *Disputed Questions on the Knowledge of Christ*, Works of St. Bonaventure IV, trans. Zachary

This twofold framework of rationality implies memory, understanding and will, a threefold understanding of the powers of the soul.[33] This threefold description of the soul's powers provides an alternative and interrelated framework through which Bonaventure can describe the human capacity for and inner orientation to infinite truth and goodness – God – as well as how the rational spirit is led back to (*reductio*) God. While the threefold framework is used below, a sense of both of these frameworks is helpful for grasping the rich complexity of Bonaventure's thought on this topic of utmost importance.

Memory (*memoria*)

"The function of memory is to retain and to represent not only things present, corporal, and temporal, but also things that are successive, simple, and eternal" according to Bonaventure.[34] In this abbreviated description of the function of memory, one can see something of our modern and more didactic sense of memory as the faculty through which we are capable of retaining, recollecting, and representing what has been learned, grasped, or experienced. One can also see something of memory's role in the comprehension of intelligible things as well as in the reception and retention of sense knowledge. What may not be so readily apparent to the contemporary reader is Bonaventure's understanding of memory as the power of the soul through which a human person is open and oriented to the triune God – "successive, simple, and eternal" things.

Bonaventure's understanding of the power and function of memory relies heavily on the thought of

---

Hayes (St. Bonaventure, NY: Franciscan Institute Publications, 2005, 1992), 171. See also q. IV, n. 29 (page 124).

[33] *Breviloquium*, pt. II, ch. 6, n. 2 (Monti, 77).

[34] *Itinerarium*, ch. III, n. 2 (Hayes, 81-82).

Augustine. In the *Confessions*, for example, Augustine describes the "faculty of memory as a great one, O my God, exceedingly great, a vast, inner recess.... This is a faculty of my mind, belonging to my nature, yet` I cannot comprehend all that I am."[35]

As Philip Cary observes: "In developing his under-standing of memory, Augustine drew on the biblical notions of seeking and finding and on philosophical notions of inquiry and discovery." This led Augustine to "think of memory as the place where the intelligible things that the lovers of Wisdom seek may be found."[36]

Memory, in the deepest sense of the word, has many dimensions and embraces a number of interrelated ideas in the thought of Bonaventure. While these ideas are not easily and neatly separated, a sense of four different meanings will be helpful for grasping the Seraphic Doctor's understanding of the soul's power of memory.

First, the power of memory (*memoria*) may be correlated with the highest point of the mind (*apex mentis*).[37] As Augustine puts it, memory "is the mind (*mens*) and this is nothing other than my very self."[38]

---

[35] Augustine, *Confessionum* book X: 8, 15; see translation by Maria Boulding (New York: Random House, Inc., Vintage Books, 1997), 206. Augustine devotes the whole of book X to a discussion of the power of memory.

[36] Philip Cary, *Augustine's Invention of the Inner Self: The Legacy of a Christian Platonist* (New York: Oxford University Press, 2000), 130.

[37] Augustine, *Confessionum,* (book X: 14, 21). See Boulding, Confessions, 210, where the text reads: "mind and memory ... are one and the same." In book X, 17,26 (Boulding, *Confessions,* 213) Augustine says that "memory ... is the mind, and it is nothing other than my very self." In *On The Trinity* (book XIV: 8,11), Augustine discusses how in the "highest part of the mind" we "discover therein an image of God." Book Fourteen of *On the Trinity* is found in *Augustine of Hippo: Selected Writings*, CWS, trans. Mary T. Clark (New York/Ramsey, NJ: Paulist Press, 1984), 342.

[38] *Confessionum* (book X, 17,26); see also book X, 14,21 (Boulding, 213 and 210).

Thus memory (*memoria / mens*) refers to the innermost dimension of the self (*homo interior*), "what I am."

Second, the *memoria / mens* is the place where God has chosen to dwell within the human person.[39] As the place "where eternal truth resides,"[40] memory may be described as the "light of the divine countenance" which the soul bears "within itself, from its origin."[41] The presence of this truth functions, as Titus Szabo put it more recently, as a kind of "secret font of the innate ideas of spiritual things."[42] Thus, following Augustine, Bonaventure could hold that "certain a priori elements [e.g., eternal laws] are present in memory."[43] *Memoria / mens* may be described, therefore, as "the ground of the soul which reflects the presence of God."[44] In this sense, memory is "the locus of a sort of preconscious contact with God," as Hayes

---

[39] *Confessionum*, (book X, 25,36); see Boulding, 221. The text reads: "You have honored my memory by making it your dwelling place." See also the *Itinerarium*, ch. III, n.1 (Hayes, 81).

[40] Ewert Cousins, *Bonaventure and the Coincidence of Opposites* (Chicago: Franciscan Herald Press, 1978), 82. This is memory in the "Platonic sense" of the term.

[41] *Commentarius in II librum Sententiarum*, d. 16, a. 1, q. 1 conclusion (II, 397). See also *Confessionum* (book X, 25,36) see Boulding, 221. For another example of this line of thought see *Itinerarium*, ch. III, n. 1 and n. 2 (Hayes, 81-83).

[42] Titus Szabo, *De SS. Trinitate in creaturis refulgente: Doctrina S. Bonaventurae*, in *The Doctrine of the Image and the Similitude in St. Bonaventure*, trans. Alvin Black (MA Thesis, The Franciscan Institute, St. Bonaventure University, 1962), 23. See also *Confessionum* (book X, 14); Boulding, 206.

[43] Zachary Hayes, *Disputed Questions on the Mystery of the Trinity*, in *Works of Saint Bonaventure* III (St. Bonaventure, NY: The Franciscan Institute, 1979), Introduction, 71.

[44] Cousins, 82.

describes it.[45] It is one of the places where one can hope to "see God."[46]

Third, memory may be described as "the source of the whole intellectual life of the soul."[47] According to Bernard McGinn, memory is the "ground of the soul prior to the discrimination of the powers of knowing and loving."[48] In this sense, it was possible, as Augustine put it, for the human person to discover within a "mental trinity" wherein "memory provides the source from which the thinker's sight receives its form ... with the will or love as the agency by which the two are linked."[49] As Bonaventure expressed it:

> [T]he mind (*mens*) loves itself most fervently. But it cannot love itself if it does not know itself. And it would not know itself unless it remembered itself, for we do not grasp anything with our understanding (*intelligentia*) if it is not present to us in our memory.[50]

---

[45] Hayes, *Mystery of the Trinity*, 71. See also Etienne Gilson, *The Christian Philosophy of St. Augustine* (New York: Random House, 1960), 103.

[46] *Itinerarium*, ch. III, nn. 1-2 (Hayes, 81-83); *On Governing the Soul*, n. 2; Augustine, *Confessionum*, book X, 25 and 17, 26; Boulding, 212-14. See also book X, 25,35 and 25,35 (Boulding, 220-21). On this point, see Cary, 129. Bonaventure's understanding of the soul's ability "to see God" will be explained in greater detail below as part of the discussion of the nature of higher reason (*ratio/intellectus/intelligentia*).

[47] Szabo, *De SS. Trinitate* (Black, 21). See also Augustine, *On The Trinity*, book XIV, 7,9 (Clark, 339-40).

[48] Bernard McGinn, "Contemplation in Gregory the Great," in *Gregory the Great: A Symposium*, ed. John Cavadini (Notre Dame: Notre Dame University Press, 1995), 151. See also Szabo (Black, 24).

[49] Augustine, *On the Trinity*, book XIV, ch. 6 (Clark, 339).

[50] *Itinerarium*, ch. III, n. 1 (Hayes, 81).

In a general way, then, both Augustine and Bonaventure indicate how this trinity of powers, in their order, origin, and interrelationship unfold from within the highest/ deepest part of the self, the *mens / memoria.*

Fourth, in the depths of its innermost being (*mens / memoria*), the creature made in the image of God is *capax Dei*, that is, "capable of God" and "can actually grasp God."[51] The creature endowed with intelligence is, therefore, capable of "grasping not only the created essence, but even the creating essence."[52] Thus, all human beings, "however little" a person might be "partake in light, has been made to attain God through knowledge and love...."[53]

Given this understanding of memory, Bonaventure expects the human person who is made "in the image" of the triune God to make the best possible use of the soul's capacity for God, that is, to exercise the powers of the soul in cooperation with grace – "the God likening flow" – so one might merit a greater measure of likeness to and union with God. Thus Bonaventure can claim that in the measure the soul partakes of the gift of grace, the human person becomes more

> like God, it sees God clearly through the intellect, and loves God through the will, and retains God forever through the memory. The soul is then wholly alive, totally transformed in its three

---

[51] See *Itinerarium*, ch. III, n. 2 (Hayes, 83) and Augustine, *On The Trinity*, book XIV, ch. 8,11 (Clark, 342).

[52] *Breviloquium*, pt. II, ch. 9, n. 1 (Monti, 84).

[53] *Breviloquium*, pt. II, ch. 12, n. 2 (Monti, 97). In the *Commentary on Book II of the Sentences,* prol., n. 13, Bonaventure states that even in its fallen state, the human person "lost rectitude itself, but not the tendency to rectitude ... the habit but not the appetite."

faculties, wholly conformed to God, fully united to God, completely at rest in God.[54]

Through the soul's worthy and faithful participation in the life of grace then, a person may begin to attain a measure of the "eternal happiness" of which every person is made "worthy."[55] In "the proximity of similitude to the Creator," the soul becomes more fully itself. This is not to suggest, however, that the creature can ever be "identified with the Creator."[56]

There are obviously a number of important, at times subtle but nonetheless significant, theological and philosophical assumptions embedded in the thought of Bonaventure with respect to the power of memory in the deepest sense of the word. A measure of sensitivity to the different meanings and aspects of *memoria* is critically important, therefore, for grasping how the soul is empowered to make the spiritual journey of the soul (*mens*) into God through knowledge and love.

The Power to Know (*Intelligentia*)

The intellective power refers to the human capacity for knowing. It is oriented toward the discernment of

---

[54] *Breviloquium*, pt. VII, ch. 7, n. 3 (Monti, 294); *Commentary on Book II of the Sentences*, prol. nn. 2-5. See J.A. Wayne Hellmann's discussion of the soul's transformation in *Divine and Created Order in Bonaventure's Theology*, trans. J.A. Hammond (St. Bonaventure, NY: The Franciscan Institute, 2001), 151-69.

[55] *Breviloquium*, pt. V, ch. 1, n. 3 (Monti, 170-71).

[56] In *Divine and Created Order* Hellmann discusses how Bonaventure understood the soul to be conformed to the Trinity under three different aspects, namely as, the ordered soul (*anima ordinata*), the hierarchical soul (*anima hierarchizata*), and the contemplative soul (*anima contemplativa*)." (See Hellmann, 152-60). See also *Breviloquium*, pt. V, ch. 1, n. 3 (Monti, 170-71).

truth, the "truth in itself, or the truth as a good."[57] In an effort to describe the nature of this power, Bonaventure makes use of a variety of speculative and philosophical categories.

Here, attention will be limited to a description of reason (*ratio*).[58] It will serve to demonstrate one important aspect of the human capacity to know – an aspect of the cognitive power that holds a central place in Bonaventure's articulation of the ways in which the human intellect is designed to rise gradually and be led back into "Truth itself, and this is God," the principle of all knowing.[59]

Reason (*ratio*), broadly speaking, refers to the whole range of activities that pertain to the intellectual life.[60]

---

[57] *Breviloquium*, p. II, ch. 9, n. 7 9 (Monti, 88).

[58] The discussion of reason follows closely the clear and helpful analysis provided by George Tavard, "The Book of the Soul," chapter 4, in *Transparency and Permanence* (St. Bonaventure, NY: The Franciscan Institute, 1974, 1954), 80-102.

[59] *See Breviloquium*, pt. II, ch. 9, n. 7 (Monti, 88); *Itinerarium* (Hayes, note 8, pp. 160-61); *Collations ... Six Days,* col. 5, n. 24 and col. 22, n. 34, pp. 86-87 and p. 357. See also *Disputed Questions on the Knowledge of Christ*, q. IV, n. 28 (Hayes, 124).

[60] See John Kleinz, "Reason and Intelligence," in *The Theory of Knowledge of Hugh of St. Victor*, dissertation published in *The Catholic University of America Philosophical Studies,* vol. LXXXVII (Washington, D.C.: Catholic University of America Press, 1944), 63-86. Another way to distinguish and describe the human person's capacity to rise gradually to the Supreme Principle (God) is found in the works of Hugh of St. Victor and is frequently used by Bonaventure. Hugh describes the human person as being gifted with a threefold "mental eye," that is, the "eye of the flesh," through which the mind turns to the body and material things – what is outside; the "eye of reason," through which the human person is able to know itself and spiritual substances – what is within; and the "eye of contemplation" (*oculus contemplationis/ oculus mentis/ intelligentia),* through which the human person turns toward the vision of divine displays through understanding (*intelligentia*) and which may lead to the savoring of divine forms through the mind's highest aspect (*apex mentis synderesis*) – what is above. See *Breviloquium* II, ch. 12, n. 5

Following Augustine, Bonaventure makes a distinction between lower/inferior reason (*ratio inferior*) and higher/superior reason (*ratio superior*).[61] This distinction is used to describe the different ways the mind is able to see (*speculatio/contemplatio*) things. The terms refer to a diversity of function rather than to a diversity of powers.[62]

"Lower" reason is oriented toward temporal things, things outside the self, the world of sense reality. It refers to the mind's capacity to "apprehend" what is in the sensible world, the first operation of the intellect. Once something is brought to the attention of the mind, reason has the potential to give it further consideration. More complex kinds of consideration (e.g., reasoning, judging, abstracting, and the like) are considered, however, to be functions of higher, not lower reason. Thus, one can say that lower reason does not "understand" what is apprehended. It "never reaches the ultimate significance of what it knows."[63]

Reason may be described as "higher" in the sense that the human mind has the capacity to look at things from different perspectives. In this sense of the word, reason refers to the mind's inclination to seek to know and understand as well as its potential to discover the spiritual significance of what is known.[64]

The diverse capacities of higher reason are explained in terms of the distinction that can be made between *ratio* (reason/understanding), *intellectus* (understanding/

(Monti, 98); *Collations ... Six Days*, col. 5, n. 24 (de Vinck, 86-87), and *Itinerarium* (Hayes, note 4, pp. 186-87).

[61] *Knowledge of Christ*, q. IV, concl.; q. IV, n. 29, and Hayes's introduction (Hayes, 135, 123-24, and. 59) See also Tavard, 65.

[62] *Breviloquium*, pt. II, ch. 9, n. 7 (Monti, 88); *Itinerarium* (Hayes, note 8, pp. 160-61.

[63] Tavard, 84.

[64] Tavard, 83; *Itinerarium*, ch. III, nn. 4-6 (Hayes, 89-93).

intellect), and *intelligentia* (understanding/intelligence).[65] In the Latin, each word suggests a nuanced understanding of the intellect's capacity to know and understand things in different but interrelated ways. Unfortunately, the distinctions are difficult to convey in the English language since the meanings of the words are close; the words may even be used interchangeably in certain contexts.

Ratio, as an aspect of higher reason, points to the human capacity to comprehend what comes into consciousness.[66] It specializes in abstraction and the logical organization of abstracted information. In this sense of the term, reason implies the human capacity for higher kinds of knowing or understanding.

Intellectus – understanding or more properly speaking, the "intellect" – refers to an intermediate kind of knowing. It is the cognitive power's capacity to turn through reason (1) to know things outside itself (temporal things), (2) to consider universal abstract reasons, (3) to turn within itself as an image of God, and/or (4) to begin to know spiritual substances, that is, how all things bear a divine imprint as either a vestige or an image of God. In a more restricted sense, *intellectus* may be understood to refer primarily to the human person's capacity to know itself and spiritual substances – what is within. The intellect has the potential, therefore, to detect the "latent mark of God and knows that the objects to which they refer ... display a higher sense than what reason could discern: a resemblance to God imprinted on them."[67] Thus, the intellect enables the human person to understand what

---

[65] Bonaventure, *Collations ... Six Days*, col. 5, n. 24, (de Vinck, 86-87).

[66] See, for example, *Itinerarium*, ch. III, n. 3 (Hayes, 85-89); also *On the Reduction of the Arts to Theology*, nn. 3-4 for Bonaventure's description of both sense and philosophical knowledge (Hayes, 39-43 and Hayes's introduction, 17).

[67] Tavard, 85.

truth can teach "as long as unruly desires and sense images do not stand as impediments becoming like clouds between [the person] and the ray of Truth" – God.[68]

Intelligentia – understanding/intelligence – is the third aspect of higher reason. It is the highest part of the soul and refers to the human person's potential to perceive "divine displays" and to "savor" divine favors. It refers to the human person's capacity to strive consciously to understand the spiritual significance of what is grasped. As Tavard put it, *intelligentia* refers to higher reason's capacity to "read inside (*inter-legere*)" what it comes to know.[69]

Intelligentia is the aspect of higher reason that is "destined to see God [face to face]."[70] It is "destined to know God, the Supreme Good."[71] It is the *mens* in the most restricted sense of that word.[72] *Intelligentia* points consistently to the highest level of understanding toward which the rational soul may aspire. It refers to the mind's potential to experience contemplative knowing, that is, wisdom.

Bonaventure's distinctions are important. They demonstrate how a thirteenth-century thinker described the human capacity for knowing and understanding. He offers a detailed, even if complicated and foreign way to understand how the intellect may choose to see things from two widely divergent perspectives, that is, either in

---

[68] *Itinerarium*, ch. III, n. 3 (Hayes, 88-89).

[69] Tavard, 87.

[70] Bonaventure, *Commentary on Ecclesiastes*, ch. VIII, n. 4, in *Works of St. Bonaventure* VII, translated and edited by Robert J. Karris and Campion Murray (St. Bonaventure, NY: Franciscan Institute Publications, 2005), 294.

[71] Bonaventure, *De Regno Dei*, n. 9 (*Opera Omnia* V, 542a), quoted in Tavard, 86.

[72] *Itinerarium*, ch. I, n. 4 (Hayes, 47-48 and the notes on pp. 143-44). See also Bonaventure's discussion of *intelligentia* as the "divine power" in the *Collations ... Six Days*, col. 5, n. 24 (de Vinck, 87).

"the light of the divine significance" or apart from it.[73] Bonaventure assumes, therefore, that everyone will train (*exercito*) and make the best possible use of the intellect's capacities. In terms of spiritual development, those choices are crucial, he says:

> When our reason (*ratio*) is turned to higher things, it is purified, illumined, and brought to perfection; and, in so far as it turns to the eternal laws and to the immutability of the divine power and justice, it is strengthened and enlivened in the good.... Therefore, while the higher and inferior reason are of the same nature, they differ in terms of the degree of their strength and weakness.[74]

The Seraphic Doctor's theory of knowledge – his understanding of the rational creature's capacity to know (epistemology) – is closely related to his theory of divine illumination, his assumption that a human person can attain "certitude at least in some areas of knowledge"[75] as well as his understanding of the various modes of God's revelation and the role of Christ in all human knowing. While these other aspects of his thought are important, they are beyond the scope of this introduction and are only acknowledged here.

The limited description of one aspect of the cognitive power provides hopefully a sense of the richness and complexity of the Seraphic Doctor's thought. In considering this, or other aspects of the cognitive power, one should not lose sight of his assertion, however, that "no matter how enlightened one may be by the light of natural or acquired knowledge one cannot enter into oneself to delight in the

---

[73] Tavard, 83.

[74] *Commentarius in II librum Sententiarum* d. 24, p. I, a. 2, q. 2 (II, 564), quoted in *Itinerarium*, (Hayes, prologue notes on page 144).

[75] Hayes, Introduction, *Knowledge of Christ*, 57.

Lord except by means of the mediation of Christ...."[76] In this way, Christ became a ladder, a mediator through whom rational creatures – blind, weak, bent-over sinners – might be drawn back into relationship with God.[77]

The Capacity to Love and Choose (*affectus-voluntas*)

The affective capacity is oriented toward the "infinite good." This power is best grasped in terms of the meaning of affectivity (*affectus*) and the human capacity to choose, the will (*voluntas*).

Affection/Love (*affectus*)

The affective capacity reveals the human person's potential to be moved (*affectus*) by desire (*desiderium*) for the good (*bonum*) in different ways. The good, in turn, may be desired either as a good in itself (*bonum honestum*), as a good that may be useful to the self (*bonum conferens*), and/or as a good that delights the self (*bonum delectabile*).[78] Even though the good may be desired in different ways, one must understand that:

> desire tends above all to what moves it most. And what moves it most is what is loved most. And that which is loved most is to be happy (*beatus*).

---

[76] *Itinerarium*, ch. IV, n. 2 (Hayes, 99).

[77] See *Itinerarium*, ch. I, n. 7 (Hayes, 51) and ch. IV, n. 2 (Hayes, 97).

[78] This is a reference to Bonaventure's threefold understanding of the good, that is, the good in itself (*bonum honestum*), the good that is useful to the self (*bonum conferens*), and the good that delights the self (*bonum delectabile*). See Robert Prentice, *The Psychology of Love According to St. Bonaventure* (St. Bonaventure, NY: The Franciscan Institute, 1992), 52-53.

But happiness is attained only by reaching the best and ultimate goal. Therefore, human desire is directed at nothing but the supreme Good, or that which leads to it or reflects the Good in a certain way. The power of the supreme Good is so great that nothing else can be loved by a creature except through a desire for the supreme Good.[79]

Therefore, Bonaventure believes that the affective power is "never brought to rest except in God and in the infinite good."[80] He also argues that the highest Good, God, should be loved above all else. All created realities – one's neighbor, self, body, and creation – are to be loved in God and "for God's sake."[81]

The inner movement of the affective capacity (*affectus*) is explained in terms of its two natural impulses or appetites (*appetitus*), that is, the concupiscible appetite and the irascible appetite.[82]

The concupiscible appetite is the innate orientation to the good.[83] Through this appetite, a person is inclined to hunger for, strive after, go out to, and/or seek to acquire the good that moves it. The movement toward the good presumes (a) the experience of a need, (b) an object (good) capable of satisfying the experienced desire, and (c) the absence of the good (object) that might satisfy one's experience of desire and wherein one might find rest.

---

[79] *Itinerarium*, ch. III, n. 4 (Hayes, 89-91).

[80] *Knowledge of Christ*, q. VI, concl. (Hayes, 171). The text reads: "the intellect and affective power of the rational soul are never brought to rest except in God.... Therefore, it is true that the intellect and affectivity are directed to the infinite good and truth precisely in so far as these are infinite."

[81] *On the Perfection of Life*, ch. VII, n. 1; *Breviloquium*, p. V, ch. 8, n. 3 (Monti, 200).

[82] A distinction is being made here between the appetites of the rational soul and the sense appetites of the human person.

[83] See note 27 p. 11.

In the love which is God, the highest Good, there is established an "order of love" that must be observed. When this order is violated, desire becomes disordered (*concupiscentia*).[84] Sin comes into being and the sinner stands in need of the assistance of the cleansing, strengthening, and uplifting influence of grace, most especially sanctifying grace or charity.[85] As a consequence, there is discord rather than harmony (*concordia*).

The irascible appetite is the innate inclination to "withdraw from evil" (flight). This appetite includes the inclinations either to "defend an acquired good" (acquisition) or to "strive after the arduous good" (fight).[86] When its efforts are thwarted or blocked, it is inclined to anger (*ira*). This inclination needs the strengthening and uplifting influence of grace in the form of the virtues of hope and fortitude in particular. In the measure that these virtues are acquired, a person is empowered to face difficulty, even to accept the possibility that one's need may not be satisfied in the state of human pilgrimage.

The irascible appetite is inclined, according to Bonaventure, to the threefold weaknesses of negligence, impatience, and a lack of trust in one's own self (*diffidentia*).[87] One must be wary of these weaknesses, especially negligence, as potential obstacles to be overcome

---

[84] Bonaventure identifies a twofold kind of disorder that might exist within the concupiscible appetite as either a disorder "of the flesh" or "of cupidity" and "the latter is the root of all evil." It is "opposed to charity." He also explains that cupidity "consists in private love and disregard for the common good." *Collations ... Six Days*, col. 21, nn. 9-10 (de Vinck, 324-25). See the discussion of concupiscence, disordered love, below on pages 30-33.

[85] See *Breviloquium*, pt. V, ch. 1, n. 2 and ch. 1, n. 6 (Monti, 170, 172). Bonaventure's understanding of sin is discussed below as well as in relation to his understanding of the purgative way in the next section of this introduction.

[86] See Prentice, *Psychology of Love*, note 69, pp. 22-23, 30-32.

[87] See *Collations ... Six Days*, col. 22, n. 37 (de Vinck, 359).

if one intends to make genuine progress on the spiritual journey. These weaknesses account for some of the most significant difficulties, according to Bonaventure, that a person must face in pursuing a truly spiritual way of living, embracing a penitential way of living, resisting temptations, and/or making progress in virtue.[88]

Choice (*voluntas*)

The affective capacity is inclined naturally to pass into action (*operatio*).[89] It is then referred to as the will (*voluntas*), the elective faculty.[90] Within the will itself, Bonaventure makes a distinction between the rational soul's innate inclination to seek the good (*synderesis*) and the human potential to choose the good freely, that is, through deliberate decision.[91]

Synderesis, the natural will, is described as the inner inclination or prod (*stimulus/scintilla*) to embrace what is morally good and/or to avoid what is morally evil.[92] As an inclination within the affective aspect of the soul, it is understood to function as a kind of "spiritual weight" (*pondus spirituale*) which inclines the soul toward the good but has "nothing of deliberation" within itself.[93] At

---

[88] See *Threefold Way*, ch. I, n. 4.

[89] He assumes that "it is not the nature of grace to compel free choice but anticipate it, so that both of them pass into action together." *Breviloquium*, pt. V, ch. 3, n. 5 (Monti, 181).

[90] For an explanation of the different levels on which the will may function see Hayes, *Hidden Center*, 117-23.

[91] *Breviloquium*, pt. II, ch. 9, n. 8 (Monti, 88-89); see also *Itinerarium* ch. III, n. 4 (Hayes, 89).

[92] *Commentarius in II librum Sententiarum*, d. 39, a. 2, q. 1, ad. 4 (II, 910b) and *Breviloquium* pt. II, ch. 9, nn. 7-8 (Monti, 88-89). See also Prentice, 36-40.

[93] See Prentice, *Psychology of Love*, 38. See also *Commentarius in II librum Sententiarum*, d. 39, a. 2, q. 1 (II, 908-11).

its deepest level, it is an attempt to speak about the way in which humanity is irrevocably set to its final end of beatitude (*beatitudo*).

The Greek term *synderesis* was introduced into Latin by St. Jerome and he referred to it as the "spark of conscience" (*scintilla conscientiae*).[94] Bonaventure, like many other medieval theologians, considered it "a fourth element of the soul above and beyond reason, spirit, and desire." It was "a habit-like faculty of the will" that was distinct from conscience.[95] The distinction enabled Bonaventure to emphasize the involvement and cooperation of both the cognitive and affective powers in the process of choosing. The distinction was, however, based on a common misreading of Jerome.

In several places, for example, Bonaventure urges the spiritual pilgrim to "turn to the sting of conscience" (*stimulus conscientiae*). It is in fact an invitation to enter into one's innermost self and make good use of one's cognitive and affective powers in the struggle for wisdom. Conscience, a habit of the practical intellect, inclines the intellect to discover truth and make practical judgments about the good to be pursued. It is stimulated, pricked,

---

[94] See Allan B. Wolter, *Duns Scotus on Will and Morality* (Washington, DC: The Catholic University of America Press, 1986), 45. Researchers have now concluded that a medieval scribe made an error in transcribing *synteresis* (conservation) for *syneidesis* (conscience) when copying Jerome's commentary on Ezechiel. "The error was incorporated into the popular *Glossa ordinaria* and, through Peter Lombard's *Sentences*, passed on to scholastic theologians." For more on this see Douglas Langston, "The Spark of Conscience: Bonaventure's View of Conscience and Synderesis," *Franciscan Studies* 53 (1993): 79-96; M. B. Crowe, "The term Synderesis and the Scholastics," *The Irish Theological Quarterly* 23 (1956): 151-64; John Quinn, "St. Bonaventure's Fundamental Conception of Natural Law," *Bonaventura* III (Rome/Grottaferrata: Collegio S. Bonaventura, 1974), 572-98.

[95] Charles Curran, "Conscience," in *Themes in Fundamental Moral Theology* (Notre Dame, IN: University of Notre Dame Press, 1974), 194 and 195.

or prodded (*stimulus*/*scintilla*) to make its judgments by synderesis, the innate inclination to do what is good and to avoid what is evil as determined by conscience. When a person acts in accordance with the inner inclination to right judgment (*conscientia*) and right willing (*synderesis*), that person is inclined to cooperate with grace and has the potential to make spiritual progress.

The deliberative will is the elective faculty in the proper sense of the word. As Tavard describes it, "the faculty of desire becomes the faculty of liberality endowed with an innate longing for spiritual good."[96] It involves "the co-operation of the two faculties – reason reflecting on itself and will acting in conjunction." The cooperation of these powers gives "rise to full freedom, the source of merit or demerit accordingly as good or evil is chosen."[97]

Free choice involves deliberation, judgment, and desire.[98] As Bonaventure explained it, deliberation "consists in inquiring" which is better. What is "better" is determined in terms of "closeness" or "likeness" to the "best" – the highest Good, Christ the exemplar of all things. In judging, the mind strives to deliberate in light of the divine laws "impressed upon the mind" so that it can arrive at "a full and complete analysis." Finally, as indicated above, human desire must search honestly for "the supreme Good, or that which leads to it, or reflects that Good in a certain way." Thus, through this kind of threefold effort, "the soul tends to its end." It is drawn in cooperation with grace toward its completion and redemption.[99] When "the will is in conformity with the

---

[96] Tavard, 97.

[97] *Breviloquium*, pt. II, ch. 9, n. 8 (Monti, 89); see also *Itinerarium*, ch. III, n. 4, on the power of choice (Hayes, 89-91).

[98] *Itinerarium*, ch. III, n. 4 (Hayes, 89).

[99] *Breviloquium*, pt. II, ch. 4, n. 4 and n. 5 (Monti, 71-72).

highest Goodness" it is "rectified." The one "who loves goodness is made upright," better, more just.[100]

The Soul, Deformed by Sin

In the original state of creation, the human person was created right and upright. The powers of the soul were "turned toward God by virtuous habits."[101] Humankind's capacities to know, to love, and to choose inclined the soul naturally "to accomplish its work with God as their source, in accordance with God's norms, and with God as their end."[102] However, since rational creatures were "made from nothing," human persons were also incomplete, imperfect, and, in virtue of their freedom, capable of acting for ends other than God.[103] In fact, the first human chose to violate the "order of love" in virtue of human freedom. Sin came into being.[104]

Sin comes from "a will that is not well-ordered but disordered."[105] It is not "a desire for evil things but a forsaking of what is better," the choice of a lesser good

---

[100] *Commentary on Book II of the Sentences*, prol. 4.

[101] See *Commentary on Book II of the Sentences*, prol., n. 2. It should be noted that humankind's "right formation and uprightness," according to the Seraphic Doctor, was understood to include "uprightness" with regard to both what is above (God, what is eternal and spiritual) and those things which are below (what is temporal and material). See also n. 10.

[102] *Breviloquium*, pt. III, ch. 1, n. 2 (Monti, 100).

[103] *Breviloquium*, pt. III, ch. 1, nn. 2-3 (Monti, 99-101).

[104] *Breviloquium*, pt. III, ch. 8, n. 2 (Monti, 118-19).

[105] *Breviloquium*, pt. III, ch. 6, n. 5 (Monti, 114-15). Sin, a disorder of the will, disrupts and may even destroy, the order of justice. "When the disorder is so serious that it destroys the order of justice, it is called mortal sin.... When the disorder is slight and does not destroy but merely disturbs the order of justice, it is called venial (actual), or readily pardonable, for it does not result in a total loss of grace...." See *Breviloquium*, pt. III, ch. 8, n. 2 (Monti, 118-19).

or what is opposed directly to goodness itself.[106] The "will becomes disordered either because it desires what should not be desired, or because it seeks what it should not seek."[107] As a result, sin disrupts, and may even completely destroy the order of right willing, or justice. This is why Bonaventure argues that sin is "not any kind of essence, but a defect, a corruptive influence" within the created will of humankind, not in the will of God.[108]

Sin deforms the powers of the soul. As Bonaventure imaged it, the intellect becomes "ignorant" to the extent that the mind is not turned to the "highest truth."[109] The will becomes "disordered" to the degree that desire is not "in conformity with the highest goodness."[110] The power to act becomes weak or impotent in the measure that it is not "conjoined to the highest power" in its activity. In other words, the sinner fails to "act with God as its source, according to God's norms, or with God as its end."[111] Disorder in any one of the soul's powers leads to disorder

---

[106] *Breviloquium*, pt. III, ch. 1, n. 5 (Monti, 101). He names the threefold changeable good as that which is inferior, the flesh; that which is exterior, the world; and that which is interior, the excellence of the soul; see *Commentary Luke* I, ch. 4, n. 8, 296.

[107] *Breviloquium*, pt. III, ch. 6, n. 5 and ch. 9, n. 5 (Monti, 122).

[108] See *Breviloquium*, pt. III, ch. 1, n. 1 and ch. 6, n. 5 (Monti, 99 and 114-15). For another discussion of the nature of sin see *Commentary on Book II of the Sentences*, prol., n. 12.

[109] Bonaventure distinguished between ignorance that is a consequence of sin (*ignorantia*) and ignorance which results from a simple lack of information about a given subject (*nescientia*). See Berard Marthaler, *Original Justice and Sanctifying Grace* (Editrice *Miscellanae Francescana*: Dissertationes ad Lauream, n. 44, 1965), 23-24.

[110] In the *Collations ... Six Days,* col. 21, nn. 9-10 (de Vinck, 324-25), Bonaventure explains that "disordered desire is either of the flesh or cupidity, and the latter is the root of all evil ... cupidity consists in private love and disregard for the common good." See also Hayes, *Hidden Center*, 164.

[111] *Breviloquium*, pt. III, ch. 1, n. 2 (Monti, 100).

in the others.[112] As a consequence, the image of the triune God becomes distorted.

According to Bonaventure, the three roots of sin are (1) negligence, (2) disordered desire (*concupiscentia*), or (3) the choice of what is morally worthless or evil.[113] A brief description of each of these points will serve to illustrate more adequately his theology of sin.

The weakness of negligence lies in the person's failure to do the required good, that is, to live rightly, to act justly, to pursue a virtuous way of living. The negligent person fails typically to pray, read and meditate, guard the heart, use time well, do good works, resist evil temptations, and/ or make progress in virtue.[114]

The choice of what is morally worthless or evil involves, in varying degrees, a "withdrawal from the First Principle" – God, the highest Good, or what leads to

---

[112] *Breviloquium*, pt. III, ch. 11, nn. 2-3 (Monti, 125-26). The description of the disorder in the powers of the soul that follows is based primarily on Bonaventure's description as found in the prologue to the *Commentary on Book II of the Sentences*. From another perspective, he can also argue that the sinner's choice is not guided by purity of intention, that is, it does not come from a pure heart and a good conscience informed by charity and faith. For a helpful explanation of Bonaventure's thought on this point see Emma Thérèse Healy, *Saint Bonaventure's* De Reductione Artium Ad Theologiam, *A Commentary with an Introduction and Translation*, in *Works of Saint Bonaventure*, I (St. Bonaventure, NY: The Franciscan Institute, 1955), 140.

[113] *On the Perfection of Life*, ch. I, n. 1; *Threefold Way*, ch. I, n. nn. 4-6. In both these texts he uses the Latin *nequitia* in seeming preference to *malus*, the choice of what is known to be evil or bad. See note 116 below. In the *Breviloquium* pt. III, ch. 9, n. 1, (Monti, 121), Bonaventure identifies "pride" as "the beginning of all sin. The roots of sin are fear that badly restrains, and love that badly enflames." He then discusses sin in terms of the seven capital sins or "primary disorders," the categories preferred by many medieval authors.

[114] Other forms of weakness include (1) impatience in the face of suffering or difficulty and (2) the lack of trust in one's own self (*diffidentia*). He associates all three forms of weakness with the soul's irascible power. See *Collations ... Six Days*, col. 22, n. 37 (de Vinck, 359).

it.[115] The choice of what is morally worthless (*nequitia*)[116] is, most typically, rooted in the disordered affections of anger, envy, or laziness. In the case of what is evil (*malus*), "[w]hen the will has the power to resist, but solely out of its own corruption, chooses to do something recognized as wrong, it is committing what is known as the sin of sheer malice." The evil of malice arises, therefore, from an absolute defection of the free will. It is "opposed directly to the grace of the Holy Spirit."[117]

Concupiscence is "disordered affectivity, the tendency of natural desires and appetites to pursue their own objects in disregard of the proper order of reason," as it was generally understood by medieval theologians.[118] The term "had strong negative connotations for medieval theologians, suggesting disorder, evil, corruption, vice, stain, and blemish."[119] Concupiscence, disordered desire, manifests itself principally in the quest for carnal pleasures, curiosity, or vanity (a form of pride) in the works of Bonaventure.[120]

The disordered desire for carnal pleasure is manifest in the search for "sensual satisfaction" in that which is sweet, soft, or carnal, that is, inferior goods. As a disorder

---

[115] *Breviloquium*, pt. III, ch. 10, n. 2 (Monti, 125).

[116] Augustine says that "the ancients wanted it known that the very word *nequitia* [worthlessness], the mother of all vices, is derived from *nequicquam* [to no purpose], that is, from which is nothing. The opposite virtue of this vice is called *frugalitas* [worth]. Therefore, as the latter word is from *frux* [fruit], which in turn is from *fructus* [productive of enjoyment], because of the kind of fruitfulness of souls, so the former word *nequitia* takes it name from barrenness, that is, that which is nothing." See "The Happy Life," in Clark's *Augustine of Hippo,* 173.

[117] *Breviloquium*, pt. III, ch. 11, n, 3 (Monti, 128).

[118] Pierre J. Payer, *The Bridling of Desire: Views of Sex in the Later Middle Ages* (Toronto: Univ. of Toronto Press, 1993), 48, and n. 78.

[119] Payer, 47.

[120] *Threefold Way*, ch. III, n. 2. See *Threefold Way*, ch. I, nn. 5-6; *On the Perfection of Life,* ch. I, nn. 2-4.

arising within the affective power, concupiscence manifests itself in a will to self. It implies, to varying degrees, a lack of regard for the will of God and/or concern for the good of one's neighbor. Bonaventure associates disordered desire, or will to self, with "the lust of the flesh" and the primary disorders (capital sins) of gluttony and lust in particular.

Curiosity (*curiositas*) is the disordered desire to acquire knowledge, experiences, and/or possessions as ends in themselves or simply for one's own sake. Bonaventure associates it with the "lust of the eyes," the desire for temporal goods (*cupiditas*). He also associates curiosity with the capital sin of covetousness and the vice of avarice.[121]

Vanity (*vanitas*) is a form of pride. It involves the disordered desire for worldly favor, praise, and honor. Bonaventure associates it with the temptation to the "pride of life" (*superbia vitae*). As a primary disorder, this form of pride manifests itself in the tendency to exalt one's own self over one's neighbor.

Another form of pride (*superbia*) is "the temptation to god-like eminence," to claim equality with God.[122] This form of pride is "the beginning of all sin."[123] It reveals creatures' inordinate desire to rise above what they were.[124] Bonaventure considered it an act of "contempt for

---

[121] On the vice of avarice see Bonaventure, Sermon II, The Third Sunday of Advent, in *What Manner of Man: Sermons on Christ by St. Bonaventure,* trans. Zachary Hayes (Chicago: Franciscan Herald Press, 1974), 108.

[122] Cf. *Breviloquium*, pt. III, ch. 3, n. 4 (Monti, 104).

[123] *Breviloquium*, pt. V, ch. 9, n. 1 (Monti, 121). See Sirach 10: 12-18 where the NAB text reads: "The beginning of pride is man's [humankind's] stubbornness in drawing his heart from his Maker; For pride is the reservoir of sin, a source which runs over with vice." In *Breviloquium* (III, ch. 11, n. 5) Bonaventure argues that: "sin takes is origin in pride and has as its consummation or end in final impenitence" (Monti, 130).

[124] *Breviloquium*, pt. III, ch. 3, esp., n. 4 (Monti, 106) and ch. 8, n. 6 (Monti, 120-21). See also *The Major Legend of St. Francis* (ch. 6, n. 11)

the first Principle."[125] It violates the "the primal relation
on which all other relationships are based."[126] As Hayes
puts it, pride is the source of

> a real rupture in the harmonious relationship that
> should exist among the different orders of being.
> Sin involves both a moral and cosmic dimension;
> for sin is not only an act of the will against the
> moral order – but precisely as such – it is a
> disruption in the order of being.[127]

As Bonaventure describes it, sin destroys harmony
(*concordia*) and results in discord

> between the Creator and the creature, between
> angels and humankind, between will and conscience,
> between sensuality and reason, between flesh and
> spirit, between man and his neighbor, between the
> sinner and the entire world.[128]

The disordered desire for lesser goods and the
temptation to rise above one's humble estate as a human
being (pride) constitute the primary obstacles to spiritual
progress. Bonaventure uses a variety of word images to
describe graphically humankind's fallen condition and
the sinner's situation as a consequence of the choice of
goods and ends other than God. For example, the sinner
may be described as a person who is "blind and bent over,"
no longer standing upright and able to see the light of

---

where he states that "pride is the source of all evil, and disobedience,
its worst offspring" (FA:ED II, 576).

[125] *Breviloquium*, p. III, ch. 9, n. 2 (Monti, 122).

[126] Hayes, *Hidden Center*, 166-67.

[127] Hayes, *Hidden Center*, 167.

[128] "Sermon II on the Third Sunday of Advent," (Hayes, *What Manner*, 103).

truth; a "beggar" in misery and need; or, an "anxious-searcher" who seeks but never finds rest. The sinner is also described as a "fool" because:

> The human mind is distracted by many concerns, and hence does not enter into itself through memory. It is obscured by images of sense objects, and therefore does not enter into itself through intelligence. And it is drawn away by disordered desires, and therefore it does not turn to itself with a desire for internal sweetness and spiritual joy.[129]

These powerful word images appear frequently in Bonaventure's theological and spiritual writings. Each image seeks to indicate, in different ways, the disordering and deforming effects of sin. These carefully chosen words also highlight, therefore, the sinner's need for the purifying, strengthening, and uplifting influence of grace.

Bonaventure's understanding of sin is articulated within a framework commonly adopted by medieval thinkers. Men and women in later ages would, however, find it limited and wanting for a variety of reasons.[130]

---

[129] *Itinerarium*, ch. IV, n. 1 (Hayes, 97); *On the Perfection of Life*, ch. I, n. 6.

[130] See, for example, Anne Carr, *Transforming Grace*: *Christian Tradition and Women's Experience* (San Francisco, CA: Harper San Francisco, 1988), 8. Questions have also been raised with regard to the association Bonaventure and many other medieval thinkers made between the higher part of the mind (*mens*) and the "masculine principle" and the association made between the inferior part of the mind with sensuality, "the feminine principle." See, for example, the *Breviloquium*, pt. III, ch. 8, nn. 5-6; on women as the "weaker sex" see *Breviloquium,* pt. III, ch. 2, n. 2, and n. 4 (Monti, 102, 103).

The Soul, Reformed by Grace

Grace is a "gift divinely given." It "comes from God, conforms to God, and leads to God."[131] Its primary purpose is to "lead the soul back to its origin" (*reductio*) to the extent that it is possible in this life in anticipation of the full enjoyment of God in glory (*beatitudo*).[132] No one is worthy to attain this blessed state unless the soul is lifted above itself "through the action of God coming down to it" through the noble gift of the divine influence – grace.[133]

Quoting the letter to James, Bonaventure explains that "every good and perfect gift is from above, coming down from the Father of Lights."[134] These gifts are available to humanity through the Word incarnate, crucified, and inspirited.[135]

The Holy Spirit, the Word inspired, is designated "the giver of grace, the love proceeding from the Father and the Son." It is the Spirit who "joins us" to the Father and the Son.[136] Thus, as Bernard McGinn describes it: "We become who we were meant to be through the Spirit's action helping us to actualize the *reductio* [return to God] offered us by the incarnate Word."[137] To put it another way, those who worthily and fruitfully partake of the gift of

---

[131] *Breviloquium*, pt. V, ch. 1, n. 3 and n. 6 (Monti, 171, 172).

[132] Cf. *Collations ... Six Days*, col. 6, n. 24 (de Vinck, 104).

[133] *Breviloquium*, pt. V, ch. 1, n. 3 (Monti, 171).

[134] James 1:17; see *On the Reduction of the Arts to Theology*, n. 1 (Hayes, 37), *Itinerarium*, prol., n. 5 (Hayes, 35).

[135] *Collationes de Septem Donis Spiritus Sancti*, Seraphici Doctoris Sancti Bonaventurae, trans. Marcian Schneider, MA Thesis (NY: The Franciscan Institute, 1950), col. 1, n. 5, page 8.

[136] Schneider, translation of *Collationes de Septem Donis*, col. 1, n. 7, p. 10; see also *Breviloquium*, pt. V, ch. 1, n. 2 and n. 6 (Monti, 169-70 and 172-73).

[137] Bernard McGinn, *The Flowering of Mysticism*, vol. III in The Presence of God: A History of Western Mysticism Series (NY: Crossroad, 1998), 92.

grace are invited to realize progressively God's salvation through the experience of redemptive-completion.[138]

Grace has an individual's "spiritual progress" as its goal."[139] It is given as "an aid to meritorious action" and as a "remedy against sin."[140] It seeks to assist the "twofold rectitude" of human nature, that is, right judgment (rectitude of conscience) and right willing (*synderesis*).[141] While grace may take a variety of forms, it may be understood through the primary categories of actual grace or sanctifying grace.

Actual grace (*gratia gratis data*) is described as "knowledge enlightening" the intellect.[142] It invites the rational creature to "know" itself, God, and the world. Bonaventure presumed that this kind of knowledge, insight, understanding – enlightenment – would stir the affections and guide a person's choices.[143]

Sanctifying grace (*gratia gratum faciens*), or charity (caritas), is the gift that seeks to dispose the soul to love God above all else – one's neighbor, one's self, one's own body, and all creation – in God and for the sake of God.[144] This gift invites the faithful person, therefore, to become actively involved in the struggle to order rightly the affections in particular and to share generously

---

[138] Hayes, *Hidden Center*, 156-57.

[139] *Collationes de Septem Donis*, col. 1, n. 9 (Schneider, 11).

[140] *Breviloquium*, pt. V, ch. 2, n. 1 (Monti, 173).

[141] *Breviloquium*, pt. II, ch. 11, n. 6 (Monti, 95).

[142] Timothy J. Johnson prefers to refer to actual grace – *gratia gratis data* – as "preparatory or helping grace." He does this, he explains, "to avoid confusion between Bonaventure's understanding of the term" and later understandings of the term. See Timothy J. Johnson, *The Soul in Ascent: Bonaventure on Poverty, Prayer, and Union with God* (Quincy: Franciscan Press, 2000), 14.

[143] *Breviloquium*, pt. II, ch. 11, n. 6 and p. V, ch. 2, n. 5 (Monti, 96 and 177-78).

[144] See *Breviloquium*, pt. V, ch. 8, nn. 2-3 (Monti, 201-202); *On the Perfection of Life*, ch. VII, n. 1; *Threefold Way*, ch. I, n. 11.

(*benevolentia*) with one's neighbor.[145] One should understand, therefore, that the gift of sanctifying grace

> empowers the individual to cultivate the virtue of
> charity. Its proper function is to rectify the affective
> power and make it capable of loving everything
> that has being and to attach itself to the highest
> Good for its own sake and above all things.[146]

Sanctifying grace is directed principally, therefore,
toward free choice – the will (*voluntas*) in its most proper
sense. According to the Seraphic Doctor, it is the gift that
seeks to direct and solicit, but not force, free choice.[147]
Received worthily and used fruitfully, sanctifying grace
assists a person in acquiring merit and advancing in the
good.[148] In this way, the soul is empowered to make "what
belongs to grace its own."[149] Recalling the Apostle Paul's
exhortation, Bonaventure urges everyone to receive grace
worthily, guard it wisely, and seek its increase.[150]

The Seraphic Doctor's understanding of the operation
of grace in the soul is demonstrated in his description
of the hierarchizing of the soul through the activities of
purgation, illumination, and perfection as well as in his

---

[145] *Collationes de Septem Donis*, col. 1, n. 3, nn. 9-12 (Schneider, 7
and 11-14).

[146] Elizabeth Dreyer, "*Affectus* in St. Bonaventure's Theology,"
Franciscan Studies 42 (1982): 11. Her argument is based on
Commentarium in III librum Sententiarum, d. 27, a. 1 (III, 579b).

[147] *Breviloquium*, pt. V, ch. 3, n. 5 (Monti, 181). Bonaventure states
that "it is not the nature of grace to compel free choice but anticipate
it, so that both of them pass into act together. And so, in the process
of justification the acts of free will and grace concur in a harmonious
and orderly manner." If the will is to open itself to sanctifying grace, it
needs the arousing assistance of actual grace.

[148] *Breviloquium*, pt. V, ch. 2, n. 2 (Monti, 173).

[149] *Breviloquium*, pt. V, ch. 2, n. 4 (Monti, 177).

[150] See *Collationes de Septem Donis*, col. 1, n. 3 (Schneider, 7). The
scripture reference is 2 Cor 6:1.

description of the various ways grace branches out in the habits of the virtues, the gifts, and the beatitudes. His theology of grace challenges one, therefore, to be sensitive to the ways in which his speculative thought is eminently practical and pastoral in its implications.

While a more complete discussion of grace is beyond the scope of this introduction, a basic sense of the Seraphic Doctor's understanding of the operation of grace is essential for grasping his understanding of the threefold way to wisdom through the three hierarchizing activities. It explains how one learns to live in conformity with the pattern of life revealed in the life of Christ and how the soul becomes enlightened and inflamed with the love of God, the goal of the spiritual journey in the state of human wayfaring.

Conclusion

Bonaventure provides a way to understand how God created the human person in the image of the Word made flesh and invites every person to become a greater likeness to Christ according to the Spirit. In articulating that understanding, he drew creatively from the deep reservoir of his personal gifts, his religious experience and faith, as well as the knowledge of science, psychology, philosophy, and theology available to him as a medieval man. His writings also demonstrate his desire to invite and encourage others to discover through experience how everyone is made of his or her own accord to "praise God, serve God, find delight in God, and be at rest in God."[151]

The Seraphic Doctor's understanding of human nature reflects his indebtedness to early Christian writers and their classical world-view. Consequently, his understanding of human nature and the operations of the powers of the soul were articulated in language

---

[151] *On the Reduction of the Arts*, n. 14 (Hayes, 51-53).

and thought-forms that relied on a blending together of, among other things, Stoic ethics, Platonic metaphysics, Aristotelian logic, and the work of the early Christian theologians[152]

Later generations, even in the face of significant advances in all fields of knowledge, have found his understanding of the noble dignity of the human person and humanity's capacity for self-transcendence to be insightful, compelling, challenging, and of great enduring value. This is not to suggest, however, that his "medieval" understanding and categories are always adequate or helpful. As will be seen in the next section of this introduction, each generation of readers must be sensitive to the challenges of textual interpretation. With effort, it is a manageable task that holds rich promise of leading others to knowledge, understanding, and the "true wisdom" wherein there is knowledge and love coming through experience.

III: The Threefold Spiritual Journey into Wisdom

"In the glory [of heaven]," there is a threefold endowment wherein the gift of wisdom consists "in the possession of eternal peace, in the clear vision of the highest truth, and in the full enjoyment of ultimate goodness or charity."[153] All the saints, holy ones, and blessed of God are granted this gift in the state of glory. They are "at rest in God" as in the heavenly Jerusalem.

---

[152] See, for example, Andrew Louth, "The Body in Western Catholic Christianity," in *Mysticism and Social Transformation*, ed. Janet Ruffing (NY: Syracuse University Press, 2001), 111.

[153] *Threefold Way*, ch. III, n. 1.

In the state of human pilgrimage, the human person is created capable of and oriented to experience a measure of the wisdom that has been promised to all in glory (*beatitudo*). However, those who desire

> through merit to arrive at this blessed state ... must be modeled after this threefold likeness – in so far as it is possible in this life – in order to have: the savory taste of peace, the splendor of truth, and the sweetness of charity.[154]

Bonaventure urges every person, therefore, to (1) cooperate with the gift of grace, (2) use rightly[155] the soul's powers, and (3) make every effort "to arrive at this blessed state" through merit,[156] that is, pursue a truly spiritual way of living through the imitation of Christ.

A person merits to approach this "blessed state," he tells us, in the measure that one's "spirit (*anima*) is made hierarchical – that is, has been purified, illumined, and perfected – through the reformation of the image, through the theological virtues, the enjoyment of the spiritual senses, and the ecstasy of rapture."[157] These are some of

---

[154] *Threefold Way*, ch. I, n. 1.

[155] Right, upright, righteousness, straight, and the like are word images used consistently by Bonaventure to image the stance of the human person whose whole self, body and soul, are in their proper relationship with their source and end, God.

[156] *Threefold Way*, ch. III, n. 1: see also *Itinerarium*, ch. I, n. 8 (Hayes, 53). The performance of good moral acts (meritorious acts) should "proceed from right intention" and are "deserving of eternal reward." The performance of these acts is understood to be "rooted in sanctifying grace" and to make one worthy to receive – merit – a greater measure of the free gift of the sanctifying grace in which they are rooted. The will by choosing rightly and persevering to the end "makes what belongs to grace its own." See *Breviloquium,* pt. V, ch. 2, nn. 1-5 (Monti, 173-78).

[157] *Itinerarium*, ch. IV, n. 4 (Hayes, 101).

the different frameworks within which he identifies the practical challenges at the heart of the spiritual journey.

In this section, attention will be focused on Bonaventure's understanding of how the soul is made hierarchical. It will include a consideration of the concept of hierarchy and the three hierarchizing activities – purgation, illumination, and perfection – through which the soul is reformed in cooperation with the gift of grace. While these categories were used by numerous spiritual writers, Bonaventure articulated a nuanced understanding of them within the larger framework of his theology of the spiritual life. If one hopes to read him correctly, one will have to afford him an opportunity to speak on his own terms and within his own categories. This presumes, of course, a measure of familiarity with some of his philosophical assumptions, speculative thought, and distinctions. One is then in a better position to determine to what degree, and in what ways, the thought of this medieval Franciscan theologian might assist an individual in the struggle to make progress in his/her spiritual journey even in different times and ages.

The Meaning of Hierarchy and Its Threefold Activity

The concept of hierarchy and the hierarchizing activities, as already indicated, serve as one of the primary frameworks through which Bonaventure renders an account of how the soul, under the influence of grace, is led back (*reductio*) to God.

Quoting Pseudo-Dionysius, Bonaventure defines hierarchy as:

a divine order, a knowledge, and an action assimilated as much as possible to the deiform,

and rising proportionally in the likeness to God
towards the light conferred on it from on high....
Hence, hierarchy implies power [order], knowledge,
and action....[158]

The aim of every hierarchy, according to Dionysius,
is "to enable things to be *as like as possible* to God and
to be at one with [God]."[159] Drawing on the thought of
this important and influential thinker, Bonaventure
articulated his own understanding of the hierarchizing
activities as the dynamic and ongoing processes through
which the soul of the faithful person becomes "as like
as possible" to God, is led back to God, and comes to
experience a greater measure of union with God.[160]

The three hierarchizing activities (*operatio*) – the
purgative, illuminative, and perfective ways – provide
descriptive categories through which the Seraphic Doctor
seeks to explain, in a more detailed way, how the human
person's capacities to know, to love, and to act are actually
reformed, recreated, and/or conformed to the sacred
order, knowledge, and action under the influence of grace.
These hierarchizing activities challenge a person to
consider continually three key questions.[161] First, in what
measure is one's understanding "attuned to the highest

---

[158] *Collations ... Six Days*, col. 21, n. 17 (de Vinck, 329). See also
Pseudo-Dionysius, *The Celestial Hierarchy*, ch. III, n. 1, in *Pseudo-
Dionysius: The Complete Works*, trans. Colm Luibheid (Mahwah, NJ:
Paulist Press, 1987), 153.

[159] Pseudo-Dionysius, *Celestial Hierarchy*, ch. III, n. 2; (Luibheid,
154). Emphasis added.

[160] See *Collations ... Six Days*, col. 21, n. 18 (de Vinck, 330).

[161] See *Commentary on Book II of the Sentences*, prologue, nn. 3-5.
These questions might also be phrased in terms of the measure that
a person has learned how to live rightly (*purgatio*), knows what to
believe (*illuminatio*), and how one is to thirst with unflagging desire
as a disciple of Christ (*perfectio*). For more on what is implied here see
Zachary Hayes, *Bonaventure: Mystical Writings* (New York: Crossroad,
2001), 98.

truth in the act of knowing"? Second, in what measure is one's will "conformed to the highest good in the act of loving"? Third, in what measure is one's power for acting "connected to the highest power in operating"?

In the measure that the soul's different powers are attuned, conformed, and connected with the highest truth, goodness, and power – God – they are hierarchized in cooperation with grace. In the measure that a person's understanding, love, and choices are conformed within to the likeness of the triune God, the person is empowered with the strengthening assistance of the theological virtues of faith, hope, and love in particular to pursue a holy and just manner of life (*conversatio*). As the divine influence becomes progressively more alive within the soul, the individual comes to know through experience that he or she is, and is always, in the process of becoming more fully a "daughter," a "friend," and a "spouse" of God – a "temple of the Holy Spirit."[162] Hayes explains succinctly:

> That which is called a hierarchical act is in fact a group of interrelated actions and exercises through which the soul acquires the constitutive elements of its perfection while on earth... .The three acts or ways are not distinct periods in the ascent of the soul. Bonaventure has transferred the static model of Pseudo-Dionysius into an extremely dynamic model. The three acts on the part of the human subject constitute three efforts

---

[162] *Itinerarium*, ch. IV, n. 8 (Hayes, 107). For another helpful metaphor see ch. IV, n. 3 (Hayes, 99), where Bonaventure describes the soul as being "clothed over with the three theological virtues by which it is purified, illumined and perfected."

which enter into the ascent at all times, but with shifts of emphasis.[163]

The hierarchizing activities "constitute three efforts," therefore, toward which the faithful soul must continually turn its attention if the heart desires to be "inhabited by divine wisdom" in the state of human pilgrimage.[164] The challenges at the heart of each of these ways help one to understand, as Hayes puts it, the "continuing work" that Christ hopes to accomplish in the soul of those who desire to become his faithful disciples.[165] With the goal of the journey more clearly determined, attention can be turned to a more in-depth consideration of the various ways the faithful soul might strive to acquire the constitutive elements of its perfection on earth, that is a taste of peace, the splendor of truth, and the sweetness of charity – wisdom.

---

[163] Hayes, *Hidden Center*, 45. See also Denys Turner, *The Darkness of God: Negativity in Christian Mysticism* (NY: Cambridge University Press, 1995), 112-13; Paul Kuntz, "The Hierarchical Vision of St. Bonaventure," in *San Bonaventura Maestro di vita Francescana e di Sapienzia Christiana*, A. Pompei, ed. (Rome: Pontificia Facoltà Teologica San Bonaventura, 1976), 233-48; Andrew Louth, *Denys Areopogite* (London: Geoffrey Chapman, 1989), 105.

[164] *Threefold Way*, ch. III, n. 1; *Itinerarium*, ch. VII, n. 2 (Hayes, 107). Bonaventure's most extensive discussion of the hierarchizing activities can be found in *Threefold Way* and the *Collations ... Six Days*, col. 22, nn. 22-42; see n. 37 in particular (de Vinck, pp. 352-63, especially p. 359). For a brief comparative study of these two texts, see Jacques Guy Bougerol, *Saint Bonaventure: La Triple Voie, Traduction Française, Commentaries et Notes* (Paris: Les Éditions Franciscaines, 1998), 80-83.

[165] Hayes, *Hidden Center*, 44.

The Three Hierarchizing Ways

The Purgative Way

"Purgation leads to peace."[166] The peace to which Bonaventure refers is the peace "proclaimed and given for us by our Lord Jesus Christ," the "peace which surpasses all understanding." It is the peace that Francis "sighed for" in every experience of contemplation and "announced" in every greeting.[167]

In its most fundamental sense, peace refers to an inner quality of the human person that is characterized by right order, right willing, justice.[168] Bonaventure names the struggle for inner peace, or the building up of the right-order desired by God within the soul, as the ongoing challenge of the purgative way. A taste of this peace is merited, however, only in the measure that there is order (*ordo*), equilibrium (*aequalitas*), and/or harmony (*concordia*) between the body and the soul, the sense appetites and the rational faculties, the rational soul

---

[166] *Threefold Way*, ch. III, n. 1 and prologue, n. 1.

[167] See *Itinerarium*, prologue, n. 1 (Hayes, 35). See also ch. VII, n. 1 (Hayes, 133). The text of Sacred Scripture to which he refers includes Eph 1:18, Luke 1:19, Phil 4:7.

[168] On the different meanings of peace in the works of Bonaventure, see Hayes' notes for *Itinerarium* note 3, p. 146). His understanding of justice as right-order is taken from Anselm, see *Commentary on Book II of the Sentences*, prologue, n. 4. Augustine associates peace with right-loving; see *The City of God*, book XIX, ch. 13, and book XIX, ch. 27, trans. Marcus Dods (NY: The Modern Library, 2000), 690-92 and 707-708. The deepest and most mystical meaning of peace is described as an experience of "the kiss, the embrace, and the union to which God may lead us." It is the "ecstatic peace" experienced by Francis on La Verna. It is an experience that might be granted to anyone who is disposed to receive it. The Seraphic Doctor encourages every spiritual pilgrim, therefore, to strive for the peace "which surpasses all understanding." See *Threefold Way*, ch. III, n. 7 and ch. III, n. 2; *The City of God*, book XIX, ch. 14 (Dods, 692-92), as well as *Itinerarium*, ch. VI, n. 3 and prologue, 2 (Hayes, 127 and 37).

and the Creator, the human person and one's neighbor. It is only through right order, right willing, or justice then that "peace is effected" with God and within one's innermost self.[169] The order of justice demands that the "immutable good is to be preferred to a changeable good, the good in itself to an advantageous good, the will of God to one's own, and the judgment of right reason over sensual desire."[170]

When this sacred order is disturbed or reversed, there is disorder and discord. These come into being as a consequence of the failure to do the good that one is capable of doing either because of (1) negligence, (2) disordered desire (*concupiscentia*), or (3) the choice of what is morally worthless or known to be evil (*nequitia / malus*). These are the roots of "almost all our sins and evils"; they come into being from a "will that is not well-ordered, but disordered."[171]

Of particular concern to Bonaventure in his understanding of the purgative way is the problem of "disordered desire." Even though he believed that human desire was inclined naturally to the highest good,[172] there was the reality of the natural and ongoing struggle within the human heart to choose and to do the good.[173] He also

---

[169] *Commentary on the Gospel of Luke* Part I, ch. 7, n. 84, p. 649. There are three volumes in this work (St. Bonaventure, NY: Franciscan Institute Publications, 2001, 2003, 2004); see also Bonaventure, *Collations ... Seven Gifts*, col. 1, n. 6 (Schneider, 9).

[170] *Breviloquium*, pt. III, ch. 8, n. 2 (Monti, 119).

[171] *Threefold Way*, ch. I, n. 4; *Breviloquium*, pt. III, ch. 6, n. 5 (Monti, 114-15). Part III of the *Breviloquium* is an extended explanation of the nature of personal sin and original sin according to the mind of St. Bonaventure.

[172] *Itinerarium*, ch. III, n. 4 (Hayes, 89-91). A more complete discussion of Bonaventure's understanding of sin can be found in the previous section of this Introduction, 27-33.

[173] A reference to Bonaventure's threefold understanding of the good in itself (*bonum honestum*), the good that is useful or advantageous to

shared the commonly held belief among theologians of his time that the sin of the first human "infected" all human nature with ignorance in the mind (*ignorantia mentis*) and disordered desire (*concupiscentia carnis*) in the flesh.[174] As he put it succinctly in a sermon, "as long as the human heart is overcome by the waters of carnal affection, it will be able to have nothing of purity, nor produce the fruit of good works" – justice.[175] Thus, he believed that the powers of the soul, the will (*affectus/voluntas*) in particular, disordered as a consequence of personal sin and infected by the enduring effects of original sin, needed to be rectified, strengthened, and lifted up by right willing, justice. The way of "purgation in bitterness" became necessary, he explains, as a remedy for sin and the disorder that flows from it.[176]

Given the Seraphic Doctor's theological framework and his understanding of reality, the way of purgation may be explained both in terms of the necessity of "ridding oneself of sin" and in terms of the soul's need to be "cleansed, [strengthened, and lifted up] by justice."[177] To put it in another way, the way of purgation may be

---

the self (*bonum conferens*), and the good that is delightful to the self (*bonum delectabile*). See Prentice, 52-53, also note 78 above.

[174] *Itinerarium*, ch. I, n. 7 (Hayes, 51) and *Breviloquium*, p. III, ch. 5 (Monti, 109-12). For an extensive treatment of the doctrine of original sin and some of the contemporary issues it raises, see Tatha Wiley, *Original Sin: Origins, Developments, Contemporary Meanings* (Mahwah, NJ: Paulist Press, 2002).

[175] "Sermon on the Monday After Palm Sunday," n. 3 which may be found in the Appendix of this volume. This theme is repeated in numerous places.

[176] *Threefold Way*, ch. III, n. 9.

[177] *Threefold Way*, ch. III, n. 1 (Hayes, 51) and *Itinerarium*, ch. I, n. 6 (Monti, 172). The amplification of the text from the *Itinerarium* is an attempt to offer a more explicit description of the influence that grace seeks to exercise on the soul as described in the *Breviloquium*, pt. V, ch. 1, n. 6, and the *Collations ... Six Days*, col. 7, nn. 3-15 in particular (de Vinck, 110-17).

understood both in terms of the sin that disrupts right order and in terms of the virtue of justice (right willing) that strives for right order in all one's daily actions. A sense of both of these interrelated dynamics provides a detailed understanding of how a person, with the assistance of grace, might struggle to turn away from sin, turn towards the ways of justice, and be led to experience a taste of the peace proclaimed and given by Christ.

Considered from within the framework of the disordering effects of sin, the purgative way challenges a person to "learn to measure [one's] spirit" and to "unburden the heart" of the disordering effects of sin.[178] This requires the cultivation of the virtue of true self-knowledge.[179]

To assist those who are seeking to acquire true self-knowledge, Bonaventure offers a variety of spiritual exercises through which the "eye of one's heart" may be purified, one's mental powers be sharpened, one's understanding be expanded.[180] The struggle to cultivate this virtue provides the firm foundation, therefore, from which one is able to "ascend to the summit of perfection."[181] This is the virtue that enables a person to know "what [one] ought to be by striving industriously, and finally what one can be by the grace of God."[182]

The thoughtful and critical consideration of one's daily actions through the disciplined use of various spiritual exercises in the light of faith and through a developing consciousness of the demands of the law of love should

---

[178] *On the Perfection of Life*, ch. I, esp. n. 5, *On Governing the Soul*, nn. 3-7.

[179] *On the Perfection of Life*, ch. I, see also 1 John 1:8.

[180] *On the Perfection of Life*, ch. I, n. 5. The Latin text reads: "*exercitio cordis oculus mandatur, ingenium acuitur, intelligentia dilatatur.*"

[181] *On the Perfection of Life*, ch. I, n. 1.

[182] *On the Perfection of Life*, ch. I, esp. n. 5.

be accompanied by feelings of sorrow, shame, and fear.[183] In this way, a person ought to become painfully conscious of the ways the soul may be turned away from God. At the same time, these considerations will obviously lead to a clearer understanding of the conversion – the true change and turning back to God – that is required if one is to live rightly. Finally, this kind of consideration is also intended ultimately to arouse within the heart the "ardor of internal desire" for God and the things of God.[184] Faithfully and fruitfully pursued, this kind of effort enables the devout soul to cultivate the inner strengths of character that make right living possible. Through this kind of effort, the deepest part of the soul may be "rectified."[185] Also, through this kind of effort the faithful soul is understood to be worthy of meriting a greater measure of "spiritual joy and happiness," the peace for which the heart longs.[186]

Considered from within the framework of the soul's need to be "cleansed, [strengthened, and lifted up] by justice," the purgative way demands that one's attention and effort be directed to cultivating the virtue of justice, "the uprightness of the will which inclines a person on the way to rectitude."[187]

As a general virtue, Bonaventure defined justice as "right willing."[188] In the measure that the will is in

---

[183] See Bonaventure's outline of the spiritual exercises of meditation, prayer, and contemplation in *Threefold Way* for good examples of the kind of systematic reflection that leads to true self-knowledge and what choices a person needs to make if one desires to experience a greater measure of peace in one's life.

[184] See *Threefold Way*, ch. I-III, *On Governing the Soul*, nn. 3-7.

[185] See *Threefold Way*, ch. I, nn. 8-9, and *Itinerarium*, prologue, nn. 3-4 (Hayes, 37-41).

[186] *Threefold Way*, ch. I, nn. 8-9.

[187] *Commentary on Luke*, Part I, ch. 2, n. 60 (Karris, 187).

[188] *Breviloquium*, pt. V, ch. 4, n. 5 (Monti, 185) and *Commentary on Book II of the Sentences*, prologue, 4. The definition is taken from

conformity with "the highest goodness," it is "rectified." One is "better," he explains, to the extent that one is "more just."[189] Thus, he can describe justice as the virtue that "beautifies the whole world; it makes that which was deformed beautiful, that which was beautiful yet more beautiful, and that which was already more beautiful to be most beautiful."[190]

As a cardinal virtue, the Seraphic Doctor described justice as the virtue that "embraces" all of the powers of the soul and "directs" all of them in the human person's ongoing effort to fulfill the commands of the law of love. In the measure that justice is cultivated as an inner strength of spirit, one is empowered increasingly to judge rightly (prudence), discipline desire (temperance), struggle in the face of difficulty (fortitude), and choose to do what is good and right (justice).[191] These are the inner strengths that empower a person of faith to render to God, neighbor, and self what is due each of them in accordance with the demands of ordered loving, justice.[192]

Anselm's work *On Free Will*, ch. 3, in *Anselm of Canterbury; Major Works*, Brian Davies and G. R. Evans, eds. (NY: Oxford University Press, 1998), 179.

[189] *Commentary on Book II of the Sentences*, prol. 4.

[190] *Collations ... Six Days*, col. 1, n. 34. The translation here is from Bonaventure Hinwood's article entitled "'Justice' According to St. Bonaventure," *The Cord* 31.11 (1981): 335.

[191] See the *Breviloquium*, pt. V, ch. 4 (Monti, 183-86) for Bonaventure's discussion of the cardinal and the theological virtues as well as the way he correlates each with a different power of the soul and with one of the seven basic virtues that guide all life. He is assuming that the cardinal virtues order the soul towards its end, rectify its affective dispositions, and heal (cleanse) all of the soul's powers. See *Collations ... Six Days*, col. 7, n. 5 (de Vinck, 111).

[192] *Breviloquium*, pt. V, ch. 4, n. 5 (Monti, 185-86); see also *Collations on the Ten Commandments, Works of Saint Bonaventure* VI, trans. Paul Spaeth (St. Bonaventure, NY: The Franciscan Institute, 1995), col. 1, n. 21, 26.

Justice is the virtue through which the good is pursued, evil is avoided, difficulty is borne with, and one learns to be wary of prosperity.[193] In the measure that the powers of one's soul are "set right" in cooperation with the reforming, restoring, and recreating influence of grace, one is able to live a holy way of life (*sancte vivendum / conversationem sanctam*).[194]

Bonaventure stresses the necessity of striving for a virtuous way of living. This emphasis provides the broader context within which one can better grasp the rich variety of virtues he associates with right living.[195] These include the theological and cardinal virtues as well as the virtues of true self-knowledge, humility, poverty, austerity, and the "restrictions of discipline" in particular. Each of these inner strengths of character points to a different but closely related set of virtues that Bonaventure considered of critical importance if one desired to develop the capacity to will rightly and to merit "a taste of peace." The challenge of cultivating each of these virtues provides even deeper insights into the demands of the purgative way and the effort it requires of those who seek the peace to which it leads. In the measure that these virtues are alive within the soul, the one who

---

[193] *Collations ... Six Days*, col. 18, n. 16 (de Vinck, 275).

[194] See *Itinerarium*, ch. 1, n. 8 (Hayes, 53), and the sermon *On the Way of Life*, n. 2 which may be found in the Appendix of this volume. In Bonaventure's medieval understanding of personal sin and the enduring effects of original sin in particular, he assumes that the soul needs to be cleansed, strengthened, and uplifted. The challenge of cultivating an always more holy and just manner of life may offer a more helpful way to understand the ongoing challenges of the purgative way and how one might struggle for a "taste of peace" in different times and ages.

[195] See, for example, the early chapters of *The Major Legend of St. Francis* and *On the Perfection of Life addressed to the Sisters*, the texts *On Governing the Soul* and the *Soliloquium* as well as the sermons *On the Way of Life* and *On Holy Saturday* in particular. Both of these sermons are included in the Appendix of this volume.

possesses them is disposed increasingly to live rightly, to seek a greater knowledge of truth and goodness, and to strive for an even more perfect love of God.

Bonaventure acknowledges that the way of purgation is "painful" and "bitter." At the same time, he assures the spiritual pilgrim that it leads to the "affection of spiritual joy."[196] The way of purgation demands, therefore, that one do all that one is able to do under the influence of grace to "set right" the soul's powers of understanding, affection, and choice, that is, to choose in faith and love to live a holy, upright, and just manner of life.[197]

The Illuminative Way

The way of illumination "leads to truth." It consists in the "imitation of Christ."[198] Those who desire to pursue the right ordering – hierarchizing – of the soul's powers through the pursuit of this way must turn their attention to struggling for the highest and most spiritual understanding (*intelligentia*) of all things and choose a pattern of life in conformity with Christ.

In the pursuit of this kind of understanding, Bonaventure presumes that one shares his assumptions with regard to (a) how one knows,[199] (b) what a human being can know with certitude, (c) the different modes of God's revelation, and (d) the role of Christ in all human knowing. While a comprehensive exploration of these important topics is beyond the scope of this introduction, a brief review of three of his assumptions with respect

---

[196] *Threefold Way*, ch. I, n. 9 and ch. III, n. 10.

[197] See Michael Blastic, "The Conversation of Franciscans: Ministry in Cosmic Context," *The Cord*, 46.2 (1996): 55-63.

[198] *Threefold Way*, prologue, and ch. III, n. 3, n. 8, and n. 10.

[199] Some aspects of Bonaventure's theory of knowledge are explained in greater detail in the Introduction above, pp. 18-24.

to human knowing will be helpful in coming to a clearer understanding of the illuminative way.

First, Bonaventure assumes that he is writing to instruct and encourage a person of faith – an individual who is seeking greater knowledge (*scientia*) and understanding (*intelligentia*) of those things that lead to true wisdom (*sapientia*).

Second, the Seraphic Doctor presumes that there is an integral connection between knowledge and affection within the human person (*anima rationalis*).[200] He believes, for example, that reading, speculation, investigation, industry, knowledge, intelligence, and study must be joined with unction, devotion, admiration, piety, charity, humility, and divine grace.[201] In other words, the struggle to know and understand must be pursued with the intention of arousing affective desire for ultimate Truth and Goodness. At the same time, he assumes that this kind of knowledge and the movement of love which ought to accompany it inclines a person to live in conformity with what is believed, understood, and loved.

Third, while the Seraphic Doctor has the highest respect for the human capacity to know, he also believes that the "light of the created intellect itself is not sufficient for the comprehension of anything without the light of the eternal Word."[202] Thus, he asserts confidently that this "light of the eternal Word" and the "manifold wisdom of God" are revealed in various ways. In fact, this wisdom "lies hidden in all knowledge and things."[203]

---

[200] For more on the close connection Bonaventure perceives between knowledge and affection see, for example, *Threefold Way*, ch. I, n. 10 and 14; ch. III, n. 3 and n. 13; *On the Perfection of Life*, ch. 5, n. 6; *Collations ... Six Days*, col. 8, n. 10 (de Vinck, 126).

[201] See *Itinerarium*, prologue, 4 (Hayes, 39).

[202] Bonaventure, "Christ, the One Teacher of All," n. 10, (Hayes, *What Manner*, 29).

[203] *On the Reduction of the Arts*, n. 26 (Hayes, 8, notes 3 and 4).

He believes, for example, that God "the First Principle made this sensible world in order to make itself known, so that the world might serve as a footprint and a mirror to lead humankind to love and praise God, it Maker.[204] The person who desires to be "illumined" by "the splendor of created things" is encouraged to "open [one's] eyes, alert [one's] spiritual ears, unlock [one's] lips, and apply [one's] heart so that in all creation [one] might see, hear, praise, love and adore, magnify and honor" God.[205] In the pursuit of this kind of enlightenment, therefore, one is expected to do what is within one's own power to contuit (*contuere*), that is, to know the true reality of a created thing as it stands in itself, and more deeply, to grasp something of its relation to its divine origin and end.[206] One must struggle, therefore, to behold (*contuere*) the uniqueness of every thing that can be seen and also be led by all created things to their joy-producing source – God.[207]

He believed that the wisdom of God was "clearly revealed in Sacred Scripture."[208] In addition to its literal meaning, he understood Sacred Scripture to have a threefold meaning. Thus, Scripture held the potential to teach the intelligent creature what to believe, how to live, and how to be in union with God, that is, how the soul must be illumined, purified, and perfected.[209] This threefold interpretation, according to the Seraphic Doctor,

---

[204] *Breviloquium*, pt. II, ch. 11, n. 2 (Monti, 94).

[205] *Itinerarium*, ch. I, n. 15 (Hayes, 61).

[206] Hayes, *Knowledge of Christ*, Introduction, 58.

[207] For more on the concept of contuition see *Itinerarium* (Hayes, Introduction, 26-27); Ewert Cousins, "Bonaventure's Mysticism of Language," in *Mysticism and Language*, Steven Katz, ed. (NY: Oxford University Press, 1992), 250.

[208] *Itinerarium*, ch. IV, n. 6 (Hayes, 106), *Breviloquium*, prologue, n. 4 (Monti, 4); *Threefold Way*, prologue. This was a common approach to the interpretation of Sacred Scripture among medieval theologians.

[209] See in particular *On the Reduction of the Arts to Theology*, n. 5 (Hayes, 45), and *Itinerarium*, ch. IV, n. 6 (Hayes, 106).

was "called for and suited to [humankind's] capacity for understanding."[210] In this way, Scripture gives us human wayfarers as much knowledge as we need to achieve salvation.[211]

Bonaventure believes firmly that Christ is the "Word and Wisdom of the Father." He is the "central point of all understanding" and the "fontal principle of all cognitive illuminations."[212] As the Incarnate Word, for example, Christ reveals both humankind's capacity for God and how the rational creature is led back to God.[213] One should understand clearly, therefore, that in the mind of the Seraphic Doctor, Christ is "the Light" that "comes down to enlighten our cognitive faculty, build our affectivity, and strengthen [our activity]."[214]

Christ, the crucified Word, assumes a particularly central role in illuminating the mind because, according to Bonaventure, "all things are revealed through the cross." It is "the key, the gate, the path, and the guiding light of truth. Anyone who takes it up ... will have the light of life."[215] One should look upon and desire that the eyes of the heart "be fixed with unending devotion on Christ dying on the cross."[216] One should struggle to understand these things and make every effort to realize that Christ "bore all of this in order *to set aflame his love in you*, so that for all these things you might love him with all your heart, all your soul, and all your mind."[217]

---

[210] *Breviloquium*, prologue, n. 3 and n. 5 (Monti, 3-4 and 4-5).

[211] *Breviloquium*, prologue, n. 3 (Monti, 3).

[212] See Bonaventure's sermon entitled "Christ, the One Teacher of All," (Hayes, *What Manner*, 21).

[213] *Itinerarium*, ch. IV, n. 2 (Hayes, 97-99).

[214] *Collationes de Septem Donis*, col. 9, n. 5 (Schneider, 134).

[215] *Threefold Way*, ch. III, n. 5.

[216] *On the Perfection of Life*, ch. VI, n. 1.

[217] *On the Perfection of Life*, ch. VI, n. 9, emphasis added.

Bonaventure is convinced, therefore, that illuminating Truth is shining forth in all things, most especially in Christ, the light of truth.[218] This light / truth is accessible to the human mind. As Hayes puts it:

> [Bonaventure] assures us that in giving ourselves to Christ and to his cause and his values, we are defining our reality in a way that will be ultimately life-giving and fulfilling since it opens us in a most radical sense to the mystery of the divine."[219]

The hierarchizing activities associated with the illuminative way emphasize the struggle to acquire a deeper knowledge and understanding of God, Christ, spiritual things, "the truth as such and the truth as a good."[220] As is evident in the *Itinerarium Mentis in Deum, The Tree of Life,* and in other works, the emphasis in the illuminative way is on seeking the enlightenment of the cognitive capacity in a manner that arouses affective desire and strengthens one's resolve to choose a pattern of life that is always in greater conformity with the pattern of life revealed in the life of Christ.

The struggle for a greater knowledge and understanding of God, and the person of Christ in particular, is the heart of the illuminative way. This kind of knowledge provides an accurate understanding of the measure against which one's spirit might be judged rightly, the central concern of the purgative way. At the same time, progress in right willing and right knowing, the goals of the purgative and illuminative ways respectively, prepares and disposes the soul to seek and desire an even

---

[218] For another argument through which one may to come to this conclusion see *Itinerarium*, c, I, n. 7 (Hayes, 51); *Collations ... Six Days*, col. 1, nn. 10-39 (de Vinck, 5-19).

[219] Zachary Hayes, "Christ, Word of God and Exemplar of Humanity," *The Cord* 46.1 (1996): 12.

[220] *Breviloquium*, pt. II, ch. 9, n. 7 (Monti, 88).

greater experience of true wisdom and to desire an even greater measure of its perfection through the love which surpasses all understanding – the kind of inner ordering (hierarchizing) – of the soul's powers toward which the way of perfection seeks to lead the spiritual pilgrim.

The Way of Perfection/Union

The way of perfection (*perfectio / unio*) leads to charity. It consists in the experience of the soul "being joined to the Spouse" through the "sweetness of charity," that is, the "highest Goodness" being joined to the human will through the reception of the Spirit of God's love and goodness.[221] This experience of union (*unio*) "takes place through charity."[222]

The way of perfection is concerned primarily with the desire to allow the affections and will, in particular, to be connected with and drawn upward into ever greater conformity with the "highest goodness." It is essentially a challenge to strive for "an increasing depth of loving union with God as one becomes aware that 'through love there is realized the supremely desirable presence of the Spouse.'"[223] In the pursuit of the love (*caritas*) to which this way leads, one's effort must be turned to "enkindling the fire of love" in so far as it is possible in the state of human pilgrimage.[224] This aspect of wisdom and Bonaventure's understanding of how one might struggle for it presumes

---

[221] *Threefold Way*, ch. III, n. 1 and n. 6. He explains "Sweetness is attributed to the Holy Spirit because of will and goodness. Where highest goodness is joined to the will, there is highest charity and sweetness" (n. 12). See also "The Evening Sermon on St. Francis, 1267" (FA:ED II, 762).

[222] *Threefold Way*, ch. III, n. 1; see also ch. II, n. 9.

[223] Hayes, *Hidden Center*, 44. His statement includes a quotation from *Threefold Way*, ch. I, n. 16.

[224] The "enkindling of love" is the subtitle, and in many manuscripts the title, given to *Threefold Way*.

familiarity with his understanding of (a) the nature of love (*caritas*), (b) the dynamic process through which the power of loves unites and transforms the soul, and (c) how one might seek to make "progress in the love of God" and come to experience a measure of "the union to which God may lead [one]."[225]

Charity is "righteous and well-ordered love." It is directed to that "good in Whom it finds its enjoyment and repose" – God.[226] It alone "leads a person to perfection," which is essentially a question of making "progress in charity."[227] Therefore, this is the virtue that "must be pursued more than all the other virtues, and not just any charity but that whereby we love God above all things and our neighbor for the sake of God."[228] It is the virtue that enables the soul "to do everything that pertains to perfection" and the one that "brings to perfection all good things."[229]

In the *Breviloquium*, Bonaventure describes love (*amor*) as "the measure of the soul (*mens*) and the origin of all its affections." The highest form of love, charity (*caritas*), is described as

---

[225] *Threefold Way*, ch. II, 9 and ch. III, n. 7.

[226] *Breviloquium*, pt. V, ch. 8, n. 2 (Monti, 201).

[227] *On the Perfection of Life*, ch. 7, n. 1 and *Threefold Way*, ch. II, n. 11. In the *Defense of the Mendicants,* Bonaventure states that the "origin of all perfection is love" (ch. III, n. 19) and demonstrates the variety of perfections that there are "according to the degree of their participation in the supreme Good itself" (ch. II, n. 12). See *Works of Saint Bonaventure* IV, trans. José de Vinck (Paterson, NJ: St. Anthony Guild, 1963), 52 and 30. See also Hayes' discussion of perfection in *Hidden Center*, 134-35.

[228] *On the Perfection of Life*, ch. VII, n. 1. See also *Breviloquium*, pt. V, ch. 8, n. 2 (Monti, 201).

[229] *Threefold Way*, ch. II, n. 11. See also *Breviloquium*, pt. V, ch. 8, n. 2 (Monti, 201) and *On the Perfection of Life*, ch. 7, n. 1; *Threefold Way*, ch. II, 11. As indicated above, in the *Defense of the Mendicants* (ch. II, n. 12), he describes perfection as a question of the degree to which someone "participates in the supreme Good itself" (p. 30).

the root, form, and end of all the virtues, relating (*unio*) them all to the final end and binding (*vinculum*) them all to one another simultaneously and in orderly (*ordo*) fashion. That is why we can say that charity (*caritas*) is the weight and measure (*pondus*) of ordered inclination and the chain of perfect unity, preserving within itself the order to be observed with respect to the diverse things we should love, both with regard to emotions felt and actions taken (*affectus / effectus*).[230]

In this descriptive definition of love, Bonaventure uses a number of important word images in an attempt to describe the nature, function, dimensions, and dynamic qualities of the power of love. For example, the medieval use of the Latin word *pondus* (weight or measure) images charity as the natural tendency, inner pull, that inclines the soul in an "orderly" way toward its deepest, most spiritual part (*anima / mens*). At the same time, charity is understood to be a kind of weight (*pondus*) that inclines the soul back to its source and end, God.[231]

According to Bonaventure, the most distinctive aspect of love is the fact that through the power of affection the soul is drawn beyond itself and is capable of clinging through affection (*affectus adhaesio*) to the desired good.[232] The affection of love, the "origin of all [the heart's]

---

[230] *Breviloquium*, pt. V, ch. 8, n. 5 (Monti, 202).

[231] See also *Itinerarium*, ch. I, n. 11, (Hayes, note 16, p. 167); David N. Bell, *The Nature and Dignity of Love: William of St. Thierry*, trans. Thomas X. Davis (Kalamazoo: Cistercian Publications, 1981), 6.

[232] This is an attempt to summarize briefly Bonaventure's psychology of love that is explained in detail in Prentice, *Psychology of Love*, chapter three, esp. p. 66. Prentice believes that Bonaventure's affective psychology is based on the principle *affectus adhaesio respectu obiecti*. This principle asserts that "Love is an act of the will (as indicated by '*affectus*'), since affection pertains to will whereby it unites itself through the concupiscible appetite (as indicated by

affections," has many objects, admits to varying degrees of intensity, and is moved for various reasons. In the form of love most properly called charity, the soul desires the experience of being united – *unio, adhaesio, copulo, jungo, suscipio* – with the highest Good, its ultimate end, God. By his deliberate choice of a variety of Latin words, Bonaventure conveys effectively the depth, intensity, and significance of this experience. For this reason, he can describe charity as "the weight of a properly ordered attraction and the bond of perfect union."[233]

One must also understand that "somehow by the association of love [one is] transformed (*transformatus*) to the likeness of the very one to whom [one is] joined by affection."[234] This means that the lover is "changed according to the pattern" of the good to which the heart is joined by affection.[235] The change is, in fact, conditioned by the good that is loved. Thus, Bonaventure can say that the "one who loves goodness is made upright."[236]

Bonaventure's understanding of love as a power that unites and transforms is based on a principle articulated and developed in the works of Hugh and Richard of St. Victor.[237] This principle assumes, as indicated above, that

---

'*adhaesio*') to any of the three goods [the honest good, the useful good, and the good that delights the self] (as indicated by '*obiecti*')."

[233] *Breviloquium*, pt. V, ch. 8. n. 5 (Monti, 202).

[234] *Commentary on Book II of the Sentences*, prol. 4. Bonaventure is quoting Hugh of St. Victor here and in a number of other places. See also *Soliloquium*, ch. 2, II, n. 12; "The Morning Sermon on St. Francis, 1255" (FA:ED II, 515).

[235] See Prentice, *Psychology of Love,* 73-74.

[236] *Commentary on Book II of the Sentences*, prol. 4. In his "The Evening Sermon on St. Francis (1267 (FA:ED II, 762), he explains: "When the soul is united by love to a creature, it takes on the creature's likeness."

[237] See, for example, *Soliloquium*, ch. 1, § II, n. 3 and ch. 2, § II, n. 12, and the "Morning Sermon on St. Francis, 1255" (FA:ED II, 515). He is drawing on the understanding of love articulated in the twelfth century by Hugh and Richard of St. Victor. See, for example,

the soul is drawn progressively upward through the power of love into experiences of joyful union with God. At the same time, the soul's experience of union effects a true change, that is, it transforms the person into a greater likeness of the "humble Christ."[238] For the Seraphic Doctor, Francis was the exemplar of this principle. He described Francis after his mystical experience on La Verna, for example, as a man who was "being borne aloft into God" by the "Seraphic ardor of his desires" and through compassion was "being transformed into him who chose to be crucified because of 'the excess of his love.'"[239] In another chapter, he describes Francis as "fixed with Christ to the cross" in that he "burned with a Seraphic love of God and also 'thirsted' with Christ crucified for the salvation of [all men and women.]"[240]

Love is like a fire (*ignis*),[241] according to Bonaventure, and he invites everyone to allow one's affections to be set "afire" with love (*caritas*) through the reception of the sweetness of the Spouse and to struggle for the perfection of charity. This "requires," he explains, that the "beloved friend of Jesus Christ" struggle to love God with one's

---

Hugh of St. Victor, *Soliloquy on the Earnest Money of the Soul*, trans. Kevin Herbert (Milwaukee: Marquette University Press, 1956) and Richard of St. Victor in "On the Four Degrees of Passionate Love," in *The Catholic Tradition*, Charles Dollen, James K. McGowan, James J. Megivern, eds. (Wilmington, NC: McGrath Publishing Co., 1979), 235-54.

[238] See Richard of St. Victor, *Degrees of Passionate Love* (Dollen, 252).

[239] *The Major Legend of St. Francis*, ch. 13, n. 3 (FA:ED II, 630). The Seraphs are angelic spirits who are "burning with the fire of love." They occupy the highest rung among the nine choirs of angels. See also "Sermon on St. Francis, 1262" in FA:ED II, 515.

[240] *The Major Legend of St. Francis*, ch. XIV, n. 1 (FA:ED II, 640). See also his description of the affection of Francis's piety, ch. VIII, n. 1 (FA:ED II, 586) and the fervor of Francis's charity, ch. IX (FA:ED II 596-604.

[241] *Breviloquium*, pt. V, ch. 6, n. 6 (Monti, 194).

whole heart (*cor*), soul (*anima*), and mind (*mens*) "so that not the smallest part" of the self does not share Christ's love.[242] This means that (1) the "heart is not inclined to love anything else but God" and that one finds no delight in worldly things; (2) the soul loves God without alternative, not for what one wants for the self, what the world advises, or what the flesh craves; and (3) the heart loves God faithfully from the depths of its innermost being. Thus, Bonaventure proposes that one do what one can, in an exercise of meditation, for example, to concentrate, nourish, and lift up the affections if one hopes to reach the summit of the perfection of charity.[243]

The affections are "concentrated," he explains, in the measure that desire is turned away from the love of creatures and created goods. Although all good things are gifts of God's creative activity, lesser goods must never be loved more than God, that is, in a disordered way. The desire for self-centered or temporal goods can easily become, however, sources of distraction and preoccupation in a heart that longs for them. They divert one's attention and scatter one's affections in ways that impede progress in the love of spiritual goods. As a consequence, the heart finds no peace or rest. The person's desire for union with God is weakened.

Love is "nourished" in the devoted soul, according to Bonaventure, by "turning the affections to the love of the Spouse." This "occurs when the soul" through love is drawn into "the presence of the One who is most highly desirable. These are the things that inflame the affections."[244]

Finally, one must also struggle to lift up the affections "beyond everything that can be sensed, imagined, or

---

[242] *On the Perfection of Life*, ch. VII, nn. 2-4.

[243] See *Threefold Way* (ch. I, nn. 15-17). See also his outlines of the spiritual exercises of prayer (ch. II, nn. 9-11), and contemplation (ch. III, nn. 6-7).

[244] *Threefold Way*, ch. I, n. 16.

understood" to God wherein there is discovered "awesome depth, marvelous beauty, and desirable sweetness."[245] One should hope, therefore, that in its fervent desire," just like a fire, the soul is ready to be "carried beyond itself into darkness and ecstasy."[246]

In a reflection on Francis's "love without limit," Bonaventure makes a rather harsh judgment and poses a pointed question that, paradoxically, places the challenge of the way of perfection in bold relief. He asks:

> How is it that we, wretched as we are, have such cold hearts that we are not prepared to endure anything for our Lord's sake? Our hearts neither burn nor glow with love. Ardent love is a quality of the heart and the stronger this love burns in a person's heart, the more heroic and virtuous are [that person's] deeds. Do you desire to imprint Christ crucified on your heart? Do you long to be transformed into [Christ] to the point where your heart is aflame with love?[247]

Francis embodied the "burning" and "ardent love" of the triune God that every heart is capable of seeking and meriting. In Bonaventure's development of the way of perfection, he describes how one might strive to allow the heart to become "aflame with love." He hopes that, through the inspiration of Francis and dedicated personal effort with the assistance of grace, others will embrace the demands and challenges of struggling for charity, a quality of the heart that expresses itself in virtuous deeds in imitation of Christ.

---

[245] *Threefold Way*, ch. III, n. 12.

[246] *Breviloquium*, pt. V, ch. 6, n. 7 (Monti, 196); *Threefold Way*, ch. III, n. 6.

[247] "The Evening Sermon on St. Francis, 1262" in FA:ED II, 726-27).

In the measure that the soul has been "cleansed by justice" and "illuminated by truth," it is disposed more readily, at least in theory, to seek its perfection in the highest good. At the same time, the soul that is gifted with or merits to experience "the kiss, the embrace, and the union to which God may lead" can expect to gain deeper insight into one's as yet unrealized and/or underdeveloped potential to know, to love, and to imitate Christ. The way of perfection demonstrates then how one might exercise oneself in those kinds of activities that are intended to lead one towards a greater measure of the "enjoyment of ultimate goodness or charity" for which one longs.[248] One should also understand that progress in charity prepares and disposes the soul for ecstasy (*excessus mentis*) and even more mystical kinds of experience (*raptus*).

Conclusion

If one desires the "true wisdom that leads to eternal life," one should also understand that no one is led to this wisdom unless the "intellect knows what truths to accept," the "will chooses the good to be done," and the "affections yearn to see, to love, and to enjoy God."[249] This is what sacred scripture seeks to teach every man and woman, "so that [wisdom] may win over every mind, meeting each at its own level while remaining superior to all, *illuminating and setting afire* with shafts of love every mind that searches it with care."[250] To put it another way, sacred scripture teaches that the human spirit must be hierarchized, that is, "cleansed by virtuous deeds,

---

[248] *Threefold Way*, ch. III, n. 1.
[249] *Breviloquium*, prologue, seec. 4, n.5 (Monti, 16).
[250] *Breviloquium*, prologue, sec. 4, n.3 (Monti, 15).

illumined by shining faith, and made perfect by burning love" if it desires to be guided to "true wisdom."[251]

What is taught must be internalized through personal effort in cooperation with grace. In this way, the intellect, the will, and the heart's affections become attuned, conformed, and connected within to the sacred order, knowledge, and activity – hierarchized – to the extent that it is possible in the state of human pilgrimage.

Drawing on his theology of the spiritual life, Bonaventure developed a threefold way for understanding the struggle for peace, truth, and love – the constitutive elements of wisdom. He also offered some practical guidance and a variety of spiritual exercises through which the faithful soul could do what was within its own power to dispose itself to make progress toward this goal in cooperation with grace. In his writings, then, one can expect to find a variety of orderly and systematic conceptualizations of a complex and ongoing process that depends on grace and requires strenuous personal effort.

The conceptual clarity of the teacher is, however, only helpful to the extent that an individual is able to use creatively Bonaventure's teaching as a guide to discovering how grace might be at work in one's life and drawing one's soul to a greater measure of justice, knowledge, and ardent love in the ordinary, sometimes extraordinary, circumstances of life.

Bonaventure's threefold way seeks to enlighten the intellect and arouse loving desire to follow Christ after the example of St. Francis through right willing, right knowing, and an excess of love that likens one to Christ to the extent that this might be possible in the life of any individual. To put it another way, it is intended to lead the soul to "true wisdom" through experience. For those who desire this wisdom and are willing to struggle for

---

[251] *Breviloquium*, prologue, sec. 4, n.5 (Monti, 16).

it, the Seraphic Doctor offers a way of meriting a measure of the wisdom to which the spiritual journey leads the faithful and devout soul.

IV
The Texts in Translation

This section is divided into three parts. The first section treats in an abbreviated way the challenges of interpreting medieval texts. The second section provides technical information on the methodology used in the preparation of this volume. The third section names some of the obstacles readers in different historical periods face in reading Bonaventure and other classic authors.

THE INTERPRETATION OF CLASSIC TEXTS

The texts included in this volume are considered "wisdom texts," true "classics" within the Franciscan-Bonaventurian tradition. Successive generations of Franciscans in particular have found in these texts, in the words of David Tracy:

> something valuable, something "important"; some disclosure of reality that must be called one of "recognition" which surprises, provokes, challenges, shocks, and eventually transforms us; an experience that upsets conventional opinions and expands the sense of the possible; indeed a realized experience of that which is essential, that which endures. Their actual effects in our lives endure and await ever-new appropriations, constant new interpretations.[252]

As a result, their "existence has been trusted to time, to generations of capable readers and capable inquirers" who must continually face the challenges of both checking

---

[252] Tracy, *Analogical Imagination,* 108-109.

their enthusiasm and ensuring the emergence of some communal sense of texts such as these.[253]

There are significant challenges to be faced, however, in any attempt to understand, appropriate, and use these Franciscan – Bonaventurian "wisdom texts" in radically different historical – social – psychological – theological contexts. As Philip Sheldrake reminds us, the interpretation of texts (hermeneutics) requires both "a receptive and at the same time critical dialogue with a spiritual text in order to allow the wisdom contained in it to challenge us and yet to accord our own horizons their proper place."[254]

With regard to the reception of a text (the hermeneutics of consent), Elizabeth Dreyer suggests that one "let the figures of the past speak to us from their own times and within their own structures of meaning – both sometimes foreign to us."[255] At the same time, she urges readers to enter into a critical dialogue with a text (the hermeneutics of suspicion). This "involves the recognition that the questions provoked by our contemporary situation may well be critical of the text and its theological and social assumptions."[256] An informed yet critical dialogue with the text challenges one to ask, therefore, not only what does it mean, but also: is it relevant to a Christian way of living in another time and context? The critical interpretation of a text demands that a person's consciousness, understanding of what it means to be human and the

---

[253] Tracy, *Analogical Imagination,* 109.

[254] Philip Sheldrake, *Spirituality and History: Questions of Interpretation and Method* (NY: Crossroad, 1992), 165.

[255] Elizabeth A. Dreyer, *Earth Crammed with Heaven: A Spirituality of Everyday Life* (Mahwah, NJ: Paulist Press, 1994), 37. See also Margaret Miles, *Practicing Christianity: Critical Perspectives for an Embodied Spirituality* (NY: Crossroad, 1988) and *The Image and Practice of Holiness: A Critique of the Classical Manuals of Devotion* (London: SCM Press, 1989).

[256] Sheldrake, 175.

like, empower each individual to take a critical stance in the face of the text's theological, conceptual, and practical assumptions. In this way, the reader is forced to confront the challenges of arriving at a faithful reading of the text. At the same time, the reader is challenged to struggle to arrive at a creative synthesis that is appropriate and relevant in another time.

Sheldrake, Dreyer, and others offer helpful and more adequate discussions of the two primary challenges of interpretation. Hopefully, readers will be sensitive to these important and sometimes complicated questions as they enter into a critical and creative dialogue with these classical texts and encounter their enduring wisdom and their excess of meaning. Ideally, this knowledge will invite the reader into a deeper understanding of his or her own experience of God, Gospel love, and the practical demands of living the Christian life after the example of Francis, Clare, and those who have been inspired by them for centuries.

THE TEXTS IN TRANSLATION: SOME TECHNICAL NOTES

The texts in this volume are translations of the critical edition of the Latin texts found in Bonaventure's *Opera omnia* as prepared by the Quaracchi editors or later editions as indicated in the notes and bibliography. The volume and page numbers in the *Opera omnia* are noted in the introduction to the different texts. References to the *Opera omnia* are limited to the volume and page number(s) included within parentheses throughout this volume. Primary Latin sources are included in the notes accompanying each text. When available, English-language translations of primary texts have also been included. A number of notes and cross-references have also been provided to assist the interested reader in better grasping or further exploring the richness and complexity of Bonaventure's thought.

The translator of Bonaventure's Latin faces a number of significant challenges. Ewert Cousins succinctly described Bonaventure's style as "highly complex, composed of long stately sentences, with rhythmically balanced phrases and clusters of symbols whose meaning is enhanced by the subtle relations suggested by their position in the rhetorical structure."[257] Bonaventure's poetic style, subtle use of Latin words, and creative use of word images is indeed difficult – at times impossible – to convey in readable contemporary English translation. Dr. Girard Etzkorn has striven, however, to provide reliable and accurate translations that closely follow the Latin text. When necessary, adjustments and interpretations of the text have been noted to clarify Bonaventure's meaning.

The translation of *The Threefold Way* makes extensive use of "sense lines." Following the example of Cousins, they are used "in order to make [the text] more available for meditative reading." These visual patterns, which occur frequently in this text, often supply what "non-inflected English grammar could not do."[258] For the most part, "sense lines" have not been used in the formatting of the other texts.

Numerous texts of Sacred Scripture are embedded in Bonaventure's writings. In this translation, the texts are italicized to assist the reader in identifying them. Translations are made from the Latin Text that Bonaventure used. That is, in fidelity to Bonaventure's use of Sacred Scripture no modern translation of Scripture has been employed. In general, the reader will discover frequently that the references to Sacred Scripture provide

---

[257] Cousins, *Bonaventure,* 47.

[258] Cousins, *Bonaventure,* 47.

helpful clues toward achieving a better understanding of Bonaventure's intended meaning.

It will be helpful to recall also that medieval methods of editing and copying texts as well as the author's reliance on transcribers and secretaries did not always produce a text that would meet the standards of accuracy, precision, and completeness expected today. At the same time, it must be acknowledged that medieval authors "could take liberties with their sources" and quotations often present complicated questions.[259] It is also possible that authors or transcribers may not always have had access to original sources and they had to rely frequently on the translations as well as the interpretations of others. Furthermore, it should be noted that Bonaventure – perhaps a secretary, transcriber or redactor – may not have recalled accurately a text. As a consequence, various technical difficulties are found in the Quaracchi edition of Bonaventure's *Opera omnia* which was prepared near the end of the nineteenth century and in accordance with the standards of that time.

Jacqueline Hamesse has discussed many of these problems in her cited article. While they are not insignificant technical concerns, for the most part they do not undermine the basic value of the Latin text prepared by the Quaracchi editors. Those who intend to work closely with these texts are cautioned, therefore, that one may encounter some discrepancies that are only acknowledged here.

The density and brevity of Bonaventure's treatment of many points in the works contained in this volume suggested the desirability of additional notes to aid

---

[259] Jacqueline Hamesse, "New Perspectives for Critical Editions of Franciscan Texts of the Middle Ages," *Franciscan Studies* 56 (1998): 174. See also Zachary Hayes, "Bonaventure: Mystery of the Triune God," in *The History of Franciscan Theology*, Kenan Osborne, OFM, ed. (St. Bonaventure, NY: The Franciscan Institute, 1994), 44-45.

the reader in grasping his meaning. When possible, a definition found in another place and in Bonaventure's own words has been used to clarify his meaning. In addition, a number of cross-references to other writings of Bonaventure have been included. The references are intended to guide the reader to other texts in which Bonaventure discusses a topic in a similar, related, or more developed way.

The meaning of some words (e.g., *mens*, *synderesis*), for example, is difficult to render in contemporary English. In other instances, the common understanding of the term has shifted over time. An attempt has been made to note some of these difficulties and/or provide descriptive definitions as much as possible. At the same time, one should realize that words like *sapientia* and *mens* are often used by our author to communicate a variety of simultaneous meanings. A glossary of terms is provided at the end of this volume.

Finally, brackets [ ] have been used to indicate either that a word has been supplied to clarify Bonaventure's thought or that the existing translation has been modified to make the translation more gender inclusive.

READING THE TEXTS IN A DIFFERENT HISTORICAL CONTEXT

In addition to the historical and textual problems of interpretation we have noted briefly, readers of Bonaventure in different historical moments will no doubt encounter other obstacles in their attempts to understand his medieval thought and to grasp the categories within which he worked. Subsequent generations of readers invariably bring a different consciousness to the text. They may understand concepts and categories in different ways and use words that may have acquired different meanings over time. All of these present potential problems in grasping Bonaventure's intended meaning. For example, the word "hierarchy" is a technical term used to describe a sacred order, understanding, and activity. Bonaventure makes use of this Pseudo-Dionysian concept to account for the dynamic and ongoing processes through which the soul is reformed by grace. His understanding of the word is far removed from, for example, the common twentieth-century understanding of the word "hierarchy" and the tendency to associate it with levels of value or structures of power sharing and decision-making. Similarly, the word "perfection" would conjure up idealized notions of precision performances in the minds of men and women in later centuries. In the works of Bonaventure, perfection is understood typically in relation to love (*caritas*), in terms of "degrees" of likeness or unlikeness to Christ. The "perfective way" treats of the soul's potential to be drawn into a transforming union of love with God. It may be difficult, therefore, for readers in radically different times to allow the Seraphic Doctor to use his own terms and speak from within his own structures of meaning.

As these and other examples would illustrate, readers of Bonaventure must be sensitive to these concerns in relation to their personal readiness to read the texts fruitfully and accurately and understand them in the context of medieval theology or spirituality. There can be no doubt that the richness, diversity, theological-philosophical categories, as well as the world-view of an author like Bonaventure are formidable, but not insurmountable, difficulties to successive generations of readers. At the same time, one should also be challenged by the fact that generations of readers have found in these texts enduring wisdom and helpful guidance in searching for theological understanding or spiritual guidance on their own journeys into wisdom.

V
Some Conclusions

The self-described "wanton Gospeller" Nancy Mairs dared to ask and explore several important questions: "What does it mean to live in the presence of God? Present to God? What responsibilities do I bear for the creation of my life? What choices must I make to sustain it?"[260] Posed in her twentieth-century memoirs, these questions are essentially variations on those posed by most spiritual seekers.

While Mairs does not look to Bonaventure for guidance in answering her questions, one can assume rightly that in him she would have found a dialogue partner who could have offered her a theological framework within which she might consider her questions. He could also have offered her some practical guidance with regard to the kinds of choices she might make in the pursuit of a Gospel way of life even in her radically different historical circumstances.

The Seraphic Doctor's theology of the spiritual life provides a detailed and well-developed understanding of how a person might "fix [one's] heart only on God" and "single-mindedly set out for God."[261] In his various works of theology and spiritual writings, he is always inviting the reader into a better personal understanding of the different ways one might partake worthily of the gift of grace and enter more deeply through experience into the

---

[260] Mairs, *Ordinary Time*.

[261] The images are taken from Francisco de Osuna, *The Third Spiritual Alphabet*, trans. Mary E. Giles (NY: Paulist Press, 1981), 47-48. Osuna was an influential sixteenth-century Franciscan spiritual director and writer. His work reflects his indebtedness to the Franciscan theological tradition and it also represents a new and creative synthesis that was articulated in the historical circumstances in which he lived.

wisdom of God. As noted above, Bonaventure achieved a new and creative synthesis of the theological tradition he inherited. His insights and perspectives were significantly influenced by his own religious experience and the life of St. Francis, his spiritual father and brother.

The retrieval of Bonaventure's medieval thought in radically different historical times presumes, of course, that an individual not only has access to the texts but also, more often than not, a teacher or mentor who is able and ready to invite a spiritual seeker (1) to read and explore the texts and (2) to critically and creatively explore the enduring wisdom embedded in those texts. In this way, successive generations of Franciscans have been empowered to understand Bonaventure's teachings and to consider how he was inviting them to follow Christ after the example of St. Francis.

This kind of "formative learning experience" is best pursued in the company of brothers and sisters – formators, spiritual directors, preachers, teachers, ministry supervisors and the like – who look to the Franciscan-Bonaventurian tradition as a source of inspiration and guidance and who give an authentic witness to its truth and relevance in different ages and times.

This introduction and the texts contained in this volume provide yet another generation of English-speaking spiritual seekers with an opportunity to enter into an informed reading of some of Bonaventure's texts. Hopefully, this volume will, with its texts, notes, and indexes, offer many helpful ways of entering into a fruitful dialogue with the spiritual wisdom of the thirteenth-century Franciscan spiritual master, St. Bonaventure of Bagnoregio.

THE TEXTS IN TRANSLATION

THE THREEFOLD WAY

DE TRIPLICI VIA

Introduction to the Text

The Threefold Way: On Enkindling Love contains Bonaventure's "most extensive reflections on the human response"[1] to grace. In this text, he briefly and concisely unfolds the inner dynamic processes through which a human person is empowered by grace to make the journey into the wisdom which is God.

Originally addressed to an unknown individual,[2] it became a widely influential text. A measure of its enduring significance lies in the practical guidance it offers in understanding Bonaventure's (1) vision of the spiritual life and (2) the personal effort required to make the spiritual journey. The text reflects in numerous ways Bonaventure's basic conviction that every human person is gifted with the potential to respond in faith and love to the ongoing and generous outpouring of God's grace through the correct use of the soul's three principal powers – memory, understanding, and will.

In Bonaventure's view, the human person is created with a unique nobility and dignity. This dignity is most evident in the soul's inner orientation and capacity to

---

[1] Hayes, *Hidden Center*, 45.

[2] There are indications in the text that it was addressed originally to a man (n. 5), perhaps a priest (n. 12). In the Latin text, the common noun *homo* is used frequently when Bonaventure is attempting to explain to the individual the kind of spiritual effort that is required of any man or woman within his understanding of the nature of the spiritual journey. In numerous paragraphs he explains simply that this is what "you" – any reader of the text – must do or what "we" – all spiritual pilgrims including Bonaventure – must do in the pursuit of spiritual wisdom. In other paragraphs, he explains what the faithful "soul" (*anima*) or the "heart" (*cor*) must do to make progress on the journey. In an effort to provide a more inclusive language translation of this text and to maintain Bonaventure's focus on the personal effort required of every spiritual pilgrim on the spiritual journey into God, this translation strives for consistency and clarity by using the second person personal pronoun "you" and "soul" as the context permits.

know, love, and choose freely a greater fullness of life with God in Christ through the power of the Spirit. Formed upright and "right," Bonaventure believed that the human person–soul–is "upright" only in the measure that the individual's (1) intelligence is consonant with the highest truth in knowing, (2) will is in conformity with the highest good through the love of goodness, and (3) powers are conjoined to the highest power in acting.[3] In the measure that all of the soul's powers are struggling to cooperate with grace, spiritual growth and progress may be made "in as far as it is possible in our pilgrim state and by the exercise of our mind (*mens*)."[4]

However, this noble ideal is difficult to achieve. Humanity is incomplete and imperfect in its created nature. In addition, Bonaventure recognized the reality of sin and its disordering effects, humanity's fallen condition, and the fact that individuals make sinful choices. As a consequence, he believed that humanity's growth in knowledge is impeded by ignorance, loving-desire becomes disordered and distracted by the choice of lesser goods, and the will experiences a certain weakness and instability in its effort to make the best use of the graces given to assist it in striving to reach its noble destiny.

In light of his understanding of humankind's noble dignity, fallen condition, and the negative impact of sin on the soul's readiness to respond to grace, Bonaventure explains in this text how a spiritual pilgrim might strive to train (*exercitare*) and reform the soul in cooperation with grace to struggle for "true wisdom wherein there is knowledge coming from true experience."[5]

---

[3] See Bonaventure, *Commentary on Book II of the Sentences*, prologue, nn. 3-5; see translation in the Appendix.

[4] See *Itinerarium*, ch. VII, n. 1 (Hayes, 133); *On the Reduction of the Arts*, n. 12 (Hayes, 51); *Breviloquium*, pt. V, ch. 1, nn. 1-6 (Monti, 169-73).

[5] *Threefold Way*, ch. I, n. 18.

This "true wisdom" is merited to be experienced in the measure that the soul acquires the constitutive elements of its perfection – Peace, Truth, and Love.[6] These constitutive elements of its perfection are to be sought through the faithful and ongoing pursuit of the "hierarchizing activities" he associates with the Ways of Purgation, Illumination, and Perfection.[7]

The Way of Purgation, he explains, leads to Peace. The pursuit of this way requires a graced confrontation with one's human-spiritual incompleteness and, even more importantly, the reality of one's own sin. Thus, this way is described as "painful" and is to be "pursued in bitterness." It leads to inner peace and "ends in the affection of spiritual joy." Through the various activities associated with this way, a person learns to "avoid sin," to live an upright and just life, or, as it might also be phrased, to live in an obedience of faith to the Divine Law through a deepening knowledge and love of God.

The Way of Illumination leads to the Truth and "consists in the imitation of Christ." It demands that the spiritual pilgrim pursue Truth and imitate Christ in so far as it might be possible by training (*exercitium*) (1) "the gaze of truth" to look upon the "first Truth," (2) the "affections of charity" to be raised up to God and expanded to one's neighbor, and (3) one's "virtuous acts" to be ordered according to the pattern of life revealed in the life of Christ. In the pursuit of the Way of Illumination, therefore, the mind seeks to be illumined with Truth and enflamed with love for that

---

[6] *Threefold Way*, prologue, n. 1 and ch. III, n. 1.

[7] It should be noted that, in *On the Perfection of Life* and *The Major Legend of St. Francis* in particular, Bonaventure approaches these concerns from the perspective of the necessity of developing the virtues (strengths of human-spiritual character) that he considered essential for the pursuit of a truly spiritual way of living.

Truth. The faithful soul is thus inclined and disposed increasingly through this kind of spiritual effort to imitate evermore closely the pattern of life revealed in the life of Christ Jesus.

The Way of Perfective Union is concerned principally with "enkindling the fire of love" – charity. In this way, then, the spiritual pilgrim is encouraged to struggle for union with God through love, a union which transforms the soul into an ever clearer image of the humble and poor Christ. The activities associated with this way are intended, therefore, to arouse ever-greater degrees of wonderment, gratitude, and delight within the soul for God's goodness and love.

Through the pursuit of the differing but interrelated movements of the three hierarchizing ways, the spiritual pilgrim learns through effort and experience to live more faithfully, lovingly, and freely in accordance with the wisdom which is God. This struggle for wisdom is the most noble and appropriate human response that any person can make to God's loving presence according to Bonaventure.

The Threefold Way is divided into three chapters. Each chapter is organized around one of three spiritual exercises, that is, reading with meditation, prayer, and contemplation. Bonaventure proposes these exercises as the practical means through which a person ought to strive for the "perfection of wisdom" in accordance with the three "hierarchizing activities." While each of the spiritual exercises has its unique and distinct character, they have the common purpose of rectifying, strengthening, and enlivening the powers of the soul.

Bonaventure outlines briefly the nature of each of these spiritual exercises in the text. He also demonstrates, in a rather abbreviated way, how the fruitful use of these exercises can lead the spiritual pilgrim toward a greater measure of peace, truth, and love – the goals of the Ways of Purgation, Illumination, or Perfective Union.

The tightly argued and complex organization of The Threefold Way makes it a rich and demanding challenge for students of the spiritual life. Bonaventure uses an economy of words to express his thought. He also relies on numerous word images that are embedded with layers of theological meaning and are intended to invite the spiritual pilgrim into always deeper levels of conversation with this classic text.

At the end of the prologue to *Itinerarium Mentis in Deum*, Bonaventure encouraged his readers to weigh his intentions, the meaning of his words, and the truth he sought to express. He suggested that the reader "not run through these reflections in a hurry, but that you take your time and ruminate over them slowly."[8] These words of instruction, encouragement, and caution might also serve as a practical guide to reading The Threefold Way. In approaching this text, the devout soul might begin most fruitfully, even if tentatively and cautiously, by turning to the Lord in prayer and, from a humble heart, cry out:

I seek you, in you I hope;
I desire you, in you I rise up;
I embrace you,
I exult in you, and finally,
I cling to you.[9]

---

[8] *Itinerarium*, prol. 5 (Hayes, 41).

[9] *Threefold Way*, ch. III, n. 8.

THE THREEFOLD WAY:
On Enkindling Love[10]

PROLOGUE

1. *Behold, I have described it for you in a threefold manner, etc.*[11]

Since all forms of knowledge bear the insignia of the Trinity, so what is taught in Sacred Scripture should represent in itself traces of the Trinity. This is why the wise man has described this sacred science in a threefold way because of its threefold spiritual meaning; namely, moral, allegorical, and anagogical.[12]

---

[10] The Latin text is *De triplici via;* alias *Incendium Amoris* as found in *S. Bonaventurae, Decem Opuscula* (Quaracchi: Collegium S. Bonaventurae, 1965), 3-34; *S. Bonaventurae Opuscula Varia ad Theologiam Mysticam et Res Ordinis Fratrum Minorum Spectantia*, Tomus VIII (Quaracchi: Collegium S. Bonaventurae, 1898), 3-18. The text is found in numerous manuscripts and codices where it is assigned various titles. The Quaracchi editors collated some 22 manuscripts and described 277 others. Since the 1898 publication of volume VIII of the Opera Omnia, additional manuscripts have been discovered. The text is considered an authentic work of Bonaventure even though it does in fact pose some problems. See Bougerol, *La Triple Voie*, 7-8. *The Three-fold Way* is one of the most ancient titles and the title by which the text has been known traditionally.

[11] See Prov 22:20. The Vulgate reads *tripliciter* ("threefold").

[12] Bonaventure, as did other medieval theologians, held that all the books of sacred Scripture, beyond the literal meaning which the word expresses outwardly, have a threefold meaning: namely, allegorical, by which we are taught what to believe concerning the divinity and humanity; the moral (tropological), by which we are taught how to live; and the anagogical, by which we are taught how to cling (*adhaerendum*) to God. See *On the Reduction of the Arts*, n. 5 (Hayes, 45); also

This threefold meaning corresponds to three acts hiearchically ordered, that is, purgation, illumination, and perfection.[13]

> Purgation leads to peace,
> Illumination to truth,
> Perfection to charity.

When these are perfectly acquired, the soul is beatified; and to the extent that it concentrates on these, the soul is rewarded the more. All understanding of Sacred Scripture depends on the knowledge of these three, as do the rewards of eternal life.

It should be understood, therefore, that there is a threefold manner of exercising the powers of the soul in attaining this threefold goal, namely:

> reading and meditation,[14]
> praying, and
> contemplating.

Itinerarium, ch. 4, n. 6 (Hayes, 105); *Breviloquium,* prol., n. 4 (Monti, 4); *Collations ...Six Days,* col. 2, n. 13 (de Vinck, 28).

[13] Cf. Pseudo-Dionysius, *Celestial Hierarchy,* ch. III, n. 2; ch. VII, n. 3; ch. IX, n. 2 (Luibheid,154-55, 165, and 170-71).

[14] Cf. Hugh of St. Victor, *Eruditiones Didascalicae,* III, ch. 11 (PL 176: 772); *The Didascalicon of Hugh of St. Victor*, trans. Jerome Taylor (NY: Columbia University Press, 1961). Hugh describes meditation as "sustained thought along planned lines: it prudently investigates the cause and the source, the manner and utility of each thing. Meditation takes its start from reading but is bound by none of reading's rules or precepts.... The start of learning, thus, lies in reading, but its consummation lies in meditation." (Taylor, *Didascalicon*, book III, ch. 10, 92-93). Hugh also explains that "there are four things in which the life of just men is now practiced and raised, as it were by certain steps, to its future perfection – namely, study or instruction, meditation, prayer and performance (*operatio*). Then follows a fifth, contemplation, in which, as by a sort of fruit of the preceding steps.... " (Taylor, *Didascalicon*, V, ch. 9, 132).

Chapter I: On Meditation
Whereby the Soul is Purged, Illumined, and Perfected

2. Let us now first look at the program of meditation. It must be understood that within yourself there are three things which, if employed, help you to exercise yourself along this threefold way, namely the 'sting' of conscience,[15] the ray of understanding, and the little flame of wisdom. Therefore,

> if you wish to be purged,
>   turn to the sting of conscience;
> if you wish to be illuminated,
>   turn to the ray of understanding;
> if you wish to be perfected,
>   turn to the little flame of wisdom,

according to the counsel of blessed Denis to Timothy, where he exhorts him saying: "Turn to the ray" and so forth.[16]

On the Purgative Way and its Threefold Exercise

3. Regarding the sting of conscience, you ought to proceed as follows. You need to stir it up; you need to

---

[15] The Latin text reads *stimulus conscientiae* and combines two important ideas on the nature of the rational creature. Conscience is that part of the cognitive capacity which both seeks to discover the truth and make practical judgments about the good to be pursued. It is "stung" or "prodded" by synderesis, the active orientation found in the affective appetite to desire what is good and avoid what is evil. For a more detailed explanation of these concepts see section II of the General Introduction.

[16] Cf. Pseudo-Dionysius, *Mystica Theologia*, ch. 1, par. 1 (PG 3: 998); translated by Colm Luibheid, *The Mystical Theology*, ch. 1, n. 1, in *Pseudo-Dionysius, The Complete Works* (Mahwah, NJ: Paulist Press, 1987), 135.

sharpen it; and you need to direct it [toward a goal].
Conscience is stirred up by recalling your sins; it is
sharpened by full vigilance; and it is given direction by
the consideration of the good.

4. Recalling its sins, the soul must proceed as follows:
it must accuse itself of its manifold negligence, disordered
desire,[17] and evil. Almost all your sins and evils, whether
in thought or in deed, can be reduced to these three.

Regarding negligence,[18] you must first reflect on
whether you have been negligent within yourself:

in watching over your heart,
in using your time, and
in concentrating on your goal.

These three must be carefully observed with the
utmost diligence, namely, so that the heart is well
guarded,[19] time is usefully spent, and the desired goal is
kept in mind in all that you do.

---

[17] Concupiscence (*concupiscentia*) may refer to the fundamental
inner orientation of the human spirit to the good. The order of love
demands that God, the highest Good, be loved above all things, one's
neighbor, oneself, and all other things and persons are to be loved in
God and for the sake of God. More typically, *concupiscentia* refers to
"disordered desire," that is, the human tendency to pursue goods that
are useful or delightful to the self without due regard to the demands
of love that is ordered properly. When the term has this negative con-
notation, it is translated "disordered desire."

[18] Bonaventure understood negligence to be a form of weakness
that implied difficulty in doing the good. Other types of weakness included impatience and a lack of trust (*diffidentia*) in one's own self.
He associates these weaknesses with the soul's irascible power. See
Collations ... Six Days, col. 22, n. 37 (de Vinck, 359).

[19] For more on guarding one's heart see *On Governing the Soul,*
nn. 3-4 where Bonaventure says that the heart must be humble, devoted, and unburdened.

Second, you must reflect [and see] if perhaps you may have been negligent:

in praying,
in reading, and
in carrying out good works,

because the soul must most diligently cultivate and exercise itself in these three if it wishes to *yield fruit in due season*;[20] and no one of these [three] is in any way sufficient without the others.

Third, you must reflect whether it may have been negligent:

in being penitent,
in resisting [temptations], and
in making progress [in virtue].

With utmost diligence, the soul ought to weep over evils committed, repel diabolical temptations, and progress from one virtue to another,[21] so that you might arrive at the promised land.

5. Regarding disordered desire,[22] you must reflect [and see] if within you thrives the disordered desire for [carnal] pleasure, the disordered desire for curiosity, or the disordered desire for vanity which are the roots of all evil.

First, you must reflect on the disordered desire for [carnal] pleasure present within yourself: whether there exists in the soul

---

[20] Cf. Ps 1:3: "That person will be like a tree that is planted near running waters, that will bring forth its fruit in due season."

[21] See Ps 83:8: "For the lawgiver will give a blessing; they will go from virtue to virtue."

[22] See note 17 above p. 92.

a desire for what is sweet,
a desire for what is soft,
a desire for what is carnal,

that is, whether the soul seeks savory food, fine garments, luxurious delights. It is not only reprehensible to desire all these things, but you must resist them from the very start.

Second, you must reflect [and see] if there is the disordered desire of curiosity present within yourself.[23] This is discovered when the soul desires

to know the occult,
to see the beautiful, and
to possess what is expensive.

In all of these matters, the vice of avarice and curiosity is most reprehensible.

Thirdly, the soul must reflect [to see] whether there is the disordered desire of vanity, which is or was present in it: namely, whether there might be

a desire for favors,
a desire for praise,
a desire for honors,

---

[23] Curiosity is the intellectual capacity's natural inclination to know and to see. It is "ordered rightly" when it is joined with a sense of devotion, that is, is directed to God above all else and strives to know the divine significance of all things for the sake of deepening one's sense of devotion. Curiosity is "disordered" when the desire to know, to see, or to possess is directed to what is advantageous and desirable to the self. See *Collations ... Ten Commandments*, col. V, n. 1 (Spaeth, 72); *Collations ... Six Days*, col. 19, nn. 3-6 and col. 1, n. 8 (de Vinck, 284-86 and p. 4); *On the Perfection of Life*, ch. VII, n. 1; *Itinerarium*, prologue, n. 4 (Hayes, 39).

all of which are vain and make one vain.[24] They must be avoided like the desire for women.[25] Regarding all of these things, conscience should accuse the heart.

6. Regarding evil,[26] you must reflect [and see] if within itself there might thrive, or at one time thrived anger, or envy, or laziness, all of which make the soul evil.[27]

First, you must reflect on the evil of anger, which consists in its attitude, in certain signs, in words; or in the heart, the face, the voice; or, in the affections, words, or deeds.

Second, you must reflect on the evil of envy, which languishes when faced with the prosperity of others, which rejoices in their adversity, and turns cold in the time of another's need.

Third, you must reflect on the evil of laziness from which arise evil suspicions, blasphemous thoughts, and wicked detractions. All such evil must be totally detested. –From this threefold reflection, the sting of conscience ought to be sharpened and the soul embittered.

---

[24] Vanity is pride (*superbia*). See below *Threefold Way*, ch. III, n. 2.

[25] This is an indication that the original treatise was addressed to a man, most likely to a priest as suggested in note 36 below.

[26] The Latin *nequitia*, translated as evil, is frequently used by Bonaventure in this text. It seems to emphasize a person's failure to choose freely to do what is good, right, and just. The choice of what is morally worthless is rooted in a failure of power (will). It is closely linked with the Latin word *malus*, translated here as wicked. *Malus* implies the choice of what is understood to be opposed to what is good, right, and just. See also *Breviloquium*, pt. III, ch. 9, n. 5 and ch. 11, n. 3 (Monti, 122-23, 127-30); *On the Perfection of Life*, ch. I, n. 4. See also the Introduction, note 107, page 30 above.

[27] Bonaventure argues that the envious (*invidia*) person "turns every good into evil" and the angry (*iracundia*) person "turns every evil into good and considers good the rendering of evil. See *Collations ... Six Days*, col. 1, n. 7 (de Vinck, 4) and *Breviloquium*, pt. III, ch. 9, n. 5 (Monti, 122-23).

7. Having seen how "the sting" ought to stir up conscience by the recalling of sins, the soul must now see how [its conscience] is to be sharpened by being circumspect. With regard to its own self, the soul must be circumspect regarding three matters; namely, the imminent day of death, the recent [flow of Christ's] blood on the cross,[28] and the present face of [the divine] judge. In these three ways, the sting of conscience is sharpened against every evil.

First, it is sharpened by considering the day of death, because it is unknown, inevitable, and irrevocable. If the soul diligently considers this, it will labor most diligently while there is time,[29] so that the soul will be purged of all negligence, disordered desire, and evil. Who would dare remain at fault, if one is not certain about the morrow?

Second, [conscience] is sharpened when the soul considers the blood of the cross shed to arouse the human heart, to cleanse it, and finally to soften it. It was shed

> to wash away human uncleanliness,
> to bring life to what is dead, and
> to make fruitful what is arid.

Who then is so lifeless as to allow to reside within the faults of negligence, or disordered desire, or evil when the soul realizes that this most precious blood was shed for it?

Third, [conscience] is sharpened when the soul considers the face of the judge who is infallible, inflexible, and inescapable. No one can trick God's wisdom, deflect God's justice, or flee God's punishment. Since therefore

---

[28] See Col 1:20: "And that through him he would reconcile all things to himself, whether on the earth or in the heavens, making peace through the blood of his cross."

[29] See Gal 6:10: "While we have time, let us do good to all people, but especially to those who are of the household of faith."

no good goes un-repaid, no evil unpunished, who is there – if a soul reflects on this – whose [conscience] is not sharpened against every evil?

8. Now we must see how, and in what way, the sting of conscience is rectified by considering the good. We must meditate on three goods in whose acquisition the sting of conscience is rectified; namely, the strenuous effort needed against negligence, uncompromising effort against disordered desire, and resolute goodness against evil.[30] Once possessed of these three, the conscience is rectified and good. This is what the prophet says: *I will show you, O man, what is good, and what the Lord requires of you; Only to do justice, to love mercy, and to walk solicitously with your God,*[31] which touches upon the three aforesaid matters. The Lord says the same thing in Luke: *Let your loins be girt.*[32]

9. You must first start with the struggle which opens the way to the others. This effort can be described as follows: struggle is a certain vigor of the mind, excising all negligence, and preparing the soul to carry out all God-like deeds vigilantly, confidently, and gracefully. These are the things that open the way to all subsequent goods.

---

[30] The Latin reads *strenuitas contra negligentiam, severitas contra concupiscentiam, benignitas contra nequitiam.* The Latin *severitas* is translated "uncompromising" to emphasize the severity – strict and disciplined effort – that is required; for more on this point see *The Threefold Way,* ch. III, n. 2. The Latin *benignitas* is translated "resolute goodness" to emphasize the intention to do what is right and good as well as the unwillingness to accept or yield to evil.

[31] See Micah 6:8. In *On Governing the Soul* (n. 8) Bonaventure urges that every effort be made to preserve internally a humble, devoted, and unburdened heart and "behave externally in all modesty, justice, and piety" (Titus 2:12) as a means of being constant in a spiritual way of living – having a rectified and good conscience.

[32] See Luke 12:35.

Uncompromising effort follows, which is a certain steadfastness of mind, restraining all disordered desire and preparing [the soul] for the love of hardship, poverty, and lowliness.

Third is resolute kindness which is a certain sweetness of the soul, excluding all evil and preparing the soul for benevolence, tolerance, and internal joy.

Thus you reach the goal of purgation along the way of meditation. Every clean conscience is joyful and happy.

Whoever wishes to be purged must turn to the sting of conscience as outlined. In the course of these exercises, however, your meditation can begin with any one of the aforesaid points. The soul must go from one to the other and then rest there until tranquillity and serenity are attained and from which arises spiritual happiness. Once this is acquired, the soul is ready to climb to the heights. Therefore, this way begins with the sting of conscience and ends with the affection of spiritual joy. While the exercise is painful, it is consummated in love.

THE ILLUMINATIVE WAY AND ITS THREEFOLD EXERCISE

10. In the second place, following the purgative way is the illuminative whereby the soul must exercise itself towards [attaining] the ray of understanding as follows. This ray must

first, be focused on getting rid of evil; second, be expanded to doing good deeds; and third, be reflected back on the rewards promised.

The ray is focused when the soul considers carefully evils done, regarding which the Lord has been so indulgent:[33] so many are they, so many sins every one of us has committed, and such big ones! To the very extent that the soul is bound to evil, to that extent it has been rightfully deprived of good. This meditation is obvious from what has been said before. Now the soul must not reflect on this alone, but also consider how many evils it might have fallen prey to if God had so allowed.

When the soul has diligently reflected on these matters, its shadows will be illuminated by the ray of understanding.[34] Moreover, such illumination must be joined with affectionate gratitude, otherwise it is not a celestial illumination from whose splendor the soul sees that warmth follows. Hence such "graces" are to be activated in order to get rid of evils committed, [including] those which might be committed by compulsion, weakness, and perversity of the will.

11. Second you must see how this ray ought to be amplified by considering the good things to be done, which are of a threefold sort. Some look to complement nature, some to the help of grace, some to the gift of superabundance.

Complementing nature are those things which God has given to the body, namely, the integrity of its members, the health of the organism, and the nobility of sex. On the

---

[33] Evil may become a source of spiritual growth when the failure to do what is good, right, and just is acknowledged, understood, and enables a person to see the good that might be done.

[34] Cf. Bernard, *Sermo 2 pro Dominica VI post Pentecosten*, n. 3, in *Sancti Bernardi Opera* 5, ed. J. Leclercq (Rome: Editiones Cisterciensis, 1955-1977), 210. See also translation by A Priest of Mount Melleray, "Second Sermon for the Sixth Sunday after Pentecost, n. 3," in *St. Bernard's Sermons for the Seasons and Principal Festivals of the Year*, vol. II (Westminster, MD: The Carroll Press, 1950), 332-33. The text in translation reads: "For who does not perceive that, many are the sins into which I fell, I should have fallen into many more had I not been restrained by the mercy of the Almighty."

part of the senses, God gave clarity to vision, sharpness to hearing, and discreteness to speech.[35] On the part of the spirit, God endowed it with clear insightfulness, rightful judgment, and a good spirit.

12.   Regarding the help of grace, God first gave the grace of Baptism whereby [original] fault was erased, innocence restored, and justice brought back which makes the soul worthy of eternal life. Secondly, God gave the grace of repentance with regard to the opportunities afforded by time with a willingness of the mind and with regard to the sublimity of religion. Thirdly, God gave sacerdotal grace whereby [some are made] a dispenser of doctrine, a dispenser of indulgence[s], and a dispenser of the Eucharist.[36] In all of these, to a greater or lesser extent, the words of life are dispensed.

13.   It pertains to the gift of superabundance that God first gave humankind the entire universe: namely [God created] inferior things as submissive, equal things as matter for merit, and superior beings as protectors. Secondly, God gave humanity his Son as brother and friend; he gave him as ransom; he gives him daily: first in the incarnation, secondly in the passion, and thirdly in the consecration. Thirdly, God gave the Holy Spirit as a seal of acceptance, as a privilege of adoption, and as a ring of espousal. The Christian soul becomes a friend, a daughter, a spouse. All of these are wonderful and

---

[35] The Latin *sermonem discretum* is translated "discreteness to speech" to avoid a lengthy circumlocution; what is meant, it seems, is the ability of the mouth, tongue, teeth, palate, and lips to form meaningful sounds in a given language.

[36] The Latin text reads: "God gave sacerdotal grace whereby you were made...." A clear indication that the text was addressed originally to a priest in all probability. See note 25 above.

inestimable, and the soul will be pleasing to God as long as it meditates on them.

14. Finally, regarding the illuminative way, you must see how this ray of understanding needs to be reflected back so that it can return to the font of all goodness by recalling the rewards promised it. Therefore, you must solicitously consider and frequently reflect that God, who does not lie, has promised to those who believe in God and love God: the removal of all evils, the company of all the saints, the fulfillment of all desires in God who is the font and the final goal of all goods – God who is so good as to exceed every wish, every desire, every imaginable estimation. Moreover, God regards [you] as worthy of such a good, if indeed you love and desire God above all else, and for the sake of God alone; and so you must struggle to reach God with every desire, affection, and choice of resolute goodness.

THE PERFECTIVE WAY AND ITS THREEFOLD EXERCISE

15. Next follows how you must exercise your souls in order [to acquire] the little flame of wisdom. This is to be accomplished in the following way:

first, this little flame is to be concentrated;
second, it must be nourished; and
third, lifted up.

It is concentrated by turning the affections away from all love of created things.[37] Since there is no advantage

---

[37] The Latin *reductionem affectionis* reflects Bonaventure's understanding that "well-ordered" affections are "turned toward" God or lead a person back (*reductio*) to God. All created things are to be loved "in God" or "for the sake of God." A correct understanding of Bonaventure's point here presumes that a person understands and

to be found in the love of creation, it is necessary that your affection be drawn away from this sort of love. If there is no advantage to be found in such love, then it does not refresh; and if it does not refresh, it does not satisfy. Therefore, all love of this sort must be removed from your affection.

16.   Second, the [little flame] is to be nourished by turning the affections to the love of the Spouse. This happens when you consider love in relation to yourself, to the heavenly citizens, or to the Spouse himself. The soul does this when it considers the fact that every need can be satisfied by love, that because of love the abundance of every good is in the blessed, and that through love the soul is in the presence of [the One] who is most highly desirable. These are the things that inflame the affections.

17.   Third, [the little flame] must be lifted up beyond everything that can be sensed, imagined, or understood. This should be done in the following order. The soul should meditate first on the God whom it wishes to love perfectly. It will see immediately that this God cannot be sensed, seen, heard, smelled, or tasted, and therefore is *not an object of sense perception; and yet is totally desirable.*[38] Second, the soul must understand that this God cannot be imagined because God has no limits, no figure, no number, no quantity, no changeability, and therefore *cannot be imagined, and yet is totally desirable.* Third, the soul must reflect on the fact that God is beyond our understanding, because God is beyond demonstration, definition, opinion,

---

accepts the "order of love" described in the preceding paragraph and the two points which follow. For a further discussion of the "order of love" see, for example, On the Perfection of Life, ch. VII.

   [38] See Cant 5:16: "His throat is most sweet, and he is totally desirable.... "

estimation, or investigation. So this God *is beyond our understanding and yet is totally desirable.*[39]

COROLLARY

18.   From what has been said, it is perfectly clear how the soul arrives at the wisdom of Sacred Scripture by meditating along the purgative, illuminative, and perfective ways. Therefore, your reflections should not concentrate solely on the contents of Sacred Scripture, but all your meditations must revolve around all the aforesaid matters as well. For every meditation of the wise soul focuses on: either *human deeds* by thinking about what you might have done, and what you ought to do, and what your motives are; or *divine acts* by thinking about how much God has given over to [humanity] – because God made all things for the rational creature – and how many things God has forgiven, and what great things God has promised. In these are included the [divine] works of creation, redemption, and glorification; or regarding the sources of both, namely, God and the soul, and how they ought to be joined. On this all of your meditations must focus, because it is the goal of all of your knowledge and your deeds, and it is the true wisdom wherein there is knowledge coming from true experience.[40]

19.   Our entire soul must concentrate on this sort of meditation, by using all its powers; namely, reason, synderesis,[41] conscience, and will. In this sort of meditation, reason by gathering together forms the

---

[39] Cf. I *Sent.*, d. 22, a. 1, q. I (I:391); *Itinerarium*, ch. VII (Hayes, 133-39); *Breviloquium*, pt. V, ch. 6 and ch. 7 (Monti, 191-96, 196-200).

[40] Bonaventure, *III Sent.*, d. 35, q. 1 (III:772A-773B).

[41] Synderesis is the natural inclination, prod, sting, or stimulus to desire good and avoid evil. For a discussion of this concept, see the Introduction, 27-29.

proposition; synderesis by sensing [correctly] offers the definition; conscience by witnessing draws the conclusion; the will by choosing provides the solution. For example, if a person meditates on the purgative way, reason must ask: "What will become of the one who violates the temple of God?" Synderesis responds that either the soul must utterly perish or be purged by the tears of repentance. Conscience assumes "You are [the one]; therefore you must be damned or you must be beaten with the prods of repentance." Finally, the will chooses, namely, that because it refuses to be eternally damned, it voluntarily takes upon itself the sorrows of penitence. The other ways must be understood in like fashion.

Chapter II: On Prayer
Whereby You Deplore your Miseries, Implore Mercy, and Offer Worship

1. Having explained how reading and meditation can lead to true wisdom, it must now be shown how prayer can lead to the same wisdom. You should know that in prayer there are three levels or parts. The first consists in deploring your miseries, the second in imploring mercy, and the third in offering worship. You cannot offer the cult of worship to God unless the soul receives grace from God. However, you cannot persuade God's mercy for giving grace except by deploring and revealing your misery. And so, every perfect prayer must have these three parts; no one is sufficient without the others, nor will you perfectly attain the goal. Hence these three must always be joined.

ON THE THREEFOLD DEPLORING OF OUR MISERY

2. Deploring any misery occurs with respect to the commission of sin, the loss of grace, or the delaying of glory. Thus the soul must have these three, namely sorrow, shame, and fear.[42] Sorrow, because of the harm or disturbance; shame, because of disgrace or dishonesty; fear, because of danger or guilt. Sorrow arises from the memory of things past, when the soul recalls what it has omitted through failure to observe the precepts of justice; what sins it has committed in violation of the prohibitions; and what it has lost, namely the gift of life. Shame arises from the understanding of present matters when the soul realizes where it is; that is, now in the depths whereas it had been close to the summit; when it realizes what sort of thing it has become, because it is now in filth and mud whereas it had been a beautiful likeness; and when it realizes who it is, because it is now a slave whereas it had been free. Fear arises in looking to the future, when you foresee where you are going, because its steps are leading to hell;[43] what will happen, because there will be the inevitable but just judgment; what the soul will obtain, namely, the 'payment' of eternal death.

ON THE THREEFOLD IMPLORING OF MERCY

3. Imploring mercy, regarding any grace whatsoever, must be accompanied with an outpouring of desire which the soul receives from the Holy Spirit who pleads for it

---

[42] In a slightly different order, Bonaventure names these as the first three of the seven steps whereby the *Taste of Peace* is acquired, ch. III, n. 2.

[43] See Prov 5:5: "Her [the harlot's] feet go down into the depths, and her steps are leading to hell."

with inexpressible groanings;[44] with the confidence of hope which the soul has from Christ who died for all; and with a diligence in imploring help which the soul asks of the saints and of all good people. – The first it owes to the Holy Spirit, because through [the Spirit] from the Father and in the Son everyone is eternally predestined, reborn spiritually in Baptism, and united in one spirit within the Church. – The second [that is, confident hope] the soul owes to Christ who offered Himself for all on the cross on earth, appeared before the face of God the Father in heaven in glory,[45] and offers Himself in the Sacrament to the Church our mother. – The third the soul owes to the company of the saints, that is the patronage of the ministering angels, the prayers of the triumphant blessed, and the merits of the militant just [on earth]. When these three concur, then divine mercy is implored in an efficacious way.

---

[44] See Rom 8:26: "But in like manner the Spirit also helps our weakness. For we do not know what we should pray for as we ought, but the Spirit himself pleads for us with inexpressible groanings." Bonaventure argues that everyone must become a person of desire; he also explains that "desires are enkindled by an outcry of prayer which makes us call aloud in the groaning of our heart and by the flash of insight by which the mind (*mens*) turns most directly and intently toward the rays of light." See *Itinerarium*, prologue, n. 3 (Hayes, 39).

[45] See Hebr 9:24: "For Jesus has not entered into a Holies made by hands, a mere copy of the true, but into heaven itself, to appear now before the face of God on our behalf."

ON THE THREEFOLD OFFERING OF WORSHIP[46]

4. When God is worshipped on account of any gift bestowed, three things are required. First, in asking for grace the heart must bow down in reverence and adoration of God. Secondly, the heart must expand in acts of resolute goodness and thanksgiving. Thirdly, the heart must rise up to a pleasing sense of harmony[47] and mutual conversation as between Spouse and bride, as we are taught by the Holy Spirit in The Song of Songs. If these things occur in an orderly fashion, there is wondrous exultation and jubilation, such that the soul is led outside itself and is made to say: *It is good that we are here.*[48]

This is the final goal of prayer. Our prayer must stop here and must not cease beforehand, until *it enters the place of the wonderful tabernacle, even to the house of God* where there is *the voice of joy ...and of feasting.*[49]

5. So that you may bow down in reverence, you should admire the divine immensity and look to your

---

[46] In his *Collations on the Ten Commandments* Bonaventure makes a distinction between *latria* and *dulia*. *Latria* is the reverence, honor, or worship which is due to God alone; it "is shown in such a way that it cannot be owed to anyone else" (col. II, n. 17). *Dulia* is the honor due to "all in whom there is power, wisdom and holiness" (col. 3, n. 12) because of God's creative activity. (Spaeth, 37, 51). See also *Breviloquium*, pt. IV, ch. 5, n. 2 (Monti, 146-47).

[47] The Latin has *complacentia* for which the English "complacency" is not only inadequate but actually distorts the meaning. Bonaventure's use of *complacentia* seems to allude to something like the mutual pleasure and enjoyment which husband and wife (or two good friends) find in one another's company; a peaceful and often wordless sharing. The phrase "pleasing harmony" was suggested by Zachary Hayes.

[48] Matt 17:4.

[49] See Ps 41:5. The Vulgate reads *transibo* ("I will go over") while Bonaventure has *ingrediatur* ("it enters"). Bonaventure also provides extended discussion of prayer in, for example, *On the Perfection of Life*, ch. V, and *Itinerarium*, ch. VII (Hayes, 133-39).

own meagerness. In order to expand it in goodness, turn to the divine generosity and your own unworthiness. Thus you may rise up to pleasing harmony, recall divine charity, and consider your own lukewarmness. By these considerations you will rise to ecstasy.[50]

6. However, the soul should know that it must show reverence to God in a threefold way. First, to the Father by whom the soul was formed, reformed, and educated. Second, to the Lord by whom the soul was plucked from the mouth of the enemy, ransomed from the prison of hell, and led into the vineyard of the Lord. Third, to the judge before whom the soul is accused, convicted, and confessed: the cries of conscience accuse you; the evidence of your life convicts you; you confess at the sight of divine wisdom. Hence, the judgment ought justifiably to go against you. The first reverence must be great, the second greater, the third greatest. Thus, the first is a simple bow; the second, a genuflection; the third, prostration. In the first you submit; in the second you put yourself down; in the third you are absolutely abject. In the first you consider yourself to be little, in the second least,[51] and in the third [you consider yourself to be] nothing at all.

---

[50] When Bonaventure speaks of "rising up," it seems he wishes to include the idea of transcending selfishness and self-centeredness in order to be able to take the viewpoint of others, particularly the "viewpoint" of God.

[51] See Bernard, *De diligendo Deo* (SBOp 3: 132). See also the translation of Bernard's discussion of the second and third degrees of love in *On Loving God,* ch. 10, n. 27, in *Bernard of Clairvaux; Selected Works,* CWS, translated by G. R. Evans (Mahwah, NJ: Paulist Press, 1987), 195: "To lose yourself as though you did not exist and to have no sense of yourself, to be emptied out of yourself (Phil 2:7) and almost annihilated, belongs to heavenly not to human love."

7. In like fashion, you must show resolute goodness toward God in three ways; that is, great, greater, and greatest:

Great, by considering your unworthiness;
greater, by considering the bountifulness of God's grace;
greatest, by considering the immensity of God's mercy.

Or from another viewpoint:

great, because of what you have done;
greater, because of how much [you have] been forgiven;
greatest, because of what [you have] been promised.

From still another view:

great, for the gifts of nature;
greater, for the endowments of grace; and
greatest, for the gifts of superabundance.

In the first, the heart is expanded or extended; in the second, the heart is opened; in the third, the heart is poured out, according to Lamentations 2:19: *Pour out your heart like water.*[52]

8. You must show your pleasure or enjoyment to God in three ways. First, so that you might make your pleasure harmonize with that of God, so that you find pleasure only in God. Secondly, so that you take pleasure in what makes you pleasing to God. Thirdly, that you take pleasure in sharing your joy with others.[53] The first

---

[52] See Lam 2:19: "Arise, give praise in the night, in the beginning of the watches. Pour out your heart like water before the face of God ...."

[53] See *Sermo* 19, ns. 2 and 4 of Gilbert of Hoyland, *Sermones in Canticum Salomonis* (PL 184:97B and 184:99BC).

is great, the second greater, the third greatest. In the
first is found gratuitous love; in the second a love that is
required;[54] in the third a blend of the previous two. In the
first, the world is crucified to you; in the second, you [are
crucified] to the world;[55] in the third, [you are] crucified
for the world, such that you wish to die for all so that all
might please God.

This, then, is the stage and level of the perfection
of charity, prior to which the soul ought not to consider
itself perfect. Such perfection is achieved when the heart
is found to be not only willing, but most ready to die for
the salvation of your neighbor, as Paul said: *I will most
gladly spend and be utterly spent for your sakes.*[56] The
soul cannot attain this perfect love of neighbor unless it
has first attained to the perfect love of God, on whose
account the soul loves its neighbor, who is lovable only
because of God.[57]

ON THE SIX STEPS MOUNTING TO THE LOVE OF GOD

9. On this account, in order to understand what it
means to make progress in the love of God, the soul must
realize that there are six steps whereby, in gradual and
orderly fashion, it arrives at perfect love.[58]

---

[54] See Gal 6:14: "But as for me, God forbid that I should glory save
in the cross of our Lord Jesus Christ, through whom the world is crucified to me, and I to the world."

[55] See Richard of St. Victor, *De Trinitate*, V, ch. 16 (PL 196: 961);
Cf. Bernard's discussion of the degrees of love in, for example, *On Loving God,* chapters 6, 9, and 12. The Latin text uses the common noun
homo in this sentence.

[56] See 2 Cor 12:15: "But I will most gladly spend and be spent
myself for your souls.... "

[57] Bernard, *On Loving God,* ch. 8, n. 25 (Evans, 193); Bonaventure,
III Sent., d. 27, a. 2, q. 3 and q. 4 (III, 607-11).

[58] See also *On the Perfection of Life*, ch. VII.

The first is sweetness, whereby the soul learns to *taste and see how sweet the Lord is.*[59] This takes place by setting aside leisure time and "sabbath" time for [God] by holy meditations because, as you can read in Psalm 75:11: *those who keep you in mind will celebrate your festivals.* This happens when meditating on the love of God brings sweetness to the heart.

The second step is eagerness; namely, when the soul first begins to be satisfied with this sweetness, there arises in it such a thirst that nothing else can satisfy [the soul] except the one whom it loves and possesses perfectly. However, since this cannot be attained in the present life—because it is at such a distance—the soul continually strives higher to leave itself in ecstatic love, crying out, and saying with blessed Job: *My soul has chosen hanging and my bones death,*[60] because *as the hind longs for the fountains of water, so my soul longs for you, O God.*[61]

10. The third level is satiety which arises from avidity. For because the soul most vehemently desires God and to be raised up, then already whatever ties it down [to this earthly life] becomes loathsome. Thus satisfied, it can find refreshment in nothing other than its beloved. Just as a person who has eaten well yet continues to eat will experience disgust for food rather than satisfaction, so the soul at this level of charity will react in a similar way with regard to all earthly things.

The fourth level is intoxication[62] which arises from satiety. Intoxication consists in this, namely, that the soul has such love for God that not only does it find solace

---

[59] See Ps 33:9: "Oh, taste and see that the Lord is sweet."

[60] Job 7:15.

[61] See Ps 41:2.

[62] Bonaventure uses the Latin word *ebrietas*, literally "drunkenness"; perhaps the colloquial expression "peak experience" might better express Bonaventure's meaning.

tedious, but even delights in and seeks pain rather than solace. And, for [the One] loved, rejoices in punishments, insults, and scourgings, just like the Apostle.[63] Hence, just as a drunk man takes off his clothes without shame and sustains beatings without pain, so it is with the [intoxicated] soul.

11.   The fifth level is security which arises from [spiritual] intoxication. At this stage the soul realizes that it loves God so much that it would gladly undergo for God any loss and any insult. Fear is cast aside.[64] The soul has such hope in divine assistance, that it is inconceivable for it to be separated from God. The Apostle was at this stage when he said: *Who will separate us from the love of Christ? ...For I am convinced that neither death, nor life ... will be able to separate us from the love of God in Christ Jesus our Lord.*[65]

The sixth level is true and complete tranquility, in which there is such peace and quiet, that the soul is somehow in silence and sleep, in the ark of Noah as it were, where it cannot be disturbed in any way. What can disturb a mind that is not disquieted by any sting of cupidity; that cannot be upset by any arrows of fear? In such a mind there is peace and quiet and the final stage, and there the true Solomon rests, because "his abode is in peace."[66] Consequently, it is most appropriate that these levels are signified by the six steps leading up to the throne of Solomon.[67] This is why we read in The Song

---

[63] See 2 Cor 11:24-25: "From the Jews five times I received forty lashes less one. Thrice I was scourged."

[64] See 1 John 4:18: "There is no fear in love. But perfect love casts out fear.... "

[65] See Rom 8:35-39.

[66] See Ps 75:3.

[67] See 1 Kings 10:18-20 and 2 Chron 9:18 [Paraleipomenon in the Septuagint.]; see also *Itinerarium*, ch. 1, n. 5 (Hayes, 49).

of Songs 3:10: *He covered the stairs with purple and the middle with charity,*[68] because it is impossible to attain this tranquillity without charity. Once attained, it is easy for the soul to do everything pertaining to perfection, whether doing or suffering, whether living or dying. You must struggle, therefore, to make progress in charity, since progress in [charity] brings about the perfection of all good things; which perfection may [God], who lives forever and ever, deign to grant to everyone. Amen.

SUMMATION

12. In order, therefore, that the soul may have the aforesaid distinctions ready at hand, note that whoever wishes to make progress towards perfection must in meditating turn to the sting of conscience by arousing it, sharpening it, and rectifying it. The soul must turn to the ray of understanding by focusing it, broadening it, and having it reflect back. The soul must also turn to the little flame of wisdom by gathering it, firing it up, and raising it up.

And so by praying the soul must first deplore its miseries with sorrow for the harm done, with shame because of the disgrace, and with fear because of the danger. – Secondly, the soul must beg for mercy with vehement desire through [the intervention of] the Holy Spirit, with confident hope through Christ crucified, and with the assistance of patronage through the intercession of the saints. – Thirdly, the soul must offer worship by showing reverence, resolute goodness, and enjoyment to God, so that, on the part of God there will be divine approval, the major proposition [of the syllogism] as it were; followed on its part by a [careful] consideration, as an assumed [minor premise of the syllogism] so to speak;

---

[68] Cant 3:10 is describing Solomon's most ornate litter.

and so there will be the full demonstration of worship, as the conclusion. Whoever continuously and intently practices this will make progress in charity up the six aforesaid steps whereby the soul arrives at the perfection of tranquillity, where there is an abundance of peace, and a sort of quiet finish, which the Lord left with the apostles.[69] Take note, therefore, that the Apostle [Paul] in every salutation offers wishes of grace and peace; grace as primary and peace as complementary.[70] But in writing to Timothy he inserts "mercy" as [necessarily] presupposed for both.[71]

Chapter III: On Contemplation
Whereby the Soul Arrives at True Wisdom

1. After having shown how the soul must struggle for wisdom through meditation and prayer, we will now briefly touch upon how the soul arrives at wisdom through contemplation. Because, by contemplation the mind reaches the heavenly Jerusalem,[72] in whose likeness the

---

[69] See John 14:27: "Peace I leave with you; my peace I give you."

[70] See, e.g., Rom 1:7 and 1 Cor 1:3.

[71] See 1 Tim 1:2 and 2 Tim 1:2.

[72] In the *Collations on the Six Days* (col. 20. n. 24), Bonaventure describes the soul as being "as lovely as Jerusalem, for it is likened to Jerusalem through the disposition of the hierarchical levels." (de Vinck, pp. 313-314). See also *Itinerarium*, prologue, n. 1, and ch. VII, n. 1 (Hayes, 35, 133; Pseudo-Dionysius, *The Ecclesiastical Hierarchy*, ch. I, n. 2, in *Pseudo-Dionysius, The Complete Works*, 196-97; Bonaventure, *Collations ... Six Days*, cols. 20-23 (de Vinck, 299-380).

The soul (*mens*), the deepest part of the spiritual being is inclined to and capable of entering into the heavenly Jerusalem, the symbolic place of rest with God. It is also a way of speaking analogously about the final goal of the spiritual journey when the soul in glory rests in Jerusalem, God's dwelling place. It was one of the favorite themes found in the monastic mysticism of the Middle Ages. See Jean Leclercq, *The Love of Learning and the Desire for God*, trans. C. Misrahi (NY: Fordham University Press, 1974), 69.

Church was modeled, according to what is said in Exodus 25:40: *Look and make it according to the pattern shown you on the mountain.*[73] For it is necessary that the Church militant conform to the [Church] triumphant, that merits [correspond] to rewards, and pilgrims to the blessed insofar as possible.

In the glory [of heaven] there is a threefold endowment wherein the perfection of rewards consists, namely,

in the possession of eternal peace,
in the clear vision of highest truth, and
in the full enjoyment of ultimate goodness or charity.[74]

Accordingly, one finds a threefold distinction in the highest celestial hierarchy, that is, Thrones, Cherubim, and Seraphim. Therefore, anyone who wishes through merit to arrive at this blessed state, must be modeled after this threefold likeness – insofar as this is possible in this life – in order to have:

the savory taste of peace,
the splendor of truth, and
the sweetness of charity.

God Himself resides in these three as upon his own throne. Consequently, it is necessary to ascend step by step through each of the aforesaid levels according to the threefold way [I have proposed], namely,

---

[73] Ex 25: 40; Cf. Pseudo-Dionysius, *The Ecclesial Hierarchy,* c. 1, n. 2 (Luibheid, 196-97).

[74] Cf. *IV Sent.*, d. 49, p. 1, q. 5 (IV, 1009); *Breviloquium,* pt. VII, ch. 7 (Monti, 290-301); *Collations ... Six Days,* col. 20, n. 10 (de Vinck, 305). Bonaventure is connecting here the Pseudo-Dionysian concept of the good and Hugh of St. Victor's concept of love.

the *purgative way*
which consists in ridding oneself of sin;
the *illuminative way*
which consists in the imitation of Christ; and
the *unitive way*
which consists in being joined with the Spouse.

And so, each has its own levels beginning from the bottom and rising to the top.

ON THE SEVEN STEPS
WHEREBY THE TASTE OF PEACE IS ACQUIRED

2. The steps for acquiring the taste of peace are the following seven. First, there is shame which arises from considering your sins, and this with respect to four things, namely their magnitude, their multitude, their turpitude, and their ingratitude.

Second, there is fear in contemplating the visage of the judge, and this is likewise fourfold, namely the lost opportunities to do good, the blinding of the powers of reason, the stubborn hardness of the will, and final condemnation.[75]

Third, there is sorrow in estimating the damage done, which again is fourfold, namely, regarding the loss of divine friendship, the loss of innocence, the wounding of nature, and the wasted life in the past.

Fourth, there are the cries imploring a fourfold assistance, that is, of God the Father, Christ the Redeemer, the Blessed Virgin, and the Church triumphant.

Fifth, there is uncompromising effort in extinguishing passion or desire in a fourfold way; that is, the extinction of:

---

[75] Cf. Bonaventure, *Collationes de Septem Donis*, col, II: "The Gift of the Fear of the Lord," esp. nn. 10-11 (Schneider, 20-25, esp. pp. 27-28).

aridity which is apathy,
perversity which is malice,
carnal desires which are disordered,
and vanity which is pride.[76]

Sixth, there is ardor in the desire for martyrdom,[77] and this for four reasons, namely, in order that the offenses might be perfectly forgiven, that the stains be perfectly eradicated, that there might be perfect satisfaction for the punishment incurred, and finally that there might be perfect sanctification in grace.

In the seventh place, there will be repose in the shade of Christ, where the soul remains and finds rest, where the soul realizes that it is protected by the shadows of the divine wings,[78] and so it will not be burned by the heat of passion or the fear of punishment. [The soul] cannot attain to this unless martyrdom is desired, and the soul cannot desire martyrdom unless passion is extinguished; nor can this happen if the soul does not beg for help; and this will not work unless it deplores the harm it has done; and the soul will not do this unless it fears divine judgment; nor will this succeed unless the soul recalls and is ashamed of its crimes. Therefore, whoever wants to have the repose of peace must proceed in the orderly fashion as we have indicated.

ON THE SEVEN STEPS
WHEREBY YOU ARRIVE AT THE *SPLENDOR OF TRUTH*

3. There are seven steps for arriving at the splendor of truth by imitating Christ, namely,

---

[76] See *Threefold Way*, ch. I, n. 9.

[77] See *Threefold Way*, ch. II, n. 8 and n. 4 above; See also E. Randolph Daniels, "The Desire for Martyrdom: A Leitmotiv of St. Bonaventure," *Franciscan Studies* 32 (1972): 74-87.

[78] See Ps 16:8: "Protect me in the shadow of your wings."

the assent of reason,
the affection of compassion,
the gaze of admiration,
the ecstasy of devotion,
the investing[79] in likeness,
the embrace of the cross, and
the intuition of the truth.

According to these, you must proceed in an orderly fashion.

First, consider who it is who suffers, and submit to him by the assent of reason, in order that you may firmly believe that Christ is truly the Son of God, the origin of all things, the Savior of humankind, the dispenser of all rewards.

Second, [consider] what sort of person it is who suffers, in order that you may cling to the Son with affectionate compassion and suffer along with the Son of God who is totally innocent, meek, noble, and lovable.

Third, [consider] how great is the One who suffers in order that you may approach with a gaze of admiration and realize that God is of enormous power, beauty, and happiness forever and ever. Stand in awe at the fact that this immense power is reduced to nothing; this beauty is drained of its color; this happiness is tormented; and this eternity is brought to death.

Fourth, [consider] why Christ suffered, and so forget yourself in an ecstasy of devotion, because he suffered for your redemption, illumination, sanctification, and glorification.

Fifth, [consider] the way in which Christ suffered, and thus strive to put on Christ by studious imitation. He suffered freely for his brethren, most painfully as far as he was concerned, most obediently with regard to

---

[79] Cf. Rom 13:14: "Put on the Lord Jesus Christ."

God [his Father], and most prudently with respect to his
enemies. Strive therefore to have the habit of kindness
regarding your neighbor, uncompromising effort in
discipline regarding yourself, humility in the presence of
God, watchfulness regarding the devil: all according to
the pattern of imitating Christ.

Sixth, you should realize what great things Christ
suffered so that you might embrace the cross with a
desire for suffering. The All-Powerful One suffered being
chained as one helpless; goodness suffered as a vile convict;
wisdom suffered mockery as one stupid; justice suffered
torments as one who is evil. So you ought to desire the
sufferings of the cross, that is in full recompense for the
harm done to things, for verbal insults, for gestures of
mockery, and painful tormentings.

Seventh, consider what Christ accomplished through
his sufferings, and so gaze upon the ray of truth through
the eye of contemplation. Because, from the fact that the
Lamb has suffered, the seven seals of the book have been
opened, according to Revelation 5.[80] This book contains
a comprehensive knowledge of all things. In it, the
knowledge of seven things was hidden from humankind,
but opened up by the efficacy of Christ's passion; namely

the admirable God,
the intelligent spirit,
the sensible world,
the desirable heaven,
the horrible hell,
laudable virtue, and
culpable guilt.[81]

---

[80] See esp. Rev 5:8.

[81] See Bonaventure's sermon "Christ, the One Teacher of All"
where he states his conviction that "'our Teacher is one,' namely,
Christ, because He is the Way, the Truth, and the Life" (see Hayes,
What Manner, n. 14, p. 34).

4. First of all, God – through the cross – is seen to be of the highest and inscrutable wisdom, of the highest and irreprehensible justice, and of the highest and unspeakable mercy. By the highest wisdom God has deceived the devil, by the highest justice obtained the price of redemption, and by the greatest mercy sent the Son. If all these things are diligently considered, they will manifest God to everyone in the clearest of ways.

Second, an intelligent spirit was revealed through the cross according to a threefold distinction; namely, God's great generosity regarding the angels, great dignity regarding humankind, and great vengeance[82] regarding the demons. For the angels allowed that their Lord be crucified; the Son of God was crucified for the sake of humankind, and this at the instigation of the demons.

Third, the sensible world was made manifest through the cross, because it is the place in which blindness prevails, since it did not acknowledge the highest and true light;[83] sterility prevails, because it despised Jesus Christ as fruitless; evil prevails, because it damned and killed its God and Lord, the innocent one and a friend.

Fourth, through the cross it was made clear that paradise is desirable, for there resides the height of all glory, the panorama of all joy, the storehouse of all opulence. In order to open up this home [paradise] to all, God became a vile, miserable, and poor man. Here the heights plunged to the depths, justice submitted to [accusations of] guilt, and opulence became destitute. The supreme Emperor condescended to abject slavery so that all might be sublimated to glory; the most just judge submitted to the most severe punishments of one guilty

---

[82] The Latin has *crudelitas*. The English "cruelty" denotes the inflicting of undeserved and excessive pain; "vengeance'" may better reflect the just requiting of evil.

[83] See John 1:9: "It was the true light that enlightens every person who comes into the world."

so that all might pass from sin and be justified; the Lord most opulent became destitute in the extreme so that all might be showered with abundance.[84]

Fifth, it became obvious through the cross that hell is a terrible place, full of dire need, degradation, ignominy, calamity, and misery.[85] If indeed it were necessary for Christ to suffer all these things to wipe out and make satisfaction for sin, then all the more must the damned suffer in just retribution and recompense for their evil deeds.

Sixth, it became obvious through the cross that virtue is laudable and how it is precious, beautiful, and fruitful. It is precious because, before Christ gave life to all, all had what was contrary to virtue; it is beautiful, because it shines resplendently in the midst of insults; it is fruitful, because a single act of perfect virtue conquered hell, opened heaven, and restored the earth.

Seventh, it became clear through the cross that evil is culpable and just how detestable it is, because to redeem sin it demanded such a great price, such a tremendous sacrifice, such difficult begging. Why? Because God and the most noble of [human beings] in the oneness of his person[86] had to make satisfaction for arrogance (there was never any greater) by the most abject degradation; for cupidity (never was there any greedier) by the most admirable poverty; for licentiousness (none was more dissolute) by the bitterest of pains.

---

[84] Augustine, *Confessionum*, XIII, ch. 8, n. 9 (CCSL xxvii, 246); *The Confessions*, book XIII, 8,9 (Boulding, 309-10).

[85] See Job 10:21-22: "Before I go, and return no more, to a land that is dark and covered with the mist of death: a land of misery and darkness, where the shadow of death, and no order, but everlasting horror dwells."

[86] An allusion to the hypostatic union, that is, Christ is one person with two natures, divine and human.

5. Thus, all things are made known in the cross, since all things can be included in this sevenfold division. From this it follows that the cross is the key, the gate, the path, and the very splendor of truth. Anyone who takes it up and follows in the way that has been described does *not walk in darkness, but will have the light of life.*[87]

ON THE SEVEN STEPS
LEADING TO THE *SWEETNESS OF CHARITY*

6. There are seven steps for arriving at the sweetness of charity through the reception of the Holy Spirit, namely,

solicitous vigilance,
comforting confidence,
the passion which enkindles,
the ecstasy which surges upward,
the tranquility of pleasure,
the joy which delights, and
the inseparable adherence [to your beloved].

You must progress in an orderly way up these steps if you wish to reach the perfection of charity and the love of the Holy Spirit.

It is first necessary that vigilance should make you solicitous in readiness for your Spouse, so that you can say: *O God, my God, for whom I watch at break of day;*[88] or again as in The Song of Songs: *I sleep, and my heart keeps vigil;*[89] or finally with the prophet: *My soul has yearned*

---

[87] See John 8:12.

[88] Ps 62:2.

[89] Cant 5:2.

for you in the night. Yes, and with my spirit within me I will keep watch for you early in the morning.[90]

Second, that confidence comfort you because of the surety of your Spouse, for then you can say: *In you, O Lord, I have hoped. Let me never be confounded;*[91] or again with Job: *Even if he should kill me, I will hope in him.*[92]

Third, that passion might set you afire because of the sweetness of your Spouse, so that you can say: *As the hind longs for fountains of water, so my soul longs for you, O God;*[93] and again in The Song of Songs: *Love is strong as death,*[94] and again: *I am faint with love.*

Fourth, that ecstasy might raise you up to the heights of your Spouse so that you may say: *How lovely is your dwelling place, O Lord of hosts;*[95] and to your Spouse: *Draw me after you, etc.,*[96] or again from Job: *My soul has chosen hanging.*[97]

Fifth, that on account of your Spouse's beauty you should find pleasurable repose, so that you can say to him: *"My lover belongs to me and I to him";*[98] and again: *"My lover is radiant and ruddy, chosen among thousands."*[99]

Sixth, that joy may delight you because of the [bounteous] plenitude of your Spouse, so that you can say: *According to the multitude of sorrows in my heart, your consolations have gladdened my soul;*[100] and again: *How*

---

[90] Isa 26:9.

[91] Ps 30:2.

[92] Job 13:15.

[93] Ps 41:2.

[94] Cant 8:6.

[95] Ps 83:2.

[96] Cant 1:4.

[97] Job 7:15.

[98] Cant 2:16.

[99] Cant 5:10.

[100] Ps 93:19.

great is the multitude of your sweetness, O Lord,[101] and in the words of the Apostle: *I am filled with consolation; I am overflowing with joy, etc.*[102]

Seventh, that you may cling inseparably because of the strength of the love of your Spouse, so that you may say: *But to adhere to God is my good*; and again: *Who will separate us from the love of Christ?*[103]

7. There is order to these steps; you must not stop before reaching the topmost step, nor can this [uppermost step] be reached except by way of the intermediary ones. In the first, [reflective] consideration prevails; in the remaining ones the affections predominate. Vigilance understands how appropriate, how helpful, and how delightful it is to love God;[104] from this arises confidence which in turn begets passion, and the latter [gives way to] ecstasy, until you arrive at the kiss, the embrace, and the union[105] to which you may be led by God [who lives and reigns forever and ever].

SUMMATION

8. The steps above may be summarized as follows. First the steps of purgation are distinguished in the following way:

> be ashamed of your crimes,
> be fearful of judgment,

---

[101] Ps 30:20.

[102] 2 Cor 7:4.

[103] See Ps 72:28; Rom 8:35.

[104] Aristotle, *Nicomachean Ethics,* book II, ch. 3, in *The Complete Works of Aristotle,* Bollinger Series, vol. II, ed. Jonathan Barnes (Princeton, NJ: Princeton University Press, 1984),), 1744-45. Cf. Bonaventure, *On the Reduction of the Arts,* n. 14 (Hayes, 51).

[105] Bonaventure uses the Latin *copulam* in completing the comparison of spiritual to carnal love.

groan because of the harm,
beg for help to be cured,
extinguish passion because of your adversary
    [the devil],
yearn for martyrdom to attain the prize,
draw near to Christ and be shaded.

The steps of illumination are distinguished as
follows:

consider who it is who suffers
    and so believing grasp him;
consider what sort of person suffers
    and suffer with him;
consider how great he is who suffers
    and admire with stupefaction;
consider why he suffers
    and confidently give thanks;
consider the way in which he suffers
    and follow his example;
consider what great things he suffers
    and embrace him ardently;
consider what follows from all of this
    and think on it intelligently.

The steps of the unitive way are distinguished in this
way:

vigilance prompts you to be solicitous
    because your Spouse is at hand;
confidence strengthens you
    because you are assured of [his love];
passion inflames you
    because of his sweetness;
ecstasy raises you up
    because of his loftiness;

pleasing harmony quiets you
    because of his beauty;

joy intoxicates you
    because of the fullness of his love;
cling to the Spouse
    because of the fortitude of his love.

Thus the devoted soul from the heart can say to the Lord:

I seek you, in you I hope;
I desire you, in you I rise up;
I embrace you,
I exult in you, and finally
I cling to you.

ANOTHER DISTINCTION
CALLING FOR NINE STEPS TO PERFECTION

9. It should be noted that there is another way for distinguishing the steps to perfection, that is, according to the tripling of a threefold difference, harmonious with a threefold hierarchy, wherein three steps are necessary for each, namely

bitterness,
gratitude, and
likeness.

If humankind had not sinned, two of them would be sufficient, that is, gratitude and likeness; gratitude for grace, likeness because of justice. Now, however, bitterness is necessary as medicine. Sins perpetrated for pleasure cannot be wiped out unless contrite affliction intervenes

In bitterness, there must be a pondering over the evils caused by sins; there must be the recalling of sorrows because of Christ's sufferings; there must be the begging for remedies on account of the miseries [caused to] your neighbor.

In gratitude,[106] there must be a wonderment concerning the absolute goodness of creation from nothingness, the wiping out of penalties because of reparation for sins, and thanksgiving for being raised up from hell. Creation was to the image [and likeness of God]; redemption was accomplished by his own blood; the raising up went to the summit of heaven.

In likeness, there must be the gaze of truth looking to what is above, there must be the affections of charity expanded to externals, there must be the virtuous acts[107] ordered to what is internal. Thus you will be raised up above yourself by the gaze of truth, that is, by contemplating divine things; there will be understanding by looking about at the universe; there will be knowledge, formed by faith, by taking judgments captive.[108] – Likewise, reaching outside yourself must be diligently fostered by the affections of charity out of desire for celestial delights; friendship, by embracing what is reasonable; modesty, out of contempt for carnal pleasures. – Also, the struggle within yourself must occur by means of virtuous acts; by striving, when taking on difficulties; by magnanimity, through acts of praise; by humility, in embracing what is lowly.[109]

---

[106] On the sin of ingratitude see the *Soliloquium*, ch. I, § IV, n. 35.

[107] From an etymological perspective the Latin *actus virilitatis* would more traditionally be translated "manly acts."

[108] See 2 Cor 10:4-5: "For the weapons of our warfare are not carnal, but powerful before God to the demolishing of strongholds, the destroying of reasoning, indeed, of every lofty thing that exalts itself against the knowledge of God, bringing every mind into captivity to the obedience of Christ."

[109] See Rom 12:16: "Do not set your mind on high things, but condescend to the lowly." In a later discussion of the six most important good habits – middle ways or virtues – Bonaventure defines magna-

10. Purgation in bitterness, wherein there is contriteness within and you are sorrowful because of the evils pressing down upon you, Christ, and your neighbor. – Compassion for Christ must be in fear [and trembling] out of respect for the as yet hidden judgments which are true, although uncertain as to the time, the day, and the hour. –Commiseration for your neighbor must cry out in confidence because of the patronage always at hand in God, in Christ, and in the intercession of the saints.

Illumination in likeness, wherein the gaze upon the first truth is raised up to the incomprehensible, expanded to the intelligible, emptied outside itself by the believable. Here also there is the affection of charity raised up to God, expanded to your neighbor, and emptied of all that is worldly. There is also the act of courage raised up to what is commendable, expanded by sharing, emptied of the contemptible.

Perfection in gratitude, wherein there is vigilance bursting out in song because of useful benefits; a joy exulting jubilantly because of the precious value of gifts; resolute goodness hastening to an embrace because of the liberality of the giver.

On the Twofold Contemplation of Divine Things

11. Note that the gaze of truth must be directed to the incomprehensible, and these are the mysteries of the high Trinity, to whom the soul is raised up by contemplation.

---

nimity as "the good habit through which great things are appreciated and vile things despised. Humility is [the virtue] which despises the appearance of greatness and appreciates what seems to be small, but is great in reality. The philosopher says that a man is magnanimous in that he desires honor. Whatever he says, it is not the teaching of truth, unless to the word 'honor' there be added 'of eternal things.'" *Collations ... Six Days,* col. 5, n. 10 (de Vinck, 80).

This is twofold: either by affirmation or by negation.[110] The first way from Augustine, the second from Dionysius.

First of all, by affirmation we understand that in the divinity, certain things are common, certain proper, certain appropriated[111] which fall between the aforesaid two. You must understand, therefore, and contemplate–if you can – what is common in God, and see that God is the first essence, a perfect nature, and a blessed life; all of which follow necessarily.[112] – Also, reflect and see, if you can, that God is present eternity, complete simplicity, and moving stability; which also follow from one another and have a natural connection. – Finally, think how God is inaccessible light,[113] an unwavering mind, and incomprehensible peace; which include not only the unity of essence, but also the most perfect Trinity. Light is a sort of parent engendering splendor; splendor and light produce warmth, such that warmth proceeds from them both, although not as an offspring. If, therefore, God is truly inaccessible light, where splendor and warmth are as substance and hypostasis, then in God there is the Father and the Son and the Holy Spirit, which are proper

---

[110] The Latin *per positionem vel per ablationem* is rendered "affirmation" and "negation.'" "Positing" and "taking away" do not do justice to Bonaventure's thought. It is more in line with the Pseudo-Dionysian affirmative and negative theology; see below paragraphs nn. 12-13 where Bonaventure uses the phrases *via affirmationis* and *via negationis*. See Augustine, *The Trinity*, V (Hill, 189-204) and Pseudo-Dionysius, *Mystical Theology*, ch. I, n. 2 (Luibheid, 136).

[111] Cf. Bonaventure, *I Sent.*, d. 34, q. 3 (I:592-93) and d. 36, a. 1, q. 2 (I, 662); *Collations ... Ten Commandments*, col. III, n. 4 (Spaeth, 31-32). See Zachary Hayes's discussion of the concept of appropriation in *Mystery of the Trinity*, 65-66.

[112] See *Itinerarium*, ch. 5, n. 5 (Hayes, 115-16); *Breviloquium*, pt. I, ch. 2 (Monti, 29 ff).

[113] See 1 Tim 6:16: "who alone has immortality and dwells in inaccessible light."

to the divine persons.[114] – Also, as the source, the mind conceives and from itself forms the word, from which the gift of love emanates; such is to be found in every 'perfect' mind. If, therefore, God is an unchangeable mind (as is obvious) then in the divine being there is the first Principle, the eternal Word, and the perfect Gift which are proper to the divine persons.[115] –Peace involves the coalescence of many things, and only things which are similar can coalesce; things are not similar unless both stem from a third or one from another. But in the divinity, both cannot stem from a third in the same fashion. Therefore, it is necessary, if in the divinity there is true peace, that there be a first origin, its image, and the union of both.[116]

12. Appropriation is found in the divinity according to a threefold difference. The first things appropriated are unity, truth, and goodness. Unity is attributed to the Father, because he is the origin; truth to the Son, because he is the image; goodness to the Holy Spirit, because he is the union.[117]

The second things appropriated are power, wisdom, and will. Power to the Father, because he is the source;

---

[114] Cf. Isidore, *Differentiarum sive de proprietate sermonum libri duo*, II, ch. 2, n. 3 (PL 83: 70); see also *Collations ...Six Days*, col. 13, n. 22 and col. 21, n. 2 (de Vinck, 195-96 and 319).

[115] In *The Trinity,* Augustine also describes the trinity of activity involved in an act of seeing in book XI, ch. I, n. 2 (Hill, 304-05) and the human capacity for an indirect vision of the triune God through the mind as an image of God with its trinity of powers in book XV, ch. III, n. 17 (Hill, pp. 407-408); Bonaventure, *Mystery of the Trinity,* q. 1, a. 2 (Hayes, 122-37); *Itinerarium,* ch. III, n. 5 (Hayes, 91).

[116] Cf. Bonaventure, *I Sent.*, d. 2, q. 4 and d. 10, a. 2, q. 2 (I:56s and 202s).

[117] Augustine, *De doctrina Christiana,* I, ch. 5, n. 5 (PL 34: 21). See the translation of D. W. Robertson, *On Christian Doctrine,* I, ch. V, n. 5 (NY: The Liberal Press, 1958), 10. See also Bonaventure, *Breviloquium*, pt. I, ch. 6 (Monti, 44 ff.); and *Collations ... Six Days,* col. 21, nn. 2-4 (de Vinck, 319-21).

wisdom to the Son, because he is the Word; will to the Holy Spirit, because he is the gift.

The third things appropriated are loftiness, beauty, and sweetness. Loftiness [is attributed] to the Father because of unity and power. Loftiness is nothing else but singular and sole power.[118] Beauty [is attributed] to the Son on account of truth and wisdom. Wisdom includes a plethora of ideas, truth includes equality: "Beauty is nothing other than numbered equality."[119] Sweetness [is attributed] to the Holy Spirit because of will and goodness. Where highest goodness is joined to the will, there is the highest charity and sweetness. – Therefore, in God there is a terrifying loftiness, marvelous beauty, desirable sweetness; and there we [ought to] rest. – This then is a raising up according to the affirmative way.

13.   There is another way which is more eminent because, as Denis says, "Affirmations can be disjoined; negations are true;"[120] the latter, while they appear to say less, actually say more. And this is the method of raising oneself up by the abnegation of all things, such that in these denials there is an order, beginning with the lowest and rising to the higher. Also, this involves

---

[118]   Cf. Augustine, *"Enarratio in Psalmum CXXXI,"* n. 27, in *Sancti Avrelii Avgvstini Enarrationes in Psalmos CI-CL,* edited by Eligius Dekkers and Johannes Fraipont, CCSL xl (Turnhout: Brepols, 1956), 1925.

[119]   Cf. Augustine, *De musica,* VI, ch. 13, n. 38 (PL 32:1183); translated by Robert Taliaferro, *On Music,* VI, ch. 13, n. 38, in *Writings of St. Augustine, Fathers of the Church Series* 2 (New York: Fathers of the Church, Inc., 1947), 363-364. In the tradition of the seven liberal arts, music was the fourth of the numerical arts.

[120]   Pseudo-Dionysius, *De Caelesti Hierarchia,* ch. II, n. 3 (PG 3:155); *The Celestial Hierarchy,* ch. II, n. 3 (Luibheid, 149-50) and *De Mystica Theologia,* ch. 1-5 (PG 3: 998ss); see also *The Mystical Theology,* chapters one through five (Luibheid, 135-41).

a super-eminent affirmation,[121] as for example, when
we say that God is not something sensible, but God is
supersensible; nor is God imaginable or intelligible or
existing, but *above* all these things. Thus, the gaze of
truth leads to the warming of the mind where it is raised
higher and penetrates deeper, because it rises above itself
and all created things.[122] This then is the most noble of
ascents. However, for this to be perfect, something else
is required: just as perfection requires illumination, so
negation requires affirmation.[123] This manner of rising
up is stronger to the extent that the power of ascent is
more intimate; it is more fruitful to the extent that the
affections are more closely bound. Consequently, it is
most useful to practice these exercises.

14.   Note that in the first hierarchy, truth must be
pleaded for in groaning and prayer, and this is the task
of the Angels; it must be listened to studiously and
willingly, and this is the task of the Archangels; it must
be proclaimed by example and preaching, and this is
the task of the Principalities. – In the second hierarchy,
truth must be sought as a refuge and a commission,
and this is the task of the Powers; it must be grasped
by zeal and emulation, which pertains to the Virtues; it
must be assimilated by self-contempt and mortification,
which belongs to the Dominions. – In the third hierarchy,
truth is to be adored by sacrifice and praise, which is the

---

[121] Here Bonaventure returns to the use of the word *positio*, that
is, positive statement or affirmation; the medieval logical exercise of
'obligation' began with a *positum* by the first of the participants, after
which the adversary would try to draw the one who spoke first into
contradicting what had previously been said.

[122] Cf. *Itinerarium,* ch. VII, n. 5 (Hayes, 115-16) and *Collations
...Six Days,* col. 2, n. 29 (de Vinck, 35-36).

[123] Aristotle, *Posterior Analytics*, book I, n. 21 in *The Complete
Works of Aristotle*, vol. 1, Jonathan Barnes, ed. (Princeton, NJ: Princeton University Press, 1984), 134-35.

task of the Thrones; it must be admired by ecstasy and contemplation, the domain of the Cherubim; it must be embraced with kisses and love, which pertains to the Seraphim. – Note diligently what has been said here, because therein is the font of life.

ON THE PERFECTION OF LIFE

DE PERFECTIONE VITAE AD SORORES

Introduction to the Text

Bonaventure wrote On the Perfection of Life Addressed to the Sisters in response to the request of the abbess of the Poor Clares at Longchamps, France, as an instruction "for the sake of devotion" in 1259.[1] Apologizing for his "brevity because of the preoccupations" of his other responsibilities, Bonaventure begins by reminding the sisters, indeed all of us, that happiness (*beatitudo*) is found in the "law of the Lord." It teaches us what is to be done, avoided, desired, prayed for, and feared in seeking true happiness – a fullness of life in the Lord. As Bonaventure writes in several places, God's wisdom is taught by the Spirit and is found in the affections of a devout mind (*per devotae mentis affectum*). In that context, he offers words of instruction on some key disciplines of the heart (virtues) which will lead the sisters – and others – to the perfect love of God (*de perfecta Dei caritate*).

Those "who wish to rise to the summit of the perfection of life" are instructed to make a faith-filled and conscious effort to develop eight virtues (strengths of character). They include: self-knowledge, humility, poverty, silence, prayer, the remembrance of

---

[1] Isabella, the sister of Louis IX, the King of France, founded the Poor Clare monastery at Longchamps near Paris in 1255. While it was traditionally assumed that she was the abbess to whom the letter was addressed, there is some doubt as to whether or not she ever professed vows within the community. See Ignatius Brady, "Two Sermons of St. Bonaventure," *Franciscan Studies* 28 (1968): 12, note 34. Isabella's name is not listed among the sisters or abbesses according to Henri Gaston Duchesne in *Histoire de L'Abbaye Royale de Longchamps 1255 à 1789*, H. Daragon, ed. (Paris: n. p., 1906).

There is no doubt that Isabella was involved in writing a rule for the community of "minor sisters" in consultation with Bonaventure and four other Franciscan Masters in Paris. Initially approved in 1259 by Alexander IV, the rule was approved definitively in 1263 by Urban IV and is associated with her name.

the passion of Christ, and charity. The first six are the interrelated and mutually helpful virtues which lead a person, through a disciplined training of the mind, heart, and spirit, to strive for the perfect love of God which is charity (*caritas*). The virtue of charity enables the devout mind to "love God above all things and our neighbor for the sake of God." To these seven virtues, the perfect number, is added an eighth virtue, perseverance. This is the virtue that reminds us that we must continually strive to make our way into God so that we might become radiant in the sight of God.

This short letter of instruction succinctly highlights essential virtues that ought to characterize the spiritual life of the sisters. They reflect, in sometimes nuanced ways, the core virtues which play a central role in the daily living of Bonaventure's theology of the spiritual life.[2] The text is of great practical interest to all who desire to follow the example of Francis and Clare in the different forms of Franciscan life. It is one of the few places where Bonaventure discusses at any length his understanding of the important virtue of self-knowledge. The chapter on the "perfection of love" provides a succinct summary of his theology of love (*caritas*) and what it means to say that one must love God with one's whole heart, soul, and mind.

---

[2] Compare with *The Major Legend of St. Francis* (1263), chaps. 5-13 (FA:ED II 560-639). In *Threefold Way*, III, nn. 1-10, Bonaventure identifies seven steps leading to peace, truth, and love – the constitutive elements of wisdom. Within each of these different schemata, Bonaventure demonstrates how a person might come to a better understanding of the differing but interrelated ways through which a person might arrive at wisdom. The subtle nuances and various ways of expressing his vision of the journey into wisdom reveal the depth and richness of Bonaventure's thought on these different and closely interrelated ways. However, *On the Perfection of Life* is a text that has been given little critical attention except for Marianne Schlosser's introduction to a 1994 German translation of the text in "Bonaventura, De perfectione vitae," *Wissenschaft und Weisheit* 57.1 (1994): 21-75, esp. 21-36.

On the Perfection of Life[3]

PROLOGUE

1. *Blessed is the person whom you will instruct, O Lord, and whom you will teach by your law.*[4] I consider no one to be wise unless [that person] has been taught by the anointing of the Holy Spirit.[5] According to the words of David the prophet, the only one who is truly blessed, the only one who is truly wise, is the one whose mind has been instructed by the Lord, whose spirit has been educated in the law of the Lord. *Only the law of the Lord is unspotted*; it alone is above reproach, converting souls to salvation.[6] The teaching or the erudition of this law is not only to be found in its external literal expression, but is rather found in the affections of the devout mind. This law must be desired *in power and in the holy Spirit*[7] so that only the Spirit might teach within;[8] the Spirit alone knows how to turn the external severity of the law into interior sweetness. The law of the Lord teaches what must be done, what must be avoided, what must be believed, what to pray for, what to desire, what to fear. It teaches us to be immaculate and above reproach. It teaches us to keep our promises, to weep over our offenses; it teaches us to despise worldly things, to reject what is carnal. It teaches

---

[3] The Latin text is Bonaventure's *De perfectione vitae ad sorores*, Opera Omnia VIII: 107-27.

[4] See Ps 93:12.

[5] See 1 John 2:20: "But you have an anointing from the Holy One and you know all things."

[6] See Ps 18:8: "The law of the Lord is unspotted, converting souls."

[7] See 1 Thes 1:5: "For our gospel was not delivered to you in word only, but in power also, and in the holy Spirit."

[8] See Augustine, *Tractate* 3, n. 13 in *Sancti Avrelii Avgvstini In Iohannis Evangelivm Tractatvs CXXIV*, edited by Radbodvs Willems, (Turnhout: Brepols, 1954), CCSL xxxvi, 26.

the whole heart, the whole soul, the whole mind to turn to Jesus Christ.[9] Compared to this doctrine, all worldly wisdom is stupid and vain.[10] As Bernard says: "No matter what others may say, I will not call anyone wise as long as he does not fear or love God."[11] Whoever listens to this doctrine and does not forget it is truly wise and truly happy. *Blessed is the person whom you will instruct, O Lord, and whom you will teach by your law.*[12]

2. And so, my beloved Reverend Mother,[13] you have asked me that, from the meager resources of my heart, I write you a little something whereby I might instruct you for the sake of devotion.[14] As far as I am concerned, I consider myself rather deficient to give such instruction, especially since in me the outward life is not resplendent, nor is there devotion aflame within, nor does my knowledge favor this. However, urged by your desire for devotion, I

---

[9] See Matt 22:37: "Jesus said to him: You shall love the Lord your Lord with your whole heart, and with your whole soul, and with your whole mind."

[10] Bonaventure, *Soliloquium*, ch. II, §1, n. 5.

[11] See *Sermo* 73, SBOp 6, 311-12: "Let a person learn as much as he wants, but I do not call anyone wise as long as he does not fear or love God."

[12] Ps 93:12.

[13] Bonaventure's instructions are addressed to the "reverend mother" in the feminine gender even though he frequently uses the masculine gender.

[14] Devotion (*devotio*) is an inner disposition of the soul that inclines a person through humble love (*affectus*) to be drawn up into God and to turn one's attention toward spiritual things. See *The Major Legend of St. Francis*, ch. 8, n. 1 (FA:ED II 586-87). See also *On the Perfection of Life*, ch. 5, n. 1 and ch. 6. See further Bonaventure's Sermon 48 "De S. Maria Magdalena" in *Sermones de diversis* II, edited by Jacques Guy Bougerol (Paris: Editions Franciscaines, 1993), 630: "In these words the glorious sinner and penitent is praised for her triple excellence: first, for the humility of her discipline; second, for the harshness of her penitence; third, for the abundance of her internal devotion." Devotion plays an important role in Bonaventure's understanding of the spiritual life. Prior to receiving his title as the Seraphic Doctor, he was referred to as the Doctor of Devotion.

have humbly agreed to do what you asked. Nonetheless, I ask your reverence, most holy mother, that you look more to the affection of my intentions rather than to whatever effects may result, that you look more to the truth of what is said rather than the charm and beauty of speech, such that while I might have less satisfactorily satisfied your desire, you will be so kind as to indulge me and forgive me for my brevity and because of the preoccupations which have taken my time.

So that you may more easily find what you are seeking, I list the titles of the chapters which follow:

> the first deals with the true knowledge of oneself;
> the second with true humility;
> the third with perfect poverty;
> the fourth with silence and taciturnity;
> the fifth with prayer;
> the sixth with remembering the passion of
>   Christ;
> the seventh with the perfect love of God;
> the eighth with final perseverance.

CHAPTER I: THE TRUE KNOWLEDGE OF SELF[15]

1. For the spouse of Christ who desires to ascend to the summit of the perfection of life, it is first necessary that she begin with herself. This is done as follows: by being forgetful of all external matters, she might enter with diligent consideration into the secret recesses of her conscience,[16] so that there she might discuss, examine, and look carefully at all her defects, all her customary habits, all her affections, her behavior, all her sins both past and present. If then she should find there something remiss,

---

[15] See also *Soliloquium*, ch. I, § I, n. 2.

[16] For a more complete discussion of the nature of conscience, see Introduction, 28-29.

she might immediately weep in the bitterness of her heart. In order that you might arrive at this knowledge, dear Mother, you ought to know that we commit all of our sins and evils either through negligence, or through disordered desire, or through the choice of what is morally worthless.[17] Your reflections regarding all of your faults must turn upon these three [sources], otherwise you will never arrive at the perfect knowledge of yourself.

2. If therefore you wish to know yourself, and knowing the faults you have committed, weep over them, you must first try to reflect if there might be or might have been in you any negligence. You must reflect, I say, about how negligently you have kept watch over your heart, how negligently you spend your time, and how you do what you do for a bad reason or goal. These three must be observed with the greatest diligence, namely how one's heart might be well guarded, how one's time might be passed usefully, and how a good and fitting goal might be pursued in every deed.

You must also reflect about how negligent you have been in prayer, in reading, and in carrying out your deeds. In these three you must most diligently exercise and cultivate yourself, if you wish to produce good fruit in timely fashion;[18] no one of these things is sufficient without the others.

Also, you must reflect about how negligent you are or have been regarding repentance, how negligent in resisting [temptations], and how negligent in making progress. You should with all diligence weep over the faults committed, repel the temptations of the devil, and progress from one virtue to another so that you may

---

[17] A standard framework for understanding the primary roots and nature of sin within Bonaventure's theological system. See above, the Introduction, 29-39. See also *Threefold Way*, ch. I, nn. 4-6.

[18] See Ps 1:3 and Matt 3:10.

arrive at the promised land.[19] And so your thoughts must revolve around your negligence.

3. If you wish to know yourself better, you must secondly reflect and see if in you there thrives or has thrived a disordered desire (*concupiscentia*) for pleasure, or curiosity, or vanity.[20]

Certainly the disordered desire of pleasure thrives in a religious person when she desires what is sweet, namely tasty food; when she seeks what is soft, namely sensuous garments; when she seeks what is carnal, namely luxurious delights.

Surely the disordered desire of curiosity thrives in the servant of God when she desires to know the occult, when she yearns to see the beautiful, and when she wants to possess what is rare.

Obviously the disordered desire of vanity thrives in the spouse of Christ when she seeks the favor of others, when she yearns for their praise, and desires to be honored by them. The maid of Christ must flee like poison all of these things because they are the roots of all evil.

4. Likewise, if you wish to have certain knowledge of yourself, you must thirdly diligently reflect as to whether there thrives or has thrived in you the wickedness of anger, the wickedness of envy, or the wickedness of laziness. Listen carefully to what I say. Certainly anger thrives in a religious person when either in mind, or heart, or affection, or outward sign, or by facial expression, word, or shout one shows the least indignation or rancor of one's heart to one's neighbor.

Also, envy reigns in someone when she rejoices over the adversity of her neighbor or is saddened over her prosperity; when she is glad about the evils befalling

---

[19] See Ps 83:8.
[20] See also *Threefold Way*, ch. I, n. 5.

her neighbor and is crestfallen about the good things happening to them.

Laziness thrives in a religious person when she is tepid, sleepy, idle, tardy, negligent, remiss, dissolute, undevout, sad, and wearisome. The spouse of Christ must detest and flee all these things as deadly poison, because herein consists the loss of body and soul.

5. If therefore, loving friend of God, you wish to arrive at a perfect knowledge of yourself, return to yourself, "enter into your heart, and learn to measure your spirit.[21] Discuss with yourself what you now are, what you were, what you ought to be, what you can be; discuss with yourself what you have been by nature, what you now are by your faults, what you ought to be by striving industriously, and finally what you can be by the grace of God."[22] Listen, dear Mother, to David the prophet who proposes himself as an example to you: *In the night I meditate in my heart; I searched and probed my spirit.*[23] He meditated in his heart and so should you. He searched and probed, and so should you. Till this field; look to yourself. There can be no doubt that whoever persists in this endeavor will find

---

[21] On this point see *On Governing the Soul*, n. 2, note 2, and the *Soliloquium*, ch. I, §IV, n. 38; ch. I, §I, n. 2; ch. I, §III, n. 10.

The instruction to "enter within," in other places, "return to" or "re-enter" one's very self must be understood in the context of Bonaventure's understanding of the rational spirit's capacity to look *outside* itself to what is material and temporal, *within* itself as to an image of the triune God, and *beyond* itself to what is eternal, most spiritual and above. See *Itinerarium*, ch. I, nn. 1-2 (Hayes, 45-47) and ch. III, n. 5 (Hayes, 91); *Breviloquium*, pt. II, ch. 12 (Monti, 96-98); *Soliloquium*, ch. I, §I, n. 2; *On Governing the Soul*, n. 2. Humanity's capacity for "seeing" may be impaired, however, by sin. Then, the assistance of grace is more urgently needed if one hopes to enter into the self as an image of God and/or rise above the self. See the text below n. 6, and *Itinerarium*, ch. IV, n. 1 (Hayes, 97).

[22] This is almost a verbatim citation from Pseudo-Bernard, *Tractatus de interiori domo,* ch. 36, n. 76 (PL 184: 545BC).

[23] See Ps 76:7.

the precious hidden treasure.[24] From such endeavors an abundance of gold is accumulated, knowledge multiplies, wisdom grows; from such exercises the eye of one's heart is purified, one's mental powers are sharpened, one's understanding is expanded. No one judges rightly who does not know herself, who does not reflect on the dignity of her state. Whoever does not first think about her own spirit is totally ignorant of what she should know about God or the angels. If you are incapable of returning to yourself, how can you deem yourself capable of examining what is above you? If you are not ready to enter the first tabernacle, how can you be so bold as to presume to enter the second tabernacle?[25]

6. If you wish to be raised up to the second and third heaven,[26] you must first pass through the first, namely your own heart. How you can and must do this, I have shown above. But blessed Bernard can teach you about this in the best way when he says: "Be a curious explorer of your integrity, diligently and assiduously examine and think about your life as to how you are progressing and how you are failing, about how you stand morally and where your affections lie, how like God and unlike him, how close or how far away."[27]

---

[24] See Matt 13:44: "The kingdom of God is like a treasure hidden in a field...."

[25] Richard of St. Victor, *Benjamin Major,* IV, ch. 23 (PL 196:167B) refers to the three tabernacles. See also translation by Grover Zinn, "The Mystical Ark," in *Richard of St. Victor, The Twelve Patriarchs, The Mystical Ark, Book Three of the Trinity,* (NY: Paulist Press, 1979), 306. Cf. *Itinerarium,* ch. V, n. 1 (Hayes, 111).

[26] See 2 Cor 12:2: "I know a man in Christ who fourteen years ago ... was caught up to the third heaven."

[27] This is an almost verbatim citation from Pseudo-Bernard, *Meditationes piissimae de cognitione humanae conditionis,* ch. 5, n. 14 (PL 184: 494D). Hereafter *Meditationes piissimae.*

O how close to perdition and burial is a religious who wants to know so many things and yet be ignorant of herself; who is curious to know [external] things and so solicitous to judge the consciences of others while being so ignorant of herself.[28] My God, how can such blindness prevail in a religious person? The reason is easy to find: the mind of human beings is distracted by worries and does not use memory to enter within itself; obfuscated by the imagination, it does not return to itself by its intelligence; because it is enticed away by illicit desires, it is at a complete loss as to how to return to itself by the desire for internal sweetness and spiritual joy.[29] Consequently, being totally preoccupied with sensible things, it does not know how to return to itself as to the image of God, and is thus totally miserable because it is ignorant of and does not know itself.[30] Having set all these things aside, remember and know yourself. Blessed Bernard himself prayed for this when he said: "May God grant me to know nothing else but my very self."[31]

CHAPTER II: ON TRUE HUMILITY

1. Because of the defects in the eyes of someone wishing to examine her heart, it is necessary to "humble yourselves *under the mighty hand of God.*"[32]

Therefore, I admonish you, friend of Christ, that on account of the assured knowledge of your own faults and defects, you humble your spirit and despise yourself. "Humility is a virtue," says the blessed Bernard,

---

[28] Bonaventure, *Soliloquium*, ch. I, § I, n. 2.

[29] See Bonaventure, *Itinerarium*, ch. IV, n. 1 (Hayes, 97).

[30] See *Sancti Avrelii Avgvstini De Ordine*, I, ch. 3, n. 3, CCSL, xxix, (Turnhout: Brepols, 1970), 90.

[31] This exact citation occurs nowhere in Bernard. But see Sermo 40, n. 3, *Sermones de diversis* (SBOp 6: 236): "The first step and first level along this way is knowledge of self."

[32] See 1 Peter 5:6.

"whereby a person, knowing himself most truly, demeans himself."[33]

With such humility our blessed father Francis vilified himself, and loved and sought humility from the beginning of his religious life until the end. Out of humility he left the world, he commanded that he be dragged naked through the streets; out of humility he waited on the lepers; he openly manifested his sins in his preaching; and, ordered others to upbraid him. O mother devoted to God, you must learn this virtue most of all from the Son of God, because he says: *Learn from me, for I am meek and humble of heart.*[34] "For whoever seeks to accumulate virtues without humility, carries dust in the wind," as blessed Gregory says.[35] Just as the beginning of all sin is pride, so the foundation of all virtues is humility. Learn to be truly humble and do not feign humility, as the hypocrites who maliciously dissimulate humility, of whom Sirach says: *There is a person who wickedly humbles himself, but is full of guile within.*[36] "For a person who is truly humble," says the blessed Bernard, "always wishes to be held in no esteem rather than be spoken of as humble."[37]

---

[33] Bernard, *De gradibus humilitatis et superbiae,* ch. I, n. 2 (SBOp 3:17); *On Humility and Pride*, ch. I, n. 2, in *Bernard of Clairvaux: Selected Works*, CWS, 103. See Bonaventure's definition of humility in *Questiones disputatae de perfectione evangelica*, q. 1 (V, 117-24); for Bonaventure on the humility of St. Francis see "The Evening Sermon on St. Francis, 1255" in FA:ED II, 519-24; and *The Major Legend of St. Francis*, ch. 2. in FA:ED II, 536-41 and ch. 6 FA:ED II, 569-76.

[34] Matt 11:29. This Gospel text is read on the feast of St. Francis. For a reflection of Bonaventure on the text and the life of Francis see "The Morning and Evening Sermon on St. Francis, 1255" in FA:ED II, 508-24.

[35] See *Homilia* 7, n. 4 of GGHG (CCSL cxli, 52).

[36] Sir 19:23.

[37] See *Sermo* 16 in *Cantica*, n. 10 (SBOp 1:95); translated by Kilian Walsh, *On the Song of Songs*, Cistercian Fathers vol. I (Spencer, MA: Cistercian Publications, 1971), 121. Bonaventure's citation is not verbatim.

2. If therefore, beloved Mother, you wish to arrive at perfect humility, you must follow a threefold path.[38] – The first path is that of considering God. You must consider God as the author of all good and because God is the author of all good, we must say to God: *You have done all our works in us, O Lord.*[39] And because God is so good, you must attribute all good to God and not to yourself, considering that it is not *by your own power and the strength of your hands*[40] that you have accomplished the good things which you possess, because "The Lord made us, and not we ourselves."[41] Reflections like these should suffice to destroy totally the pride of those who say: "Our mighty hand, and not the Lord, has accomplished all these things."[42] Such pride banished Lucifer from the glory of heaven. Lucifer refused to consider that he had been made from nothing, but rather looked to his own elegance and beauty, such that *every precious stone was your covering*[43] and thus the pride of his heart raised him up. But since "humiliation follows the proud,"[44] so he was immediately cast down from the throne of his nobility into a place of extreme degradation, and he who had previously been the most excellent of angels became the most miserable of devils.

---

[38] See note 33, p. 147.

[39] See Isa 26:12 where the Vulgate reads *nobis* ("for us") while Bonaventure has *in nobis* ("in us").

[40] See Deut 8:17: "Lest you should say in your heart: My own power and the strength of my own hand have achieved all these things for me."

[41] See Ps 99:3.

[42] See Deut 32:27. See Augustine, *Enarratio in Psalmum* CVI, n. 15 (CCSL xi, 1852); translated by Maria Boulding, in WSA III/19, *Expositions of the Psalms* 99-120 (Hyde Park, NY: New City Press, 2003), 238: *"The wise will treasure these things.* And what are the wise to treasure? These wise persons must be poor if they are to keep it all; they must not be proud or puffed up, or they will never treasure these things."

[43] See Ez 28:13. Cf. Bernard, *On Humility and Pride*, X: 31, (Evans, 126).

[44] See Prov 29:23.

3. How many imitators of Lucifer we find today, sons and daughters of pride, whom the Lord patiently tolerates! Since however, as Bernard says, "pride is more tolerable in a wealthy person than in a poor person,"[45] therefore, the handmaid of Christ ought always to be most humble so as to take the place of a repudiated angel. Whether in an angel or in a human being, only humility pleases God. You should not think that virginity without humility will please God. Certainly Mary would not have become the mother of God had she had any pride in her. Therefore, blessed Bernard says: "Without humility, I dare to say, the virginity of Mary would not have pleased God."[46] Hence, it is a great virtue without which there is not only no virtue, but it rather bursts into pride.

4. The second path consists in recalling [the life of] Christ. You should remember that Christ was humbled even to the most disgraceful sort of death,[47] and became so humble as to be considered a sort of leper. Thus the prophet Isaiah said: *We have thought of him, as it were, as a leper, and as ... humiliated by God.*[48] He had become so

---

[45] See Bernard, *Sermo* 54 in *Cantica*, n. 8 (SBOp 2: 107); translated by Killian Walsh, *On the Song of Songs*, Cistercian Fathers vol. II (Kalamazoo, MI: Cistercian Publications, 1979), 76: "Who would not reckon pride more tolerable in a wealthy person than in a poor person?"

[46] See *Homilia* 1, n. 5, of "In laudibus Virginis Mariae" (SBOp 4: 18): "But without humility, I dare to say, the virginity of Mary would not have been pleasing." See translation by Community of St. Mary's at York, "On the 'Missus Est'" (The Praises of the Virgin Mother), in *Sermons of St. Bernard on Advent and Christmas* (London: R. and T. Washbourne, Ltd., 1909), 29. Hereafter, *St. Bernard on Advent and Christmas*. Cf. Bernard's *Epistola* XLII, ch. 5 n. 17 or *De moribus et officio episcoporum* (SBOp 7: 114): "From the fullness of all virtues Mary singles out her humility in Luke 1:48: *God has regarded the humility of his handmaid.*"

[47] See Phil 2:8: "He humbled himself, becoming obedient to death, even death on a cross."

[48] See Isa 53:4.

humiliated that at the time no one was thought to be viler than he. And so the same Isaiah says: *In his humiliation justice was denied him,*[49] as if to say: so great was his humility, so much had he debased himself that no one could render him true justice and no one would believe that he was God. *If therefore "our Lord and master" himself says: No slave is greater than his master nor any messenger greater than the one who sent him,*[50] so if you are a handmaid of Christ, a disciple of Christ, then you must be vile, contemptible, and humble.

O how despicable to God is the religious who wears humble vestments and has a proud heart! What a useless Christian is she who sees her humble and despised Lord while *exalting her heart ... and busying herself with great things that are too sublime for her.*[51] What is more despicable in the spouse of Christ, what ought to be punished more in the handmaid of Christ than [having seen] the very highest made lowest, the greatest made the smallest and become man, she who is decayed and worm-like should extol herself? Of such Augustine says: "O deathlike membrane, what do you cover? O putrid bloody matter, why are you puffed up? Is the head humble and the members proud?"[52] As if to say: Such is not becoming.

---

[49] See Isa 53:8 in the LXX. The Vulgate has: "He was taken away from distress and from judgment."

[50] See John 13:14 and 16.

[51] See Ps 130:1: "My heart is not exalted ... I have not busied myself with things that are too sublime for me." Cf. Bernard, *Sermo* 1, n. 1, *In nativitate Domini* (SBOp 4: 245): "For is there a greater indignity, is there something more detestable, is there something deserving of more severe punishment than the person who sees the God of heaven becoming a little child and exalts himself so greatly as to soar above the earth?" See also "Sermon I on the Birth of the Lord" (*Sermons of St. Bernard on Advent and Christmas*, p. 102).

[52] See Augustine, *Sermo* 304, ch. 4 (PL 38: 1396). The last question: "Is the head humble and the members proud?" is not found in Augustine, but in the Glossa Ordinaria apud Lyranum on Phil 2:8. See Augustine, *Sermon* 304, ch. 4, in *Sermons (273-305A) on the Saints,*

5. The third path which you must take if you wish to arrive at perfect humility is to be circumspect regarding yourself. You are circumspect, dearest Mother, when you realize whence you came and where you are going.[53]

Consider then where you came from. You should know that you stem from a mass of perdition, from the dust and slime of the earth, frequently in sin and exiled from the happiness of paradise.[54] Such reflections suffice to lance and exclude the tumors of pride, so that you can begin to shout with the three young men in Daniel 3:37: *We are humbled in the entire world this day because of our sins.* You ought also to consider where you are going. You are going to corruption and ashes, *for you are dirt, and to dirt you shall return.*[55] Why then are you proud, O dirt and ashes? Today you are, tomorrow you will not be; if today you are healthy, perhaps tomorrow you will be sick; if today you are wise, perhaps tomorrow you will be stupid; if today you are rich in virtue, perhaps tomorrow you will be a beggar and miserable.[56] Who then is this Christian who would dare to be proud when seeing herself surrounded by such misery and calamity?

6. Learn then, O consecrated virgins, to have a humble spirit, a humble gait, humble senses, a humble demeanor. Only humility will placate divine anger, only humility will find divine grace. *For humble yourself the more in all things, the greater you are,* as Sirach 3:20 says, *and you will find favor with God.* This is how Mary found favor

---

trans. Edmund Hill, WSA III/8 (Brooklyn: New City Press, 1994), 317.

[53] See Pseudo-Bernard, *Meditationes piissimae,* ch. 1, n. 1 (PL 184: 485A).

[54] All these are oblique allusions to Gen 3.

[55] See Gen 3:19.

[56] The images of the sinner as the beggar and the miserable one appear frequently in the spiritual writings of Bonaventure. For example, see *Commentary on Book II of the Sentences*, prologue, n. 12ff. See above, Introduction, 30-36, esp. 35-36.

with God, as she herself testified when she said: *For he has looked upon his handmaid's lowliness.*[57] Nor is this surprising, because humility paves the way for charity, and purges the mind of vanity. This is why Augustine says: "The more we have drained the tumors of pride, the fuller will we be with love."[58] Just as water flows down into the valleys, so the grace of the Holy Spirit flows into the humble; and just as water flows more forcefully, the greater the slope of descent, so she who proceeds with a totally humble heart will more closely approach to God in order to pray for grace. This is why Sirach 35:21 says: *The prayer of the lowly pierces*[59] *the clouds, and the lowly will not be comforted until his prayer reaches the Most High,* because the Lord *will do the will of those who fear him and will hear their prayer.*[60]

7. Therefore, friends of God and handmaids of Christ, be humble so that you will never allow pride to prevail in your hearts,[61] because you have a humble master, namely the Lord Jesus Christ; and you have a humble mistress, namely the virgin Mary, queen of all. Be humble because you have a humble father, namely blessed Francis; be humble because you have a humble mother, namely blessed Clare, an exemplar of humility.

Be humble then in such a way that patience will be the witness to your humility. The virtue of humility grows with patience and there is no true humility that is not joined to patience. Augustine testifies to this when he

---

[57] Luke 1:48.

[58] See Augustine, *De Trinitate*, VIII, n. 12 (CCSL l, 287); Edmund Hill, trans., *The Trinity*, 253: "And the more cured we are from the tumors of pride, the fuller will we be with love."

[59] The Vulgate reads *penetrabit* ("will pierce") while Bonaventure has *penetrat* ("pierces").

[60] See Ps 144:19.

[61] See Tob 4:14: "Never allow pride to reign in your mind or in your words."

says: "It is easy enough to put a veil over your eyes, to put on ragged and ugly clothes, to walk around with bowed head; but patience is the test of true humility."[62] As Sirach 2:4 says: *In your humiliation show patience.*

Alas, I say with sorrow, many are we who are proud in the cloister, whereas we were surely humble in the world. Hence blessed Bernard says:

> Sad to say, I see that many, having spurned the pomp of the world have rather learned pride in the school of humility, and under the wings of a meek and humble master have become more haughty and impatient in the cloister than they were in the world. What is more perverse, many in the house of God tolerate no contempt, who in their own homes could be nothing but contemptible![63]

8. I advise you, loving mother, that you also advise your daughters, your consecrated virgins, that they preserve their virginity in humility and their humility in virginity. Virginity coupled with humility is like a gem set in gold. This is why blessed Bernard says: "Virginity coupled with humility is a beautiful mixture. The soul greatly pleases God wherein humility supports virginity and virginity adorns humility."[64]

Listen then to the advice of your brother, listen mother, and it will please you: flee proud companions like vipers, spurn proud virgins like demons, despise the company of the proud like deadly poison. Why? Hear

---

[62] See Augustine, *Epistola* 17, ch. 20 (PL 33: 1113). Bonaventure's citation is more a summary than a quotation. For example, Augustine writes: "Patience amidst injury is the test of true humility."

[63] See Bernard, *Homilia* IV, n. 10, "*In laudibus Virginis Mariae*" (SBOp 4: 55). Bonaventure's citation is virtually verbatim.

[64] See *Homilia* I, n. 5, "In Laudibus Virginis Mariae" (SBOp 4:17). See also "On the *Missus est*," homily 1, n. 5 (*St. Bernard on Advent and Christmas*, pp. 29, 32). Bonaventure's citation is virtually verbatim.

why! There was once a wise man who described a proud
person as follows: "Every proud person is intolerable. His
clothing is extravagant, his gait pompous, head erect,
visage grim, fierce-looking eyes. He pushes toward the
places of honor, deems himself better than others, flaunts
his opinions, words and deeds, and has no respect [for
others]."[65] Consequently, friend of God, spouse of Christ,
virgin of the Lord, you must flee the companionship of
the proud, lest you become like them. As Sirach 13:1 says:
"The person that *associates with the proud person will
become proud.*"[66]

CHAPTER III: ON PERFECT POVERTY

1. The virtue of poverty is necessary for perfect integrity in the sense that no one can be altogether perfect
without it, as vouched for by the Lord in the Gospel: *If
you wish to be perfect, go and*[67] *sell what you have and
give to the poor.*[68] Since the summit of evangelical perfection consists in the excellence of poverty, no one ought to
believe that she has reached the highest peak of perfection who has not yet become a perfect imitator of evangelical poverty. For Hugh of St. Victor says: "Whatever
one might be able to find of perfection in religious, nev-

---

[65] See Julius Pomerius, *De Vita Contemplativa*, III, ch. 8, n. 1 (PL
59:484BC) among the works of Prosper. Bonaventure's citation is at
best a summary. See also Julianus Pomerius, *The Contemplative Life*,
Book III, ch. 8, n. 1, translated and annotated by Mary Josephine Suelzer, ACW 4 (Westminster, MD: Newman Bookshop, 1947), 118-19.

[66] The Vulgate reads *communicaverit* ("associates") while Bonaventure's text has *communicat* ("associates"). Further, the Vulgate
reads *inducet superbiam* ("will learn pride") whereas Bonaventure
has *induet superbiam* ("will become proud").

[67] The Vulgate does not have *et* ("and").

[68] See Matt 19:21.

ertheless one ought not believe they have reached the integrity of perfection unless there be a love of poverty."[69]

2. There are two things which ought to motivate any religious, or any person whatever for that matter, to love poverty. The first is the "divine example" which is above reproach; the second is the "divine promise" which is priceless.

The first, I say, which ought to move you, friend of Christ, to the love of poverty is the love [for it] and example of our Lord Jesus Christ. He was born poor, lived poor, and died poor.

3. Look at the example of poverty [Christ] left you, so that by his example of poverty you may become its friend. Our Lord Jesus Christ was born poor in that he had neither shelter, nor clothing, nor nourishment. For shelter he had a stable, for clothing he had rags, for nourishment his mother's milk. Hence Paul the Apostle in considering poverty breathlessly [as it were] exclaimed to the Corinthians: *For you know the gracious act of our Lord Jesus Christ, who, although he was rich, became poor for our sake, so that by his poverty we might become rich.*[70] And blessed Bernard says:

> An eternal affluence of all goods was present in heaven, but poverty was not found among them. But on earth this kind of good was abundant, even superabundant, yet human beings were ignorant of its value. So the Son of God, desiring poverty,

---

[69] QuarEd state (p. 112, n. 10) that they did not find this reference among the works of Hugh of St. Victor and offer three parallel passages. See, e.g., Jerome, *Epistola* 14, n. 6 (PL 22: 351): "Now the perfect servant of Christ possesses nothing except Christ. Or if he has something besides Christ, he is not perfect."

[70] See 2 Cor 8:9: "For you know the gracious act of our Lord Jesus Christ, that, although he was rich, he became poor for your sake, so that by his poverty you might become rich."

descended to earth and chose it for himself. Through his evaluation of poverty he made it precious in our sight."[71]

4. Our Lord Jesus Christ showed us an example of poverty while living among us in the world. Listen, blessed virgin, listen all who profess to be poor.[72] See how poor was the Son of God, the King of the angels, while he lived here on earth. He was so poor that at times he had no shelter, but with his apostles had to sleep outside the cities and villages. Thus the evangelist Mark says: *He looked around at everything and, since it was already late, went out to Bethany with the twelve.*[73] Regarding this text the Gloss says: "He looked around to see if someone might offer him shelter. But because he was in such dire poverty and yet would not resort to base flattery, he could not find any hospitality in such a [big] city."[74] And Matthew 8:20 says: *Foxes have dens and birds of the air have nests, but the Son of Man has nowhere to rest his head.*

5. Thus not only was the Lord of the angels born poor and lived poorly, but, so that he might enkindle the love of poverty in us, he died in direst poverty. All of you, who have vowed poverty, *look and see.*[75] How poor at the time of his death, for our sakes, the King of heaven had become! He was despoiled and deprived of all that he had. He was despoiled of his clothing, I say, when *they divided his*

---

[71] See Bernard, *Sermo* 1, n. 5, "*In vigilia nativitatis Domini*" (SBOp 4: 197). Bonaventure's citation is virtually verbatim. See translation as "First Sermon on Christmas Eve," in SBSermons I, 315.

[72] For a parallel discussion of the content of nn. 4-6 see St. Bonaventure, "Sermon on St. Anthony," translated by Brad Milunski, *The Cord* 36 (1986): 182-91; also *Defense of the Mendicants*, ch. VII, nn. 6-8 (de Vinck, 131).

[73] Mark 11:11.

[74] Cf. Nicholas of Lyra, *Biblica Sacra cum Glossa interlinearis*, Mark 11:11 (Ed. Basiliea, 1506, V, 110).

[75] See Lam 1:12.

garments and cast lots over his tunic.[76] He was despoiled of body and soul when, through the suffering of the bitterest sort of death, his soul was cast from his body. He was even despoiled of his divine glory when *they did not accord him glory as God,*[77] but treated him as a criminal, as Job lamented: *They have stripped me of my glory.*[78] Regarding such examples of poverty, blessed Bernard says: "Look at the poor Christ: born without shelter, lying in the crib between an ox and an ass, wrapped in rags, fleeing to Egypt, seated on an ass, hanging naked on the cross."[79]

6. Who then is the miserable Christian, this hopeless and senseless religious, who still loves riches and loathes poverty, when she sees and hears the God of gods, the Lord of the world, the King of heaven, the only begotten of God sustaining such poverty? As blessed Bernard says: "What a great abuse it is, unimaginably great, that a vile worm would wish to be rich, on whose account the God of majesty and Lord of the Sabbath wanted to become poor."[80] "Let the pagan who lives without God seek wealth; let the Jew seek riches who accepts promises of worldly possessions."[81] But you, virgin of Christ, handmaid of the Lord, what can you be thinking of in seeking riches, when you have vowed poverty, while you live among the poor of

---

[76] Bonaventure's citation is a blending of Matt 27:35 and Ps 21:19. Neither text, however, has *vestem* ("tunic").

[77] See Rom 1:21.

[78] See Job 19:9 where the Vulgate reads *spoliavit* ("he has stripped") whereas Bonaventure has *spoliaverunt* ("they have stripped").

[79] See Bernard, *Sermo* 3, n. 1-2, *"In Resurrectione Domini"* (SBOp 5: 104) for a weak parallel to Bonaventure's citation. See also a parallel in Augustine, Sermon 14, n. 9, in *Sermons (1-19) on the Old Testament*, translation and notes by Edmund Hill, WSA III/I; (Brooklyn: New City Press, 1990), 321.

[80] See *Sermo* 3, n. 1, *"In Resurrectione Domini"* (SBOp 5:104). Bonaventure's quotation is virtually verbatim.

[81] See Bernard, *Sermo* 1, n. 7, *"In festivitate omnium Sanctorum"* (SBOp 5:332). Bonaventure's citation is virtually verbatim. See also: "First Sermon the Feast of all the Saints," n. 7 (SBSermons, III, 338).

Jesus Christ, when you wish to be the daughter of father Francis, when you promised to imitate your poor mother Clare? And so, beloved mother, your avarice and mine are put to shame because, although we profess poverty, we [often] trade poverty for avarice, desiring what we ought not, yearning for what is forbidden by the rule, whereas the Son of God *became poor for our sake*.[82]

7. I realize that the more fervent lovers of poverty you have been and the more closely you have imitated evangelical poverty, so also will you be showered with both temporal and spiritual goods. If, however, you should turn to the contrary, and despise the poverty you have professed, then indeed you will be destitute of all goods both temporal and spiritual. Once the poor mother Mary of the poor Jesus said: *The hungry he has filled with good things; the rich he has sent away empty.*[83] The most holy prophet attests to this when he says: *The rich grow poor and hungry, but those who seek the Lord want for no good thing.*[84] Have you not read or have you not heard the Lord Jesus speaking to his apostles in the Gospel of Matthew when he says: *Do not worry and say: What are we to eat or what are we to drink? ... For your Father knows what you need"*[85] Again, listen to what he says to you in the Gospel of Luke: *When I sent you forth without a moneybag or a sack or sandals, were you in need of anything? And they replied: Nothing.*[86] If then the Lord fed his disciples without solicitude in the midst of the tough and unbelieving Jews, why is it surprising if he nourishes the Friars Minor as professing the same perfection, why [surprising] if he nourishes the

---

[82] See 2 Cor 8:9.

[83] Luke 1:53.

[84] Ps 33:11.

[85] See Matt 6:31-32. Bonaventure's text of Matt 6:32b differs from the Vulgate: "For your Father knows that you need all these things."

[86] See Luke 22:35.

poor sisters who imitate evangelical poverty while living among the Christians and the faithful? Therefore, cast[87] all your worries upon him, because he cares for you.[88]

8. Since, therefore, God the Father has shown such solicitude and care for us, it is puzzling why we should be so worried about these temporal affairs, these curious and transient things. I find no other cause than avarice that is the mother of confusion and damnation. I find no other cause than that our affections have strayed from God, our salvation.[89] There is no other cause than the fact that the fervor of divine charity has grown cold and congealed in us. Certainly, if we were truly fervent, then naked we would follow the naked Christ.[90] When people are exceptionally hot, they are accustomed to shed their garments. The fact that we accumulate temporal goods is a sign of great frigidity in us. My God! How can we be so hard-hearted regarding Christ, who "went forth from his homeland," that is from heaven and "from his kinfolk," that is from the company of the angels; "and from his father's house,"[91] that is from the bosom of the Father, and became poor, abject, and despised for us? And for him we are reluctant to leave one miserable and fetid world! We may indeed leave the world 'bodily,' and yet our hearts, minds, and desires are totally preoccupied and absorbed with the world.

---

[87] The Vulgate does not read *itaque* ("therefore"). Further, the Vulgate reads *proicientes* ("casting") while Bonaventure has *proiicite* ("cast").

[88] See 1 Peter 5:7.

[89] See Deut 32:15: "The beloved grew fat ... forsook God who made him and departed from God his savior."

[90] See Jerome, *Epistola* 125, n. 20 (PL 22: 1085) where he has *nudus* ("naked") while Bonaventure has *nudi* ("naked"). In paragraph n. 20, Jerome cites Gen 12:1. See the next note.

[91] Here Bonaventure is giving a Christological interpretation of Gen 12:1: "And the Lord said to Abram: Go forth from your homeland, and from your kinfolk, and from your father's house...."

9. O blessed friend of God, call to mind the poverty of the poor Lord Jesus Christ, imprint upon your heart the poverty of your poor father Francis, recall the poverty of your mother Clare, and then with all your strength and resolve cling to poverty, embrace Lady Poverty. Nor should you wish to love anything else under heaven for the sake of the Lord than poverty: not honors, nor any temporal things, not riches. Take great care to observe the holy poverty which you have vowed. It is fruitless to have and love riches; to love and not to have is dangerous; to have and not to love is laborious. Therefore, it is sure that it is not useful to have nor to love riches. What is delectable is the act of perfect virtue. Consequently, both the advice of the Lord regarding poverty[92] and his example should move and incite every Christian to the love of poverty. O blessed poverty, how beloved of God, how secure in the world to the one who loves you! "For whoever," says Gregory, "has nothing he loves in the world, has nothing to fear from the world."[93] Thus, as we read in *The Lives of the Fathers*[94] there was a certain brother who had a mat of rushes, half of which he put under himself at night and the other half he covered himself with. One time, when it had become very cold, the father of the monastery who happened to be out at night overheard him saying: "I thank you, Lord, that there are so many wealthy people in prison, seated in iron, or chained in iron, or with feet in

---

[92] See Matt 19:21.

[93] See *S. Gregorii Magni Moralia in Iob Libri* I-IX, X, ch. 21 n. 39, edited by Marcus Adriaen, CCSL cxliii, (Turnhout: Brepols, 1979), 565: "When he has nothing in the world that he desires, he has nothing to fear from the world." Bonaventure's citation is not verbatim. See also *Morals on the Book of Job* Book X, ch. 21, n. 39, Library of Fathers of the Holy Catholic Church, vol. I (Oxford: J.H. Parker, 1844-50), 607-608. Hereafter references to the Latin edition will be in the shortened form *Moralia in Iob*; references to the English translation will be to the *Morals* with the volume and page number indicated.

[94] Cf. "Vita Ioannis Eleemosynarii," *Liber Primus De Vitis Patrum*, ch. 20 (PL 73: 355BC).

stocks, and I am like an emperor, stretching my feet and walking where I will." – And so you have the first, namely the example of poverty.

10. The second thing which should enkindle in you the love of poverty is the divine promise which is priceless. O Lord *enriching all*,[95] O good Lord Jesus, who can express adequately in words, or understand in her heart, or write down by hand about the celestial glory you have promised to your poor ones? By their voluntary poverty, they deserve "to participate in the glory of the Creator";[96] they deserve "to enter into the powers of the Lord,"[97] into the eternal tabernacles, into those resplendent mansions. They deserve to become citizens of that [heavenly] city whose architect and builder is God. With your blessed lips you have promised them this when you said: *Blessed are the poor in spirit, for theirs is the kingdom of heaven.*[98] The kingdom of heaven, Lord Jesus Christ, is none other than you yourself, who is the *King of kings and the Lord of lords.*[99] You will give yourself to them as recompense, as reward and as joy; and they, in turn, will enjoy you and rejoice with you and be satisfied in you. *The poor will eat their fill, and they who seek the Lord will praise him. Their hearts will live forever.*[100] Amen.

---

[95] See Rom 10:12.

[96] See *Homilia* 37, n. 1, in GGHG (CCSL cxli, 348).

[97] See Ps 70:16. The Vulgate reads *introibo* ("I will enter) while Bonaventure has *intrare* ("to enter"). Also the Vulgate reads *potentiam* ("the power") whereas Bonaventure has *potentias* ("powers").

[98] Matt 5:3.

[99] I Tim 6:15.

[100] Ps 21:27.

Chapter IV: On Silence

1.   The virtue of silence[101] contributes much to the perfection of the religious person because, just as *where words are many, sin is not wanting*,[102] so where speaking is brief and rare, humans are spared many a sin. And just as from constant prattle comes frequent injury to God and man, so justice is nourished in silence, as the fruit of peace is gathered from its tree. Because peace is greatly needed for those in the cloister, so silence is most necessary whereby their peace of mind and body is preserved. This is why the prophet Isaiah, reflecting on the virtue of silence, says: *The work of justice will be peace, the service of justice will produce silence*;[103] as if to say: silence is such a great virtue that among humans it preserves the justice of God and nourishes and conserves peace among one's neighbors. Unless a person watches diligently over [her] mouth[104] and the precious gifts [she] possesses, [she] will be quickly dissipated and deteriorate into many evils. *Indeed, the tongue*, says blessed James in his canonical epistle, *is a small member and yet has great pretensions.... Our*[105] *tongue is also a fire, a world of malice.*[106] The Glossa comments: "Through the tongue almost all crimes are perpetrated ... or committed."[107]

---

[101] Compare Bonaventure's discussion of the essential value of the virtue of silence in the life of the cloistered sisters and his instruction on silence for the friar novices in the *Instruction for Novices*, ch. 15, in *Writings Concerning the Franciscan Order*, (Monti, 173-74).

[102] See Prov 10:19.

[103] Isa 32:17. Cf. Gregory, *Moralia in Iob,* VII, ch. 37, n. 58, CCSL cxliii, 378; *Morals*, I, 462-64. Gregory also cites Prov 10:19 and Isa 32:17. See also Bernard of Clairvaux, *Epistola* 89, n. 2 (SBOp 7: 236) where Bernard cites Isa 32:17 and *Epistola* 385, n. 4 (SBOp 8: 353) where Bernard quotes Isa 32:17.

[104] See Ps 39:2.

[105] The Vulgate does not read *Nostra* ("Our").

[106] See James 3:5-6.

[107] This is the Glossa Ordinaria (PL 114: 676B). The Glossa Ordinaria is dependent upon Bede. See PL 93: 27C.

Would you like to know, O friend of God, what evils come from the tongue which is not carefully guarded? Listen and I will tell you. From the tongue comes blasphemy, complaining, the defense of sin, perjury, lying, detraction, flattery, cursing, insults, quarreling, mocking what is good, bad advice, rumors, boasting, disclosing secrets, idle threats, vain promises, garrulousness, and crude jokes. In truth it causes great disorder to the feminine sex and it is most unbecoming for consecrated virgins not to watch over their mouths and not to discipline their tongues, since so much harm is perpetrated by tongues disturbing the peace. Certainly, I dare say, it is useless for a religious to boast about having a virtue in her heart while dissipating the discipline of silence by noisy and garrulous speech. *For*[108] *if anyone*, Scripture says, *thinks he is religious and does not bridle his tongue but deceives his heart, his religion is in vain.*[109]

2. O lovable spouses of Jesus Christ, look to your mistress and mine, look to the mirror of virtues, Mary, and learn from her the discipline of silence! It is obvious that the blessed Virgin was quite taciturn. If we peruse the Gospels, we will find few places where she spoke and with few words. We find that she talked only to four persons and then only in seven phrases: to the angel with two, to her Son with two, to Elizabeth with two, and to the servants at the wedding with one. This should put to shame our loquacity whereby we are prone to many words, whereas silence is greatly useful.

3. It is useful in one way because it induces compunction. When silent, a person reflects about her ways[110] and

---

[108] The Vulgate reads *autem* ("but") whereas Bonaventure has *enim* ("for").

[109] James 1:26.

[110] Cf. 118:59: "I have reflected on my ways."

allows time for thinking about how manifold are her defects and how little progress has been made, and from this compunction arises. Thus the prophet David says: *I was dumb and humiliated and could speak of nothing good. And my sorrow was renewed.*[111]

Silence is also useful in another way because it shows that [a human being] is also a celestial being. An almost irrefutable argument is as follows: if [someone] is in Germany and does not speak German, [she is] known not to be a German. So if someone is in the world and does not speak 'worldly', it shows clearly that she is not of this world. For *the one who is of the earth ... is earthly and speaks of earthly things,* as we read in the gospel of John.[112]

Nothing is more helpful to the religious person wishing to preserve silence than to flee the company of [others] and lead a solitary life. The one who has already raised herself above the status of men [and women], need have no other consoler or anyone with whom to converse other than God alone. And so you must be solitary and silent, and because you have God for your companion, you need not worry about human companionship. This is why it is said in Lamentations: *He will sit alone and will be silent, because he has raised himself above himself.*[113] Let [her] sit alone, I say, avoiding the company of others; in silence, meditating upon things celestial; and she has raised herself above herself by tasting heavenly sweetness.

4.   Even though silence is necessary for all religious for achieving the perfection of [all] virtues, it is most necessary that virgins betrothed to God and friends

---

[111] Ps 38:3.

[112] See John 3:31. See also Bernard of Clairvaux, *Epistola* 78, n. 4 (SBOp 7:203): "Put on the yoke of silence, and perpetual quiet compels meditation on heavenly matters away from all the clamor of worldly concerns."

[113] Lam 3:28.

of Jesus Christ preserve silence. Their speech must be so precious that they be shy about speaking, and then only when great necessity requires it. Therefore, blessed Jerome says: "Let the speech of the virgin be modest and rare; nothing is more precious in eloquence than modesty."[114] The philosopher gives the same advice when he says: "To attain the highest perfection, I want you to speak briefly, rarely, and in a quiet voice."[115]

Listen, talkative friend; listen noisy and garrulous virgin! What you must certainly do in order to get used to keeping silence, is what Agathon the abbot did, as we read in *The Lives of the Fathers*, "he kept a stone in his mouth for three years until he learned to keep silence."[116] You too should tie a stone to your tongue, affix your tongue to your palate. *Put your finger over your mouth,*[117] so that you may learn to keep silence, because it is most unbecoming for a spouse of Jesus Christ that she should desire to speak with anyone but with her spouse.

5. Therefore, speak rarely, with few words, and briefly; speak timidly and shyly; moreover "speak rarely in your own defense."[118] Cover your face with the veil of modesty,

---

[114] *See Epistola* 1, n. 19 (PL 30: 34B): "Now let the speech of a virgin be prudent, modest, and rare; nothing is more precious in eloquence than modesty."

[115] This seems to be a summary of Seneca, *Epistle* XL, n. 14 in *Seneca Ad Lucilium Epistulae Morales,* translated by Richard M. Gummere (LCL; London: William Heinemann, 1934), 271: "But words, even if they came to you readily and flowed without any exertion on your part, yet would have to be kept under control. For just as a less ostentatious gait becomes a philosopher, so does a restrained style of speech, far removed from boldness. Therefore, the ultimate kernel of my remarks is this: I bid you be slow of speech."

[116] See *De Vitis Patrum*, V, libellus 4, n. 7 (PL 73: 865B).

[117] See Judges 18:19.

[118] See Sir 32:10. See also Clare of Assisi on silence in her "Form of Life," ch. V, in *The Lady: Clare of Assisi, Early Documents*, revised edition and translation by Regis Armstrong (New York: New City Press, 2006), 116-17. Hereafter CA:ED.

tie up your lips with the thread of discipline, and let your speech be brief, precious and useful, let it be modest and humble. Friend of God, speak rarely and little, because *Where words are many, sin is not wanting.*[119] Do not speak the idle word, because *On the day of judgment people will render an account for every careless word they have spoken.*[120] "The idle word," says the Gloss, "is the one uttered without necessity by the speaker and without usefulness to the listener."[121] Hence, it is always better and more useful to keep silence than to speak. As the wise man says: "I sometimes had regrets for having spoken, but never for having kept silence."[122]

CHAPTER V: ON PRAYER

1. It is most necessary for the spouse of Christ who wishes to make progress that she set herself assiduously to practice prayer and devotion. A religious, who is not devout and who is tepid, is not assiduous in frequent prayer. Consequently, she is not only miserable and useless, but in the eyes of God carries around a dead soul in a living body. Since the virtue of devotion has such efficacy that it alone is able to conquer the temptations and wiles of the evil enemy, who alone impedes the friend of God from rising to the heavens, it is not surprising then that one who is not assiduous in the practice of prayer often succumbs miserably to temptations. Thus blessed Isidore says: "This is the remedy for one who is burning with the

---

[119] See Prov 10:19.

[120] Bonaventure has smoothed out the Vulgate of Matt 12:36: "Because every careless word that people have spoken, they will render an account of it on the day of judgment."

[121] This is the Glossa Interlinearis apud Lyranum on Matt 12:36. See also PL 114: 128A: "The idle word is one that does not benefit rectitude and has no just cause."

[122] Attributed to Xenocrates by Valerius Maximus, *Dictorum factorumque memorabilium*, VII, ch. 2 ab externis n. 6.

temptations of vice: as often as he is but touched with any vice, so often should he set himself to pray, because frequent prayer repels the attacks of the vices."[123] And this is what the Lord says in the gospel: *Watch and pray that you may not enter into temptation.*[124]

Devout prayer has such power that a person can profit from it in all things and at all times: in winter and in summer, in tranquil and rainy times, night and day, on feast days and ordinary days, in sickness and in health, when young and old, standing, sitting and walking, in the choir and outside the choir. What is more, sometimes one hour of prayer is worth more than the whole world, because by a brief devout prayer a person gains the kingdom of heaven. However, in order that you may know how you ought to pray, to the extent that the Lord has endowed me, I will instruct you – although in this matter it is rather I who need instruction than you.

2. You should know, worthy friend of God, that to arrive at perfect prayer three things are necessary.[125] The first is that when you are prepared to pray, then standing erect with an upright heart and shutting down all your senses, you must noiselessly reflect from a heart bitter and contrite about all of your miseries, present, past and future.

You must first carefully reflect about the great and many sins you have committed all the days of your life; about the great and many good things you have failed to accomplish in the world and in the Order; about the great

---

[123] Isidore, *Liber* III *Sententiarum*, ch. 7, n. 1 (PL 83: 671B-672B).

[124] Bonaventure's citation is based on Matt 26:41, Mark 14:38, and Luke 22:40 and 46, but agrees verbatim with none of them.

[125] In *Threefold Way*, ch. II, n. 1, Bonaventure describes the three parts of prayer as: Deploring our Misery, Imploring God's Mercy, and Offering Worship. See also his discussion of prayer in the *Instruction for Novices*, ch. II; see *Writings Concerning the Franciscan Order*, (Monti, 151-56).

and many graces of your Creator you have frequently lost.[126]

You must also reflect how far you have strayed from God by sin, although you were once close to him; how different you have become from God although you were once like him; how once your soul was beautiful, but now is filthy and foul.[127]

You must reflect as to where you are headed by your sins, namely to the gates of hell; what will happen to you, that is, in the fearful day of judgment; what you will receive for all of this, namely, the fires of eternal death.

Because of all these things you ought immediately with the publican[128] beat your breast and with the prophet David *roar with anguish of heart*[129] and, as Mary Magdalen did to the Lord Jesus, *bathe his feet with [your] tears*.[130] Nor should there be any method to your tears[131] because there was no method [to your madness] when you offended your beloved Jesus. And this is what blessed Isidore says: "When we pray to God, we must groan and weep, remembering the serious [sins] we have committed and the painful torments of hell which we fear."[132] Your prayer must begin with these tearful meditations.

---

[126] See *Threefold Way*, ch. II, n. 2.

[127] Bonaventure's thoughts echo those of Pseudo-Bernard, *Meditationes piisimae,* ch. 1, n. 1 (PL 184: 485-508). Cf. Bonaventure, *Soliloquium*, ch. I, n. 2.

[128] See Luke 18:13.

[129] See Ps 37:9: "I am afflicted and exceedingly humbled. I roared with the groaning of my heart."

[130] See Luke 7:38. Bonaventure erroneously gives the name of Mary Magdalen to the unnamed sinful women of Luke 7:36-50.

[131] The Latin reads *nec debes aliquem modum habere in lacrimis,* where Bonaventure seems to be saying that weeping ought not to be feigned or confected.

[132] See Isidore, *Liber* III *Sententiarum* ch. 7, n. 5 (PL 83: 673A): "And therefore, when we stand before God, we must groan and weep, remembering how serious are the sins we have committed and how horrible the torments of hell which we fear." See also Bonaventure, *The Threefold Way*, ch. II, n. 2; *Itinerarium*, prologue, n. 3 (Hayes, 39).

3. The second thing necessary for the spouse of God in praying is that she be grateful, namely that in all humility she be thankful to her Creator for all the benefits already received and those yet to be received.[133] This is what the apostle Paul enjoined: *Persevere in prayer, being watchful in it with thanksgiving.*[134] Nothing makes a person more worthy of divine gifts than that she always give thanks to God for the gifts received. Thus, blessed Augustine writing to Aurelius says: "What can be better than that we bear in mind, proclaim with our lips and express with our pen our thanks to God? This cannot be said more briefly, heard more joyfully, understood more grandly, or done more fruitfully."[135]

Therefore, when praying you ought to reflect with thanksgiving that God made you a human being, made you a Christian, and was indulgent regarding your innumerable sins. Because you would have committed many sins, if God had not watched over you;[136] [He did watch over you] because he did not allow you to die in the world, because he chose you to enter the highest and most perfect [state of] religious life, because he supported and nourished you; because he became [a human being] for you, was circumcised, and baptized; because for you he became poor and naked, humble and despised; because for you he fasted, hungered, thirsted, labored, and became tired; because for you he wept and sweated blood; he fed you his most holy body and gave you his most precious blood to drink; because for your sake he was beaten, spit on, derided, and scourged; because for you he was crucified, wounded, suffered a most loathsome

---

[133] On the importance of gratitude, see *Threefold Way*, ch. III, n. 9.

[134] Col 4:2.

[135] *Epistola* 41, n. 1 (PL 33: 158).

[136] Cf. Bernard, *Sermo* 2, *Dominica VI post Pentecosten*, n. 3 (SBOp 4:321-22); "Second Sermon for the Sixth Sunday after Pentecost," (SB-Sermons, II, 332) for some parallels to the thoughts expressed here.

and bitter death, and so redeemed you; because [for you] he was buried, rose and ascended to heaven and sent the Holy Spirit; and finally because he promised you and all the elect the kingdom of heaven.

Such thanksgiving in prayer is useful beyond measure and without it prayer is of no value, because "ingratitude," says blessed Bernard, "is a scorching wind, drying up ... the font of piety, the dew of mercy, and the flow of grace."[137]

4. The third thing necessary for perfect prayer is that there be nothing else in your mind except what you are praying for. It is most indecent that someone should pray to God with her mouth while thinking of something else, where half the heart is in heaven and half on earth. Such a prayer will never be heard by God. Hence on the text of the Psalm, *I cried with all my heart. Answer me, O Lord*,[138] the Gloss says: "A divided heart does not get [what it seeks]."[139] At the time of prayer the friend of God must turn her heart away from all external worries, all worldly desires, and the love of all carnal things in order to get [her mind] back to interior things and focus on them with all her heart and mind, and thus return to the One toward whom her prayer is directed.[140] This is what your spouse Jesus advises when he says in the gospel: *But when you pray, go into your room, and having closed the door, pray to your Father in secret.*[141] You have 'entered the room,' when you have collected all your thoughts, desires, and

---

[137] See Bernard, *Sermo* 51 in *Cantica*, n. 6 (SBOp 2: 87); Sermon 51, n. 6; *On the Song of Songs* (Walsh III, 45). Bonaventure's citation is almost verbatim.

[138] Ps 118:145.

[139] This is the *Glossa Interlinearis apud Lyranum*.

[140] On the necessity of having an "unburdened heart" see *On Governing the Soul*, n. 3.

[141] See Matt 6:6. The Vulgate reads *orabis* ("you pray") whilst Bonaventure has *oraveris* ("you pray"). The Vulgate reads *ostio tuo* ("your door") while Bonaventure has *ostio* ("door").

affections into the secret [chamber] of your heart; you have 'closed the door,' when you guard your heart diligently, so that you will not be hampered in your devotion by a flood of imagery. For "prayer," says Augustine, "is a turning of the mind to God in pious and humble affection."[142]

5.   Listen, most blessed Mother. Listen, friend of Jesus Christ. "And incline your ear to the words of my mouth."[143] Do not be mislead or deceived: you will not lose the bountiful fruit of your prayer, you will not be deprived of the pleasure or cheated of the sweetness which you should draw from prayer. Prayer is a deep well and the font of the boundless sweetness of the most blessed Trinity from which the grace of the Holy Spirit is drawn up. The most devout prophet David experienced this when he said: *I have opened my mouth and drew breath.*[144] The Gloss interprets "I have opened my mouth" to mean "by praying, seeking, knocking." The Gloss interprets "and drew breath" to mean "I have drawn [from the deep]."[145] Did I not tell you what prayer is? Listen again: "Prayer is the turning of the mind to God." Do you want to know how you should turn your mind to God? Pay attention. When you are in the midst of praying, you must recollect yourself totally, enter into the cubicle of your heart, and

---

[142] The reference is actually to Alcher of Clairvaux, *Liber de spiritu et anima,* ch. 50 (PL 40: 816): "Prayer is the devotion of the mind, that is, a turning to God in pious and humble affection."

[143] Bonaventure has combined two psalms: Ps 44:11: "Hear, daughter, and see, and incline your ear" and Ps 77:1: "Incline your ears to the words of my mouth."

[144] Ps 118:131.

[145] This is the Glossa Ordinaria (from Augustine); see Exposition 27, n. 4, of Psalm 118 in *Expositions of the Psalms* 99-120, translation and notes by Maria Boulding, in WSA III/19 (New York: New City Press, 2003), 473: "He opened his mouth to ask, seek, and knock; he thirsted, and he drank in the good Spirit, through whom he would be able to do what he could not do unaided: observe the command that was holy, and just, and good."

dwell alone with your spouse; and, forgetful of all external affairs, you must raise yourself with total devotion above yourself[146] with all your heart, all your mind, all your affections and desires. Nor ought you to let your mind 'relax' from praying, but it should continually ascend on high ignited by the fire of devotion until you enter "into the place of the wonderful tabernacle, even to the house of God,"[147] and there, whenever you gaze upon your beloved with the eye of your heart, whenever you *taste and see how sweet the Lord is*,[148] and realize *how great and abundant the Lord's sweetness is*,[149] you may fall into his arms and kiss him with the lips of intimate devotion. And so totally alienated from yourself, totally raised up to heaven, totally transformed into Christ, you will be unable to restrain your spirit, but will exclaim with the prophet David and say: *My soul refused to be consoled. When I remembered God, I was delighted.*[150]

6. If your heart, beloved Mother, by way of devout prayer is to be raised higher toward God and become more fervent, you should note carefully that there are three ways whereby we may experience mystical ecstasy:[151]

---

[146] See Lam 3:28: "He will sit solitary and keep quiet, because he has raised himself above himself."

[147] Ps 41:5

[148] See Ps 33:9.

[149] See Ps 30:20: "How great and abundant is your sweetness, O Lord."

[150] Ps 76:3-4.

[151] The text of Bonaventure reads *in mentis alienationem deducimur* which he borrowed from Richard of St. Victor, *Benjamin Major*, V, ch. 5 (PL 196: 174A): "Now it seems to me that there are three ways whereby we may experience mystical ecstasy." See also "The Mystical Ark" (Zinn, 316). It likely refers to the apostle Paul's being raised up to the third heaven where he did not know whether he was in or out of the body (2 Cor 12:2-5). The phrase is translated here as "mystical ecstasy"; in some instances it might refer to rapture. In *Itinerarium* (ch. IV, n. 3) Bonaventure writes, in a similar way, about the

sometimes on account of great devotion, sometimes
because of great admiration, sometimes because of great
exultation.

7. Sometimes, I say, because of great devotion as "when
the mind is beside itself, raised above itself, and is
transformed ... when we are so inflamed with the fire of
heavenly desires that everything external becomes bitter
and boring, when the flame of intimate love transcends
human powers which like melted wax renders the soul of
itself helpless and then lifts it on high and sends it forth
to the heights like aromatic smoke."[152] Then we are forced
to exclaim with the prophet and say: *Though my flesh
and my heart waste away, you are the God of my heart
and the God that is my portion forever.*[153]

8. Sometimes this occurs because of great admiration,
"when the mind is illumined with divine light and
suspended in admiration of the highest beauty, when it
is stricken with a powerful stupor, as it were, and totally
torn away from its [worldly] state – much like a flash of
lightning[154] – the more deeply it penetrates its gaze into
the beauty it beholds, the more quickly and sublimely it
is raised above itself by the ardor of its loftiest desires."[155]
Then it is forced to exclaim with the most holy Esther: *I

---

soul being prepared for spiritual ecstasy [*excessus mentis*]; see Hayes,
101. See also *Soliloquium*, ch. II, § III, nn. 15-17.

[152] See Richard of St. Victor, *Benjamin Major,* V, n. 5 (PL 196:
174AB; "The Mystical Ark" (Zinn, 316). Bonaventure's citation is not
verbatim.

[153] Ps 72:26.

[154] See Ez 1:14: "And the living creatures ran and returned like
flashes of lightning."

[155] See Richard of St. Victor, *Benjamin Major,* V, n. 5 (PL 196: 174B;
"The Mystical Ark" (Zinn, 316). Bonaventure's quotation is almost verbatim. Philotheus Boehner notes the important function of *admiratio*
in Bonaventure's theology of the spiritual life. See *Itinerarium* (Hayes,
note 13, pages 151-52).

saw you, O Lord, as an angel of God, and my heart was troubled for fear of your majesty. For you, O Lord, are very admirable and your face is full of graces.[156]

9. Sometimes rapture occurs because of great exultation, when "having drunk from the abundance of internal sweetness, even completely inebriated thereby, the mind is oblivious as to what is going on or what has happened ... and is transformed into a certain super-worldly affection and enraptured by a certain wonderful happiness."[157] Then the mind is constrained to exclaim and say with the prophet: *How lovely are your tabernacles, O Lord of hosts! My soul yearns and faints for the courts of the Lord. My heart and my flesh have rejoiced in the living God.*[158]

10. In this way, then, a friend of God ought to exercise her soul in pursuit of devout prayer and thus learn through the frequent use of prayer, through the eye of a clean and purified heart, through a tireless spirit of devotion, how to become worthy to contemplate what is divine and savor with pleasure divine sweetness. For it is unbecoming for a soul stamped with the image of God, adorned with the likeness of God, redeemed by the blood of God, and capable of heavenly bliss to gravitate toward temporal things.[159] She ought rather to "mount a cherub and fly, borne on the wings of the wind,"[160] that is, up to the orders of angels and there to contemplate the Trinity and the humanity

---

[156] Esther 15:16-17.

[157] See Richard of St. Victor, *Benjamin Major,* V, n. 5 (PL 196: 174BC; "The Mystical Ark" (Zinn, 317). Bonaventure's citation is not verbatim.

[158] See Ps 83:2-3. The Vulgate reads *exultavit* (have rejoiced") whereas Bonaventure has *exultaverunt* ("have rejoiced").

[159] Bonaventure adapts the language of Pseudo-Bernard, *Meditationes piissimae*, ch. 3, n. 7 (PL 184: 489C).

[160] See Ps 17:11: "And he mounted upon the cherubim, and he flew. He flew upon the wings of the wind."

of Christ while meditating on the glory and joy of the supernal citizens, angels, and all the saints.

But who are those today, who use their time to meditate, who explore the celestial joys, who body and soul are preoccupied with heavenly things?[161] Rare are they! As a result we can fittingly say of certain religious what blessed Bernard says:

> Their concerted efforts should be to penetrate the heavens with their devotion, to stroll about in spirit in the celestial mansions, to toast in admiration the triumphant ... apostles and the choirs of prophets and martyrs ... if they fail to do these things, they are foul and enslave themselves to the servitude of the body, to the obedience of the flesh, in order to satisfy their gluttony and their bellies....[162]

Chapter VI: On Remembering Christ's Passion[163]

1. Since the fervor of devotion is nourished and preserved in a person by the frequent remembering of Christ's passion, hence it is necessary that frequently, or rather that always she should want the eyes of her heart to be fixed with unending devotion on Christ dying on the cross. The Lord says in Leviticus 6:12: *The fire on my*[164] *altar shall always burn, and the priest shall feed it,*

---

[161] See Phil 3:20: "But our preoccupation is with heavenly things."

[162] This is an abbreviation of Bernard, *Sermo* 35 in *Cantica*, n. 3 (SBOp 1:250); Sermon 35, n. 3, *On the Song of Songs* (Walsh, II, 167).

[163] Ignatius Brady notes that much of this chapter is based on earlier work in, for example, the *Breviloquium*, pt. V, ch. 9. See Brady's article entitled "Two Sermons of St. Bonaventure," *Franciscan Studies* 28 (1968): 25.

[164] QuarEd indicate rightly (p. 120, n. 7) that the Vulgate does not read *meo* ("my").

putting wood on it every day. Listen, most devoted Mother, the 'altar of God' is your heart; on this altar the 'fire' of fervent devotion must never go out, because you must feed it every day with the wood of the cross of Christ and the remembrance of his passion. This is what the prophet Isaiah is talking about: *With joy you will draw water from the fountains of* the Savior,[165] as if to say: whoever desires from God the waters of grace, the waters of devotion, the waters of weeping, let her draw them from the fountains of the Savior, that is from the five wounds of Jesus Christ.

2. Approach, O friend, with the feet of your affections to your wounded Jesus, to Jesus crowned with thorns, to Jesus affixed to the tree of the cross, and with blessed Thomas the apostle not only gaze at the wounds in his hands made by the nails, not only put your finger into the holes made by the nails, not only put your hand into the wound in his side,[166] but totally through the opening in his side enter the very heart of Jesus where, transformed into Christ by your most ardent love for the crucified, pierced with the nail of the fear of God, transfixed by the lance of cordial love, thrust through by the sword of intimate compassion, you may seek nothing else, desire nothing else, or be consoled by nothing else except that you may die on the cross with Christ. Then you will be able to exclaim with the apostle Paul and say: *I have been nailed to the cross with Christ. It is*[167] *now no longer I who lives, but Christ lives in me.*[168]

---

[165] See Isa 12:3.

[166] John 20:25 and 27.

[167] The Vulgate reads *Vivo autem iam* ("But it is now") whereas Bonaventure does not have *autem* ("But").

[168] See Gal 2:19-20. Bonaventure describes Francis as a person who experienced both this kind of desire and personal transformation. See *The Major Legend of St. Francis*, ch. 9, n. 2 and ch. 13, n. 3, FA:ED II, 597, 632. In *Itinerarium*, prologue, n. 3 (Hayes, 37), Bonaventure describes how "the burning love of the Crucified" had totally "absorbed the soul of Francis." A similar invitation to enter into and share the

3. This is how you must remember the passion of Christ, namely in order that you may understand how his passion was most ignominious, most bitter, pervasive, and lengthy.

First consider, worthy friend of God, how the death of Jesus Christ your spouse was most ignominious. He was crucified as a thief and robber. No one under the Old Law was punished by such a death unless he were the worst of criminals, thieves, and robbers.[169]

Think about Christ's great ignominy. He was crucified in the worst and vilest of places, namely on mount Calvary,[170] among the bones and skeletons of the dead. This place was reputed to be for the death of the condemned, where the worst of men were beheaded and hanged.

Even greater was the ignominy of Christ, because he was hanging between thieves as if he were the prince of robbers. Hence Isaiah said: *He was counted among the wicked.*[171]

Gaze still more at the greater ignominy of your spouse, because he was hung in mid-air as if unworthy to live or die on earth. What shame and insult! The Lord of the earth is denied the earth, while no one is considered more vile in the world than the Lord of the world. And so the death of the Son of God was most ignominious because of the sort of death he suffered while hanging on a cross; because of his companions in death since *he was counted*

---

sufferings of Christ can be found in Bonaventure's *The Tree of Life,* The Seventh Fruit, nn. 25-26; Cousins, *Bonaventure,* 147-49).

[169] Cf. Deut 21:22-23.

[170] See Matt 27:33, Mark 15:22, Luke 23:33, John 19:17. Cf. *Commentarius in Evangelium S. Ioannis* 19:17, n. 29 (VI: 495); *Commentary of the Gospel of Luke* Part III, Luke 23:33, n. 39 (Karris, III, pp. 2147-50, esp. pp. 2148-49): "So it is called *the place of the Skull* (Calvary) because it contained the skulls of the condemned whose heads were cut off there and hung on a pole."

[171] Isa 53:12.

among the evildoers[172] and condemned; because of the place of his death, because he was crucified on mount Calvary, the foulest of places.

4. O good Jesus, O loving Savior, not once but many times you were put to shame! The more [times and] places one is put to shame, the more ignominious he becomes to the world. Behold, you Lord Jesus, were tied up in the garden, buffeted in the house of Annas, spit upon in the atrium of Caiphas, mocked in the court of Herod, made to carry your cross along the way, and crucified on Golgotha. Woe is me! Woe is me! Behold, the freedom of captives is captured; the glory of the angels is mocked; the life of human beings is killed! O miserable Jews, you have accomplished what you promised! For you said: *Let us condemn him*[173] *to a most shameful death.*[174] This is why the blessed Bernard said: *"He emptied himself, taking the form of a slave.*[175] He was a son and became a slave. Not only did he accept the role of a slave in order to be subservient, but became a bad slave to be beaten ... and thus remit the punishment, since he had no sin."*[176] Not only was he the "servant of the servants of God" – as the Pope is called[177] – but he even became the servant of the servants of the devil, by serving in order to expurgate the foulest sins of sinners. Nor was even this enough for him, but he chose the most shameful of deaths, so that you would not be afraid to suffer in like

---

[172] See Luke 22:37 where the Vulgate reads *iniustis* ("unjust") while Bonaventure has *iniquis* ("evildoers").

[173] The Vulgate reads *illum* ("him") whereas Bonaventure has *eum* ("him").

[174] Wis 2:20.

[175] See Phil 2:7.

[176] See *Sermo in feria IV Hebdomadae sanctae*, n. 10 (SBOp 5: 63). Bonaventure's citation is not verbatim.

[177] Cf. John Diacono, *S Gregorii Magni Vita*, II, n. 1 (PL 75: 87A): "He was the first one to define himself at the beginning of his letters in a very humble way as 'the servant of the servants of God, thus leaving for all his successors a testimony of his humility....'"

fashion. *He humbled himself, becoming obedient to death, even death on a cross,* "which is more ignominious" as the Gloss says.[178]

5. Secondly, consider and realize, O virgin devoted to God, how the passion of Christ was most bitter. The cross did not allow those blessed limbs stretched to their limits in the torture of death to be folded – considered to provide solace and comfort for anxious hearts – nor did that most revered head find a place to rest at the time of death.

Look even more closely at how bitter was the death of Christ. The more delicate suffer more. Never was there a body so delicate for sustaining sufferings than was the body of the Savior. The body of women is more delicate than that of men. The flesh of Christ was completely virginal because he was conceived of the Holy Spirit and born of the Virgin. Consequently, the passion of Christ was the bitterest of all, because he was more delicate than all virgins.[179] If then the mere thought of his death made his *soul sorrowful,*[180] because of the tenderness of his flesh, such that the sweat of his body *became like drops of blood falling on the ground;*[181] how much more sorrow and pain was inflicted on him in the suffering of his bitter passion. And so the blessed Bernard says: "O Lord Jesus Christ, the bloody sweat that flowed ... onto the ground from your most holy flesh while you prayed was a most certain witness to the terrors of your heart."[182] "What have you done, sweetest boy, that you should be treated so? What [evil] have you committed, beloved youth, that you should be so judged? ... Behold it is I who am the cause of your

---

[178] This is the *Glossa Interlinearis apud Lyranum* on Phil 2:8.

[179] Cf. Bonaventure, III *Sent.*, d. 16. a. 1. q. 2 (III: 349).

[180] See Matt 26:38: "My soul is sorrowful, even unto death."

[181] See Luke 22:44.

[182] See Pseudo-Bernard, *Sermo de vita et passione Domini,* n. 6 (PL 184: 958B). Bonaventure's citation is not verbatim.

suffering. It is I who am the blow behind your murder."[183] Look even more carefully how bitter was Christ's death. The more innocent a person, the more difficult it is to tolerate punishment. If Christ had sustained such pain because of his own sins, his death might have been more tolerable. But *he committed no sin, but no deceit was found in his mouth.*[184] Even Pilate testified to this when he said: *I find no crime deserving of death in him.*[185] For he is *the refulgence of eternal light, the spotless mirror of the power of God, the image of his goodness,* as Wisdom 7:26 says.

6.   Reflect more fully about how painful was the death of your beloved spouse Jesus Christ. The more pervasive the pain, the more bitter. Christ, your spouse, suffered in every part of his body, such that not the smallest part of his body was without its special pain; there was not the smallest place which was not filled with bitterness. *For from the sole of the foot to the top of the head, there was no sound spot.*[186] Because of the overpowering and excruciating pain he cried out saying: *Come, all you who pass by the way, look and see whether there is any suffering like my suffering.*[187] Truly, Lord Jesus Christ, never was there pain comparable to your pain. So massive was your bleeding that it covered your entire body.

O good Jesus, O sweetest Lord, since not drops but great waves of blood flowed from five parts of your body:

---

[183] See Anselm, *Oratio* 2 (PL 158: 861AB). Bonaventure's citation is not verbatim.

[184] See 1 Peter 2:22. The Vulgate reads *in ore ipsius* ("in his mouth") whilst Bonaventure has *in ore eius* ("in his mouth"). See also Clare of Assisi, "The Third Letter to Blessed Agnes of Prague," n. 12, *CA:ED*, 51 and the "Fourth Letter to Blessed Agnes of Prague," n. 14, *CA:ED*, 55.

[185] Luke 23:22.

[186] See Isa 1:6.

[187] Lam 1:12. See also Clare of Assisi's use of this passage in her description of an approach to contemplative prayer in "The Fourth Letter to Agnes of Prague," nn. 24-27, *CA:ED*, 56-57.

from your hands and feet during the crucifixion, from your head crowned with thorns, from your entire body during the flagellation, and from your heart opened by the lance. It is surprising that there was any blood left in you at all. Tell me, I pray, my beloved Lord, tell me, since one drop of your most sacred blood would have sufficed to redeem the whole world, why did you suffer so much blood to flow from your body? I know, Lord, I really know: you did this for no other reason than to show me how much you love me.

7. So *what will I render to the Lord for all the things he has* rendered *to me?*[188] "Surely,[189] Lord, as long as I live, I will remember the labors you sustained in preaching, the weariness in traveling about, the vigils in prayer, the tears of compassion ... the pain, the abuse, the spitting, the blows, the mockery, the nails and the wounds...." Otherwise "you will require from me *the blood of the just one that has been shed upon the earth.*"[190] *Who, then, will give water to my head and a fountain of tears to my eyes,*[191] that I might weep day and night over the death of my Lord Jesus who suffered death, not for his sins, but for mine. *He was wounded for our iniquities, crushed for our sins*" as the prophet Isaiah says.[192]

8. Finally, reflect and attend carefully, because the death and passion of Christ were pervasive. From the first day of his birth to the last day of his death he was always in

---

[188] Ps 115:12.

[189] Bonaventure includes here a long citation from Bernard's *Sermo in feria IV Hebdomadae sanctae*, n. 11 (SBOp 5: 64). It is an abbreviation and rearrangement of Bernard's words.

[190] Bernard has adapted Matt 23:35: "That upon you may come all the just blood that has been shed on the earth."

[191] Jer 9:1. Bonaventure does not follow Bernard's sequence of thought in citing Jer 9:1 here.

[192] Isa 53:5. While Bernard quotes Isa 53:3, he does not cite Isa 53:5.

pain and suffering, as he testified through the prophet who said: *I am poor and in labors from my youth*;[193] and elsewhere: *I have been scourged all day long*,[194] that is, during my entire life.

Also consider how morose was Christ's passion. He was hanged in such fashion that the pain would endure longer, so that his suffering would not end quickly, so that death would come more slowly and he would be tortured longer and suffer more pain.

9. From all of what I have told you, O virgin of Christ, O friend of God, you can glean how shameful, how painful, how extensive, and how morose was the death and passion of your beloved spouse Jesus Christ. What is more, he bore all of this in order to set aflame his love in you, so that for all these things you might love him with all your heart, all your soul, and all your mind.[195] What could be more benevolent than that the Lord should take on the form of a servant to assure the salvation of a servant?[196] What could more apprise someone of his salvation, than the example of undergoing death for the sake of justice and divine obedience? What could incite a person more to love God than such benign condescension[197] whereby the Son of the most high God *should lay down his life*[198] for us who have merited nothing; in fact, we have much

---

[193] Ps 87:16.

[194] Ps 72:14.

[195] See Matt 22:37: "Jesus said to him: You shall love the Lord your God with your whole heart, and with your whole soul and with your whole mind."

[196] See Phil 2:7.

[197] The Latin *benignitas* means a generous, gift-giving goodness to one who is undeserving. It is translated here as "benign condescension" to emphasize God's generosity in stepping down (*condescendere*) in relation to humanity's need.

[198] See John 10:15: "I lay down my life for my sheep."

for which we ought to be punished.[199] Such was his loving condescension that nothing can be thought more kind, more benign, or more amicable. Such condescension is seen to be even greater to the extent that he chose to sustain such great pain and abjection. For "God ... who *did not spare his own Son but handed him over for us all, how has he not given us everything else along with him?*"[200] And so we are invited to love him and imitate our beloved.

10. Woe to those who are ungrateful after having received the benefits of such kindness, in whose souls the death of Christ has had no effect. "Look at the head of Christ," says Bernard, "bowed to kiss you, the arms open to embrace you, the pierced hands full of gifts for you, the open side to love you, his entire body open to cover you."[201] Also, woe to those who by their sins *are re-crucifying Christ*[202] *for themselves.*[203] *They add pain to the pains of his wounds.*[204] Thirdly, woe to those who cannot soften their hearts to grieve, who cannot arouse themselves to kindness, for whom such a loss of blood, such an enormously priceless gift cannot inflame them to the virtue of good works. Certainly, such are *enemies of the cross of Christ.*[205] What is more, they blaspheme Christ the Son of God now seated

---

[199] This phrase is a preferred rendering of *immo cum multis nostris demeritis*.

[200] See Rom 8:32. The Vulgate reads *donabit* ("will give") while Bonaventure has *donavit* ("has given").

[201] See Pseudo-Augustine, *Sermo 32, Sermones ad fratres in eremo commorantes, et quosdam alios* (PL 40: 1293): "What other things could we want to see but his head inclined to summon us and forgive us, his heart open to love us, his arms extended to embrace us, his entire body exposed to redeem us?"

[202] The Vulgate reads *Filium Dei* ("Son of God"), Bonaventure has *Christum* ("Christ").

[203] See Hebr 6:6.

[204] Bonaventure adapts Ps 69:27: "They have added to the pain of my wounds."

[205] See Phil 3:18.

at the right hand of the Father in heaven, more than the Jews of old did when he was hanging from the cross. To such persons and concerning them, Christ complains, speaking through the blessed Bernard who says: "Look, man, at what I have endured for you. See the pain that torments me. I cry out to you for whom I died: look at the sufferings I endure; look at the nails that pierce me. And if my external pains be so great, my internal grief is greater still as long as I know you are ungrateful."[206]

11. Beware, Mother, lest you be ungrateful regarding such a gift, beware lest you experience no devotion regarding such a priceless treasure. What you should do is to put Jesus Christ crucified *as a seal on your heart*[207] and, just as a seal in soft wax, so you should imprint your spouse Jesus in your heart and say with the prophet: *My heart has become like wax melting away.*[208] "Put him *as a seal on your heart*"[209] so that "you may never desist from doing good and never grow tired of working in the name of the Lord Jesus."[210] Then when you have done all good things, begin anew as if you had done nothing. If at times something sad happens, something bad, something tedious, something bitter, and certainly if sometimes a good thing happens by chance,[211] then you should immediately look

---

[206] In Book III, d. 16 a. 2. q. 3 of his *Sentence Commentary* Bonaventure attributes this "hymn" to Philip the Chancellor (d. 1237). See Opera Omnia 3:359 n. 6 and 8:123 n. 6 for reasons why Bonaventure attributed these verses to Bernard.

[207] See Cant 8:6: "Put me as a seal on your heart, as a seal upon your arm, for love is strong as death...." See Bonaventure, "Sermon on St. Francis, 1266 Part II," FA:ED II, 734-35 on the text from Haggai 2:23: "I take you ... and make you like a seal, for I have chosen you." He describes here the way in which Francis "became like a seal."

[208] See Ps 21:15.

[209] See Cant 8:6.

[210] See Gal 6:9: "And in doing good, let us not grow tired."

[211] The Latin text reads *aliquod bonum desipuerit*; literally "something good be accomplished foolishly."

to the crucified Jesus hanging on the cross. Look there at
the crown of thorns, the iron nails, the lance in the side;
gaze at the wounds in his feet and hands, the wounds
to his head, his side and his whole body, and recall that
this is what he suffered for you, what he bore for you, so
that you may know how much he loved you. Believe me:
after gazing in such a way [at the crucifix], you will find
that everything sad becomes joyful, everything heavy
light, everything boring lovable, everything harsh sweet
and soothing. Then can you begin to cry out with blessed
Job and say: *What my soul previously refused to touch, is
now my food because of the dire need*,[212] of the passion of
Christ. As if you were to say: the good things which my
soul formerly found tasteless, have now become – because
of the distress of the passion of Christ at which I gaze
– for me sweet and delectable.

We read about a certain person who, having entered
religious life, had become dissatisfied with the coarse food
and the other hardships of religious life. Thus overcome
with great dissatisfaction, he threw himself at the feet
of the crucifix and began to recount with many tears
the intolerable harshness and labors of the Order, the
insipidness of the bread and drink. Immediately from the
side of the crucifix came a flow of blood, and when he –
weeping profusely – repeated the account of his miseries,
the image of Christ answered and said: Whenever you
experience harshness in food or drink, dip it into the
[savory] seasoning of the blood of Christ.[213]

---

[212] See Job 6:7. The Vulgate reads *nolebat tangere* ("refused to
touch") while Bonaventure has *noluit tangere* ("refused to touch"). Cf.
Gregory, *Moralia in Iob*, VII, ch. XV, n. 18 (*Morals*, I, 376).

[213] See *Chronica XXIV Generalium Ordinis Minorum,* ed. Bernard
a Bessa in *Analecta Franciscana* III (1897): 306-307. Bonaventure's
abbreviated version of this story accentuates food.

Chapter VII: On the Perfect Love of God[214]

1. Previously, as the Lord has inspired me, I taught you, O friend of God, how you need to cultivate your mind so that gradually you can ascend and progress *from virtue to virtue.*[215] Now, in the seventh place, something remains to be said about the form of the virtues, namely charity, which alone leads a person to perfection. Nothing can be said to be better, nothing can be thought to be more useful in ridding oneself of vices, in progressing in grace, or in achieving the highest perfection of all the virtues than charity. Hence, Prosper says in the book *On the Contemplative Life*: "Charity is the life of the virtues and the death of the vices;"[216] and just as wax melts before the flame, so vices perish in the face of charity. Charity is so powerful that it alone closes the gates of hell, it alone opens the heavens, it alone gives hope for salvation, it alone makes one a friend of God. Charity is so powerful that it alone among the virtues deserves the name "virtue";[217] whoever has it is rich, affluent, and happy; whoever lacks it is poor, a beggar and miserable.[218] Consequently, commenting on the phrase from Corinthians: *If I do not have love,*[219] the Gloss says: "Pay heed as to how great is charity: if it is absent, everything else is useless; if it is

---

[214] For more on the sources of Bonaventure's thought on the nature of love see *Threefold Way*, ch. II, nn. 9-11, ch. III, nn. 6-7; and *Soliloquium*, ch. I, § IV, nn. 42-46; On the seven steps leading to the sweetness of charity see *Threefold Way*, ch. II, nn. 9-11.

[215] See Ps 83:8.

[216] The quotation is from Julius Pomerius, *De Vita Contemplativa*, III, ch. 13, n. 1 (PL 59: 493B); *The Contemplative Life*, book III, ch. 13: "Love is ... the death of sins, the life of virtues" (Suelzer, 131). Cf. Bonaventure, III *Sent.*, d. 36. q. 6 (III: 805-807).

[217] Literally, the Latin has *"sola inter virtutes 'virtus' nominata est"* ("it alone among the virtues is called virtue").

[218] See Rev 3:17: "Because you say: 'I am rich and have grown wealthy and have need of nothing,' and do not know that you are wretched and miserable and poor and blind and naked."

[219] 1 Cor 13:1.

present, one has everything; whoever begins to acquire it will have the Holy Spirit."[220] And blessed Augustine says: "If virtue guides us to the blessed life, yet I take nothing whatever to be virtuous except the highest love of God."[221] Therefore, since charity is such a [powerful] virtue, it must be pursued more than all the other virtues, and not just any charity but that whereby we love God above all things and our neighbor for the sake of God.

2. In the Gospel your spouse teaches you how you must love your Creator when he says: *You shall love the Lord, your God, with all your heart, with all your soul, and with all your mind.*[222] Listen carefully, most beloved friend of Jesus Christ, how much love your beloved requires of you. Your most loved one requires that you give your whole heart, your whole soul, and your whole mind to his love, such that in all of your heart, in all of your soul, in all of your mind, there is not the smallest part in you which does not share his love. What ought you to do so as to be sure to love the Lord your God with your whole heart? What does *with your whole heart* mean? Listen to what blessed Chrysostom has to say: "To love God with your whole heart means that your heart is not inclined to love anything else but God, that you find no delight in worldly things other than God, not in honors ... nor in parents.... If the love of your heart is taken up with any of these things, then you do not love God with all your heart."[223] I entreat you, handmaid of Christ, do not be deceived concerning

---

[220] The *Glossa Ordinaria apud Strabum and Lyranum* provide only the first part of this citation which stems from Peter Lombard and ultimately from Augustine, *Tractate* 9, n. 8, on John's Gospel; see CCSL xxxvi, 95.

[221] See *De moribus Ecclesiae catholicae*, I, ch. 15, n. 25 (PL 32: 1322). Bonaventure's citation is verbatim. See also *Breviloquium*, pt. V, ch. 8, nn. 1-5 (Monti, 200-03).

[222] The closest Gospel parallel is Matt 22:37.

[223] See *Homilia* 42, on Matt 22:37, *Opus Imperfectum* (PG 56: 873). Bonaventure's citation is not verbatim.

love. It is a certainty that if you love something, but not in God or because of God, then you do not love God with all your heart. Thus Augustine says to the Lord: "for anyone who loves something else along with you, but does not love it for your sake, loves you less."[224] Or again, if you love something and because of this love you do not progress in the love of God, then you do not love God with all your heart. Or if you love something and neglect something which you ought to hold dear for the love of Christ, then you do not love with all your heart. Therefore, love the Lord your God with all your heart.

3. Our Lord Jesus Christ must be loved, not only with all one's heart but also with all one's soul. What does it mean *with all your soul*? Listen to blessed Augustine: "To love God with all your soul," he says, "means to love God with all your will without alternatives."[225] You assuredly love with all your soul, when it is not what you want, or what the world advises, or what the [desires of the] flesh suggest, but when you gladly do without contradiction what you know the Lord God wants you to will to do. Surely you then love God with all your soul when, for the love of Jesus Christ, you gladly put your life at stake if that should be necessary.[226] If in any of these ways you have been negligent, then you do not love with all your

---

[224] See *Confessionum*, X, ch. 29, n. 40, or *The Confessions*, book X, ch. 29, n. 40 (Boulding, 223).

[225] QuarEd imply that these and similar words do not occur in Augustine. See Opera Omnia (I: 81, n. 8; III: 613, n. 7; VIII: 125, n. 1). The closest parallel is *Sermo* V *in communi de uno martyre* (PL 217: 616D-617A): "'With the mind,' that is, they love the Father through their memory, 'whole,'" that is, without forgetting. 'With the heart,' that is, they love the Son through their intellect, 'whole,' that is, without error. 'With the soul,' that is, they love the Spirit with their will, 'whole,' that is, without alternatives."

[226] Bonaventure's understanding of the perfect love of God provides the context for understanding his treatment of "the desire for martyrdom" as the greatest act of love and a distinct step in the fol-

soul. Therefore, love the Lord your God with all your soul, that is, conform your will to the divine will in all things.

4. You should love your spouse the Lord Jesus not only with all your heart and all your soul, but also with all your mind. How *with all your mind*? Again, listen to blessed Augustine teaching you: "To love God with all your mind," he says, "is to love him with your entire memory and without forgetting."[227]

Chapter VIII: On Final Perseverance

1. After you have undertaken the pursuit of all virtues, still you are not radiant in the sight of God unless there be perseverance, the consummation of all virtues. No mortal man, no matter how perfect, is worthy of praise in his life, unless he brings to a good and happy end the good he had begun. Perseverance is the end and "consummation of all virtues, the nurse of merit and the mediator of reward."[228] Hence the blessed Bernard says: "Take away perseverance, and no amount of obedience or beneficence will guarantee grace, nor will courage warrant praise."[229] It will count for little if a person has been a religious, patient and humble, devout and celibate, to have loved God and acquired all the virtues unless she perseveres. For even though all the virtues run the race, only perseverance *gets the prize*,[230] because it is not [the one] who begins, but *the one who*

---

lowing of Christ. See, for example, *The Threefold Way*, ch. III, n. 8, and *The Major Legend*, ch. 9, FA:ED II, 596-604.

[227] See n. 225 above.

[228] See Bernard, *Epistola* 129, n. 2 (SBOp 7: 323). Bonaventure's citation is verbatim.

[229] *See Epistola* 129, n. 2 (SBOp 7: 323). Bonaventure's quotation is not verbatim.

[230] 1 Cor 9:24.

perseveres ... will be saved.[231] Hence John Chrysostom says: "Of what use are the seeds of flowers if later they die?" as if to say, none whatever.[232]

2. If therefore, most beloved virgin of Christ, you have acquired the virtues for performing good works, even if you have many virtues, then [by all means] persevere in them, make progress in them, struggle courageously in them to the death like the [good] soldier of Christ, so that when the last day and the end of your life comes, he will give you the crown of glory and honor as payment and reward for your work. Thus Jesus Christ, your only true love, speaks to you in Revelation saying: *Remain faithful until death, and I will give you the crown of life.*[233] This crown is none other than the reward of eternal life, the acquisition of which ought to be the desire of every Christian. It is so great that no one can fathom its greatness, as blessed Gregory says.[234] It is so much that no one can count it. It is so long and enduring that it can never be terminated or ended. Your spouse, Jesus Christ, in The Song of Songs invites you to this reward, to this crown when he says: *Come from Lebanon, my bride, my friend, come from Lebanon. Come, and you will be crowned.*[235] Therefore, *arise, my beloved, my beautiful one,* friend of God, spouse of Jesus Christ, "dove" of the eternal King. "Come! Hasten"[236] to the nuptials of the Son of God,

---

[231] See Matt 10:22.

[232] See *Homilia* 33, n. 5 on Matt 10:22 (PG 57: 394): "For what work is it for seeds to flower initially, but after a short time to burn up?" Bonaventure quotes the sense of Chrysostom, not the exact words.

[233] Rev 2:10.

[234] See *Homilia* 9, n. 2, and *Homilia* 37, n. 1 in GGHG (CCSL cxli, 60 and 348) for two possible parallels. Bonaventure is not quoting Gregory verbatim.

[235] See Cant 4:8. Bonaventure has adapted the Vulgate of this verse by adding "my" to bride and inserting *amica mea* ("my friend").

[236] See Cant 2:10, 14.

because the whole celestial assembly is waiting for you, because *everything is now ready.*[237]

3. There is a handsome and noble servant waiting to serve you; there is savory and tasty food to refresh you; likable and most friendly companions to rejoice with you.

Therefore, arise and hasten to the nuptials; because there a handsome servant is waiting to serve you. This servant is none other than the angelic hosts, yes even the Son of the eternal God, as he himself avers in the Gospel when he says: *Amen, I say to you, he will gird himself, have them recline at table, and proceed to wait on them.*[238] O what great splendor then for the poor and outcast, when they shall have the Son of God and the most high King as their servant, as well as the whole assembly of the heavenly kingdom.

4. There you will find tasty and savory food to refresh yourself. The Son of God himself will set the table with his own hands, just as he said in the Gospel: *And I confer a kingdom on you, just as my Father has conferred one on me, that you may eat and drink at my table in my kingdom.*[239] O how tasty and delicious is the food that "God has provided with sweetness for his poor."[240] O how blessed is he who in the kingdom of heaven will eat the bread baked in the vessel of the virginal womb and fired by the Holy Spirit.

---

[237] See Rev 19:9 and Matt 22:4, for the imagery of the wedding banquet. The nuptial banquet as a metaphor for contemplative union is more developed here than in Bonaventure's "Letter to the Abbess and Sisters of St. Clare," in *Writings Concerning the Order,* (Monti, 68-69). Cf. *Soliloquium,* c.4, § I, n. 3, towards the end.

[238] See Luke 12:37 where the last word in the Vulgate is *illis* ("on them") while Bonaventure has *eis* ("on them"). See also *Soliloquium,* ch. 4, § III, n. 12.

[239] See Luke 22:29-30. The Vulgate reads *in regno* ("in the kingdom") while Bonaventure has *in regno meo* ("in my kingdom").

[240] See Ps 68:11: "O God, you have provided in sweetness for your poor."

Whoever eats this bread will live forever.[241] The King of heaven will feed and refresh his chosen ones with such food and such bread, as we read in the book of Wisdom: *You fed your people with the food of angels and gave it*[242] *bread from*[243] *heaven prepared without labor, having in it all that is delicious and the sweetness of every taste.*[244] Behold, such is the nourishment of the divine table.

5. Moreover, most pleasant and amiable companionship awaits you so that they may join in your joy. There will be Jesus with the Father and the Holy Spirit; Mary will be there with the flower-bearing assembly of virgins; the apostles, martyrs, and confessors will be there together with the entire heavenly host. A person will be miserable indeed, if not a member of such a noble society; she is void of desire who does not yearn to join such a society.

6. But I know that you, O most resplendent friend of Christ, desire Christ; I know how you have striven with all your might to seek the companionship and the embraces of the eternal King. So now arouse your heart and soul, raise up your mind and think 'as hard' as you can.... For if you find individual good things so enjoyable, how delightful do you think that great good will be which contains the happiness of all good things? ... if created life is good, how good is the life-creating God? If the happiness of acquired salvation is great, how great is the happiness of the One who created all salvation?[245]

---

[241] John 6:52.

[242] The Vulgate reads *illis* ("them") whereas Bonaventure has *ei* ("it").

[243] The Vulgate reads *e* ("from") while Bonaventure has *de* ("from").

[244] Wis 16:20; see also *Soliloquium*, ch. 4, § III, nn. 11-12.

[245] See Anselm, *Proslogion,* ch. XXIV, in *S. Anselmi Opera Omnia,* I, Franciscus Salesius Schmitt, ed. (Edinburgh: Thomas Nelson and Sons, 1946), 117-18. Bonaventure's citation is not verbatim. See also Davies and Evans, *Proslogion,* in *Anselm of Canterbury,* 101.

Whoever enjoys this good, what will it be and not be for him? Certainly whatever he wishes will be and whatever he does not wish will not be. There will be all the goods of body and soul, such as *eye has not seen nor ear heard and nor the human heart understood.*[246] Why then, friend of God, are you wandering around in search of delights for your soul and body? Love the One good in whom resides all goods, and let that be enough. Desire the undivided good which is all good, and be satisfied.[247]

7. "There you will find what you love, my mother; there what you desire, blessed virgin.[248] What do you love, my mother; what do you desire, blessed virgin? Up there is all that you love, all that you desire. If beauty delights you, *the just will shine like the sun*[249].... If a long and healthy life pleases you, up there is healthy eternity ... because *the just will live forever*[250] and *the salvation of the just*[251] is eternal. If satiety makes you happy, they will be satisfied when the glory of God appears. If you wish to be inebriated, they will be inebriated from the abundance of the house of the Lord.[252] If sweet melodies delight you, there the choirs of angels sing ceaselessly in praise of God .... If you desire friendship, there the saints will love God more than themselves and others as much as themselves,

---

[246] See 1 Cor 2:9. The Vulgate reads *in cor hominis ascendit* ("it has entered the human heart") while Bonaventure has *cor hominis intellexit* ("the human heart understood"). Anselm has *cor hominis cogitavit* ("the human heart thought").

[247] This is an almost verbatim citation from Anselm's *Proslogion*, ch. XXV (Schmitt, I, 118; Davies and Evans, 101).

[248] Bonaventure adapts Anselm by adding "my mother" and "blessed virgin." See n. 256.

[249] See Matt 13:43: "Then the just will shine like the sun in the kingdom of their Father."

[250] Wis 5:15.

[251] See Ps 36:39: "The salvation of the just is from the Lord."

[252] See Ps 35:9: "They will be inebriated from the abundance of your house."

and God will love them more than they love themselves. If peace and concord please you, then all [in heaven] have but one will and they have none other than the will of God. If honors and riches delight you, [know that] God will place his good and faithful servants and handmaids over many.[253] Nay more, you will be called and will be sons and daughters of God....[254] Wherever God will be, there will they also be:[255] "indeed, *heirs of God and joint heirs with Christ.*"[256]

8. "What great joy there is, where there is such great good!"[257] "Surely, Lord Jesus, *eye has not seen nor ear has not heard nor has it entered into the human heart*[258] in this life, how much your blessed will love you and will rejoice with you in that blessed life."[259] The more one loves God here below, the more [that person] will rejoice with God hereafter. Therefore, love God much here below and you will rejoice much with Him there. May the love of God grow within you here, that you may there possess fully his joy. And so, "may your mind meditate on this, may your tongue speak of this, may your heart love this, your mouth preach this, may your soul hunger for this, may your flesh thirst for this, and may your whole substance desire this, 'until you *enter into the joy or your God,*'[260]

---

[253] See Matt 25:21, 23.

[254] See Matt 5:9: "Blessed are the peacemakers, for they will be called sons of God." Bonaventure has adapted Matt 5:9 to his audience by adding "daughters."

[255] See John 12:26: "And where I am there also will be my servant."

[256] See Rom 8:17. All of paragraph 7 is Bonaventure's adaptation of Anselm's *Proslogion*, ch. XXV (Schmitt, I, 118-19); *Proslogion* (Davies and Evans, p. 102).

[257] See Anselm's *Proslogion*, ch. XXV (Schmitt, I, 120); *Proslogion* (Davies and Evans, 101).

[258] 1 Cor 2:9.

[259] This is Bonaventure's adaptation of Anselm's *Proslogion,* ch. XXVI (Schmitt, I, 121); *Proslogion* (Davies and Evans, 103).

[260] See Matt 25:21: "Enter into the joy of your Lord."

until you are embraced by your loved one, until he leads you into the inner chambers of your beloved spouse, who with the Father and the Holy Spirit lives and reigns one God forever and ever. Amen."[261]

---

[261] This is Bonaventure's adaptation of Anselm's *Proslogion*, ch. XXVI (Schmitt, I, 121-22); *Proslogion* (Davies and Evans, 103-04). Bonaventure also uses this prayer at the conclusion of the *Breviloquium* and the *Soliloquium*.

On Governing the Soul

De regimine animae

INTRODUCTION TO THE TEXT

On Governing the Soul is a brief and tightly argued treatise. It addresses three questions of central importance to individuals who are seeking to live holy lives: namely, Who is God? What does God ask of humankind? How might a person live an authentically human and truly spiritual life in a particular historical-cultural context?

Bonaventure's answers to these questions demonstrates how his spiritual-pastoral theology reflects the central convictions of his theological vision. The text is divided into two parts. In part one, Bonaventure invites the faithful soul to believe in, reflect on, and contemplate with admiration the most high God. He then provides a succinct articulation of his understanding of the primary attributes of the triune God. It is an invitation that, in effect, challenges the believer to consider his or her own image of God.

In the second part of the text, Bonaventure encourages the believer to turn his or her attention to the commands of the "law of God." In the mind of Bonaventure, this law instructs one to strive to have a heart that is humble, devoted, and unburdened as well as to live moderately, justly, and in a God-like manner (*pietas*). In this way, he effectively articulates a basic plan for living an authentically human and deeply spiritual life which is easily adapted to the circumstances of different times and to various styles of life.

De regimine animae was most likely composed between 1264-1274. It may have been written for Blanche, the Queen of Spain and daughter of Louis IX. Whether an individual has an extensive or limited knowledge of Bonaventure's theological vision, there is much that can be learned from this spiritual writing.

ON GOVERNING THE SOUL[1]

1. Above all else it is necessary, beloved soul, that you have the highest, most pious, and holiest regard for the most high God,[2] by believing with sure faith, by reflecting with an attentive mind, and by contemplating with admiration through the insightful intuition of your mind.[3]

2. You will have the highest regard for the most high God if by way of a faithful, pious, and penetrating intuition you believe, admire, and praise God's vast power creating everything from nothing and preserving all things, God's infinite wisdom governing and ordaining all things, God's unswerving justice in judging and meting out retribution. You must first leave yourself, then return to yourself, and finally transcend yourself[4] so that you may sing with the

---

[1] The Latin text is in Opera Omnia (VIII:128-30).

[2] *Breviloquium*, pt. I, ch. 2 (Monti, 29-33); *Collationes ... Septem Donis*, col. III, n. 5 (Schneider, 39); and *Mystery of the Trinity*, q. 1, a. 2 (Hayes, 122-37) where Bonaventure discusses "the credible truth that God is a Trinity."

[3] In his sermon, "Christ, the One Teacher of All," Bonaventure makes reference to Hugh of St. Victor's assertion that, just as there are "three degrees of true and certain knowledge" so there are "three levels in the development of faith." The first is "to choose through piety; the second the approval of reason; and the third to apprehend by truth." Bonaventure goes on to assert that "accordingly it appears that there are three ways of knowing. The first is through the faith of pious assent; the second is through the approval of right reason; and the third is through the clarity of pure contemplation." See Opera Omnia (V: 567); *What Manner* (Hayes, 21-22). See also *Mystery of the Trinity*, q. 1, a. 2 (Hayes, 122-37).

[4] This is a reference to Augustine's understanding of the soul's capacity for interiority. Following the thought of both Augustine and Hugh of St. Victor, Bonaventure held that the rational spirit (soul) had the innate capacity to look *outside* itself to what is material and

prophet: *The daughters of Judah rejoiced because of your judgments, O Lord. Because you, O Lord, are the Most High over all the earth, exalted far above all gods.*[5]

You will have the most pious[6] regard for the most high God, if you admire, embrace, and bless God's immense mercy as being most benign whereby the Son took on our mortal humanity, as being so compassionate in the Son's suffering of the crucifixion and death, as being so generous in giving of the Holy Spirit[7] and instituting the Sacraments, especially in communicating himself so liberally in the Sacrament of the Altar. Then from your very soul you can sing with the psalmist: *The Lord is sweet to all and his mercies are upon all his works.*[8]

You will have the holiest regard for the most high God, if you reflect on, admire, and praise God's mind-transcending holiness proclaiming it with the blessed Seraphim[9] [by singing]: *Holy, holy, holy.*[10] The first "holy" refers to the highest and purest sanctity which God possesses such that it is impossible for God not to will and approve what is holy. The second "holy" refers to the holiness which God loves perfectly in others, such that it is impossible for God to deny the gifts of grace or the rewards of glory to those who strive for sanctity. The third "holy" has to do with God's severe abhorrence for what is

---

temporal, *within* itself as to an image of the triune God, and *beyond* itself to what is eternal, most spiritual, and above. See *Itinerarium*, ch. I, n. 1 and ch. 3, nn. 4-6 (Hayes, 45 and pp. 89-91); *Breviloquium*, pt. II, ch. 12 (Monti, 96-98); *On the Perfection of Life*, ch. 1, note 19; and *Soliloquium*, ch. I, § I, n. 2.

[5] Ps 96:8-9.

[6] See note 33 below, p. 209.

[7] See Sir 11:17: "The gift of God abides with the just."

[8] Ps 144:9.

[9] Isa 6:2 refers to the Seraphim, and Isa 6:3 to their threefold praise of God: Holy, Holy, Holy.

[10] On the intellect being made to resemble the Seraphim, see *Collations ... Six Days,* col. 8, nn. 9-11 (de Vinck, 125-27).

opposed to sanctity, such that it is impossible for God not to reprove sin or to leave it unpunished. If indeed you believe this, then you will sing with the legislator: *God is faithful and without any iniquity, just and upright.*[11]

3. After this you must turn the eyes of your soul[12] to the law of God which commands you to exhibit a humble heart to the most high, a devoted heart to the most pious, and an unburdened heart to the most holy.

You must show to the most high a humble heart, I say, by reverence in your mind, by obedience in your deeds, and by paying God respectful honor in your words and signs, according to the rule and teaching of the Apostle: *May you do everything for the glory of God.*[13]

You must show a devoted heart to the most pious One by persisting in fervent prayers, by tasting spiritual sweetness, and by acting according to the manifold graces given you. Then your soul may continually *ascend through the desert* to God, *like a pillar of smoke from aromatic spices and myrrh.*[14]

You must exhibit an unburdened heart to the most holy Spouse, so that in you, neither in your senses nor in your affections, will you entertain any love for bodily pleasures; nor will there be any desire for worldly delights; nor any affection for malicious thoughts. Then, having banished all the blemishes of sin, you are able to sing with the Psalmist: *Let my heart be perfect in your statutes, that I be not put to shame.*[15]

---

[11] Deut 32:4.

[12] The "eyes of the soul" (*oculos mentis*) refers to the soul's deepest/highest capacity to see what is most spiritual, eternal, and above. See note 4 above.

[13] See 1 Cor 10:31: "Therefore, whether you eat or drink or do anything else, do all for the glory of God."

[14] See Cant 3:6. See *Itinerarium*, ch. IV, n. 3 (Hayes, 101).

[15] Ps 118:80. See *On the Perfection of Life* (ch. V, n. 4) for a description of the "divided heart."

4. Reflect, therefore, diligently and see if you have observed all these things from your youth. If in your conscience[16] you find this to be so, then do not attribute this to yourself, but to the gift of God, and then give thanks to God. If, however, you should find that whether once or many times, in one or many of the above or perhaps in all of them, you have been seriously or less seriously deficient, whether because of weakness or ignorance or even knowingly, then you should strive to be reconciled with God *with inexpressible groanings*[17] by showing God that you have taken on a repentant spirit so that you can truly sing with the penitent Psalmist: *For I am*[18] *ready for beatings, and my sorrow is before me always.*[19]

5. Sorrow of the soul must have two companions so that it can purge the soul and appease God: namely, fear of divine judgment and the ardor of internal desire.[20] Thus you can recuperate a humble heart by fearing, a devoted heart by desiring, and an unburdened heart by sorrowing.

Be fearful then of *divine judgments* which are *a mighty deep.*[21] I say fear vehemently, lest perhaps you

---

[16] Conscience, a dimension of the cognitive capacity, seeks to both discover the truth and make practical judgments about the good to be pursued. It is "prodded" by *synderesis* which was understood to be a natural inclination within the affective capacity to desire the good and avoid evil. See Introduction, 28-29.

[17] See Rom 8:26.

[18] The Vulgate does not read *sum* ("am").

[19] See Ps 37:18.

[20] Bonaventure explains that "through the ardor of desire, the soul is rendered godlike, and the mind and reason, in so far as it is possible, dominate over all bestial movements of sensuality." See Appendix, "The Monday after Palm Sunday," n. 2.

[21] See Ps 35:7. Bonaventure argues that "through the fear of judgment, [a person] is confirmed in goodness and is kept safe from the flux of the worldly." See Appendix, "The Monday after Palm Sunday," n. 1. In the *Collationes ... Septem Donis*, col. 2, nn. 10-13 (Schneider, 27-29), Bonaventure explains that the "fear of the Lord" will take "root

still displease God even though you are repentant. Fear even more vehemently, lest you offend God again. Fear most vehemently, lest you depart from God in the end where you will always be without light, always burning with fire and never without [being consumed by] worms, unless by true repentance you depart in final grace and are then able to sing with the Prophet: *Pierce my flesh with fear of you, for I am afraid of your judgments.*[22]

6. Be sorrowful also and seek to repay for your past sins. Be vehemently sorrowful, I say, because all the divinely-bestowed gifts given you have been wiped out. Be more vehemently sorrowful because you have insulted Christ who was born and crucified for you. Be most vehemently sorrowful because you have vilified God. You have dishonored his majesty by transgressing his laws, you have denied his truth and offended his goodness by rendering the entire universe dishonest, deformed, and disordered. And so by setting yourself against the divine statutes, commands, and judgments – all meant to have you serve God – you have abused nature, Scripture, justice, mercy, and the gratuitous gifts and rewards promised you. Therefore, think seriously on these things: *Mourn as for an only child with bitter wailing.*[23] *Let your tears flow like a torrent day and night. Let there be no respite for you, no repose for your eyes.*[24]

7. Nevertheless, you must desire divine charisms, the flames of divine love toward God who has reached down to you, patiently sustaining you when you were a sinner,

---

in us" through a threefold consideration of God's power, wisdom, and judgments. It is a gift that makes a person very aware of his or her need for the assistance of grace.

[22] Ps 118:120.

[23] Jer 6:26.

[24] Lam 2:18.

waiting for you with forbearance, mercifully bringing you back to repentance, pardoning you, giving you grace, promising you the crown [of glory]. Nevertheless, since you are so dependent upon God – or better, since you have received from God that which you owe back to God – *A sacrifice is an afflicted spirit, a heart contrite and humbled*,[25] you must desire [the divine charisms] through bitter compunction, through genuine confession, and appropriate satisfaction. You should desire vehemently, I say, divine approval through the bountiful sending of the Holy Spirit. You should desire more vehemently conformity to the divinity by expressly imitating Christ crucified. You should desire most vehemently to comprehend the divinity by a clear vision of the eternal Father, so that you may truly sing with the Prophet: *Athirst is my soul for God, the living God. When shall I go and appear before the face of God?*[26]

8. Moreover, in order that you might preserve this spirit of fear, sorrow, and ardor internally, make every effort to behave externally in all modesty, justice, and piety in accord with the teaching of the Apostle: *Rejecting godless ways and worldly desires, may you live temperately, justly, and devoutly in this age.*[27]

---

[25] See Ps 50:19: "A sacrifice to God is an afflicted spirit, a contrite and humbled heart."

[26] See Ps 41:3. The Vulgate reads *parebo* ("shall appear") while Bonaventure has *apparebo* ("shall appear").

[27] Titus 2:12. The pastoral epistles to Titus and Timothy provide the Scriptural foundations for Bonaventure's teaching on this point. Temperance is the "firm and measured dominion of reason over desire and other wayward motions of the soul. Its parts are sobriety in taste, chastity in touch, modesty regarding our senses, which modesty is called discipline by the theologians." See *Collations ... Six Days*, col. 6, n. 15 (de Vinck, 102). While these virtues can be distinguished by reference to their differing objects, Bonaventure seems to be principally concerned with their interrelatedness in that each requires disciplined striving and the responsible choice of what is morally good

Therefore strive to acquire all modesty, according to the doctrine of the Apostle: *Your modesty should be known to all.*[28]

Therefore, you should strive for modesty, I say, by striving for nothing more than an adequate measure in your use of food and clothing, in sleep and waking, in leisure and work, so that your behavior will in no way be excessive.

You should strive for modesty in discipline by moderating silence and speech, sadness and joy, gentleness and rigor, as opportunity requires and right reason dictates.

You should strive for modesty by honestly regulating, ordering, and composing your acts, movements, gestures, clothing and garments, your bodily members and senses as required by moral integrity and right living. Then you will rightfully be numbered among those of whom the Apostle says: *Everything must be done properly and in order among you.*[29]

---

within the proposed framework. See also *Collations ... Six Days*, col. 1, n. 11 and nn. 31-33 (de Vinck, 6 and 16-17); *Threefold Way* (ch. I, n. 8) on the necessity of having "a good and right conscience" with reference to Micah 6:8.

See in the Appendix the sermon entitled "On the Way of Life," n. 2 where Bonaventure explains that "an honest and holy life consists in two things, namely, the strengthening of justice and the restrictions of discipline." There he describes the "fourfold restrictions of discipline," another way of describing how one lives modestly.

[28] Phil 4:5. For Bonaventure, modesty and moderation (or purity) are concerned principally with ethics, the choice of what is morally good. As a virtue, it involves choosing to avoid the extremes of too much or too little. See *Collations ... Six Days*, col. 1, n. 11 and nn. 31-33 (de Vinck 6, 16-17). See also Bonaventure's *Commentary on Book II of the Sentences,* prologue, n. 5 in the Appendix.

[29] See 1 Cor 14:40. The Vulgate does not read in *vobis* ("among you").

9.   You should also strive after justice,[30] so that the prophetic dictum may truly apply to you: *For the sake of truth and for meekness and justice,* etc.[31] You should strive for true justice, I say, through zeal for the honor of God, through the observance of the divine law, and through the desire for the salvation of your fellow human beings.

You should strive for orderly justice through obedience to your superiors, through good relationships with your peers, and through the [assistance of those who are in need].[32]

---

[30] Justice is "rectitude of the will" (*rectitudo voluntatis*), the "exercise of perfect virtue." In this sense, it may be referred to as a general virtue. Justice is also said to "embrace every power" and, in this sense, is referred to as one of the cardinal virtues. See *Breviloquium*, pt. V, ch. 4, n. 5 (Monti, 185-86); Bonaventure's *Commentary on Book II of the Sentences, prol.,* n. 4 in the Appendix. The aim of justice is to serve the common good. See *Collations ... Six Days*, col. 6, n. 18 (de Vinck, 102).

[31] Ps 44:5.

[32] Justice "orders" the human person's relationship to God, neighbor, self, those who are in need (*inferiores*). With regard to one's neighbor, there is a twofold justice, a command of kindness and a command of blamelessness. Justice is concerned principally, therefore, with right order. It is a question of what is due to God, to neighbor, or to self in love. See *Collations ... Ten Commandments*, col. 1, nn. 21-23 (Spaeth, 26-27); *Questiones disputatae de perfectione evangelica* q. 1, conclusion (V:121A-B).

The Latin phrase *per castigationem ad inferiores* is rendered "assistance to those who are in need." In a parallel passage, Bonaventure states that "[t]he righteousness of justice consists in the upright will to give each what is due them: to superiors submission and honor, to equals adaptability and kindness, to [inferiors] graciousness and thoughtful care." See in the Appendix, *On the Way of Life*, n. 2; *Breviloquium*, pt. V, ch. 4, n. 5 (Monti, 185). For more on the "order" of right relationships see *Collationes ... Septem Donis*, col. 1, n. 9; on the fullness of justice, see col. 1, n. 15 (Schneider, 11-12 and 15-17).

In *Questiones disputatae de perfectione evangelica,* q. IV, art. II, conclusion (Opera Omnia V:185-186). Bonaventure discusses "righteousness" and connects it with submitting/subjecting one's will to another in the context of his understanding of the virtues of obedience and humility. He also notes there that, following the example of Christ, becoming a servant is best achieved when one subjects one's

You ought to strive for perfect justice so that you might assent to every truth, favor goodness, and oppose malice both internally as well as in word and in work, doing nothing to others that you would not have done to yourself, denying nothing to others which you would like to have for yourself. Then you will perfectly imitate those of whom it is said: *Unless your righteousness surpasses that of the Scribes and Pharisees, you will not enter the kingdom of heaven.*[33]

10. Finally you must strive after piety[34] because, as the Apostle says: *Devotion is valuable*[35] *in every respect, since it holds a promise of life both for the present and for the future.*[36] Be attentive to divine worship, I say, by saying the canonical hours devoutly and reverently, by confessing and deploring your daily sins, by receiving the most holy Eucharist regularly and hearing Mass daily.

---

own will to a person who is in greater personal and/or spiritual need than oneself and/or someone who is like one's own self.

[33] Matt 5:20. Obviously Bonaventure intends to quote this passage in favor of those whose righteousness does indeed surpass those whom Christ proscribes.

On the "four acts of justice" see *Collations ... Six Days*, col. 18, nn. 16-20 (de Vinck, 275-77).

[34] *Pietas* (piety, god-likeness, filial love) is a threefold strength of character which involves: (1) rendering reverent worship to God and offering faithful obedience to the laws of God, (2) guarding holiness within oneself, as well as (3) feeling compassion for and extending oneself in good works (dutiful service) toward those who are "made in the image (*imago*)" or "bear a trace (*vestigium*)" of the Creator God. See *Collationes ... Septem Donis*, col. III and col. 1, n. 9 (Schneider, 11-12). In III *Sent.*, d. 35. q. 4 (III: 784) Bonaventure focuses on the first and third characteristics in this section. In section three above, he treats those things which are integral to guarding holiness within one's own self.

[35] The Vulgate reads *utilis* ("useful") while Bonaventure has *valet* ("is valuable").

[36] See 1 Tim 4:8.

Attend to the piety of saving souls, now by aiding them through your frequent prayers, now by sharing information with them through your words, now by inspiring them with your exemplary deeds: *Let the hearer say: Come.*[37] This, however, must be done wisely so that you do not incur the loss of your own salvation.

You must strive after piety by relieving the bodily necessities [of your fellow human beings] by patiently providing support, by giving friendly consolation, by rendering humble, joyful, and merciful service. In this way, you will fulfill the divine law, as the Apostle says: *Bear one another's burdens, and so you will fulfill the law of Christ.*[38] In pursuit of all this, it is most helpful – so I believe – to keep in mind [the One] crucified as your beloved, so that your beloved "may rest" continually like *a sachet of myrrh* between "the breasts" of your mind.[39] And may he deign to preserve you who is blessed for all ages. Amen.

---

[37] Rev 22:17.

[38] Gal 6:2.

[39] Bonaventure has adapted Cant 1:13. Bonaventure uses this image to describe Francis's love of Christ in *The Major Legend*, ch. IX, n. 2 (FA:ED II: 597).

SOLILOQUIUM
De quatuor mentalibus exercitiis

SOLILOQUIUM
A Dialogue
on the Four Spiritual Exercises

Bonaventure wrote the *Soliloquium: A Dialogue on the Four Spiritual Exercises* (1259-1260) while serving as the Minister General of the Order. It contains a series of spiritual exercises which were intended to lead the "devout soul" (*anima devota/mens devota*) to a knowledge of the length, breadth, depth, and height of God's love (see Eph 3:14-19). While the purpose of this treatise is similar to that of an earlier work entitled the *Breviloquium* (1255), the *Soliloquium* was specifically prepared for "less [theologically] sophisticated persons" (*simpliciores*).[1] It is an excellent example of Bonaventure's creative use of his theological knowledge to serve the different spiritual-pastoral needs of the friars at that time.

The *Soliloquium* is arranged as a series of mental exercises (*meditationes*) that take the form of a dialogue. The dialogue unfolds as the soul (*anima*) poses questions to the "innermost self" (*homo interior*). The "innermost self" is understood to mean that deepest, most spiritual part of the self, the human person "made in the image of God" in its three faculties of memory, understanding, and will.[2]

The "innermost self" responds to the questions raised by the soul by drawing on the words of wisdom that have been handed down by the saints. The writings of Augustine, Gregory the Great, Bernard of Clairvaux, Hugh of St. Victor, and others are liberally quoted. Indeed, the treatise is a storehouse of the wisdom of

---

[1] See Prologue, n. 4 below, pp. 220-21.

[2] The Latin phrase *homo interior* is translated "innermost self." Bonaventure's vision of spirituality has deep roots in the world of St. Augustine's thought, the pre-eminent master of the spirituality of the "inner way." Bonaventure's language here reflects that tradition and readily lends itself to a literary dialogue between the outer person and the inner person, two dimensions of the one person.

the saints. Their thoughts are literally strung together at some points in this text in an effort to make, clarify, or stress the point that Bonaventure intends to make. The number and variety of quotations make the reading of this text a true exercise of meditation (*meditatio*).

Throughout the *Soliloquium* Bonaventure invites the reader into different levels and circles of reflection – within and without, below and above. The exercises literally stretch the soul in every possible direction. In the course of these different mental exercises, Bonaventure never loses sight of his primary goal; namely, that the reader be strengthened in faith and rooted in love, centered-in, as well as lifted-up into, a contemplative knowledge and love of God. All of this so that the devout soul will become "filled unto the fullness of God" (Eph 3:19). A person experiences this, Bonaventure says, "when God is to the will an abundance of peace, to the mind the fullness of light, and to the memory endless eternity."[3]

The person who desires to know and love God in this way must "turn back to God"[4] and earnestly strive for it. That is, desire it as Anselm did when he prayed:

> O, my God, that I might know you, and that I might love you, so that I might rejoice over you for all eternity.... I ask you, O Lord, ... that my mind might reflect on [this joy], that my tongue might speak of it, that my heart might love it, that my speech might preach it, that my soul hunger for it, my body thirst for it and my

---

[3] See Prologue, n. 3 below. pp. 219-20.

[4] The Latin *revertere* is translated "turn back" and/or "return." Both words accurately express Bonaventure's understanding of conversion. On the level of a metaphor, the word images also suggest correctly the movement of the *reductio*, the person's return to God as to the Source. See *Soliloquium*, ch. I, § IV, n. 38 below. pp. 260-61.

whole being desire it, until I might share the joy of my God, who is forever three and one, who is blessed forever. Amen.[5]

Outline of the *Soliloquium*

---

[5] See *Soliloquium*, ch. IV, V, n. 27 below, p. 344.

SOLILOQUIUM[6]

For this reason I kneel before the Father of our Lord Jesus Christ, from whom all fatherhood in heaven and on earth is named, that he may grant you in accord with the riches of his glory to be strengthened with power through his Spirit in the innermost self, and that Christ may dwell in your hearts through faith; that you, rooted and grounded in love, may be able to comprehend with all the holy ones what is the length, breadth, height, and depth, and to know also the love of Christ that surpasses knowledge, so that you may be filled unto all the fullness of God.[7]

1. Paul, the apostle, a vessel of eternal election,[8] sacred depository of divine sanctification, mirror and exemplar of heavenly contemplation, in the passage quoted above shows us the origin, the object, and the fruit of exercising our mental powers.[9] The exercising of our mental powers, if it is to be pious and salvific, must have supernaturally comforting power, regulatory wisdom, and consoling clemency. Thus the devout soul, fired by the love of divine contemplation, in spirit kneels before the throne of the most blessed and incomprehensible Trinity, humbly

---

[6] The Latin text is *Soliloquium: De quatuor mentalibus exercitiis,* Opera Omnia VIII: 28-67.

[7] See Eph 3:14-19. There are some minor differences between Bonaventure's citation and the Vulgate, e.g., the Vulgate reads *latitudo* ("breadth") before *longitudo* ("length").

[8] See Acts 9:15: "This man is a chosen vessel to me."

[9] For an overview of Bonaventure's understanding of the human person – rational spirit – as an image of triune God with a trinity of powers see the Introduction, pp. 12-30 above.

knocks and wisely begs of God the Father his strengthening
power lest, depressed by its struggles, it succumb; of God
the Son [it begs] for guiding wisdom lest, seduced by
error, it deviate from the truth; of God the Holy Spirit [it
begs] for consoling affection and mercy lest, overcome by
weariness, it give up [the struggle]. For *all good giving
and every perfect gift is from above, coming down from
the Father of lights*.[10] And, according to Augustine: "Every
good of ours is either God or from God."[11] Therefore it is
fitting that, at the beginning of every undertaking, God
should be invoked from whom every good thing originates,
through whom every good thing is exemplarily produced,
and toward whom every good thing is ultimately directed.
This is the ineffable Trinity, Father, Son and Holy Spirit,
alluded to by the Apostle when he says: *I kneel ... so that
you may comprehend*.[12]

2.   Second, he shows us the fourfold *object* of the mental
exercises. The object of the devout exercising of one's
mental powers must be [directed to the] *interior* and
exterior, *inferior* and *superior*. The devout soul, by means
of a mental exercise of contemplation, must first direct its
rays [of enlightenment] to what is *interior* to it, so that
the soul may see how it was formed by nature, deformed
by sin, and reformed by grace. – Second, it must direct the
rays of its contemplation to *external things*, so that it may

---

[10] James 1:17.

[11] See *De Doctrina Christiana*, I, ch. XXXI, n. 34, in *Sancti Avrelii
Avgvstini De Doctrina Christiana, De Vera Religione,* Joseph Martin
and K.-D. Daur, eds. (Turnhout: Brepols, 1962) CCSL xxxii, 26: "For
every good of ours is either God himself or from him." See translation
by R. Green, *De Doctrina Christiana* (Oxford: Clarendon Press, 1995),
45. See also *De Vera Religione,* ch. XVIII, n. 35 (Turnhout: Brepols,
1962) CCSL xxxii, 209: "But every good is either God or from God." See
the translation by John Burleigh, "Of True Religion," in *Augustine:
Earlier Writings*, LChC (Philadelphia: The Westminster Press, 1953),
244.

[12] Bonaventure alludes to Eph 3:14-18.

understand how unstable is worldly affluence, how fickle worldly preeminence, and how miserable worldly luxuries. – Third, it must direct the rays of its contemplation to *inferior things*, so that it may understand the inevitable necessity of human death, the fearful strictness of the final judgment, and the intolerable suffering of the pains of hell. – Fourth, it must direct the rays of its contemplation to *superior things*, so that it may understand and taste[13] the inestimable pricelessness, the ineffable savoriness, and the unending eternity of heavenly joy. – This indeed is that *blessed cross*, with its four ends, upon which, you, O devout soul, must hang in contemplation together with your most dear spouse Jesus Christ. This is that *fiery chariot*[14] with its four wheels, in which you in assiduous contemplation, and clinging to your most faithful friend, ascend to the heavenly palace. These are those four regions, namely east, west, north and south, through which you, my soul, must daily wander in search of your most special beloved, so that you can say with the bride: *On my bed at night I sought him whom my heart loves.*[15] The Apostle touches upon these four things when he says: *That you may he able to comprehend with all the holy ones what is the length, breadth, height, and depth.*[16]

3. Third, he [the apostle Paul] shows us the *fruit* of this exercise. The fruit of this salvific exercise, if worthily and laudably followed, is eternal blessedness which is the very best and most beautiful and totally sufficient, requiring

---

[13] Here Bonaventure uses the verb *sapere*, a cognate of the Latin for wisdom, *sapientia*.

[14] See 2 Kings 2:11: "And as they (Elijah and Elisha) went on, walking and talking together, behold a fiery chariot and fiery horses divided them, and Elijah went up by a whirlwind into heaven."

[15] Cant 3:1.

[16] See Eph 3:18. The Vulgate has *latitudo* ("breadth") before *longitudo* ("length") and has *et* ("and") between the first and second and second and third dimensions.

nothing else whatever. Therein: "We will see and we will love. We will be at peace and we will praise"[17] forever and ever[18] [the One] who is blessed forever. The Apostle promised this fruit when he concluded his sermon saying: *So that you may be filled with all the fullness of God.*[19] We will find this fullness when: "God will be to our will the abundance of peace, to our minds the fullness of light, to our memories endless eternity."[20] Then God will be "all in all":[21] "When all error will depart from the mind, all sorrow from the will and all fear from the memory. In its place will come that for which we hope: wonderful serenity, divine happiness, and eternal security."[22]

4. At the suggestion of my conscience, I have compiled this treatise for the sake of the *less sophisticated*[23] by using the words of the saints in the form of a dialogue, in which the devout soul as a disciple of eternal truth asks [questions] reflectively, and the "innermost [self],"[24]

---

[17] See *Sancti Avrelii Avgvstini De Civitate Dei, Libri XI-XXII,* XXII, ch. 30, Bernardus Dombart and Alphonsus Kalb, eds. (Turnhout: Brepols, 1955) CCSL xlviii, 866: "There we will be at peace and we will see. We will see and we will love. We will love and we will praise." Also *The City of God* (Dods, 867).

[18] The rare phrase *in aeternum et ultra* ("forever and ever") also occurs in Ex 15:18: "The Lord will reign forever and ever."

[19] Eph 3:19.

[20] See Bernard, *Sermo 11,* in *Cantica,* n. 5, (SBOp 1: 57); *On the Song of Songs* (Walsh, I, 73). Bonaventure's citation is not verbatim.

[21] See 1 Cor 15:28: "... that God may be all in all."

[22] See Bernard, *Sermo 11,* in *Cantica,* n 6, (SBOp 1: 58); *On the Song of Songs* (Walsh, I, 73-74). Bonaventure's citation is not verbatim.

[23] Because of the complexity of this text we have decided to highlight key points of the text by means of italics, so that readers may find their way more easily through this text.

[24] The Latin *homo interior* is translated "innermost [self]" throughout this work. See note 2 above, p. 213.

reflecting internally, responds.[25] – However, in order that we may succeed in reaching the heights of contemplation by means of this exercise of our mental powers, let us from the start humbly approach by invoking the Father of lights, kneel devoutly in our hearts before the throne of the eternal Majesty, and incessantly cry out with tears and groans before the royal pedestal of the undivided Trinity, so that God the Father through his blessed Son in the Holy Spirit may grant us the grace of exercising our mental powers in order that we might know *what is the length, breadth, height, and depth*[26] and thereby rise up to [the One] who is the end and completion of every desire. Amen.

---

[25] Other examples of this approach can be found in Hugh of St. Victor, *Soliloquium de arrha animae* (PL 176: 951-70); *Earnest Money; De Cognitione verae vitae,* among the works of Augustine (PL 40: 1006-32); Isidore, *Synonima de lamentatione animae peccatricis* (PL 83: 826-68).

[26] Eph 3:18.

CHAPTER I
How the Soul Must Reflect Internally

§ I: PREAMBLE

1.   *SOUL*. Tell me, if after devoutly invoking divine munificence and humbly begging for divine wisdom, and after tearful supplication for heavenly affection and mercy, how might I obtain the grace of exercising my mental powers regarding these four matters, namely the length, the breadth, the height, and depth? Where should I begin in orderly fashion, lest I lose the fruits of this exercise by ignorantly proceeding in the wrong way? For according to blessed Ambrose:

> Ignorance of order disturbs ... the form of merit ... [n]or should we imagine that we possess perfect knowledge of something that we know ought to be done, and yet be ignorant of the order in which we ought to proceed.[27]

2. *INNERMOST SELF*. O soul, according to blessed Bernard [writing] to Pope Eugene: "Your reflections ought to begin with yourself, lest neglecting yourself, you uselessly turn to other things."[28] Also, in his *Meditations*:

> Many people know many things and are ignorant of themselves; they look to others and desert themselves; seeking God through external things and neglecting what is within them where God

---

[27] See Ambrose, *Expositio in Psalmum* 118:27, *Sermo* 4, n. 12 (PL 15: 1311BA). Bonaventure's citation is not verbatim.

[28] See *De Consideratione*, II, ch. 3, n. 6 (SBOp 3: 414). Bonaventure's quotation is verbatim. See translation by John Anderson and Elizabeth T. Kennan, *Five Books on Consideration: Advice to a Pope*, CFS 13 (Kalamazoo: Cistercian Publications, 1976), 52. Hereafter *On Consideration*.

is. Hence I turn from exterior things to interior
things and I rise from inferior things to superior
things, so that I may know from whence I come
and where I am going, from whence I am and what
I am. And so, from the knowledge of myself, I rise
to the knowledge of God.[29]

Likewise, Chrysostom *On Matthew* says: "Not the least
part of philosophy is the knowledge of oneself."[30] Also,
Ambrose in *Hexaemeron*: "Know what you are. Look to
yourself, ... so that you might reflect as to what enters
into your thoughts and what goes out in your speech."[31]
– So:

Examine your life, O soul, with daily reflections.
Look diligently as to how you progress and
regress; how you are doing morally; how [orderly]
your affections; how you are like God and unlike
him; how close and how far... .Know this always
for sure that you are much better off and more
praiseworthy if you know yourself, than if by
neglecting yourself you know the course of the
stars, the powers of plants, the complexities of
humans, and the natures of animals; if you have
scientific knowledge of everything celestial and
terrestrial. Return to yourself, if not always, at

---

[29] See Pseudo-Bernard, *Meditationes piissimae,* ch. 1, n. 1 (PL 184:
485A). Bonaventure's citation is not verbatim.

[30] See *Homilia* 25, n. 4 (PG 57: 332): "It is truly not the least part
of philosophy when we can recognize our merit, for that person who
considers himself nothing especially knows himself."

[31] See *Hexaemeron*, VI, ch. 8, n. 50 (PL 14: 278A). Bonaventure's
citation is not verbatim. See note 121 below.

least occasionally. Rule over your affections, direct your acts, correct your missteps.[32]

Therefore, O soul, accept the counsels of the saints and first direct the rays of your contemplation to the *East*, that is, to the consideration of your condition. Diligently consider, therefore, how generously the supreme artisan has *formed you in your nature*, how maliciously through your will you have been *deformed through your faults,* and how graciously by divine goodness you have often been *reformed through grace.*

§ II: How the Nature of the Soul has been Generously Endowed by the Supreme Artisan

3. Consequently, you should *first* consider *how your nature has been so generously formed.* As I see it, your natural generosity consists in the fact that you have naturally been imprinted with the image of the most blessed Trinity. Hence, Anselm says in his *Proslogion*: "I understand, O Lord, and I give you thanks, that you have created me in your image in order that I may remember you, think of you, and love you."[33] Bernard in his *Meditations states*:

Within my innermost [self], I find three things whereby I am reminded of God, whereby I gaze upon him and desire him. These three are memory, intelligence, and will. For when I am reminded of God... .I delight in him. For I remember him

---

[32] Pseudo-Bernard, *Meditationes piissimae*, ch. 5, n. 14 (PL 184: 494D-495A). Bonaventure's citation is not verbatim.

[33] See *Proslogion*, ch. I (Schmitt, 100); *Proslogion* (Davies and Evans, 87). Bonaventure's citation is not verbatim.

more than wine.[34] When I gaze upon him with
my intelligence, I understand how in himself he
is incomprehensible because he is the beginning
and the end; [I understand] how desirable he is
to the angels because of things into which angels
longed to look.[35] [I understand] how delightful he
is to all the saints because they constantly rejoice
in him; [I understand] how admirable he is for all
creatures, because he creates powerfully, governs
wisely, and is benignly generous.[36]

When I see these things, I desire him: "When I love God
with my will, I transform myself into him."[37] Therefore,
realize, O my soul, what a marvelous and inestimable
dignity it is to be not only a vestige of the Creator, as
is common to all creatures, but to be God's image which
is peculiar to rational creatures. So, my soul, *praise the
Lord. Praise your God, O Zion.*[38] "Wake up and praise,
exult and rejoice, because you are stamped with the
image of God, decorated with his likeness, participant of
his reason, capable of eternal beatitude."[39]

4. However, because all these things might rightfully be
judged to be of little value if they were to end in death,
exult and give praise because along with these things

---

[34] Bonaventure has inserted into his quotation an allusion to Cant
1:3: "... we will be glad and rejoice in you, remembering your breasts
more than wine...."

[35] The original contains an allusion to 1 Peter 1:12: "Into these
things angels desire to look."

[36] See ch. l, n. 1 of Pseudo-Bernard, *Meditationes piissimae* (PL
184: 485AB). Bonaventure's citation is not verbatim.

[37] See ch. 18, n. 61 of Pseudo-Bernard, *Tractatus de caritate* (PL
184: 614C) for a parallel: "The person who loves God ... transubstantiates himself to his beloved."

[38] See Ps 147:12.

[39] See Pseudo-Bernard, *Meditationes piissimae,* ch. III, n. 7 (PL
184: 489C). Bonaventure has adapted the quotation.

God has given you an immortal nature, an incorruptible substance, an interminable duration, a perpetual life. As Augustine states in *On the Trinity*: "You would not be the image of the eternal Trinity, if for you death ended all."[40] As Augustine says in another place:

> Take heed, O soul, that your Creator, after having given you being, gave you beautiful being, perpetual being; God gave you the capacity to live, to sense, to discriminate; he decorated you with senses and enlightened you with wisdom.[41]

Augustine further states:

> So look to your beauty, so that you may understand what sort of beauty you should love... .For if, as is fitting, you are not sufficiently competent to understand yourself, then why do you not at least depend on someone else's judgment in estimating what you ought to be? You have a spouse whose beauty you are able to know if you have any doubts, who is so beautiful and comely, the sole Son of God who ought to capture your gaze, even if your own singular beauty, over and above all others, would not attract you.[42]

---

[40] See *Sancti Avrelii Avgvstini De Trinitate* (Libri XIII-XV), XIV, ch. 8, n. 11, W. J. Mountain, ed. (CCSL 50 a) (Turnhout: Brepols, 1968), 436: "It is God's image in so far as it is capable of him and can participate in him." See also translation by Edmund Hill, *The Trinity*, in WSA I/5 (NY: New City Press, 1991), 379.

[41] Cf. *De Trinitate*, XIV, ch. 2-4, n. 4-6, CCSL la, 425-29; *The Trinity* (Hill, I/5, 374-87). For a closer parallel see ch. 18 of Alcher of Clairvaux, *De spiritu et anima* (PL 40: 793-94).

[42] See Pseudo-Augustine, *De diligendo Deo*, I, ch. 4 (PL 40: 851) for the closest parallel, which also occurs in Hugh of St. Victor, *Soliloquium de arrha animae* (PL 178: 954C); *Earnest Money* (Herbert, 22-23 and 16).

precious little. In the *third* place, therefore, hear about your *admirable dignity,* which is of such simplicity that nothing else can dwell in the house of your mind, nothing else can make its home there except the simplicity and purity of the eternal Trinity. Here is what the Spouse says: *My Father and I will come to him and we will make our dwelling with him.*[43] And elsewhere: *Come down quickly, for today I must stay at your house.*[44] It is impossible for anything to fill the mind except God alone who created it. It is he who is more intimate than your most innermost being, as Augustine testifies.[45] Therefore, rejoice, O happy soul, that you can be host to such a guest. Bernard says: "O happy soul, which daily cleanses its heart so as to receive God as its guest. But this guest needs no goods because he is the author of all good things."[46] Bernard states:

O what a blessed soul, wherein God finds rest, because it can say: *He who created me has found rest in my tabernacle.*[47] Thus he could not deny the rest of heaven for him[48] who prepared a place of rest for him in this life.

---

[43] See John 14:23: "If anyone loves me, he will keep my word. And my Father will love him, and we will come to him and we will make our dwelling with him."

[44] Luke 19:5.

[45] See Augustine, *Confessionum*, III, ch. 6, n. 11 (CCSL xxvii, 33); see also Boulding, *Confessions,* 44-45. Bonaventure has adapted Augustine's statement.

[46] Cf. Bernard, *Sermo 2, de dedicatione Ecclesiae*, n. 2 (SBOp 5: 376-77) for a parallel, whose gist Bonaventure cites. See also Second Sermon for the Dedication of a Church (SBSermons, II, 395-396).

[47] Sir 24:12.

[48] See Pseudo-Bernard, *Meditationes piissimae*, ch. 1, n. 2 (PL 184: 486BC). Bonaventure's citation is virtually verbatim.

O soul, you are much too greedy if the presence of such a guest is not enough for you, because you ought to know how liberal he is, since he shared his goods with you; how pious he is, because he endowed you with his gifts. It would in no way be appropriate for such a prince to send his guest away needy. "Decorate your bridal chamber and receive Christ the king,"[49] in whose presence your whole family will exult and rejoice. O most marvelous and admirable idea! "O King, whose beauty the sun and moon admire,"[50] whose greatness heaven and earth revere, by whose wisdom the hosts of heavenly spirits are enlightened, by whose clemency the college of all the blessed is satisfied. Such a one, O soul, desires your hospitality; longs for and hopes for your dwelling more than his celestial palace. For his *delights* are *to be with human beings.*[51]

6. If all of the above have not yet moved you to praise your Creator, then turn the beam of your reflections to the *fourth* benefit and realize that your capacity is such that no creature besides God is sufficient to satisfy your desires. Hugh of St. Victor says: "Every happiness, every sweetness, every beauty of created things can affect the human heart, but cannot satisfy it."[52] Anselm states: "Every abundance, that is not God, is penury to me."[53]

---

[49] See *Roman Missal* for the procession on the Feast of the Purification of the Blessed Virgin Mary, February 2.

[50] See *Roman Breviary*, Feast of St. Agnes, first antiphon of the Third Nocturn, January 21.

[51] See Prov 8:31.

[52] See Hugh of St. Victor, *Homilia 2, In Salomonis Ecclesiasten Homiliae XIX* (PL 175: 142D). Bonaventure's citation is virtually verbatim.

[53] A weak parallel is found in Anselm, *Meditatio* 14, ch. 2 (PL 158: 781A): "If you had given me all the things that you have made, it would not be enough for your servant unless you would give your very self." A strong parallel is found in Gregory, *Moralia in Iob*, XXII, ch. 38, n. 73

According to Gregory: "Because the human soul was truly
made to desire God, then whatever besides God is desired,
is less [satisfying] and consequently whatever is not God
is truly not sufficient for it."[54]

7. I now believe, my soul, that you have sufficiently
understood your nobility which is most praiseworthy.
Turn now the rays of your reflections to the *power* you
have over other creatures, which is truly amazing. Hugh
observes:

> O my soul, what has your Spouse given you? ...
> Look around at this world ... all of nature has been
> directed towards this end, ... namely that it serve
> your needs and is available ... as your delights
> without ceasing throughout the ages.[55]

Realize then, O my soul, and consider diligently that your
Creator, your King, your Spouse, and Friend, has put the
whole fabric of the universe at your service. – Behold,
the *angels* purge and inflame your affections, illumine
and inform your intellect, perfect and guard your person.
It is indeed a great dignity to have such teachers, such
consolers, such guardians. Bernard says:

> O soul, if you could understand the joy and
> exaltation with which the angels assist at your

(CCSL cxliii a, 1057): "For every abundance that the holy man enjoys
while still on this pilgrimage is penury without the vision of God"
See also *Morals*, II, 506. The strongest parallel is Augustine, *Confessionum*, XIII, ch. 8, n. 9 (CCSL xxvii, 246): "Every abundance that is
not my God, is penury to me." See also Boulding, *Confessions* (309-10).

[54] See *Moralia in Iob*, XXVI, ch. 44, n. 79 (CCSL 143b, 1326); *Morals*, III.1, p. 193. Bonaventure's citation in not verbatim.

[55] See Hugh of St. Victor, *Soliloquium de arrha animae* (PL 176:
955); *Earnest Money* (Herbert, 17). Bonaventure's quotation is not verbatim.

prayers, are present at your meditations, ... how carefully they guide us on the path of good, with what longing they await us and our eternal salvation![56]

– The *heavens* serve you in their movements; the luminaries of the heavens by their influence; the sun gives you the day; the moon illuminates the night for you; *fire* tempers the coldness of the air; *air* mitigates the heat of fire; for you *water* washes what is polluted, diminishes your burning thirst and enriches the fertility of the earth. The *earth* sustains you by its solidity, refreshes you with its fertility, delights you with its beauty. – And so, my soul, you have briefly passed through each of the inferior things to what is superior. You have found that [as Hugh of St. Victor said]:

By divine ordination every creature directs its course towards this goal, namely to serve your needs and constantly give you pleasure.... But beware, my soul, lest you be an adulteress and not a bride, if you should love the gifts more than the affections of your Lover.[57]

Augustine in his book of *Confessions*:

Woe to you if you go astray, if you love your inclinations rather than him, so that you might amass temporal wealth, while not understanding what that blessed light is telling you, that light

---

[56] See Pseudo-Bernard, *Meditationes piissimae,* ch. VI, n. 16 (PL 184: 195D-196A). Bonaventure has abbreviated and adapted this quotation.

[57] See Hugh of St. Victor, *Soliloquium de arrha animae* (PL 176: 955); *Earnest Money* (Herbert, 17-18). Bonaventure's citation is not verbatim.

which is the intelligence of a purified mind, whose footsteps and beckonings adorn all creatures.[58]

And *if you* perchance still *do not know yourself, O most beautiful of women, go forth and follow the footprints of the flocks*,[59] that is, irrational creatures, which are [mere] footprints of your Creator, whereas you are the mirror of the most blessed Trinity.[60] Therefore you should understand that [your Creator] is more worthy and more excellent than all of these. *Follow the tracks of the flock and pasture the young ones near the shepherds' tents*,[61] that is, turn your reflections to the chorus of angels whom you by nature resemble in a certain way and who will be your fellow citizens in glory.

8. *Soul.* I have remained silent for some time. With some shame and embarrassment I am compelled to say and confess that I have done little to make my love worthy of this dignity. Woe is me: unhappy and miserable! I have unworthily and irreverently prostituted myself; I have lived idly and negligently. I believe what Bernard said to be true: "The more perfectly I understand my dignity to be, the more I blush with shame and am embarrassed at the degenerate life I have led."[62] I fear that the more

---

[58] This citation is not from Augustine's *Confessions*, but is an adaptation of Augustine's *De libero arbitrio*, II, ch. XVI, n. 43 (CCSL xxix, 266); translation by John H. S. Burleigh, "On Free Will," in *Augustine: Earlier Writings,* LChC VI (Philadelphia: Westminster Press, 1953), 162.

[59] See Cant 1:7.

[60] See the description of the powers of the soul in the Introduction to this volume, 17-29.

[61] Cant 1:7.

[62] See *Sermo 81 in Cantica*, n. 1, (SBOp 2: 284); *On the Song of Songs* (Walsh IV, 158). Bonaventure's quotation is not verbatim.

dignified and noble the nature, the more serious the sin.[63] I am also afraid that the offense is greater to the extent that the one offended is more excellent. I am also fearful that the injury is greater to the One who has showered me with greater benefits. Woe is me, my Lord God! From the dignity of my person, I ponder over the vileness of malice; from the beauty of nature, I realize the deformity of sin; from recalling the benefits received, I understand the ingratitude of my deeds. Miserable me! Now I see, now I know, as Gregory says, that:

> whatever I have received from the Great Donor for my use in this transitory life, I have miserably abused by depravity and sin.... The tranquility of human peace I have turned into idle security. I have wandered about the earth in preference to my heavenly home. I have degraded bodily health and welfare into the servitude of pleasures. I have turned the abundance of plenty, not to the needs of the body, but to the superfluities of miserable avarice. The serene caresses of the air I have deflected to serve my love for earthly delights. Thus, I fear, nay more I tremble greatly, that all these things will strike back in punishment which have so badly served my vices.[64]

9. *INNERMOST SELF*. O my soul, it seems to me that your thoughts are good ones. From your words I sense that my admonitions have not been in vain. It seems to me that you have been enlightened a little by divine light and truly touched by it.

---

[63] See Augustine, *Tractate* 110, n. 7 (CCSL xxxvi, 627): "Why do we not rather understand that the more sublime the nature, the more worthy of damnation their sin was judged?"

[64] See *Homilia* 35 n. 1 of GGHG (CCSL cxli, 322). Bonaventure has adapted Gregory's words.

According to blessed Gregory:

> Everyone when touched by the brightness of true
> light, sees oneself, so that thus one may know
> what is justice, and learn what is sin whereby he
> is blinded. Thus it is that holy men who progress
> upward towards God in the virtues, more clearly
> understand how unworthy they are. Because, as
> they approach the light, they then discover what
> had lain hidden in them.[65]

§ III: How the Soul has Been Deformed Perversely By Guilt Stemming from the Will

10. *Therefore, O soul, if the light of truth has illuminated
your dignity, which up to now you have not noticed, then
if you now understand and see the faults whereby you
have offended your Creator, and how generously you have
been endowed by nature, now look and see how terribly
deformed by sin you have become.* – Anselm comments:

> Therefore return, O luckless and miserable soul,
> and recall the enormity of your sin; raise your
> groans and lamentations up to the very heavens.
> Reflect, O faithless soul of God, adulteress of Christ,
> what you have done! You have deserted the chaste
> lover of yours in heaven; you have despised your
> maker; repudiated your spouse, upset your God,
> and treated your guardian angel irreverently. You
> were the temple of God, the spouse of Christ, the
> sanctuary of the Holy Spirit. What is this sudden
> conversion and rapid change? From the virgin of

---

[65] See *Moralia in Iob,* XXXII, ch. 1, n. 1 (CCSL 143b, 1625); *Morals,* III.2, 506. Bonaventure has adapted Gregory's observations, especially by rearranging the sequence of his sentences.

God you have become the corruption of Satan; from the spouse of Christ you have become a despicable prostitute; from the dwelling place of the Holy Spirit you have become a hovel of the devil.[66]

Recall, O soul, just why you have sold your beauty; why you have forsaken your honor; for what purpose you have basely defiled your face; recall the many good things you have sold so cheaply.

SOUL. I realize, O Innermost Self, that you speak the truth and you rightly upbraid me for such great transgressions.

11.   INNERMOST SELF. O soul, why have you despoiled yourself of so many goods? Why have you needlessly deprived yourself of such honors? Why have you lived so many years, so many days, so many hours fruitlessly? For Bernard says:

O Lord, my God, how much time has passed wherein I lived without bearing fruit! How indeed can I stand before you? How can I raise my face to look at your great and terrifying gaze, when [I realize] that you have ordered me to number all my days, looking for me to bear fruit therein? O Lord, my God, why have I neglected to give you any time in my heart, to embrace you with all my mind, to delight in your sweetness? Where was I when I was not with you, since from you every

---

[66] This is more a summary than a quotation from *Meditatio* 3 (PL 158: 725B-729C).

creature receives whatever is desirable, praiseworthy, and delightful?[67]

12.   *SOUL.* Lord, now I understand, but am ashamed to
confess it. The *beauty and grace of creatures deceived
my eyes* and I did not realize it. After all, you are more
beauteous than all creatures, to whom you have given
but a little drop of your inestimable beauty. Who indeed
adorned the heavens with stars, the air with birds, the
water with fishes, the earth with plants and flowers?[68]
Was it not you, most gracious Father? Through you
the hosts of heavenly spirits are adorned with various
gifts. Because of you the Seraphim are inflamed with
love; the Cherubim glow with knowledge;[69] by your gifts
the Thrones judge [rightly]; endowed with your gifts
the renowned Dominations rule; by virtue of you the
Principalities preside; because of your power the Powers
repel the malice of the devils; by your profound powers the
Virtues effect miracles; at your command the Archangels
announce the greater events, the Angels communicate
the lesser. But what are all these things but little sparks
of your beauty? O good Jesus, font of the beauty of the
universe, forgive my miserable self, because I have been
so late in acknowledging your beauty, so late in loving
you.[70] This is why I have strayed so miserably.

---

[67] The works of Bernard do not contain these words. Bonaventure
or his source put together sentences from Anselm, *Meditatio* 13 (PL
158: 776B, 774D).

[68] See Anselm, *Meditatio* 13 (PL 158: 774A).

[69] See Anselm, *Meditatio* 13 (PL 158: 774C).

[70] See Augustine, *Confessionum*, X, ch. 27, n. 38 (CCSL xxvii, 175):
"I have learned to love you late, Beauty so ancient and so new! I have
learned to love you late! You were within me, and I was in the world
outside myself.... I fell upon the lovely things of your creation." Cf.
Boulding, *Confessions*, 222.

13. Likewise, *the sweetness of creatures has deceived my sense of taste*, and I did not realize that you are sweeter than honey. You have adapted your sweetness to honey and every creature. Sweetness and every delight in creatures is nothing else but your sweetness ... *which you have hidden for those who fear you*,[71] as should be obvious. Hence, the sweetness of all creatures, if a person truly thinks about it, does no more than tickle the palate for your eternal sweetness. O Jesus, font of all sweetness and piety, forgive me for not having realized your inestimable sweetness and honey-like piety in creatures, and for not having tasted it with the interior love of my mind. And so, I have miserably strayed and sated my mind up to now with pig swill.[72] Alas, I fear that I have never eaten the bread of your sons, but have always *feasted on the delights of this world* and have remained famished. Gregory: "Because we do not want to taste interiorly the sweetness prepared for us, so as miserable, fasting, and starving we love our hunger."[73] O most sweet Jesus, now I know that all sweetness contrary to you has been great affliction and misery for me. Augustine in his book *Confessions*:

O most merciful God, even when I was raging in my sins, you were most piously with me, sprinkling with bitterness all my evil pleasures and sins, teaching me by scourgings that if I should wish to taste without bitterness, it could only be in you, O Lord.[74]

---

[71] See Ps 30:20.

[72] See Luke 15:16: *And he* (the younger son) *longed to fill himself with the pods that the swine were eating.*

[73] See *Homilia* 36, n. 1 in GGHG (CCSL cxli, 332). Bonaventure's quotation is not verbatim.

[74] See *Confessionum*, II, ch. 2, n. 4 (CCSL xxvii, 19); Boulding *Confessions*, 26. Bonaventure's citation is not verbatim.

But I did not grasp this teaching and thus I strayed. However, in all these evil pleasures I feared the betrayer, the accuser, the censurer. At times my conscience was fearful, I was often terrified of being disgraced, occasionally I was horrified at the prospect of hell and yet, miserable me, amidst all these torments my willfulness remained unchanged.

14. Likewise, the *odor of creatures has deceived my sense of smell,* and I have not known your aroma, O good Jesus, *surpassing all fragrance.*[75] O good Jesus, source of aromas, whose sweetness should make me follow after you in the fragrance of your balm.[76]

15. Also, the *sounds* of *creatures* deceived my *hearing,* and I did not know how *sweet are your words to the palates* of your chosen ones,[77] how delightful your counsels to the ears of your friends, how light-weighted your commandments in the hands of your holy ones. O Jesus, font of wisdom, author of scientific knowledge, sower of chaste counsels, now at least have me listen to your voice, for *your voice resounds in my ears.*[78] Now I recall with great bitterness how that voice singing and saying has deceived me:

> *Come, therefore, let us enjoy the good things that are real ... let us crown ourselves with rosebuds before they wither. And may not springtime blossom pass us by. Let us have our fill of premium wine and costly perfumes. Let us leave tokens of our rejoicing everywhere.*[79]

---

[75] See Cant 4:10.

[76] Bonaventure has conflated Cant 1:3 and 4:10.

[77] See Ps 118:103.

[78] Cant 2:14.

[79] Bonaventure cites and rearranges Wis 2:6-9 with the resultant versification: 2:6a, 8a, 7b, 7a, 9a.

These are the voices I listened to and I did not understand or realize that they are all *vain things, to be laughed at.*[80] All of these things and things like them quickly wither and disappear like shadows. What have all these stupid things bestowed on their lovers? *But what profit did they get from the things of which they are now ashamed and confounded?*[81]

16. However, all this while, most loving God, you were with me; I frequently heard your voice, but did not listen; I sensed your salvific inspirations, but did not consent. How often you have inspired me with your saving counsels: "You have sinned, stop, desist, and be ashamed!" Miserable me! To these I responded at times with "sleepy" words as it were, after the fashion of blessed Augustine in his book of *Confessions*:

> Now, O Lord, "soon"; "very soon"; "a little longer," I will leave all that is vain and mundane. But alas, this "soon" and "a little while" and "now" are not really little and now, and the "little" went on for a long time.[82]

Again Augustine:

> Many are eternally damned and in the end shackled in their sins, namely those who, hearing God's voice, do not mend their ways. They hear the voice of hidden inspiration, but they do not correct their lives, saying: "Tomorrow, tomorrow."

---

[80] See Jer 10:15.

[81] Bonaventure has adapted Rom 6:21: "But what fruit did you have then from those things of which you are now ashamed?"

[82] See *Confessionum*, VIII, ch. 5, n. 12 (CCSL xxvii, 120); Boulding, *Confessions,* 155. Bonaventure does not quote verbatim, but gives the gist.

Suddenly the door closes and the sinner, with the voice of a crow as it were, remains outside the haven of his heavenly home, because he refused to bemoan his sins with the dove.[83]

Gregory:

Alas, their happiness has laid low and worsened many by their sins, their daily peace has rendered them inert, and to the extent that they have been found negligent in their protracted quietude, the evil enemy has quickly stricken them more seriously.[84]

Likewise Gregory: "Some God tolerates longer in order that they might convert; those who do not turn back, he damns more severely."[85]

17. However, that I might manifest to you more clearly the history of my unhappiness, I confess that all of these were insufficient [to make me aware] of my unhappiness, but only accumulated to my damnation. Alas, *the softness of the flesh miserably deceived my sense of touch.* O good Jesus, I was unaware of how comforting was your embrace, how genuine your touch, how delightful your companionship. "When I shall have loved you, I am clean; when I shall have touched you, I am chaste; when I shall

---

[83] This citation is not found intact in one place in Augustine's writings. There are three parallels: *Sermo* 82, ch. 11, n. 14 (PL 38: 512); *Sermo* 224 ch. 4 (PL 38: 1095); *Enarrationes in Psalmos CII*, n. 16 (CCSL xl, 1467); translation, "Exposition on the Book of Psalms," in *St. Augustine on the Psalms* (London: Parker and Rivington, 1853), 17.

[84] See *Moralia in Iob,* XXXI, ch. 43, n. 84 (CCSL 143b, 1608); *Morals*, III.2, 487. Bonaventure's quotation is not verbatim.

[85] See *Homilia* 13 n. 5 of GGHG (CCSL cxli, 93). Bonaventure's citation is virtually verbatim.

have accepted you, I am a virgin."[86] O most sweet Jesus! Your embrace does not stain, but cleanses; your touch does not defile, but sanctifies. O Jesus, font of all sweetness and delight, what a wealth of delight, honesty and joy you have, when the *left hand*–of your eternal wisdom and knowledge – *is under my head* – namely, under my mind; and your *right hand* – of divine clemency and love – *embraces me*,[87] namely, in my will. Miserable me! Was there ever anything more sweet, more comforting, more delightful than to find repose in the arms of such a Spouse, than to sleep blissfully when showered by the kisses of such a King and Friend? The devout soul sensed this sweetness and hoped for it when it said: *Let him kiss me with kisses of his mouth, etc.*[88] Who will give you to me for my brother, *nursing at my mother's breasts, so that I may find you outside and kiss you, and now no one will despise me? I will take hold of you and bring you into my father's house and into my mother's bedroom.*[89] *There you will teach me*[90] the precepts of the Lord.

18. However, O Lord God, if such things are so sweet to think about, how much sweeter to savor them! If such things are so delightful to read about, how much sweeter to the affections which experience them! Augustine: "Make me, O sweetest Jesus, savor within by love what I taste

---

[86] See Pseudo-Ambrose, *Epistola* I, n. 3 (PL 17: 814C): "When I shall have loved you, I am chaste; when I shall have touched you, I am clean; when I shall have accepted you, I am a virgin."

[87] Both Cant 2:6 and 8:3 state: *His left hand is under my head, and his right hand will embrace me.*

[88] See Cant 1:1: *Let him kiss me with the kiss of his mouth, for your breasts are better than wine.*

[89] The Vulgate reads *in domum matris meae* ("into the house of my mother") while Bonaventure has *in domum patris mei et in cubiculum genitricis meae* ("into the house of my father and into my mother's bedroom").

[90] See Cant 8:1-2.

externally by knowledge; make me feel affectionately what I know intellectually."[91] O sweetest Jesus, transfix the marrow of my soul with the salvific wound of your love, so that I might truly burn, languish, dissolve, and waste away with desire for you alone, so that I might long *to depart this life and be with you.*[92] O that I might hunger only for you, the bread of heavenly life that came down from heaven![93] O that I might thirst for you, the fountain of life, the fountain of eternal light, the torrent of true pleasure![94] O that I might encircle you, seek you, find you, and finally in you find sweet repose! But what madness, what infernal insanity has kept me so long from these great comforts of my mind, these joys divine and mellifluous banquets? – Tell me, what is the cause of this evil, what are the reasons for these dangers, the occasion of such harm?

19. *INNERMOST SELF.* I see, *O soul*, that you are already fatigued by your labors and suffering from your pains, such that you cannot figure out to what you might attribute the losses you have incurred. And so I ask you to listen carefully, so that perhaps I can show you the *causes of such evils* and what have been the occasions of so much harm. O my soul, you have a *household enemy*, an inimical friend, an adversary close at hand, who renders you evil for good,[95] and who is all the more cruel an enemy because

---

[91] See Pseudo-Augustine, *Liber de contritione cordis*, ch. 2 (PL 40: 944): "Make me, I pray you, O Lord, savor through love what I taste through knowledge. To feel affectionately what I know intellectually."

[92] See Phil 1:23: *to depart and to be with Christ.*

[93] See John 6:41: *I am the bread that has come down from heaven.*

[94] See Ps 35:9-10: *You will make them drink of the torrent of your pleasure, for with you is the fountain of life.*

[95] See 1 Macc 16:17: *He committed a great treachery in Israel and rendered evil for good* and Prov 17:13: *Evil will not depart from the house of the person who renders evil for good.*

he feigns friendship and thus deprives you of these and other infinite goods. With all due respect, this enemy is your unhappy and miserable *flesh* which is so sweet and dear to you. Once you have laid this foundation, you built up this worst of enemies against you. By honoring your flesh, you provide weapons to this cruelest of enemies. When you clothe it with a varied and precious wardrobe, you despoil yourself of all interior adornment, forgetful of what blessed Gregory says in his *Homilies*: "Because the flesh lives elegantly for a time, so the spirit is eternally tormented and groans."[96] On the other hand: "The more the flesh is disciplined, the happier the spirit in heavenly hope."[97] Hence, I can no longer restrain myself concerning the great harm done by you, lest I do not reprehend severely enough the great evil heretofore passed over in silence. Bernard says:

O soul, I know someone who lived with you for many years, who sat at your table, who took food from your hand and slept on your bosom; and when he wished, he engaged in conversation with you. By hereditary right, he is your slave. But because you spoiled him and spared the rod ... he put his heel to your head[98] and reduced you to slavery.[99]

---

[96] This quotation is not from GGHG, but from *Moralia in Iob*, X, ch. 24, n. 42 (CCSL 143, 567); *Morals*, II, 610. Bonaventure's citation is not verbatim.

[97] See Gregory, *Moralia in Iob*, XXXI, ch. 38, n. 77 (CCSL 143b, 1603); *Morals*, III.2, 482. Bonaventure's quotation is almost verbatim.

[98] See John 13:18 about Judas: "'He who eats bread with me has lifted up his heel against me.'"

[99] Bonaventure has adapted Pseudo-Bernard, *Meditationes piissimae,* ch. XV, n. 38 (PL 184: 506B).

He adds:

> O miserable and wretched soul! Who will free you from the chains of this prison? God arises. The armed enemy falls and is crushed, that one who holds God in contempt, that friend of the world ... who courts with the devil. – What do you think should be done with him? If you are thinking rightly, I believe you will say with me "He is guilty of death, crucify him!"[100] Let there be no pretense, don't delay, don't spare [yourself].... "Crucify him, crucify him!"[101] But, on what cross? On the cross of our Lord Jesus Christ from which we have our salvation, life, and resurrection.[102]

Recall, O soul, your origins as Bernard says in his *Meditations*. Know that you are

> signed with the image of God, adorned by his likeness, espoused by faith, endowed with hope, chosen by charity, redeemed by his blood ... a partaker of his intelligence and capable of eternal bliss. Why do you put up with this flesh? ... If you carefully consider all its facets: what goes out from the nostrils and the other openings of the body; you have never seen anything more abominable than dung. If you care to count its miseries: how burdened with sins, itching with concupiscence, preoccupied with passions, polluted with illusory notions ... full of confusion, sated with ignominy.

---

[100] See Matt 26:66: *He is guilty of death* and Mark 15:13-14: *Crucify him, crucify him.*

[101] See Mark 15:13-14.

[102] Bonaventure has adapted Pseudo-Bernard, *Meditationes piissimae,* ch. XV, n. 40 (PL 184: 507A). The last sentence is taken from the responsorial for the fourth reading at the second nocturn for the feast of the Finding of the Holy Cross.

What do you have from the flesh but foul and dirty thoughts?[103]

Again: "O soul, image of the divine likeness, you should be ashamed to be counted as a likeness of the pigs, you should blush to wallow in filth when you are made for heaven."[104] Again, the words of Bernard:

O soul, while you are in the flesh, you are entangled in thorns and it is inevitable that you should suffer greatly from the thorns of temptation and the stings of [frequent] attacks.... So in The Song of Songs you are told: *As a lily among thorns, so is my beloved among women.*[105] O splendid lily, O soft and delicate flower! You are surrounded by unbelievers and corrupters and you dwell with scorpions. Look how you must walk carefully among the thorns. The flesh and the world are full of thorns. To walk through them and not be injured comes from divine and not human power.[106]

20. In the words of Leo, there is still another enemy – the devil, strong and cruel,

who with incredible cunning challenges customs, stirs up trouble, tests the affections, and always looks for ways of inflicting harm wherever he sees someone preoccupied. This longtime enemy of the human race from its beginning knows into whom

---

[103] Bonaventure has adapted Pseudo-Bernard, *Meditationes piissimae*, ch. III, n. 7 (PL 184: 489C-490A).

[104] Bonaventure has adapted *Sermo 24* in *Cantica*, n. 6 (SBOp 1: 158); *On the Song of Songs* (Walsh, II, 47).

[105] Cant 2:2.

[106] Bonaventure has adapted *Sermo 48*, in *Cantica*, nn. 1-2 (SBOp 2: 67-68); *On the Song of Songs* (Walsh, III, 12).

he might inject the allurements of gluttony, whom he might infect with the virus of envy, whom he might allure by the enticements of sensual pleasures, and to whom he might promise the vain inducements of pride. He knows whom he might oppress with fear, whom he might deceive by elation, whom he might seduce by flattery.... He also has companions beholden to him whose cunning and words he uses to deceive others.[107]

O soul, you are so fragile in resisting, you so easily fall, you rise with difficulty! How can you evade the snares of this cruel adversary whom you know to be endowed with such subtleties?

21. *Soul.* Now I see that "someone who is dominated by him [the devil] does not easily acknowledge his sin. But as soon as he begins to distance himself from him, he then finally realizes that he had wallowed in filth."[108] Therefore, because I have already begun to distance myself from sin, and thus know myself and my sin, I can hardly refrain from weeping. Anselm:

O Father, my God, you have stamped me with your loving image, and I have covered it with the hateful image of the devil. Alas, miserable little man that I am: I have covered the image of God with the image of the devil! ... How can I not hate

---

[107] Bonaventure has adapted Leo's *Tractatus XXVII, de natale Domini*, n. 3, *Sancti Leonis Magni Romani Pontificis Tractatvs septem et nonaginta* edited by Antonivs Chavasse (Turnhout: Brepols, 1973) CCSL cxxxviii, 134-35; translation by Jane P. Freeland and Agnes J. Conway, "On the Nativity of the Lord," in *St. Leo the Great Sermons,* FC, No. 93 (Washington: Catholic University of America Press, 1996), 112-13.

[108] Bonaventure adapts Eadmer, *Liber de sancti Anselmi similitudinibus*, ch. XCIX (PL 159: 665A).

to imitate him whose name I abhor? He lapsed willingly and I want to deteriorate. With no fault to avenge, he sinned by pride. I, having seen his punishment, sin contemptuously. He was once created in innocence; I have often been redeemed. He rose up against him who created him; I rose up against him who "re-created" me. He deserted what God had promised him; I have fled the God pursuing me. He persisted in malice in spite of God's disapproval; I run to [the devil] while God mercifully beckons me back. While both of us [rose up] against God, he did so even though God was not seeking him; I did so in revolt against him who died for me.... While this is the image I abhor, I still find that in many things I have a more horrible image.[109]

INNERMOST SELF. Flee, flee from me, O horrible person, flee yourself, flee what is external to you. You ought not to tolerate this horror without heart pangs. If you do tolerate it, you do not know yourself. This is not courage, but a weakness of the mind. This is not sanity, but obdurate iniquity.[110]

22. SOUL. "If I look at myself, I see intolerable horror; if I do not look at myself, there will be unavoidable death.... Unhappy me! To myself I am horrible, but I am much more unhappy when confronted with eternal death."[111] Also in his *Prayers* Anselm wrote: "O most patient Father, O most gracious King, I cannot hide from you, I cannot excuse myself, but I am not a little ashamed to confess. I have now discovered the cause of such evils, I now

---

[109] Bonaventure has adapted *Oratio* 8 (Schmitt, II, 27).

[110] Bonaventure has adapted *Oratio* 8 (Schmitt, II, 27).

[111] Bonaventure continues to adapt *Oratio* 8 (Schmitt, II, 28).

acknowledge what had been maliciously hidden."[112] In his *Meditations* Bernard says:

> Miserable heart! All the while you have not cared about future joy, nor have you sought divine counsel. You have become alienated from yourself and preoccupied with the love of earthly things. During all this time you have fallen into them and become entangled in them, vanity has deceived you, pleasures of the flesh have polluted you, curiosity has led you astray, you have been tormented by envy, tortured by anger, torn by avarice, and made restless by sloth; and thus you have become immersed in all the vices. All this, because you deserted the one good who could be sufficient for you.[113]

O most gentle God, may all the times I spent in evil pass into oblivion before you, and grant that the time left to me – perhaps in a very brief and momentary way – may give honor to you, be profitable to me, and edifying to my neighbor.[114] O most pious God, because of the magnitude of the evil for which I, unhappy and miserable, have been responsible, I now see and recognize that I cannot justifiably have sufficient remorse for myself and my sins, especially if the detestation of sin is not at least as great as was the pleasure in my miserable will.

23. *INNERMOST SELF.* O soul, if as you say, you cannot sufficiently regret your fault, then it is necessary for you

---

[112] QuarEd indicate (37, n. 3) that they did not find this prayer among the prayers of Anselm.

[113] See Pseudo-Bernard, *Meditationes piissimae,* ch. IX, n. 23 (PL 184: 499C). Bonaventure's quotation is not verbatim.

[114] See Anselm, *Meditatio* 13 (PL 158: 776C).

to turn to one of the saints. Do you not realize, as Bernard says:

> You have easy access to God, where the Mother faces the Son and the Son the Father. For you the Mother bares her breasts, the Son shows the Father his wounds and his side. I think that nothing can be repulsive to them, where there are so many signs of charity.[115]

Bernard:

> Therefore, in dangers and troubles and in all matters of doubt think of Mary, call upon Mary. She will not leave your heart, she will not turn away from your words.... If you follow her, you will not stray; if you ask her, you will not lose heart; if you cling to her, you will not fall down. With her protection, you have nothing to fear; if she leads you, you will not tire; with her intercession, you will be pardoned.[116]

Therefore, pray, O soul, having great faith in her, using the words of Anselm: "O Lady, if through you your Son has become my brother, then through him are you not my mother? And so, 'I will exult and rejoice in you,'[117] because in whatever way I will be judged, it will depend on the 'sentence' of my mother and my brother."[118]

---

[115] This quotation is not from Bernard, but from Ernald, *Libellus de laudibus B. Mariae Virginis* (PL 189: 1726D).

[116] Bonaventure has adapted *Homilia* 2, n. 17, *In laudibus Virginis Matris* (SBOp 4: 35); translated at St. Mary's Convent, York, "On the *Missus est*," in *Sermons of St. Bernard on Advent and Christmas*, 47.

[117] See Ps 9:3.

[118] Bonaventure has adapted *Oratio* 52 (PL 158: 957C).

24. *SOUL*. Since I have sinned against the Son, I have irritated the mother. I could not have offended her without injury to her Son. O conscience, tell me, what am I to do? As an enemy of the mother, who will reconcile me to her Son? Who will placate the mother for me, when her Son is angry?

25. *INNERMOST SELF*. [Listen to Anselm]:

> O soul, lay aside your doubts. Even though both are offended, yet both are kind, both are most pious. Let the guilty one flee the just God [and run] to the pious mother. Let the culprit flee the offended mother [and run] to the kindly Son and say: "God, you became the son of a woman because of our misery. Woman, you became the mother of God out of mercy. Either have pity on me, impious sinner, or send me to someone more merciful to whom a wretch like me might flee."[119]

26. *SOUL*. How wise is your advice, how consoling to miserable me your words! Because, when I see my sins for what they are, then I realize that I have polluted the elements,[120] I have sullied the heavens, obfuscated the stars of heaven, tortured the damned in hell, greatly disturbed the saints in heaven, and treated irreverently the angels deputed to watch over me. And so it is that I am much afraid to ask help from them. And since they are rightly angry with me, I cannot presume to turn to them.

---

[119] Bonaventure has adapted *Oratio* 6 (Schmitt, II, 17).

[120] Here Bonaventure refers to the four elements of classical and medieval times, namely earth, water, air, and fire.

27. *INNERMOST SELF.* Your fears are exaggerated, although your humility is pleasing. Do you not know that many of the saints sinned? They learned from their great sins how they ought to be compassionate towards us sinners. Think about Moses, the great prophet, despairing of God's power.[121] Think of David, that most saintly of kings, who violated divine law by adultery and homicide.[122] What of Solomon, that most wise man, who adored vain and evil idols.[123] Think about Manasses, that most evil king, who sinned more than all the kings of Israel, and yet said: "My sins are greater than the sands of the sea, and I am not worthy to see the heights of heaven because of the multitude of my iniquities."[124] Always think about these who asked for pardon. But why go on about the saints of the Old Testament? Think of Matthew sitting at the customs' post, sinner and publican, but called to be a disciple.[125] Look to Paul who stoned Stephen and yet was chosen to be an apostle.[126] Look at Peter who denied Christ and quickly begged for pardon.[127] Look to the centurion who crucified Christ and yet presumed on divine mercy.[128] Look at the thief hanging on the cross and asking for forgiveness.[129] Finally, O soul, think about that famous and impure Mary Magdalene who became a

---

[121] See Ex 4, Num 20:10-13, and Ps 105:32-33.

[122] See 2 Sam 11:2-22.

[123] See 1 Kings 11:4-13.

[124] See *Oratio Manasse* 9 [-10] in Vulgate, 1909 and the critical apparatus for verse 10.

[125] See Matt 9:9.

[126] The first account of God's choosing of Paul occurs in Acts 9:1-19. While Acts 7:58 refers to the stoning of Stephen, Acts does not describe Paul as throwing a stone.

[127] See Luke 22:56, 62.

[128] See Luke 23:47.

[129] See Luke 23:40-43.

special lover of Christ.[130] All of these, although they now reign with God, were once sinners like us, or at least they could have sinned had they not been preserved from sin by divine clemency. Because to whomever it was granted, the gift of being virtually unable to sin, such a gift is not the result of nature but of celestial grace.

28. *SOUL.* Now I can confidently ask the prophets and kings for help; now I can boldly invoke the apostles and martyrs; I can constantly plead with the confessors, virgins, and widows; but above all I can call upon in devout veneration the most holy Virgin Mary. Now I know, [as Bernard says] "how pious, how sweet and how kind Mary is. Her name cannot be uttered without enkindling [the affections], nor can those who love her even think about her without reawakening their emotions."[131] [Bernard continues]: "This is she who begged for the salvation of all and obtained the redemption of the whole world."[132] And Anselm: "O marvelously singular and singularly admirable woman! Through whom the elements are renewed, the sick healed, [humanity] saved, and the angels restored. O woman full of grace! The dew of your abundant plenitude has revivified every creature."[133]

---

[130] See Luke 7:36-50 where Luke does not give a name to the sinful woman. See Bernard, *Sermo Dominica VI post Pentecosten,* 2 n. 4 (SBOp 5:211); *Sermon* 2 "The Sixth Sunday after Pentecost" (SBSermons, II, 338) for a similar listing of forgiven sinners.

[131] Bonaventure has adapted Pseudo-Bernard, *Ad Beatam Virginem Deiparam Sermo panegyricus,* n. 6 (PL 184: 1013D).

[132] Bernard, *Sermo 4 in Assumptione B. M. Virginis,* n. 8 (SBOp 5: 249): "For she obtained the redemption of the world and begged for the salvation of all." See also "Fourth Sermon for the Feast of the Assumption" (SBSermons, III, 256).

[133] Bonaventure's citation of *Oratio* 52 is virtually verbatim (PL 158: 955C).

Again Bernard:

> O blessed discoverer of grace, generator of life, mother of salvation! Through you we have access to your Son, as through you he was given to us, so through you he may receive us. Your integrity has excused the sin of our corruption; your humility before God, O most blessed one, has obtained pardon for our vanity.... O blessed one! Through the grace which you have discovered, through the prerogative which you have merited, through the mercy which you have generated, through your intercession obtain from him who deigned to partake of our infirmities and miseries a share of your glory and bliss.[134]

§ IV: How by Divine Goodness the Soul has been Restored through Grace

29. *INNERMOST SELF.* I now believe that you have somewhat focused the rays of your contemplation so as to understand how you have been *formed by nature* and how you have been *deformed by sin.* Now turn the beam of your contemplation so as to see how you have been *reformed by grace.* You must surely realize that the more perfectly the darkness of your mind has been cleansed in the bath of contrition, the more clearly can be seen the benefits of divine redemption. Sin, according to Augustine, "is darkness which dulls the intellect and puts the entire interior of man in the shadows."[135]

---

[134] Bonaventure has adapted *Sermo 2 de Adventu Domini*, n. 5 (SBOp 4: 174). See also "The Second Sermon on the Advent of the Lord" (SBSermons, I, 20-21).

[135] These are not the exact words of Augustine. For two parallels, see his *Epistola* 55, in *S. Avreli Avgvstini Hipponiensis Episcopi Epistvlae,* Pars II, Ep. XXXI-CXXIII, A. Goldbacher, ed. (CSEL xxxiiii) (Prague: Tempsky, 1898), 178: "Now the human soul, turning away

Hence, it is necessary that you be all the more solicitous in continually dissipating the shadows of sin from your mind with the tears of compunction, to the extent that the rays of your contemplation have been overshadowed by sin. Now, O soul, that your affections are at peace, turn the beam of your contemplation on how you have been restored by grace through God's great mercy, lofty wisdom, and wondrous power.

30. First, consider how, because of the gift of redemption, *he freed you from original sin.* Are you not aware that through original sin you were despoiled of [many] natural and spiritual goods, that you were enslaved to the prince of darkness, chased from and exiled from your fatherland? But, according to Bernard:

> His exceptional majesty wanted to die so that we might live, to serve that we might reign, to be exiled that we might be repatriated; he stooped to the most menial tasks that he might put all of his works in our care.[136]

For the Son of Man has come to seek and save what was lost.[137] He has come, I say, so that he might make you, the proud one, humble.

---

from the Sun of justice, that is, from that interior contemplation of unchangeable truth, diverts all its powers to earthly matters and is thereby more and more blinded to matters interior and above." See also *De libero arbitrio*, II, ch. 16 n. 43 (CCSL xxix, 266): "Woe to those who turn themselves away from your light and delightfully abide in their own darkness."

[136] Cf. *Sermo 3 in Acensione Domini*, n. 2 (SBOp 5: 132). Bonaventure's citation is almost verbatim. See also "Third Sermon on the Ascension of the Lord" (SBSermons, II, 241-42).

[137] Luke 19:10.

Gregory:

> This is why the only begotten Son of God took on
> the form of our weakness, not only that the invisible
> might become visible, but appear despised. This is
> why he tolerated the taunting and mockery, the
> insults and the torments of his passion, so that the
> humble God might teach us not to be proud.[138]

Augustine:

> Christ ... despised all earthly goods in order to
> demonstrate [to us] that they ought to be despised.
> He endured all sorts of earthly troubles to teach
> us that they ought to be endured. He taught us
> that happiness is not to be sought in them nor
> unhappiness to be feared from them.[139]

31. Second, he came that *he might reconcile you to the
eternal Father.* Augustine:

> Since you were an enemy of the Father, I reconciled
> you.... Since you were far away, I came to bring you
> back; since you were wandering in the mountains
> and forests, I sought you out and found you
> among the rocks and woods.... I carried you on my
> shoulders and brought you back to my Father. I
> labored, I sweated, I had my head covered with
> thorns, I gave my hands to the nails, I let my side
> be opened with a lance.... I poured out my blood

---

[138] Cf. *Moralia in Iob*, XXXIV, ch. 3, n. 54 (CCSL cxliii, 1770-71); *Morals*, III.2, 658. Bonaventure's quotation is almost verbatim.

[139] Bonaventure has adapted *De Catechizandis Rudibus*, ch. XXII, n. 40 (CCSL xlvi, 164); translation by Joseph Christopher, *The First Catechetical Instruction*, in ACW 2 (Westminster, MD: The Newman Bookshop, 1946), 71.

for you. For you I bore not slight wounds, but was gravely wounded for your sake. And so! By your sin you cut yourself off from me.[140]

32. Third, *he came to buy you back [from slavery]*.

Augustine:

That we might be in awe, that we might congratulate you, love you, praise you, adore you ... because through the death of our Redeemer we have been called from death to life, from darkness to light, from exile to our homeland, from corruption to incorruption, from misery to glory, from struggle to joy.[141]

Gregory Nazianzen:

O marvelous and unheard of mixture! The Creator becomes creature, the boundless one is taken prisoner, the one "who is rich towards all"[142] becomes a pauper. He took on the image of our flesh, so that he might repair the image he had made, so that he might endow our mortal flesh with immortality.[143]

33. Wake up, O my soul, and *look at the face of your Christ*.[144] Look, I say, at that face once shining in blinding splendor, whose clarity is veiled on account of you; that

---

[140] Bonaventure has adapted Pseudo-Augustine, *Tractatus contra quinque haereses*, ch. 6 (PL 42: 1109-10).

[141] Bonaventure has adapted Ambrosius Auspertus, *Sermo in festo Assumptionis Beatae Mariae Virginis*, n. 7 (PL 39: 2132).

[142] See Rom 10:12.

[143] Bonaventure has adapted *Oratio* 38, n. 13 (PG 36: 326C).

[144] Ps 83:10 reads: "Look at the face of your anointed."

face most beautifully adorned and yet despised because
of you; that gracious and sweet face, spit upon in its
kindliness; lovingly desirable, now made abominable in its
desirability. Look and reflect what the Lord has done on
earth.[145] God is mocked that you might be honored; God is
scourged that you might be consoled; God is crucified that
you might be freed; the immaculate Lamb is sacrificed
that you might have a feast; the lance made blood and
water flow from his side that you might drink. Therefore,
look at the cost of your redemption, look at the example
[he gave] for your instruction.[146] Look carefully, O soul, and
reflect how Christ the Lord and your friend was afflicted
with every sort of pain, in all parts of his senses [body], by
men from every status. The king [Herod] mocked him; the
prefect [Pilate] judged him; the disciple [Judas] betrayed
him; the apostles deserted him; the priests, scribes and
pharisees handed him over; the pagans scourged him; the
rabble condemned him and the soldiers crucified him.

Bernard:

> That great head which makes angels tremble
> was pierced with dense thorns; that face *fairer*
> *in beauty than the sons of men* was defiled by the
> spittle of the Jews; *those eyes ten thousand times*
> *brighter than the sun*[147] were darkened in death;
> those ears which had listened to the songs of the
> angels were made to hear the insults of sinners;
> the mouth which taught the angels tasted gall and
> vinegar; those feet whose very 'footstool is adored

---

[145] See Ps 45:9: "Come and see the works of the Lord."

[146] Here Bonaventure might mean that Christ is an example as
to how we ought to be *formed*, or how we might *model* ourselves after
him.

[147] See Sir 23:28.

because it is holy'[148] were affixed to the cross with a nail; those hands which formed the heavens were stretched out and nailed to the cross; the body was beaten, the side pierced with a lance. What was left? Only his tongue so that he might pray for sinners and commend his mother to the disciple.[149]

O faithful soul, our Savior in his care for our salvation could not shelter us from the temptations of our enemy. However, the more he showed us how to emulate his love, if this we should spurn, the greater will be our damnation.

34. *SOUL.* I have kept silent long enough. What you have proposed, with devout attention I have heard with both joy and sorrow. *I rejoice heartily in the Lord,*[150] because he has loved me so much that he did not even spare his only begotten Son for me.[151] Gregory: "O inestimable love of charity! that you handed over your Son to redeem a slave-girl, nay one not even worthy of the name 'slave-girl.'"[152] O Lord Jesus Christ, who for me did not spare yourself, you have pierced my heart with your wounds and inebriated my mind with your blood. Wherever I turn, I always see you crucified for me; whatever I look at seems to me stained with your blood. And so, turning totally to you, I find nothing but you, nothing except the sight of your wounds. It would be consoling to me if I were

---

[148] See Ps 98:5.

[149] QuarEd state (n. 12, p. 39) that they cannot find this quotation among the works of Bernard. A slight parallel may be found in Bernard's *Sermo Feria IV Hebdomadae Sanctae*, n. 8 (SBOp 5: 61-62).

[150] Isa 61:10.

[151] See Rom 8:32.

[152] This citation is based on the "Praeconium Paschale" or "Exultet" of Holy Saturday: "O inestimable love of charity that you handed over your Son to redeem a slave."

crucified with you, my Lord. It would afflict me deeply
to meditate on anything other than you. Every time I
think about the wonderful condescension of divine piety
in our regard,[153] I am greatly ashamed and embarrassed
because of my ingratitude. And so, the more I realize the
great worth of the benefits of redemption, the viler are
the sins of my ingratitude.

35. *INNERMOST SELF.* Therefore, O soul, lest you be
ungrateful, look to the many and wonderful benefits
you have received. The sin of ingratitude is very great,
because, according to Bernard: "Ingratitude is like a
scorching wind, drying up the streams of divine mercy, the
font of clemency and the springs of grace."[154] Therefore,
O soul, frequently think about, mull over, and reflect on
that terrible word spoken against ingrates in the person
of our Savior:

> O soul, look how much I suffer for you; I cry out to
> you who die for you. Look at the pains I suffer; look
> at the nails that pierce me; listen to the insults
> by which I am ashamed. Although the external
> sufferings be great, still my inner torment is
> greater, when I know you to be ungrateful.[155]

Elsewhere, against ingrates: *O my people, what have I done
to you, or in what way have I grieved you? Answer me!*[156]

---

[153] See the *Exultet*: "O wonderful condescension of your piety in
our regard."

[154] Bonaventure has adapted *Sermo 51* in *Cantica*, n. 6 (SBOp 2:
87); *On the Song of Songs* (Walsh, III, 45).

[155] In III *Sent.*, d. 16. a. 2. q. 3 Bonaventure attributes this "hymn"
to Philip the Chancellor [d. 1237]. See Opera Omnia III: 359, n. 6 and
Opera Omnia VIII: 123, n. 6 for reasons why Bonaventure attributed
these verses to Bernard. Bonaventure cites this same hymn in *On the
Perfection of Life*, ch. VI, n. 11.

[156] See Micah 6:3.

Why is it that you prefer to serve my enemy rather than me? Therefore, be careful, O soul, always to give thanks; never cease to bless and magnify the only begotten Son of God for so many gifts.[157]

36. As Bernard says:

> You owe your whole life to him who gave his life for you and suffered such terrible torments to save you from eternal suffering.... Therefore when you shall have given him everything that you are and everything that you can, will you still not be like a star to the sun, like a droplet to the river, like a [speck of] dust to the mountain?[158]

37. Because, O soul, the eye of your contemplation has been purified by the grace of divine redemption, whereby your Spouse freed you from original sin, I will now show you how you have been *freed from actual sin* by divine mercy. Consequently, turn the ray of contemplation to the benefit of justification and consider the grace of the Lord your God: in fatherly fashion through hidden inspiration he strengthened you against actual sin. How kindly and amicably through your inner voice he called you back at times, saying, *Return, return, O Shulammite*,[159] that is, O soul miserably afflicted by sin.

38. Return to me, because I am your *creator*; return to me, because I am your *redeemer*; return to me, because I am your *consoler*. And if this is not enough, return to me, because I am such a liberal *benefactor*. Therefore, return to me, it is I who created you to be so noble. Return to me,

---

[157] On the need for gratitude see *Threefold Way*, ch. III, n. 9.

[158] Bonaventure has adapted *Sermo 22, de diversis,* nn. 5-6 (SBOp 6: 173, 175).

[159] Cant 6:12.

it is I who through my most bitter death so mercifully freed you from eternal death. Return to me, it is I who lavished upon you both spiritual and bodily gifts. Finally, return to me, O soul, it is I who have liberally rewarded you with the happiness prepared for you. Turn back, I say, from sins of thought; turn back from sins of speech; turn back from sins of action; turn back from your customary sins. Turn to me, O soul, the saints await you with eager longing; turn to me, the angels exult at your arrival; turn to me, the entire company of celestial paradise awaits you. O soul, turn back; Jesus Christ with arms extended on the cross beckons you; the unfathomable Trinity expects your return. O soul, this is the voice of your beloved inviting you.[160]

39. Now turn your attention to the long-suffering patience of the [God] who awaits you. How long he has anticipated your arrival! How long a time he has tolerated you in your sins! Before your conversion you were damned with so many and such great sins, and yet he mercifully awaited you the sinner. Turn, O soul, Christ on the cross with head bowed waits to kiss you, his arms are extended to embrace you, his hands open with gifts for you, his body extended to cover you, his feet affixed to stay with you, his side open to let you enter. Bernard says: "O soul, you should be like *the dove in the clefts of the rock, in the secret recesses of the cliff,*[161] fly to the hands, fly to the feet, enter the side, there you may rest safely, there be secure in peace."[162] Hugh says:

---

[160] The Latin *revertere* is translated here as both return and turn back. It immediately refers to humankind's having "turned away" from God through sin. The call to "return" should also be understood in the larger context of the whole movement of *reductio*. See also *On the Perfection of Life*, ch. I, n. 5, note 15.

[161] Cant 2:14.

[162] With slight modifications Bonaventure takes this citation from Part I, ch. 12 of Pseudo-Bernard, *Instructio Sacerdotis* (PL 184: 779B).

O soul, if you reflect clearly, you will realize the number and quality of those cast aside in comparison with yourself, who were not fortunate enough to merit the grace given you.... Your Spouse chose you and preferred you, he picked you from among all, he took you from all, he loved you above all.[163]

40. *Soul.* I confess and realize, I feel and understand that God has chosen me above so many others, but nothing is worthy of satisfying God for all such great benefits.

41. *Innermost Self.* O soul, now that you have seen the patience of him who waits for you, turn the rays of your contemplation to the *kindness* of him who justifies you. Think carefully and consider what inestimable grace your Spouse has given you. As Bernard says: "Such are the graces he gave you that you might be his friend at table, in his kingdom, in his very bedchamber."[164] Elsewhere he says:

The mercies of the Lord I will sing forever,[165] because I find in me seven mercies, whereby I most clearly recognize his inestimable compassion. First, he spared me from my sins. Second, he did not immediately condemn me when I sinned, but while I prolonged my iniquities, he prolonged his compassion. Third, he changed my heart, so that what had previously been bitter become

A slight parallel occurs in Bernard, *Sermo 61, in Cantica* n. 3 (SBOp 2: 149-50); *On the Song of Songs* (Walsh, III, 142-43).

[163] Bonaventure has adapted Hugh's *Soliloquium de arrha animae* (PL 176: 963B-D); *Earnest Money* (Herbert, 27).

[164] Bonaventure has adapted *Sermo 2 in Dominica 1 post Octavam Epiphaniae*, n. 3 (SBOp 4:321); "The Second Sermon for the First Sunday after the Octave of the Epiphany" (SBSermons, II, 45).

[165] Ps 88:2.

sweet for it. Fourth, in his mercy he took me back when I repented. Fifth, he gave me the strength to restrain myself and correct my ways. Sixth, he gave me grace for obtaining merit. Seventh, he gave me the hope of obtaining it.[166]

42. *Soul.* O Lord, my God:

Unhappy and miserable as I am, I ought to love my God who created me when I did not exist; who redeemed me while I was perishing ... and who freed me from so many dangers. When I strayed, he brought me back; in my ignorance, he taught me; when I was sinning, he upbraided me; when I was sad, he consoled me; when I almost despaired, he comforted me; when standing, he held me up; when falling, he raised me up; when I set out, he led me; when I came back, he received me.[167]

There he was watching over everything, attending to details, always present, caring for all things, in all things providential, such that he was totally occupied in watching over me as if forgetful of all else and concerned only with me.[168]

---

[166] Bonaventure has adapted Bernard's *Sermo* 2, *Dominica VI post Pentecosten,* nn. 3-5 (SBOp 5: 210-13); "The Second Sermon for the Sixth Sunday after Pentecost" (SBSermons, II, 332-34).

[167] Bonaventure seems to have adapted Anselm's *Meditatio* 7 (PL 158: 741B-742A). See also Alcher of Clairvaux, *De spiritu et anima*, ch. 17 (PL 40: 792).

[168] See Alcher of Clairvaux, *De spiritu et anima,* ch. 17 (PL 40: 792-93).

43. Since as you say, I must love God for all these things, tell me how I am to love him and repay him for all he has undergone out of love for me.[169]

Innermost Self. O soul, as Bernard says: "Let the reason to love God be God, but there are no restrictions to love God."[170] We can, however, find something of a way by searching the Sacred Scriptures. For he, who initially gave you love, shows the way of love when he says: *You shall love the Lord, your God, with all your heart, with all your soul, and with all your mind.*[171] Therefore, O soul, with a singular love, love God the Father who from nothing created you so nobly; love God the Son who reformed you in an inestimable way by dying for you; love God the Holy Spirit who so frequently in his consoling mercy redeemed you from sin and comforted you in doing good. Therefore, love God the Father *mightily*, lest you be imperiled and vanquished by any other love; love God the Son *wisely*, lest you be stealthily seduced by any other love; love God the Holy Spirit *sweetly*, lest you be poisoned and infected with any other love.

To put it another way, with Bernard:

> Learn from Christ, O Christian soul, how you must love Christ. Love *sweetly, prudently,* and *mightily.* Sweetly, so that by his love all other love will have a bad taste. May he alone be honey in your mouth, melody in your ear, joy in your heart. Love *prudently*, so that your love will burn continually

---

[169] For Bonaventure on the "Perfect Love of God" see *On the Perfection of Life*, ch. VII.

[170] Bonaventure has slightly adapted Bernard, *De diligendo Deo*, ch. I, n. 1 (SBOp 3: 119); *On Loving God* (Evans, 174): "The cause of loving God is God himself. The way to love [God] is without measure."

[171] Deut 6:5. See also Matt 22:37; Mark 12:30; Luke 10:27.

in him and in no other. Love *mightily*, so that your
fragility might joyfully bear up for his sake under
everything hard and difficult. Then you can say:
"My labors lasted hardly one hour, and if prolonged
I would not feel it because of my love." And so, the
Christian relentlessly focuses his love on Christ,
gladly sustaining everything for him, until such
time as he comes to him.[172]

44. *SOUL*. O innermost self, with all due respect – and
I ask not out of curiosity, but from humility; not out of
presumption, but out of devotion – tell me: What is it I
love, when I love my God?

INNERMOST SELF. O soul, if your question had been
presumptuous, it would have been malicious, but because
it stems from devotion, it deserves a devout answer. Hear
what that great lover of God, Augustine, had to say in his
book of *The Confessions*. He says:

When I love God, I do not love bodily beauty or
temporal harmony or resplendent light so pleasing
to the eyes. I do not love sweet melodies ... or
fragrant smelling balms, not manna or honey, not
open arms or fleshy embrace. These I do not love
when I love my God. But what do I love? I love a
light of sorts, a certain voice, a certain kind of odor,
a sort of nourishment, an internal embrace ... of
my inner being, where my soul is made bright by
that which space cannot encompass, where sweet
sounds are heard which are not dissipated by

---

[172] This is a medley of quotations. The main theme is from *Sermo
20* in *Cantica*, n. 4 (SBOp 1: 116-17); *On the Song of Songs*, (Walsh I,
149-50). See also *Sermo 14,* in *Cantica n.* 4 (SBOp 1: 78); *On the Song
of Songs*, (Walsh, I, 100). See further *Sermo 15,* in *Cantica*, n. 6 (SBOp
1: 86); *On the Song of Songs,* (Walsh, I, 110).

time, where there is fragrance not borne away by gusts of air, where taste perdures undiminished by eating, where [all this] remains unaffected by satiety.[173]

45. *SOUL.* O Innermost Self, please tell me a little about this virtue of charity so that, knowing more about it, I might burn more strongly in the love of God.

INNERMOST SELF. Truly, O soul, the fruit of charity is great indeed, but lies hidden. According to Augustine:

Charity is tolerant in times of adversity, temperate in prosperity, strong in times of great suffering, joyful in good works, careful in temptations, generous in hospitality, joyful among genuine companions, most patient among false companions ... secure in the face of insults, kindly when faced with hate, calm when angrily confronted, innocent in the midst of evil, groaning in sin, breathing deeply in truth.[174]

O happy love! From which arises moral strength, pure affections, keenly intelligent thoughts, holy desires, resplendent works, rich virtues, worthy merits and sublime rewards and honors.

O sweetness of love, and love of sweetness, may my heart feast on you, may the bowels of my soul be filled with your nectar.[175]

---

[173] Bonaventure has adapted *Confessionum*, X, ch. 6, n. 8, (CCSL xxvii, 159-60). See also Boulding, *Confessions*, 202.

[174] Bonaventure has adapted Sermon 350 (PL 39: 1534); trans. Edmund Hill, in *Sermons III / 10 (341-400) on Various Subjects,* WSA III/10 (NY: New City Press, 1995), 108.

[175] Bonaventure has adapted ch. 11 from Pseudo-Augustine, *Manuale,* ch. 11 (PL 40: 956).

Jerome says:

> Without the love of charity, even though one might
> believe rightly, one cannot attain beatitude. Charity
> is so great that without it, even prophecies and
> martyrdom are thought to be nothing; no reward
> compensates for charity. Charity takes first place
> among all the virtues.[176]

O how miserable is [the one] whose mind is taken up with
the love of temporal things which: "are acquired with
labor, possessed in fear, and lost in pain."[177]

46. But, as Augustine says:

> Blessed is he who loves you, Lord, and loves his
> enemy and his friend for your sake. Only he loses
> no one dear to him for whom all are dear ones for
> love of you.... No one will ever lose you unless he
> sends you away. But if he shall send you away,
> where would he go? From one pleased to one who
> is angry?[178]

Further on Augustine says:

> He loves you less who loves something else, but not
> for your sake. O charity which always burns and
> is never extinguished. O charity, my God, enkindle

---

[176] QuarEd refer (p. 43, n. 7) to two passages in Jerome. Neither
is exact. See Jerome, *Commentariorum in Epistolam ad Galatas* 5:14,
22, III (PL 26: 436B-438A and 446C-449D). See also *Apologia adversus Libros Rufini,* II, ch. II (PL 23: 445A-C).

[177] See Bernard, *Sermo* 42, n. 3, *Sermones de diversis* (SBOp 6:
257): "Are not riches acquired with labor, possessed with fear, and lost
in pain?" The same sermon is quoted more extensively in ch. II, § I, n.
3 below.

[178] Bonaventure has adapted Augustine, *Confessionum*, IV, ch. 9,
n. 14 (CCSL xxvii, 47); see also Boulding, *Confessions*, 63.

me ... that I might restrain my lust of the flesh, my lust of the eyes, and my worldly ambition.[179]

Hence in his book on *Morals* Gregory says:

O how happy and blessed is he who with the sole desire for eternity remains steadfast in love, who is not elated by prosperity or crushed by adversity, and since he has nothing in this world that he loves, so there is nothing in the world that he fears.[180]

Paul says in his epistle: *Love is patient, love is kind. It is not jealous, it is not puffed up, it is not pretentious. Love is never rude, it is not self-seeking, it is not prone to anger, neither does it brood over injuries. Love does not rejoice in what is wrong but rejoices with the truth.*[181] In his book on *Morals*, Gregory comments on this passage:

Love is *patient* because it tolerates injuries with equanimity. It is *kind* because it generously dispenses good things in return for evil. It is *not jealous* because, since it desires nothing from this world, it does not know how to be envious of transient earthly things. It is *not inflated* because, since it anxiously desires the rewards of eternal retribution, it takes no pride in external goods. It is *not rude* because, since it is entirely taken up

---

[179] Bonaventure has adapted *Confessionum*, X, ch. 29, n. 40-41 (CCSL xxvii, 176); cf. *Confessions,* book X, 29,40 (Boulding, 223).

[180] Bonaventure has adapted *Moralia in Iob*, X, ch. 21, n. 39 (CCSL cxliii, 565); *Morals*, I, 607-08.

[181] See 1 Cor 13:4-6. The Vulgate reads *caritas non aemulatur, non agit perperam, non inflatur* ("Love is not jealous, it is not pretentious, it is not puffed up") while Bonaventure has *non aemulatur, non inflatur, non agit perperam* ("it is not jealous, it is not puffed up, it is not pretentious").

with the love of God and neighbor, it simply ignores what deviates from rectitude. It is *not ambitious* because, being entirely preoccupied with what is within itself, it has no taste whatever for what is outside and foreign to it. It *does not seek its own interests*, because it ignores the transient things as foreign to it and acknowledges nothing as its own except what is pertinent to it. It is not *quick-tempered* because it is both tolerant of injuries and in no way arouses feelings of revenge, all the while expecting greater rewards for its greater labors. It *harbors no evil thoughts*, because its mind is firmly fixed in the love of purity and since it has uprooted all hatred, it does not know how to contaminate its mind. It does *not rejoice over wrongdoing*, because it breathes with love toward all and does not take pleasure in the downfall of its adversaries. It *rejoices with the truth*, because in loving others, it always sees the good in them, and rejoices in their accomplishments as if they were its own.[182]

---

[182] This long citation is virtually verbatim from *Moralia in Iob*, X, ch. 6, n. 10 (CCSL cxliii, 543); cf. *Morals*, I, 585-86.

Chapter II
The Soul Turned Toward External Things

*How the soul through mental discipline must turn the rays
of contemplation to external things in order to understand
how unstable is worldly opulence, how changeable worldly
excellence, and how miserable worldly splendor.*

1. *INNERMOST SELF.* O soul, you should now turn the
rays of contemplation to the things *alongside you*, that
is to the sensible world, so that you may despise it and
the things in it. Having done this, you are then able to
become aflame with the love of your spouse. You love him
less, if there is anything which you desire that you do
not love in him and for his sake.[183] According to Gregory:
"The more one separates oneself from that highest love,
the more one delights in inferior things."[184] Also, a person
is more quickly converted to God, if there is nothing in
this world which delights him. As Augustine says: "All
creatures ought to seem worthless to you, in order that
your Creator alone might sweeten your heart."[185]

---

[183] See Augustine, *Confessionum*, X, ch. 29, n. 40 (CCSL xxvii,
176); (Boulding, *Confessions*, 223). Bonaventure cited this passage at
the end of chapter I, n. 46 above.

[184] This is a virtually verbatim quotation from *Homilia* 30, n. 2 of
GGHG (CCSL cxli, 257).

[185] This citation is not found verbatim in Augustine. There are
two parallels, *Enarratio II, Sermo* 3, n. 8 in *Sancti Avrelii Avgvstini
Enarrationes in Psalmos I-L*, Eligius Dekkers and Iohannes Fraipont,
eds. (Turnhout: Brepols, 1956) CCSL xxxviii, 218: "Let everything
except God be considered worthless." See also Pseudo-Augustine,
Liber Soliloquiorum animae ad Deum, ch. 22 (PL 40: 882): "I ask that
all things become bitter to me, so that you alone may appear to be
sweet to my soul."

§ I: ON THE THREEFOLD VANITY OF EARTHLY THINGS

2. Always reflect and reconsider, not only from what you have heard but also from what you have experienced, not only from spoken testimony but also from the facts, *how unstable is worldly opulence, how changeable worldly excellence, how false and miserable worldly fame.* Everything which here below seems important is rather steeped in sorrow than honored with joy.[186] Bernard says:

> See how the lovers of this world shop in the market places of the world, some seeking riches, others honor, others fame. But what ought I say about *riches*? They are acquired with labor, possessed in fear and sorrowfully lost.... What might I say about *honor*? Placed as you are on high, will you not be judged and wounded by everyone? Is there anyone in a position of honor without pain, anyone who is a prelate without troubles; can anyone be placed in the highest positions without becoming vain? ... And what should I say of *fame*? It is nothing more than a vain puffing up of the ears! Can this escape judgment? ... Look to those whom you seek to rise above and reflect, because you have sown in them the seeds of envy.[187]

3. *SOUL.* If this is the way things are, then what is it that miserable men seek when they desire the vanities of the world? How blind they are who seek worldly fame!

---

[186] Bonaventure has adapted Gregory, *Moralia in Iob*, XXXII, ch. 20, n. 38 (CCSL cxliii b, 1657); *Morals*, III.2, 540.

[187] Bonaventure has adapted *Sermo* 42, n. 3, *Sermones de diversis* (SBOp 6: 257-58).

Innermost Self. Gregory says: "There are those who when they see the fame of certain people ... believe it to be something of great worth and hope that they too may rise to such fame. However, when witnessing their ... deaths, they realize how vain is their fame and sorrowfully say to themselves: Behold, human beings are but nothing."[188]

O blessed soul, what are these worldly things? Nothing but empty dreams. *What did pride or the boasting of riches profit those who love them? For all of them have passed like a shadow ... like a ship traversing the waves. When it has passed, no trace can be found.... For they are consumed in their wickedness.*[189] And, sad to say, how many there are who have left no trace of virtues behind them! *Where are the rulers of the nations, who lorded it over*[190] *the wild beasts of the earth ... who heaped up silver and the gold,*[191] who built up cities and encampments, who conquered kings and kingdoms in war? *Where is the wise one? Where is the scribe? Where is the debater of this age?*[192] Where is the most wise Solomon? Where the powerful Alexander? Where the most strong Sampson? Where the handsome Absalom? Where the marvelous Assuerus? Where are the most powerful caesars? Where the famous kings and princes? Bernard: "What good was empty fame for them, short-lived joy, worldly power, large families, carnal pleasures, deceitful riches, the delights of disregarded desire? Where are the smiles, the joy, the

---

[188] Bonaventure has adapted *Moralia in Iob*, VI, ch. 6, n. 8 (CCSL cxliii, 289); *Morals,* I, 317.

[189] Bonaventure has modified Wis 5:8-10, 13, esp. by changing first person plural verbs to third person plural.

[190] The Vulgate reads *dominantur* ("lord over") while Bonaventure has *dominati sunt* ("lorded over").

[191] See Bar 3:16-17.

[192] 1 Cor 1:20. The Vulgate has *conquisitor* (debater), which, for Bonaventure, more probably meant "an eager procurer of worldly goods."

boasting, the arrogance?"[193] Where is the nobility of blood-lines? Where is bodily beauty? Elegant form? Youthful comeliness? Abundant booty? Immense palaces? Worldly wisdom? All such things are of this world, *and the world loves its own*;[194] and yet all these things together with the world do not last long. The world and its enticements will pass away.[195] – Thus Bernard says:

> Therefore, if you are truly wise, ... if you have light in your eyes, desist seeking [those things] the pursuit of which is miserable, which when possessed are a burden, ... when loved contaminate, and when lost are agonizing.[196] Leave all these things behind for the sake of him who is above all.[197]

And, Bernard again:

> Flee and flee again, O soul, to the city of safe haven, that is to religious life, where you can do penance for the past, obtain grace in the present, and happily prepare for future glory. Do not let the consciousness of sin hold you back, because where sin prevailed, *grace overflowed all the more.*[198] Let not the austerity of penance frighten you. For *the sufferings of this present time are not worthy to be compared to*[199] bygone sin which is forgiven, but to

---

[193] Bonaventure has adapted Pseudo-Bernard, *Meditationes piissimae,* ch. III, n. 9 (PL 184: 491B).

[194] See John 15:19.

[195] See 1 John 2:17.

[196] Bonaventure has adapted Bernard, *Epistola* 103 n. 2 (SBOp 7: 260).

[197] Bonaventure has adapted Abbot Gaufried, *Declarationes de colloquio Simonis cum Jesu,* Admonition II, n. 2 (PL 184: 438B).

[198] See Rom 5:20.

[199] See Rom 8:18.

present grace that is infused, and to future glory which is promised.[200]

4. *SOUL*. I now recognize the falsity and instability of the world. However, not knowing by what chains I am bound, I am still unable to focus my attention as I should.

INNERMOST SELF. Certainly, O soul, if you attend diligently and prudently to the dangers you incur from the world, you will without doubt restrain your mind from worldly vanities. Worldly behavior is very serious and dangerous because, according to Bernard: "Chastity is endangered by pleasures, humility by wealth, piety by business dealings, truth by garrulity, and charity by this evil age."[201] O weak and sickly soul, how easily are you deceived, how prone to fall, and how difficult it is for you to get up again![202] Do you not know that "just as it is difficult for a tree by the wayside to keep its most beautiful fruit to maturity, so it is difficult for a [person] living near the world to preserve immaculate justice to the end"? So says Chrysostom.[203]

---

[200] Bonaventure has adapted *Ad Clericos de Conversione*, ch. 21, n. 37 (SBOp 4: 113-14); translation by Marie-Bernard Saïd, "On Conversion, A Sermon to Clerics," in *Sermons on Conversion* (Kalamazoo, MI: Cistercian Publications, 1981), 75. Bonaventure's major modification is to identify "religious life" as "the city of safe haven."

St. Bonaventure considered entrance into religious life a safe and sure way of pursuing Christian holiness. The Second Vatican Council's Constitution on the Church, *Lumen Gentium*, Ch. V: "The Call to the Whole Church to Holiness," n. 40, offers a different perspective on the call to holiness.

[201] *Ad Clericos de Conversione*, ch. 21, n. 37 (SBOp 4: 113); *On Conversion* (Saïd, 75). Bonaventure concludes this verbatim citation with a reference to Gal 1:4.

[202] Bonaventure expresses similar thoughts in chapter I, n. 20 above and chapter III, n. 3 below.

[203] Bonaventure has adapted *Homilia* 39, on Matt 21:39, *Opus Imperfectum* (PG 56: 815-16).

Likewise, Augustine in one of his epistles: "The chains of this world are truly harsh: false happiness, certain sorrow, uncertain pleasure, hard labor, fearful [peace and] quiet, abundant misery, and vain hope for happiness."[204] O soul, if you keep these things in mind, you will despise the world and what is in it. – What is it, beloved, that you love? What do you desire? What do you seek in the world? If you would like to be a prelate, what do you do but mess up your life? Do you not know that

> it is a monstrous thing to occupy the highest places with the lowest of minds; the first seat [of honor] and the lowest of lives; a talkative tongue and idle hands; many words and no action; grave demeanor and few deeds; great authority, fragile stability?[205]

Gregory in his *Pastoral Care* says: "Prelates ought to understand that if they behave perversely, then they merit to die as many deaths as the examples of perdition transmitted by them to their subjects."[206] – Perhaps you will say: "I do desire the prelacy, but I intend to live it in a goodly and holy fashion." I praise you, but I rarely find something worthy of praise. I always fear that, according to Gregory in his *Register of Letters*:

---

[204] This is Bonaventure's verbatim citation of *Epistola* 26, n. 2, in *S. Avreli Avgvstini Hipponiensis Episcopi Epistvlae,* A. Goldbacher, ed. CSEL xxxiiii (Prague: Tempsky, 1895), 85.

[205] This is Bonaventure's verbatim quotation from *De Consideratione*, II, ch. VII, n. 14 (SBOp 3: 422); *On Consideration* (Anderson and Kennan, 64).

[206] This is a slight modification of Gregory, *Regulae Pastoralis Liber,* Part III, ch. 4 (PL 77: 54B); trans. Henry Davis, *Pastoral Care,* vol. 2, in ACW 11 (Westminster, MD: Newman Press, 1950), 97.

The merits of those who preside and those whom they rule are so interconnected that frequently because of the evil deeds of the rulers the lives of the subjects are worsened, and frequently because of the good deeds of the people the lives of the pastors go bad.[207]

5.   If you seek worldly wisdom, what great dangers you court for yourself! Bernard: "How often and how many have been cast down by worldly wisdom which has likewise extinguished in them a mentality imbued with a Godlike spirit which the Lord had so vehemently wanted to inflame....[208] Do you not realize that worldly wisdom is *earthly, unspiritual and devilish,*[209] inimical to salvation, something which suffocates life and is the mother of cupidity?"[210] Augustine: "Whoever wishes to seek salvation without the Savior, and thinks he can be prudent without true wisdom, is not healthy but sick, not prudent but stupid, and struggles assiduously to remain sick."[211] "Whoever grows in knowledge and does not grow

---

[207] Bonaventure has slightly adjusted *S. Gregorii Magni Registrvm Epistvlarvm Libri I-VII*, VII, epistola 7, edited by Dag Norberg, CCSL cxl, 455 (Turnhout: Brepols, 1982). See also *Moralia in Iob*, XXV, ch. 16, n. 35 (CCSL cxliii b, 1260); Morals, III.1, 126): "But it is certain that the deserts of rulers and people are so mutually connected, that frequently the conduct of the people is made worse from the fault of their pastors, and the conduct of the pastors is changed according to the deserts of their people."

[208] See Luke 12:49: "I have come to cast fire on the earth, and what will I except that it be kindled?"

[209] James 3:15.

[210] Bonaventure has modified Pseudo-Bernard, *Declarationes de colloquio Simonis cum Jesu*, Admonitio XXVII, nn. 32-33 (PL 184: 455D-456A).

[211] This citation represents Bonaventure's adaptation not of Augustine, but of Rabanus Maurus, *De magicis artibus* (PL 110: 1097AB).

in the good life, distances himself from God,"[212] says Alghazel. Therefore, if you desire to be wise "learn such wisdom on earth that you can take with you to heaven."[213] You should now study how to reach him, because once you have seen him you will have learned everything. This is the true eternal truth "without which everything wise seems foolish, and even if you know only the eternal truth, you will have perfect knowledge."[214]

6.   However, O soul, if perhaps you still love worldly riches, secular pomp, and carnal pleasures, and thus leave the world unwillingly, listen to this: "how transitory and how fragile are these things! Tell me, where are the kings, where are the princes, where are those who love all these things?"[215] I am afraid that many of them *have been cut down and have gone down into the nether world.*[216] *What did their pride avail them? What advantage has the boasting of riches brought them?*[217] Whoever loves the world more than God, the world rather than the cloister, gluttony rather than abstinence, carnal pleasure rather than continence follows the devil and goes down with him to eternal torment. Augustine: "Those who

---

[212] QuarEd cite (p. 46 n. 9) Alghazel, *Philosophia,* II, tr. 5, ch. 5 (Venice, 1506). Alghazel (d. 1111) is discussing the unhappiness of the damned soul: "Therefore, the law says that there is a greater punishment on the day of judgment for those persons who, although they were wise, lived wretchedly. He also says that the person who grows in knowledge, but does not grow in leading a good life will be separated from God."

[213] Bonaventure has adapted Jerome, *Epistola* 53, n. 9 (PL 22: 549).

[214] Bonaventure has adapted Gregory, *Dialogorum*, IV, ch. 33 (PL 77:376B); translated by Odo Zimmerman, "Dialogues," in FC 39 (NY: The Fathers of the Church Inc., 1959), 230.

[215] Bonaventure has modified Pseudo-Anselm, *Exhortatio ad contemptum temporalium* (PL 158: 684D).

[216] Bar 3:19.

[217] See Wis 5:8.

flourish in earthly happiness, lose the virtue [power] of
God.... They flourish for awhile but perish eternally; they
flourish with prosperity that deceives and perish in true
torments."[218] Again Augustine comments: "If in this world
the possession of something delights us, then with alert
minds let us possess God who possesses all things, and
then in [God] we will have everything we desire in happy
and holy fashion."[219]

7. However, O soul, you may still find that you object to
all of the aforesaid by saying: "I despise the world, but
I cannot bring myself to abandon my friends, parents,
and acquaintances." – This is a frivolous objection, my
soul. Listen to Bernard: *"This saying is trustworthy and
deserves full acceptance.*[220] If it is impious to despise
father or mother, it is most pious to do so for the sake of
Christ."[221] "O heartless father, O cruel mother.... They are
not parents but murderers ... who prefer that you perish
with them rather than reign without them."[222] Jerome
observes:

> Even though she has thinning hair and even if she
> should open her blouse to show you the breasts
> with which she had nursed you, even though your
> father be lying on the threshold, having forsaken

---

[218] Bonaventure has adapted *Enarratio in Psalmum LIII*, n. 9
(CCSL xxxix, 653).

[219] See Pseudo-Augustine, *De salutaribus documentis*, ch. 10 (PL
40: 1050). Bonaventure's citation is almost verbatim.

[220] 1 Tim 1:15.

[221] Bonaventure has modified Bernard, *Epistola* 104, n. 3 (SBOp
7: 263).

[222] Bonaventure has adapted Bernard, *Epistola* 111, n. 2 (SBOp
7: 284).

mother and stepped on father, sally forth with dry eyes and soar up to the standard of the cross. It is actually a type of piety to be cruel in such matters.[223]

And Chrysostom: "Do you not realize, O soul, that he who has Jesus, has father, has mother, has every friend? Why do you follow the dead? Follow the living and *let the dead bury their dead.*"[224]

§ II: The Reason why many Earthly People are Blinded

8. *Soul.* I already realize from your words and from much experience that "the world of itself is falling apart; but, it flourishes in the hearts of many ... who love the bitterness of the world, who follow the fugitive, and embrace the fallen one."[225] Tell me: what is the reason for such blindness?

Innermost Self. O soul, do you not realize how you were created in such a delicate and noble way by your Spouse, the author of all things, such that you cannot be without [God's] love? Jerome: "It is difficult for the human soul not to love ... for it is inevitable that our mind be drawn to some desirable thing."[226] Hence, "it is

---

[223] Bonaventure has adapted *Epistola* 14, n. 2 (PL 22: 348).

[224] QuarEd refer (p. 47, n. 5) to *Homilia* 18 (Venice: n.p., 1583), tome II, f. 403, col 4. Matt 8:22 occurs at the end of this citation.

[225] This is an adaptation of *Homilia* 28, n. 3 of GGHG (CCSL cxli, 242-43).

[226] Bonaventure has modified *Epistola* 22, n. 17 (PL 22: 405).

inevitable," according to Bernard, "that we delight either in the highest or in the lowest."[227] Therefore, according to Gregory in his *Morals*:

> There are some who neglect their lives while desiring transitory things; nor do they understand eternal things, or if they do, they despise them; they sense no pain when they are wounded.... And so it is that, though miserable, they think all is well ... they love exile as if it were their homeland and they exult in their blindness ... as if they were in the brightness of light! The mentality of the elect, on the other hand, is such that they regard all transitory things as nothing, and seek that for which they were created. Since nothing other than God can satisfy their affections ... they find peace only in the contemplation of their Creator; they [keenly] desire to be in the company of the heavenly citizens, and even while living ... in this world strive to rise above the world.[228]

Likewise, Gregory *On Ezechiel*:

> For those who have had no experience of the sweetness of heavenly things, it seems comforting for them to be involved in worldly matters; because, the less the human mind understands

---

[227] Bonaventure has adapted Bernard, *Sermo 5 in Ascensione Domini*, n. 8 (SBOp 5:155): "Holy delight shies away from a soul preoccupied with worldly desires. There can be no commingling of true with false delights, of eternal with transient, of spiritual with sensual, of the highest with the lowest. You cannot at the same time relish things above and things that are upon the earth (Col 3:2)." See also "Fifth Sermon for the Feast of the Ascension" (SBSermons, II, 276-77).

[228] Bonaventure has modified *Moralia in Iob*, I, ch. 25, n. 34 (CCSL cxliii, 43-44); *Morals*, I, 50-51.

what is eternal, the more comfort it finds in temporal things. But once someone has tasted the sweetness of heavenly rewards with the "tongue" of his heart ... the more does he comprehend the sweetness that is within and the more what lies outside turns into bitterness.[229]

9. *SOUL.* Please do not put off teaching me about worldly and celestial joy, so that knowing more truly the nature of both, I might more perfectly despise the one and strive more studiously to attain the other. Because, I believe that, just as the good is not loved unless it is known,[230] so too evil is not avoided unless it likewise is known.

INNERMOST SELF. O soul, in my view, worldly joy – if indeed it can be called joy rather than an unknown scourge – is never perfectly known unless it is perfectly despised. Hence, as has been handed down to us by those who perfectly despised the world, earthly joy is especially held to be contemptible for five reasons. First, because its object is vile. What actually is the joy of the world? Augustine responds: "O unpunished wickedness,"[231] namely illicit sex, drunkenness, constant banqueting, preoccupation with silly vanities; and yet these people suffer nothing injurious in this life. Such wicked people think they are secure in their pleasures since they are not

---

[229] Bonaventure has modified *Homilia* 10, n. 43 (CCSL cxlii, 165-66).

[230] See Augustine, *De Trinitate*, X, ch. 1, n. 1, CCSL l, 311: "And first since no one can fully love something that is entirely unknown...." See also *The Trinity* (Hill, 286). Cf. Jerome, *Commentarius in Ecclesiasten* 1:17 (CCSL lxxii, 261): "Contraries are known by contraries. And wisdom is the first to have lacked foolishness. But a person cannot lack foolishness unless he had first known it."

[231] See *Sermo* 171, ch. 4, n. 4 (PL 38: 935); *Sermons* (Hill, III/5, 249): "what the world relishes is villainy that no one punishes."

punished for their wickedness; they are totally oblivious [of the fact].

Augustine says: "there is nothing sadder than the happiness of sinners, whereby their sinful infirmity is nourished and their bad will ... strengthened."[232]

– Second, there is impurity in the subject. The soul deformed by sins is the subject of earthly joy, which *is glad when it has done evil and rejoices in most wicked things.*[233] Hence Jerome puts it well when he says: "Laughing and rejoicing with this world does not emanate from a sane person, but from one mentally ill,"[234] because the clean heart is not happy and joyful with this unclean world, but with God and in God. The joy is brief.

– Third, of itself it is ephemeral, because *the joy of the hypocrite is but for a moment.*[235] Augustine *On John*: "The joy of the world is vanity, with great desire its advent is hoped for, but when it comes it eludes our grasp."[236] O soul, "how brief, how fragile, how fleeting is worldly joy."[237] *For the days of human beings are short,* says Job.[238]

---

[232] Bonaventure has adapted *Epistola* 138, ch. 2, n. 14 (PL 33: 531).

[233] See Prov 2:14: "who are glad when they have done evil and rejoice in most wicked things." Cf. Bernard, *De Gratia et libero arbitrio*, ch. V, n. 14 (SBOp 3: 176) where Bernard interprets Prov 2:14: "This describes what they do and how they do it ... by laughing fanatically." See also translation by Daniel O'Donovan, *On Grace and Free Choice*, in *The Works of Bernard of Clairvaux*, vol. 7, CFS 13 (Kalamazoo, MI: Cistercian Fathers Publications, 1977), 70.

[234] QuarEd refer (p. 48, n. 3) generally to Jerome's interpretation of 2:2 and 4:13-16 in his *Commentarius in Ecclesiasten*. They summarize Jerome's exposition: "Here their joy is called madness and foolishness." See CCSL lxxii, 262-63 and 288-90.

[235] Job 20:5.

[236] Augustine, *Tractate* 7, n. 1 (CCSL xxxvi, 67). Bonaventure's citation is almost verbatim.

[237] Bonaventure has modified Pseudo-Anselm, *Exhortatio ad contemptum temporalium* (PL 158: 684D).

[238] Job 14:5.

– Fourth, it ends in sadness, because *they live out their days in prosperity and in an instant go down to the nether world*.[239] *For when joy ends, mourning follows*.[240] Moreover, O soul, if you wish to be discerning, such joy is frequently mixed with sadness, since it is always necessary that *a troubled conscience forecasts grievous things*.[241]

– Fifth, it results in great misery, because it is an impediment to spiritual joy. Therefore, O soul, you should realize how miserable is this world, and those who cling to it are the most miserable of all. Worldly joy always excludes a man [or a woman] from the blessed life. Bernard: "O how vile and useless is earthly consolation! And it ought to be feared even more, because it is an impediment to true and saintly consolation."[242] "Therefore, O my soul, refrain from delighting in the world if you wish to be consoled by [clinging to] the memory of God."[243] And Augustine: "For you all creatures ought to be worthless, so that only your Creator might be sweetness for your heart."[244]

10. *Soul*. I already despise the world, its false joy; I recognize the true sadness, the false sweetness, and the true bitterness of the world. On this account, following

---

[239] See Job 21:13.

[240] Prov 14:13.

[241] Bonaventure has adapted Wis 17:10.

[242] Bonaventure has modified Bernard's *Sermo 4 in Vigilia Nativitatis Domini*, n. 1 (SBOp 4: 220); "Fourth Sermon for Christmas Eve" (SBSermons, I, 343).

[243] Bonaventure has adapted Bernard's *Sermo 4, Psalm XC* "Qui Habitat," n. 2 (SBOp 4: 398); "Fourth Sermon on Psalm XC" (SBSermons, I, 156).

[244] This citation is not found verbatim in Augustine. There are two parallels. Cf., *Enarratio II, Sermo 3*, n. 8 (CCSL xxxviii, 218): "Let everything except God be considered worthless." See also Pseudo-Augustine, *Liber Soliloquiorum animae ad Deum*, ch. 22 (PL 40: 882): "I ask that all things become bitter to me, so that you alone may appear to be sweet to my soul." Bonaventure quotes this same passage from Augustine in chapter II, n. 1 above, p. 271.

your advice, it is only right that I condemn all these things. But since, as you say, I cannot survive without love, tell me what I ought to do. Where should I turn? Where might I find the love I need.

INNERMOST SELF. O soul, if you wish to know yourself perfectly,[245] you will despise the world and everything in it. If you understand that you are made for heaven, you will doubtless find terrestrial consolation abhorrent. "You should blush to wallow in filth, when you are made for heaven."[246] You should be ashamed to delight in the lowly, when you can be satisfied only with the sublime. You are, as I believe, of a heavenly nature. And, so it seems to me, you ought to naturally desire and seek after celestial consolation, to the extent that carnal folly allows it. Bernard: "O how sweet and delightful it would be to live according to nature, with the added seasonings of divine love, if carnal folly would allow it; once healed, nature would be rightly disposed."[247]

11. SOUL. And just what does it mean *to live according to nature*?

INNERMOST SELF. Strictly speaking, to live according to nature is to live a celestial life on earth, "to return from

---

[245] See *On the Perfection of Life*, ch. I.

[246] Bonaventure has adapted *Sermo 24,* in *Cantica* n. 6 (SBOp 1: 158); *On the Song of Songs* (Walsh II, p. 47). Cf. *Soliloquium*, ch. I, n. 19 above p. 245, where Bonaventure cites this same passage.

[247] Bonaventure has adapted Pseudo-Bernard's *Epistola ad Fratres de Monte Dei*, I, ch. 8, n. 23 (PL 184: 323A). Actually this letter is by William of St. Thierry in *Opera Didactica et Spiritualia*, Stanislaus Ceglar and Paul Verdeyen, eds. (Turnhout: Brepols, 2003), CCCM lxxxviii n. 89, 246-47; translation by Theodore Berkeley, *The Golden Epistle, A Letter to the Brethren at Mont Dieu*, CFS 12 (Kalamazoo, MI: Cistercian Publications, 1976), 17. The text was attributed commonly to Bernard in medieval times.

exterior things to the interior, to rise from the inferior to the superior."[248] And "to do everything according to what is most noble, to what is excellent in humans, such is according to our intellects," as the Philosopher says in Book X of the *Ethics*. [249]

12. *SOUL*. Is it possible for man here on earth and in this *vale of tears*[250] to lead a celestial life?

INNERMOST SELF. O soul, if you doubt and are puzzled by my words as those of a sinful man, then listen to Augustine, listen to the apostle Paul. Here is what Augustine says: "Once we grasp something eternal by knowledge and love, our minds are no longer in this world."[251] Hence the Apostle says: *Our citizenship is in heaven*.[252] O soul, I believe that you are situated "where you love and not where you live;"[253] because "whatever you love, by the power of this love, you are transformed

---

[248] This is a verbatim citation from Alcher of Clairvaux, *De spiritu et animae*, ch. 14 (PL 40: 790).

[249] See Aristotle, *Nicomachean Ethics*, book X, n. 7, in *The Complete Works of Aristotle*, vol. II (Barnes: n.p., 1861): "If reason is divine, then, in comparison with man, the life according to it is divine in comparison with human life. But we must not follow those who advise us, being men, to think of human things, and, being mortal, of mortal things, but must, so far as we can, make ourselves immortal, and strain every nerve to live in accordance with the best thing in us; for even if it be small in bulk, much more does it in power and worth surpass everything."

[250] Ps 83:7.

[251] This is an adaptation of *De Trinitate*, IV, ch. 20, n. 28 (CCSL 1, 199); *The Trinity* (Hill, 174). Cf. also Bonaventure, I *Sent.*, I, d. 15. p. 2. dub. 5 (I:275).

[252] Phil 3:20.

[253] In his *De Praecepto et Dispensatione*, ch. XX, n. 60, Bernard interprets Phil 3:20 and Rom 8:24: "For our spirit is not more present where it lives, but where it loves." (SBOp 3: 292); translation by Conrad Greenia, "On Precept and Dispensation," in *Works of Bernard of Clairvaux*, vol. 1 (Spencer, MA: Cistercian Publications, 1970), 149.

into its likeness."[254] If therefore you contemplate and love the celestial, how is it that you do not yet dwell in heaven, when in life you already imitate the celestial spirits?

§ III: ON DIVINE CONSOLATION
AND THE DISPOSITION REQUIRED TO OBTAIN IT

13. *SOUL.* Woe is me so unhappy and miserable! I sense that I have been miserably blinded for a long time, while I was wandering so long in temporal and earthly things, while I bound myself by love to what was vile and mundane, from which I experienced little consolation, much bitterness and desolation, meager and precious little joy, frequently varied and heavy sadness of heart. Please tell me, what is heavenly consolation and how can I attain it in this *vale of tears*[255] and misery?

INNERMOST SELF. O soul, according to Bernard:

This consolation is nothing other than a certain grace of devotion stemming from a hope for pardon and a certain small taste of the good, but with the sweetest of pleasures whereby the benign God re-creates the afflicted soul, so that the soul is invited to seek God and to be intensely inflamed with divine love.[256]

---

[254] See Pseudo-Bernard, *Tractatus de caritate,* ch. 18, n. 61 (PL 184: 614C) for a parallel: "The person who loves God ... transubstantiates himself to his beloved."

[255] See Ps 83:7.

[256] This is an adaptation of Bernard, *Sermo I in festo omnium Sanctorum*, n. 10 (SBOp 5: 335-36); "First Sermon for the Feast of all the Saints" (SBSermons, III, 343).

And from Hugh:

> O soul, what do you think is so sweet and consoling,
> whereby in recalling their loved one, devout souls
> are touched and infused with sweetness, such
> that they already begin to be transported outside
> themselves? Consciousness is exhilarated, the
> memory of all sorrows vanishes, the mind rejoices,
> the intellect made brilliant, the heart illuminated,
> the affections gladdened. They do not know where
> they are, they cling to something within, not
> knowing what it is, and yet they desire to hold
> onto it with all their powers. The mind in some
> way pleasantly struggles so as not to lose this,
> so that it may find in it the culmination of all its
> desires.[257]

O soul, certainly this is divine consolation.

14. *SOUL*. Innermost Self, who will help me to bring this
sweet and unexperienced consolation into my heart,
so that I might forget my evil deeds, despise worldly
consolation, and happily *alienate myself from myself?*

INNERMOST SELF. O soul, what you desire is great, you
ask for a priceless gift. Hence, so I believe, it cannot be
obtained by human effort or promoted by human merit;
but with humble supplications from those worthily
disposed, it can be asked of God [who bestows it] only
from the condescension of divine piety. *Because all gold,
compared to her* [wisdom] *is a little sand, and silver in
comparison to her is regarded as nothing.*[258]

---

[257] This is a modification of Hugh of St. Victor, *Soliloquium de
arrha animae* (PL 176: 970AB); *Earnest Money* (Herbert, 35).

[258] See Wis 7:9: *Because all gold, in comparison to her, is a little
sand, and before her silver is esteemed as mire.*

15. *SOUL.* Innermost Self, tell me what sort of disposition is required so that the affections of one praying might be properly disposed?

INNERMOST SELF. Of such matters much could be said by those with much experience. However, since I consider myself inexperienced, I blush to say much. I am afraid that someone will say to me: "Why do you speak of what you have not tasted? As one unworthy, why do you praise that of which you are ignorant?"

SOUL. Do not fear to propose with reverence and humility what you have heard and read. Many people make useful proposals of great and difficult things, which they have learned, not from their own experience, but from the knowledge of others.

INNERMOST SELF. Well then, with some audacity I will speak, since charity serves to help those powers to which experience is denied. Hence, as I feel, so will I speak. Always with respect to someone with better judgment, I think that if you wish to prepare yourself to taste this heavenly sweetness, you must be *purified*, you must *practice,* and then *be raised up.*

16. First, I say, the mind must be *purified of sins, of inordinate affections, of temporal consolation and inordinate love of creatures.* Because, as Bernard says:

> Everyone errs who believes that he can mix celestial sweetness with these ashes, divine balsam with this poisonous joy, [who thinks he

can mix] the charisms of the Holy Spirit with the allurements of this world.[259]

But, after the soul has been purged and purified from such things, purged by tears, purified by sorrowful groanings, then the soul can be consoled and refreshed by the aroma of heavenly sweetness.

Second, the mind must be *exercised in doing good deeds and putting up with evil,* because those who are imbued with the love of truth will never be deterred from the exercise of good works or broken by putting up with evil. "Truly," as blessed Benedict says, "although in the beginning *the path which leads to life is narrow,*[260] with the passing of time it is broadened by the sweetness of ineffable pleasure."[261] O what blessed consolation infused in those who labor for Christ!

The third point, whereby the soul is inebriated with this sweetness, is *the raising up of the mind,* [which occurs] when the mind is happily separated from earthly matters and in some marvelous way is lifted above itself, above the world, and above every creature, so that the soul can say: The king *has brought me into his chambers.*[262] This is the wine cellar into which the soul is led, where it drinks of well-aged wine, inestimably sweetened with the divinity, [where it drinks] of the whitest milk of uncontaminated

---

[259] This is an adaptation of *Sermo 5 in Ascensione Domini,* n. 13 (SBOp 5: 158); "Fifth Sermon on the Feast of the Ascension" (SBSermons, II, 282).

[260] Matt 7:14.

[261] This is an adaptation of the Prologue to the Rule of St. Benedict, nn. 48-49. See *The Rule of Saint Benedict: Latin and English,* trans. Luke Dysinger (Trabuco Canyon, CA: Source Books, 1997), 8-10.

[262] See Cant 2:4: "He has brought me into the wine cellar."

humanity.[263] O soul, here "friends drink," but "the dearest ones are inebriated."[264] O happy inebriation, which is followed by a chaste and holy sobriety of mind and body. Like a [person] who is drunk, the soul is made joyful and happy in adversity, strong and secure in time of danger, prudent and discrete in prosperity, liberal and pious in condoning injuries, and finally quiet and somnolent in the repose of the divine embrace, where the left arm of the Spouse upholds the head in friendly fashion and the right enfolds the beloved in [loving] familiarity.[265]

17. *Soul.* I confess with humility and reverence that it has at times happened to me, although all too rarely, that with great violence during the beginning of my conversion, I was able to tear my mind away from earthly things, and with great effort to raise myself to the contemplation of the celestial. I entered with fear, looked about in shame, gazed at the choirs of angels, the palaces and joys of the patriarchs and prophets; I looked at the tabernacles of the apostles, the banquets of the martyrs, the *rewards given* the confessors and virgins; and I begged for an alms of some [small] consolation from each of them. I hoped for the scraps[266] from the table of the lords, but got none. But what is sad to hear, by all of them I was quickly repulsed as a pilgrim and stranger. What good did such a fatiguing

---

[263] See Augustine's *Enarratio II, Sermo* I, n. 9, in *Psalmum* XXX (CCSL xxxviii, 197); trans. Dame Hebgin and Dame Felicitas Corrigan, *St. Augustine On the Psalms*, vol. II, ACW 30 (Westminster, MD: The Newman Press, 1961), 201: "The Lord made his wisdom like milk for us."

[264] See Cant 5:1: "Eat, my friends, drink and be inebriated, my dearest ones."

[265] See Cant 2:6 and 8:3: *His left hand is under my head, and his right hand will embrace me.* Cf. Bernard, *On Loving God*, ch. III, n. 10 (Evans, 181-82).

[266] See Matt 15:27: *But she said: Yes, Lord, for even the dogs eat of the scraps that fall from their master's table.*

elevation of the mind do for me, when there followed no consolation?

INNERMOST SELF. O soul, such a devastating repulse did not happen without a reason. I believe that reason to be because you wanted to partake of consolation before you partook of suffering;[267] you wanted to participate in the rewards before you were an imitator of [their] virtues. First concern yourself with being a companion to the angels by purity and innocence, to the patriarchs and prophets by humility and the confidence of faith; strive to be the daughter of the apostles and martyrs by charity and patience, to the confessors and virgins by piety and continence. Then in this [life of] exile, together with the prodigal son,[268] you can confidently obtain the alms of the pious father.

18. *SOUL*: I now already know and realize how vain and insipid are all such transitory things. Because of this I despise the world, I count for little the consolation of earthly things, I flee and spurn worldly joy as a deadly poison; I lament the past as dead, I wash and purge my miserable mind by groans and tears. And if at times amidst tears and groans, I sense the aroma of divine sweetness – however so little – still as one unhappy, hungry, and thirsty I do not taste the bread of sons or the wine of friends. Bernard:

---

[267] See 2 Cor 1:7: ... *knowing that as you are partakers of the sufferings, so will you also be of the consolation.*

[268] See Luke 15:11-32.

O Lord, my God, my heart has not yet attained to abundance of the sweetness you have hidden for those *who fear you.*[269] I am buoyed up by his aroma which for me surpasses the aroma of balsam and all sorts of odiferous scents.[270]

O Lord God, if the aroma is so wonderful, imagine how savory is the taste of your sweetness! And, from Augustine, "O that you would enter into my heart and inebriate it ... that I might embrace you, the sole good."[271]

INNERMOST SELF.   O devout soul, if I might speak, begging your pardon, you are overly anxious and yet not presumptuous. Assess your powers, consider your merits, discuss your virtues. Then, if it pleases you, you might prefer to run humbly with the youth in the odor of divine balm,[272] rather than ask presumptuously for something beyond your merits.

19.   *SOUL.* How hard and burdensome at times is the consoler of my misery; how niggardly – if I may so speak – is the dispenser of divine goodness! I speak boldly and will not keep silent. The aroma is not enough for me, a little taste does not satisfy me but only upsets me; my affections yearn for and require inebriation. For I know what he says: *Drink, friends. Be inebriated, most beloved.*[273] If the unworthiness of the petitioner is depressing, the piety of the one promising raises hope. How can I doubt

---

[269] See Ps 30:20.

[270] This quotation is not from Bernard, but is an adaptation of Anselm, *Meditatio* 13 (PL 158: 773C).

[271] This is a modification of *Confessionum*, I, ch. 5, n. 5 (CCSL xxvii, 3); see also Boulding, *The Confessions*, 5.

[272] See Cant 1:2-3: "Therefore, young maidens have loved you.... We will run after you in the odor of your balm."

[273] Cant 5:1. Cf. Bernard, *Sermo* 31 in *Cantica*, n. 7, (SBOp 1: 223-34); *On the Song of Songs* (Walsh II, 130).

that he is glad to bestow his goods [on me], who did not disdain to suffer for my sins? You must be aware that you taught many about the piety of God, that you learned from blessed Augustine: "Shame on human laziness! God is willing to give more than anyone dares to ask."[274] Again in his *True Religion*: "*God gave us the pledge of the Spirit,*[275] whereby we might sense his sweetness and taste of the font of life, by which with sober inebriation we are irrigated like a *tree planted near running water.*"[276] Chrysostom:

> Nothing more clearly demonstrates the omnipotence of God than the fact that he makes omnipotent those who hope in him. For, because of the hope in God supporting the mind ... no fraud, no allurement can either throw down [the one] who is standing or overcome [the one] who is dominant.[277]

> And so, now let human despair be ashamed, and cursed be the trembling of a timidity which would believe that the rich One, and he who is greatly

---

[274] This is an adaptation of *Sermo* 105, ch. 1, n. 1 (PL 39: 619); see *Sermons,* WSA III/4, Edmund Hill, trans. (Brooklyn, NY: New City Press, 1992, 88). Cf. also Alcher of Clairvaux, *De spiritu et anima,* ch. 6 (PL 40: 784).

[275] See 2 Cor 5:5. Ps 1:3 occurs at the end of the citation.

[276] Cf. *De Vera Religione,* ch. XII, n. 24-25, in *Sancti Avrelii Avgvstini De Doctrina Christiana, De Vera Religione,* Joseph Martin and K.-D. Daur, eds. CCSL xxxii (Turnhout: Brepols, 1962), 202-203. This is actually an adaptation of Augustine's *De agone christiano,* ch. IX, n. 10, in *Sancti Aureli Augustini De Fide et Symbolo de Fide et Operibvs de Agone Christiano ...,* Joseph Zycha, ed., CSEL xxxxi, 112 (Prague: Tempsky, 1890).

[277] In reality this is a modification of Bernard, *Sermo 85* in *Cantica,* n. 5, (SBOp 2: 310-11); *On the Song of Songs* (Walsh IV, 201).

liberal *to all who call upon him*,[278] would deny
his gifts to those who place perfect hope in him.
Did not the eternal Father, *with whom there is no
alteration*,[279] send his Son solely out of his immense
liberality, with whom he entrusted all that he had,
all that he could do, all that he was? If indeed his
liberality had diminished his infinite goodness,
perhaps then our infirmity might reasonably be
fearful. But, because "of himself [God] is good
and not from some incidental gift,"[280] God] is not
diminished by communicating his goodness, nor
is he enhanced by the addition of some outside
goodness.

INNERMOST SELF. O soul, great is your faith; you are
very strong in hope and confidence. And, although a hope
which proceeds from one's own merits and confidence in
divine clemency is meritorious and holy, nevertheless
I advise you, before you rise above yourself to seek
[spiritual] inebriation, you first descend within yourself
in salutary reflection, so that you may learn to have a
reverent fear of your Spouse, before you begin to enter his
secret chamber. You ought to fear him not only when he is
angry, but also when he is most graciously flattered.

---

[278] Rom 10:12.

[279] James 1:17.

[280] Cf. *Homilia* 14, n. 1 in GGHG (PL 76: 1127C): "For behold, he
who is not from some incidental gift, but is essentially good says: 'I am
the good shepherd.'"

CHAPTER III

The Soul Turned Toward Inferior Things

How the soul through mental discipline must turn the rays of contemplation to inferior things, so that it may understand the inevitable necessity of human death, the ineffable rightness of the last judgment, and the intolerable harshness of the pains of hell.

1. *SOUL.* Briefly tell me, just what are *these inferior matters* to which I must turn my reflections? I wish to ascend quickly to be inebriated with divine consolation; I don't wish to linger long with inferior things. I want to enter *the lovely tabernacles of the Lord* and yearn with all my heart to dwell *in the courts of the Lord.*[281]

INNERMOST SELF. O soul, these indeed are inferior, so that you may turn from them to see and bemoan the *inevitable necessity of death*, be fearful of *the ineffable rightness of divine judgment*, and tremble at *the intolerable harshness of the pains of hell.*

§ I: FIRST, REGARDING THE INEVITABLE NECESSITY OF DEATH

2. Frequently consider and diligently reflect and mull over the fact that *death cannot be avoided*, that *the hour of death cannot be ascertained*, and that *the time preordained by God cannot be changed.*

Isidore says:

In human affairs what is more certain than death? What more uncertain than the hour of death? It has no pity on destitution, no respect for power,

---

[281] See Ps 83:2-3.

it is not impressed with mores or family origins, it spares neither the young nor the aged; it is at the threshold for the elderly; it lies in ambush for youths.[282]

Soul. I understand that our life is nothing more than a journey towards death.[283] Why are temporal things so loved when the time of their possession is so uncertain?

> Why do we desire this life for so long, wherein the more we live, the more we sin; the longer the life, the more numerous the failings? Daily the evils grow and the good things diminish... .Who can weigh how many evils we perpetrate during the ticking-seconds of time and how many good things we neglect?... It is a serious fault when we neither do good nor think good, but allow our minds to wander about among the inane and useless.[284]

3. *Innermost Self.* Gregory in his *Morals:* "O soul, carnal minds love temporal things because they do not realize at all that we must flee the life of the flesh. If only they would look to its fleeting nature, they would certainly not love such short-lived prosperity."[285] Or again: "My life is

---

[282] Rather this is a modification of Bernard, *Ad Clericos de Conversione,* ch. VIII, n. 16 (SBOp 4: 90); "On Conversion" (Saïd, 50).

[283] Cf. Augustine, *De Civitate Dei,* XIII, ch. 10 (CCSL xlviii, 391-92); *The City of God* (Dods, 419). Cf. also Bernard, *Sermo 17 in Psalmum Qui Habitat,* n. 1, (SBOp 4: 486): "We say that a human being is dying when he most certainly is approaching death. But what are we doing from that first moment when we begin to live except to draw near to death and begin to die?" See also "Seventeenth Sermon on Psalm XC" [*Qui Habitat*] (SBSermons, I, 298).

[284] See Pseudo-Bernard, *Meditationes piissimae,* ch. II, n. 5-6 (PL 184: 488B-489B). The citation is largely verbatim.

[285] This is an adaptation of *Moralia in Iob,* VIII, ch. 10, n. 25 (CCSL cxliii, 399); Morals, I, 433.

like that of the navigator, so that whether I am asleep or awake, I always hasten towards death."[286]

> O present life, how many you have deceived....
> While you flee, you are nothing; while you see, you
> are a shadow; when elated, you are but smoke; you
> are sweet to the stupid, bitter to the wise. They
> who love you, do not know you; those who flee
> you, understand you.... To some you promise to be
> long so that you may deceive them; to others [you
> promise] to be brief so as to induce despair.[287]

The author of the book *On Spirit and Soul*: "We ought to exercise our mind continually in meditation; we ought to reflect on our miseries.... We entered this life in pain, we live in labor, and we will leave it in ... fear."[288]

And Bernard says:

> The longer we stay in this region of shadowy death,
> in the infirmities of the body, in the conflicts and
> places of temptation, if we think about it diligently,
> we understand that we labor in this threefold
> hardship: we are easily seduced, weak in resisting,
> and frail in doing.[289]

4. *SOUL.* I now see how useless it is to live in time unless we hasten to the rewards promised us whereby we live in

---

[286] This is an abbreviation of Gregory's *Register Epistularum*, VII, n. 26, (CCSL cxl, 482).

[287] This is a modification of Pseudo-Augustine, *Sermo* 49, *Sermones ad fratres in eremo* (PL 40: 1332).

[288] This is an adaptation of Alcher of Clairvaux, *De spiritu et anima*, ch. 49 (PL 40: 816).

[289] This is a modification of Bernard, *Sermo 7 de Adventu Domini*, n. 1 (SBOp 4: 196); "Seventh Sermon for Advent" (SBSermons, I, 51-52).

eternity. Because, even though someone may be allowed to live well, nevertheless, to no one is it promised that he should live a long time. Bernard: "O life secure, where conscience pure! ... Where death is awaited without fear, where with sweetness hoped to be and with devotion greeted!"[290]

INNERMOST SELF. O soul, if you wish to understand this, listen to my counsel, and Bernard: "in this life, as long as it lasts, compare it to that life which lasts forever. While you live in the flesh, [you should] die to the world, so that after the death of the flesh you may begin to live for God."[291] You must understand that "no one joyfully and happily anticipates death, unless while he lives he prepares for it with good works."[292] Listen to what Seneca has to say: "The foolish one, namely the sinner and criminal, has already begun to die, but the wise and virtuous conquers death by dying."[293]

SOUL. I see that the death of good people is blest and that the death of sinners is unhappy and miserable.[294]

---

[290] See Bernard, *De Laude Novae Militiae*, ch. I, n. 2 (SBOp 3: 215); translation by Conrad Greenia, "In Praise of the New Knighthood," in *The Works of Bernard of Clairvaux*, vol. 7, CFS 19 (Kalamazoo, MI: Cistercian Publications Inc., 1977), 130. The citation is virtually verbatim.

[291] See *Epistola* 105 (SBOp 7: 264). The citation is virtually verbatim.

[292] See Seneca's *Epistola* 30, n. 12, in *Ad Lucilium Epistulae Morales*, 219: "No one welcomes it (death) cheerfully, except the man who has long since composed himself for death."

[293] QuarEd admit (p. 53, n.6) that they have been unable to find this citation in Seneca and give some possible parallels. Cf. *Epistola* 13, n. 15-16; *Epistola* 23, n. 8; *Epistola* 30, n. 6-13; *Epistola* 70, n. 3-4.

[294] See Ps 115:15 and Ps 33:22.

INNERMOST SELF. O soul, according to Bernard:

The death of a just man is good because [it brings] peace, it is better because of a newness [of life], it is best because of security. On the other hand, *the death of sinners worst*[295] and [their death] is truly the worst. It is bad in the loss of the world, worse in the separation from the flesh, and worst in the twofold pain[296] of worms and fire.[297]

And worst of all is the privation of contemplating God.

§ II: ON THE INEFFABLE RIGHTNESS OF THE LAST JUDGMENT

5. *SOUL.* You have said enough about death; now tell me about the last judgment.

INNERMOST SELF. O soul, I will do what you are urging, but I ask that you listen with patience. You should know that while it is terrifying to meditate on death, in my opinion, it is no less frightening to think about the last judgment, because when that time comes no one will be able to deceive wisdom, turn away justice, beg for clemency, or stave off the sentence of just retribution. Therefore, consider, my soul, with fear what it will be like for you on the last day, when your conscience will speak against you concerning your thoughts,[298] when [the very] elements[299] accuse you concerning all your actions, when

---

[295] Ps 33:22.

[296] See Jer 17:18 and Isa 66:24.

[297] This is an almost verbatim citation from *Epistola* 105 (SBOp 7: 265).

[298] See Rom 2:15-16.

[299] Earth, water, air, and fire: the ultimate constituents of nature according to the ancient and medieval philosophers of nature.

the cross will be borne in testimony against you, when
the blows will cry out against you, the wounds will be
allegations, the nails will speak and the wounds make
complaints against you.[300] From Bernard:

> O how hemmed in we are! On the one side sins
> accuse us, on the other terrifying justice, within is
> our burning conscience, below the horrifying chaos
> of hell, above the angry Judge of just judgment,
> outside the world afire, within the fearful justice
> of the judge. *And if the righteous one will barely
> be saved then, where will the godless and the
> sinner appear?*[301] Where can one turn? To hide is
> impossible, to show oneself intolerable.[302]

– Anselm in his *Meditations*: "O sinful soul, useless
and dry wood, destined to eternal fires, what will you say
on that day when you will be required to give an account
– to the very blink of an eye – of how you have spent all the
time allotted to you?"[303] What then, O my soul, what then
concerning your vain and useless thoughts, your flighty,
jocular, and ridiculous words, your useless and fruitless
deeds? Ambrose, *On the Gospel of Luke*: "Woe is me if I
do not weep over my sins! Woe is me if I do not arise *at
midnight to confess to you!*[304]*... Even now the ax lies at
the root of the trees.*[305] He ought to bear fruit who [has

---

[300] The latter phrases obviously refer to the passion and death of
Christ.

[301] See 1 Peter 4:18: "And if the righteous one is barely saved,
where will the godless and sinner appear?"

[302] This is an adaptation of Pseudo-Bernard, *Tractatus de interiori domo,* ch. 22, n. 46. (PL 184: 531D). This passage also occurs in
Anselm, *Meditatio* 1 (Schmitt III, 78-79).

[303] This is a modification of *Meditatio* 1 (Schmitt III, 77).

[304] See Ps 118:62.

[305] See Luke 3:9.

access to] grace, who needs to do penance."[306] O my soul: "Whether awake or asleep, the sound of that horrifying trumpet will always resound in your ears: 'Rise up, you dead, come to the judgment.'"[307] O soul, never banish this from your memory: *Go away, you accursed, into the eternal fire.*[308] *Come, you blessed, accept the kingdom.*[309] What can be said that is more lamentable and terrible than *Go away*? What can be more delightfully expressed than *Come*? Two words, one of which nothing more horrible, the other of which nothing more joyful can be heard! O soul, separate yourself now from the world, so that you can stay with Christ. Flee the world now, so that you can follow God. Depart now from the society and companionship of the depraved, so that you may be able to follow the hosts of the blessed.

§ III: ON THE INTOLERABLE HARSHNESS OF THE PAINS OF HELL

6. Having considered all these things, now turn the rays of your contemplation on the torments of the reprobate. See how they are of all kinds, how hard, how horrible, how intolerable they are. Bernard, [writes to] Eugene: "I

---

[306] This is a modification of *Sancti Ambrosii Mediolanensis Opera, Pars IV*, II, n. 76; *Expositio Evangelii secvndvm Lvcam: Fragmenta in Esaiam*, M. Adriaen, ed. (Turnhout: Brepols, 1967) CCSL xiv, 64.

[307] This is an adaptation of Jerome, *Epistola* 66, n. 10 (PL 22: 644-45). See also *Regula Monacharum*, XXX (PL 30: 417B): "Let that terrifying trumpet blast your ears: Rise up, you dead, come to the judgment."

[308] See Matt 25:41: *Depart from me, you accursed, into eternal fire.*

[309] See Matt 25:34: *Come, you blessed by my Father, take possession of the kingdom prepared for you from the foundation of the world.*

am in horror of the gnawing worm, the living death."[310] "O infernal region! How you are to be avoided.... There [we find] the burning fire, the numbing cold, the immortal worm, the intolerable stench, the blows of the hammer, palpable darkness, the confusion of sinners, the bonds of chains, the horrible faces of the devils."[311] Augustine: "Woe to them for whom the pain of worms will be prepared, the burning flames, thirst without something to drink, tears and gnashing of teeth, tears to the eyes ... where death is wished for but will not be given,"[312] where *there is no order, but everlasting horror dwells*.[313] "Can you imagine what lamentations, what sadness, what grief there will be when the wicked will be separated from the company of the just ... and handed over to the power of the devils, and *with them will go to eternal punishment?*"[314] In that place there will always be endless grief and groaning, far away from the joys of paradise ... never to have repose, but tormented for many thousands of years, never therefore to be freed. There the torturer and punished will never tire, there he who suffers will never die. There the fire consumes, but life always goes on; there old torments are borne so as to be always renewed.... And so without hope of pardon and mercy, they always live on, so as always to die; they will die never to be consumed.[315]

---

[310] See *De Consideratione*, V, ch. XII, n. 25 (SBOp 3: 488); *On Consideration* (Anderson and Kennan, 172). The citation is virtually verbatim.

[311] This is an adaptation of Bernard, *Sermo 42*, n. 6, *Sermones de diversis* (SBOp 6: 259).

[312] This is a modification of Pseudo-Augustine, *Liber de salutaribus documentis*, ch. 49 (PL 40: 1064-65).

[313] See Job 10:22: ... *and no order, but eternal horror dwells*.

[314] See Matt 25:46.

[315] Bonaventure has adapted Pseudo-Bernard, *Meditationes piissimae*, ch. III, n. 10 (PL 184: 491D-492A).

7. *SOUL*. Why, as you say, is death hoped for in hell and never comes? Why is there eternal punishment for [sins] committed in time?

INNERMOST SELF. "This is because life is offered them in this world and they do not want to accept it; and so in hell they will seek death and will not be able to find it."[316] Hence Gregory [says]: "The wicked would gladly live forever, so that they might always persist in sin.... However, the justice of the strict judge requires that they never be free from torment whose attitude in this life is such that they never wanted to be without sin."[317]

8. *SOUL*. "O death, how sweet you might have been for those for whom you were so bitter! They alone desire you who so vehemently abhorred you."[318] Anselm in his *Meditations*:

O loving Jesus, in your name grant me mercy; forget my provocative pride, look at this miserable one humbly invoking you.... Give benign recognition to what is yours, wipe away what is foreign. O Lord, have mercy on me while there is time for mercy, lest you damn me on the day of judgment.[319]

"It is true that my conscience [tells me] that I have merited damnation and my repentance is not sufficient

---

[316] See Augustine, *Sermo* 229, n. 4 (PL 39: 2167). The citation is virtually verbatim.

[317] This is a modification of Gregory, *Dialogues,* IV, ch. XLIV (PL 77: 404A); *Dialogues* (Zimmerman, 253).

[318] See Lothario dei Segni [Innocent III], *De Contemptu Mundi* III, ch. IX (PL 217: 741A); "The Misery of the Human Condition" (Howard, 106-08). The citation is virtually verbatim.

[319] This is a modification of *Meditatio* 1 (Schmitt III, 79).

for satisfaction, but it is nonetheless certain that your mercy overcomes every offense."[320]

> If God so acted regarding the haughty angel, what will become of me, earth and ashes? He became proud in the celestial palace, I [wallowing] in dung. Who does not believe that pride is more tolerable in a wealthy person than in a poor one? Woe is me! If pride is punished so harshly in a proud and powerful person, even though pride is always associated with the rich and powerful, how will it be judged in the miserable and poor person that I am?[321]

9. *INNERMOST SELF.* O soul, if the aforesaid seem to you to be terrible, listen to what is far more serious than the above. Chrysostom *On Matthew*: "Even if you threaten me with a thousand gehennas, I will still not consider them as worse than being banished and denied the happiness of the wonderful society of the Creator."[322] O soul, terrible indeed is gehenna, but more terrible still the face of the angry judge. But, what surpasses all terror is the exclusion from the eternal contemplation of the most blessed and enjoyable Trinity. Chrysostom: "To be excluded from the eternal goods and to be banished from those things *that God has prepared for those who love him,*[323] evokes such torment, such that even if there were no external pain, this alone would suffice, and it would be better to suffer thousands and thousands of flames rather than to look at the angry face of that most gentle Christ and depart from

---

[320] See Anselm, *Meditatio* 2 (Schmitt III, 83). The citation is virtually verbatim.

[321] This is an adaptation of Bernard, *Sermo* 54 in *Cantica* n. 8 (SBOp 2: 106); *On the Song of Songs* (Walsh, III, 76).

[322] This is an adaptation of *Homilia* 23, n. 8 (PG 58: 317).

[323] See 1 Cor 2:9.

him for all eternity."[324] Gregory in his *Homilies*: "O if man could understand how wonderful [the words]: *Behold the bridegroom is coming!*[325] How sweet: *Those who were ready went into the wedding feast with him!*[326] How bitter: *And the door was closed.*"[327] O soul, what more [need be said]? Prosper in his *The Contemplative Life*:

> Think how bad it is to be separated from the face of Christ, to be excluded from that joy of contemplating the divine, to be deprived of the most blessed society of all the saints ... to die to eternal life and to live in eternal death ... to be plunged into the depths of bubbling hell, to be torn to shreds forever by voracious worms, never to be done with tribulations, to have to listen to the waves of resounding shrieks, to be blinded by the bitter vapors of the smoky pit, and not to perceive that which illuminates, but to perceive that which torments![328]

10. *SOUL*. Already I tremble with fear, I am faint with horror. Tell me, what good is such a sad meditation?

INNERMOST SELF. O soul, I believe that the continual and devout meditation on the foregoing is a remedy for sins and a salutary bolstering up for the good things that

---

[324] QuarEd admit implicitly (n. 2) that they cannot find this passage in John Chrysostom. The closest parallels are found in his *Homilia* 23, n.7-8, in *Matthaeum* (PG 57: 316-18).

[325] Matt 25:6.

[326] Matt 25:10.

[327] Matt 25:10. This is a modification of *Homilia* 12, n. 4 of GGHG. (CCSL cxli, 84).

[328] This is an adaptation of Julianus Promerius, *De vita contemplativa,* book II, ch. XII, n. 3 (PL 59: 492BC); "The Contemplative Life" (Suelzer, 130).

must be done and the bad things that must be borne.
Bernard in one of his epistles [says]:

> You fear [long night] vigils ... and manual labor;
> but these are trivial indeed compared to thoughts
> of perpetual flames. By recalling ... shadows we
> do not fear solitude; if you think of upcoming
> conversations with [all their] idle talk, silence will
> not ... displease you; the frequent recalling of *the
> weeping and gnashing of teeth*,[329] prepares you to
> bear with the mat and pillow.[330]

Augustine in one of his sermons:

> The human spirit, bound to the allurements and
> [venal] desires of this world, flees work and expects
> pleasure, and can hardly be brought to put aside the
> habits of its past life. But when the [human spirit]
> begins to think about the inevitability of future
> judgment and the cruelty of eternal sufferings, it
> voluntarily declares war on its passions. Moved
> by the hope of reward or the fear of torments, it
> struggles mightily against his pristine desires and
> strenuously strives to conquer them.[331]

11.   *SOUL.* Well, you have sufficiently terrified my
miserable self dwelling as I am *in this valley of tears*,[332]
but your teaching has not been fruitless. Now have
mercy on me in my misery and do what you have already
promised. Introduce me gradually to perpetual felicity,
so that I might glean some solace of mind there because

---

[329] See Matt 8:12.

[330] This is a modification of *Epistola* 1, n. 12 (SBOp 7: 10). Bernard
refers to the austerities of monastic life.

[331] This is an adaptation of *Sermo* 196, n. 6 (PL 39: 2112).

[332] See Ps 84:7.

alternating [themes] is pleasant. According to Augustine: "It is always a good thing for the life of [a human being] to be corrected whether by punishment or forgiving, whether by terrifying or consoling."[333] Seneca: "The [human] mind is generous and, when recalcitrant, it is better that it be led rather than dragged."[334] Note, how generous is the [human] mind; it is often more easily led by soft and flattering [talk] than by what is frightening and adverse; it is often more enticed by consoling promises than forced with threats and fears. And so our spouse and sister – the soul[335] – desires to be drawn by the fragrance of celestial ointments, by the taste of divine charisms, and thus with the Bridegroom to run in the way of the commandments, no longer out of fear but gladly out of love.[336]

12. *INNERMOST SELF*. O soul, what you say I know to be true. Unfortunately, there are many who, when in prosperity, do not want to imitate God; and so it is necessary to frighten them with [threats of] adversity. There are many who, because of blindness, do not understand the divine charisms, or lose them through negligence while engaged in useless busy work. And so, as I see it, God out

---

[333] This is a modification of *Epistola* 153, ch. VI, n. 19. (PL 33: 662).

[334] This is a modification of Seneca, *On Clemency*, book I, ch. 24, in *Seneca Moral Essays* I, trans. John W. Basore LCL (NY: Putnam's Sons, 1928), 423: "Man's spirit is by nature refractory, it struggles against opposition and difficulty, and is more ready to follow than to be led; and as well-bred and high-spirited horses are better managed by a loose rein, so a voluntary uprightness follows upon mercy under its own impulse...." Bonaventure quotes this same passage from Seneca in his *Commentary on Luke*, Part I, ch. V, n. 5 (see Karris, Part I, 382-83).

[335] See Cant 1:3: *Draw me. We will run after you to the fragrance of your ointments.* The spouse and sister refer to the soul.

[336] See Ps 118:32: *I have run the way of your commandments when you expanded my heart.*

of the immensity of his infinite goodness would always
be ready to encourage by consolations, rather than to
terrify by harshness, if indeed men [and women] were
equally disposed to receive his divine consolation, which
is so precious and delicate that it ought not in any way
be dispensed indiscriminately to everyone. – If therefore,
after all you have heard, see to it that you have a purified
intellect and well-disposed affections because, according
to Augustine: "The highest good cannot be seen except
by totally purified minds;"[337] and I believe that even
less so is it possible to savor [the highest good] without
affections that are very well disposed. There are many
in this life who understand with great insight, but [with
their affections] they savor nothing. Augustine: "O Lord,
make me taste with my affections what I sense with
my intellect; make me sense with love what I perceive
through my understanding."[338]

13. *SOUL*. Tell me; what sort of disposition is first required
in the affections and the intellect, so that I might at least
sense a small "inebriation" of mind, so that by contemplating the celestial sweetness I might taste thereof? I
have already tried to practice mental contemplation, but,
sad to say, I fear that I have not yet sensed the smallest
drop of this celestial sweetness. I have read much about
the lives and behavior of the saints, much about nature,
about the tasks and orders of angels. I have also read
quite a bit about the unity of the ineffable divinity, about
the incomprehensible Trinity; a great deal about the

---

[337] See *De Trinitate*, I, ch. 2, n. 4 (CCSL 1, 31): "that we may learn
from actual experience that the highest good exists that is discerned
by totally purified minds." See also *The Trinity* (Hill, 67).

[338] See Pseudo-Augustine, *Liber de contritione cordis*, ch. 2 (PL
40: 944): "Make me, I pray you, O Lord, savor through love what I taste
through knowledge. To feel affectionately what I know intellectually."
Bonaventure quoted this same passage in *Soliloquium*, ch. I, n. 18
above, p. 241-42.

unbelievable happiness of all the blessed. And yet, while my mind was totally taken up with all these things, I still remain fasting and famished, and with blessed Augustine I cry out: "Make me taste, most clement Father, with my affections what I sense with my intellect."[339] And yet I have made no progress. Many times when exhausted by long [hours of] study and angry with myself, I exclaim with the prophet: *How long, O Lord, will you utterly forget me? How long will you hide your face from me,*[340] because, even though I judge myself unworthy to eat the bread of the children, nevertheless with great longing I desire to eat at least the smallest crumbs which fall [from the table];[341] but alas, more often than not, with open mouth *I toiled in vain.*[342]

14. *INNERMOST SELF.* O soul, the aforesaid things, about which you complained so sadly, happen for two reasons. Sometimes because of the goodly and salvific dispensation of divine goodness. As Gregory in his *Morals* says: "The most pious Father at times tends to defer the requests of petitioners so that their desires might grow and thus be heard because of their merits, even though what they want is not so quickly granted."[343] Again in his *Homilies*: "Holy desires grow because of delay. But if they failed because there was a delay, then they were not desires."[344] For God, although because of his piety is most forgiving, nevertheless it sometimes happens that what he has

---

[339] See previous note.

[340] Ps 12:1.

[341] See Matt 15:26-27.

[342] Isa 49:4.

[343] This is an adaptation of *Moralia in Iob*, XX, ch. 31, n. 61 (CCSL cxliii a, 1047); *Morals*, II, 495.

[344] See *Homilia* 25, n. 2 of GGHG (CCSL cxli, 207): "For holy desires, as I previously said, grow because of delay. But if they failed because there was a delay, then they were not desires."

generously granted is taken away, so that you might learn greatly and passionately to desire great things and more solicitously hold onto what you have with a grateful heart. – At other times a benefit is withdrawn because of an inordinate disposition in the petitioner. Bernard: "It is altogether wrong to try to mix celestial sweetness with these ashes, the divine balms with this poisonous joy, the charisms of the Holy Spirit with the allurements of this world."[345]

---

[345] This is a modification of Bernard, *Sermo 5* in *Ascensione Domini*, n. 13 (SBOp 5: 158); "Fifth Sermon for the Feast of the Ascension" (SBSermons, II, 282). Bonaventure also cites this passage in *Soliloquium* ch. II, n. 16 above.

.

CHAPTER IV
The Soul – Turned Toward Superior Things

How the soul by means of mental exercise ought to turn the rays of contemplation in order to reflect upon superior things, so that it might see the twelve joys of heaven arising from the contemplation of either inferior or external things, interior or superior things.

§ I: ON CELESTIAL JOY IN GENERAL

1. *INNERMOST SELF.* O soul, lest I leave you too long in suspense and afflict you with unfulfilled hope, you should purge your mind from vain and useless images, from natural and simply curious reasons, from extraneous and scientific preoccupations. Also purge your affections from sin and its consequences, from the occasions and causes of sin. *Lift up your powers of reasoning, open and expand your affections, and enter into the joy of the Lord,*[346] which in this life *eye has not seen in a perfect way, and ear has not heard, and it has not entered the human heart, what God has prepared for those who love him.*[347] Augustine says: "Therefore, O my soul, fire up with love and desire for the celestial life of the saints, where action is not tiring, repose is not slothful, life is without blemish, praise of God without interruption."[348] Consequently, rejoice and exult, and consider the reward for your labor, which is truly so great that it cannot be counted, so large that it cannot be measured, so precious that it cannot be priced, so abundant that it is boundless.

---

[346] See Matt 25:21: *Enter into the joy of your master / Lord.*

[347] See 1 Cor 2:9. Cf. Bonaventure, I, *Sent.*, d. 2. dub. 1 (I:59).

[348] This is a modification of *De Catechizandis Rudibus*, ch. 25, n. 47 (CCSL xlvi, 170); *The First Catechetical Instruction* (Christopher, 78).

2. SOUL. You have had much to say in general; please tell me now about everything more specifically, because we understand better what is said in particular than what is expressed in general.

INNERMOST SELF. O soul, what can I say? When I look to the joy awaiting us, I almost expire with admiration, because "joy will be within and without, below, above and all around."[349] You will rejoice in everything and about everything. Your joy, as I believe, was prefigured in Revelation in that blessed *woman clothed with the sun, with the moon under her feet, and on her head a crown of twelve stars.*[350] This woman, in my view, is the blessed soul; daughter, spouse, and queen of the eternal King; daughter by the creation of nature, spouse by adoption through grace, queen in attaining the [rewards] of glory.[351] Such a soul is justly characterized as *clothed with the sun*, because it is resplendent with God-like clarity and *crowned* with the dignity of eternal happiness. Involved in this happiness on account of its special decor are twelve joys, prefigured by the twelve stars wherewith heavenly happiness is decorated and furnished.

3. *INNERMOST SELF.* O soul, you must daily with devout mind think about these joys and seek no consolation while dwelling in this present misery. Moreover, in the hope [of obtaining] this joy you must gladly and with equanimity bear up with the trials of the present life. Bede states:

---

[349] See Eadmer, *Liber de sancti Anselmi similitudinibus*, 71 (PL 159: 643A): "For joy will be both within and without, joy down below and above, joy all around, everywhere will be full of joy."

[350] Rev 12:1.

[351] The preceding is a paraphrase of Jerome, *Epistola* 54, n. 3 (PL 22: 551).

O soul, do not be disturbed if evils flourish in this world, while you suffer and they rejoice, and you are perturbed. Evil ones have no place in celestial joy, nor should you worry if you have nothing here on earth. But with hope for that joy towards which you strive, your affections should joyfully and patiently sustain whatever adversity might come your way.[352]

O Soul. Jerome in one of his epistles says: "If at times worldly joys, the false prestige of this world, or its brief and fragile power delight you, at that point call to mind all of this and you will reject it as dung."[353]

Therefore, hasten, O soul, not with bodily steps, but with affections and desires, because not only the angels and blessed, but the Lord and Master of the angels and the blessed awaits you. God the Father awaits you as his most beloved daughter[354].... God the Son as his sweetest spouse, God the Holy Spirit as his most gracious friend. God the Father awaits you that he might make you heir of all goods; God the Son, that he might offer you to the Father as the fruit of his birth and the price of his most precious blood; God the Holy Spirit, that he might make you a participant of his eternal goodness and sweetness. The entire and most blessed family of all the celestial spirits of

---

[352] QuarEd give (p. 59, n. 5) two parallels for this citation, see Pseudo-Bede's *Commentary on Psalm XXXVI* (PL 93: 674) and the *Glossa ordinaria* on James 1:2 (PL 114: 671B).

[353] See *Epistola* 52, n. 10 (PL 22: 536): "Let us think of his cross, and we will consider riches mire."

[354] Referring to the soul (in Latin, in the feminine gender).

the Eternal King awaits you so that they might receive you into their company.[355]

4. Therefore, desire their company above all else. You would come there with much shame, if you had not loved their company in this *vale of tears*.[356] "As often as the useless yearning for this world pleases you and as often as you see something glorious about this world, immediately turn your thoughts to heaven and anticipate what you will be in the future."[357] I truly believe, O soul, that if you consistently concentrate on celestial joys, you will consider this life of exile as a suburb of the heavenly kingdom, wherein daily you will have a spiritual foretaste of that eternal sweetness. Because as Augustine says: "as long as we keep something eternal before our minds, then we no longer dwell in this world"[358] but we dwell in heaven. O soul, such is the power of your love that as Bernard observes: "you more truly *live where you love,* rather than where you are [simply] alive."[359] O dearest soul, *this is the kingdom of God that is within us,*[360] which we have sadly neglected while dissipated with inane and silly things outside us. "We have become dissipated with outer things while caring nothing for the kingdom of God within us

---

[355] This is an adaptation of Pseudo-Bernard, *Meditationes piissimae*, ch. 6, n. 17 (PL 184: 496BC).

[356] See Ps 83:7.

[357] This is modification of Jerome, *Epistola* 22, n. 41 (PL 22: 425).

[358] See *De Trinitate* IV, ch. 20, n. 28 (CCSL l, 199); "For when we grasp in our mind, insofar as we are able, something of eternity, we are not in this world." See also *The Trinity* (Hill, 174).

[359] See Bernard, *De Praecepto et Dispensatione,* ch. XX, n. 60 (SBOp 3: 292): "For our spirit is not more present where it lives than where it loves." Cf. *On Precept and Dispensation* (Greenia, 149).

[360] See Luke 17:21: *The kingdom of God is within you.*

.... We seek consolation outside us in silly things and *false follies*,[361] such that we have already lost the devotion of our pristine religion and now retain no trace of it."[362]

Therefore, O soul, daughter of the eternal King, listen with a devout mind, *turn your ear* to holy and salutary advice. Gaze in contemplation at the consolation of the heavenly kingdom, in contempt and disgust *forget your people and your father's house*,[363] that is, the world, the devil, and yourself.

§ II: On Heavenly Joy in particular
First, on the Threefold Joy Arising from Contemplation on the Things beneath Us

5. And so, with a devout mind look and consider how those divine and celestial spirits have avoided the perils of the present life. Although they can never turn their gaze from the splendor of that eternal sun, nevertheless they sometimes turn the rays of their contemplation to inferior matters, at other times to what is *superior*, sometimes to the *interior* and at other times to the *exterior*.

6. They turn to *inferior* things, I say, and rejoice for three reasons. First, because with the help of divine power they have overcome their impious, horrible, and cruel enemies. Second, because they have either avoided by divine wisdom all defects and sins, or they have corrected those

---

[361] Ps 39:5.

[362] See Bernard, *Apologia ad Guillelmum Abbatem*, ch. X, n. 25 (SBOp 3:102); translation by Michael Casey, *Apologia to Abbot William*, in WBC, Treatises I (Spencer, MA: Cistercian Publications, 1970), 61. The citation is not verbatim.

[363] Bonaventure interweaves Ps 44:11 throughout this paragraph: "Listen, O daughter, and see, and turn your ear. And forget your people and your father's house."

already committed. Third, by divine clemency they have escaped from the deplorable, interminable, and eternal sufferings. O soul, can you imagine how much they daily rejoice when they see how much they have surmounted the flesh, the world, and the devil, or [on the other hand] how many have been befouled by various sins concerning which they have never merited to be pardoned, as well as so many that have been damned for all eternity? I really think that having passed from death to life[364] doubles [their] joy.

7. O Lord God, if now such grave peril is found in war, how much joy, do you think, will be in the triumph, when having vanquished and triumphed over the world, having submerged the wicked Pharaoh and his army in the Red Sea, all the elect take up their tambourines with Miriam, chanting and singing psalms, praising and blessing the Lord with one voice, saying: *Let us sing to the Lord, for he is gloriously triumphant*, etc.[365]

At that time two Seraphim will be constituted, that is, two choirs of the elect, namely the innocent and the *penitent*, singing one to the other: *Holy, holy, holy is the Lord God of Sabaoth.*[366] Holy is God the Father, who so powerfully freed us from the world, the flesh, and the devil. Holy is God the Son, who so wisely redeemed[367] us from punishment and sin. Holy is God the Holy Spirit, who is

---

[364] See John 5:24: *The person who hears my voice ... has passed from death to life.*

[365] See Ex 15:1 and Jerome's *Epistola* 22, n. 41 (PL 22: 424): "how great that day will be.... When after the crossing of the Red Sea, in which Pharaoh and his army had been submerged, Mariam, holding a timbrel in her hand, chants to the choir: 'Let us sing to the Lord, for he is gloriously triumphant,' etc."

[366] See Isa 6:3: "Holy, Holy, Holy, Lord of hosts."

[367] Bonaventure uses the Latin word *iustificavit* which could be rendered by "obtained justice for us" or "rendered us just"; the phrase "justified us from" is a bit awkward.

so forgiving in preserving us from eternal torments. *All the earth is filled with his glory*,[368] who called us from the misery of this world to the joys of the celestial kingdom.

O soul, what will it be like for you on that day, when you will be raised to that happy choir, and where everything which you piously bore on earth will be changed into eternal jubilation. Then with all the others you will praise the Lord your God with exultant lips saying: *The mercies of the Lord I will sing forever*.[369] According to Augustine, in *The City of God*, "when the song is sung to celebrate the glory of Christ, by whose blood we have been redeemed, that city will have no greater joy,"[370] nor anything sweeter.

8. Therefore, when you are tried by temptations, when you struggle against persecution, when you are overcome in this world with various tribulations, then turn your mind to heaven and realize that these things are nothing more than the "raw materials" for eternal joy. And then, according to Gregory, considering your reward will mitigate the force of the scourges: For "if we consider how many and how great are the things promised us in heaven, everything possessed on earth becomes loathsome to the mind."[371] Actually, not only do the good things which we so pleasurably possess become vile, but also the bad things which at times we must so sadly tolerate become loathsome as well. "For *the sufferings of this present time are as*

---

[368] Isa 6:3.

[369] Ps 88:1.

[370] See *De Civitate Dei*, XXII, ch. 30, n. 4 (CCSL xlviii, 864): "When that song is sung to the glory of the grace of Christ, by whose blood we have been redeemed, there will certainly be no greater joy for that city." See also *The City of God* (Dods, 866).

[371] See *Homilia* 37, n. 1 in GGHG (CCSL cxli, 318). The citation is verbatim.

nothing compared[372] to the past sin which is forgiven, to the present grace which is infused, and to the *future glory* which is promised."[373] O soul, what you will then possess with joy when you understand perfectly [will compensate for] what you endured in the world so perilously whereby so many oppressed you; [will compensate] for what you have overcome in the way of the deceitful craftiness of the devil whereby so many are deceived; for the eternal sufferings you have avoided whereby innumerable [souls] are tormented.

SOUL. How sensible and salutary is this counsel of yours! Because, when I think about what you have proposed, I hopefully receive much consolation there from. But, O Lord God, what do you think it will be like for me when I will truly possess the things I now hope for?

§ III: Second, the Blessed Turn the Rays of their Contemplation upon the Things alongside Them and Rejoice over this Threefold Object

9. *Innermost Self.* O soul, what you have heard are but trifles. Comparatively speaking, what you have perceived are almost nothing. Take a moment to raise the eyes of your mind and you will understand what joys there are regarding those things *alongside* us; mull over them frequently with a devout mind. Therefore, attend carefully and consider *the beautiful place* which divine wisdom has built[374] for you; look *at the delicious food, the elegant*

---

[372] See Rom 8:18.

[373] See Bernard, *Ad Clericos de Conversione*, ch. 21, n. 37 (SBOp 4: 113-14); "On Conversion" (Saïd, 75). The citation is virtually verbatim.

[374] See Prov 9:1: *Wisdom has built a house for herself....*

decor, the precious treasure[375] which the eternal power
has gathered for you; notice also *the famous assembly* [of
the blessed] with whom your mind can rejoice eternally
over divine clemency.

10. O soul, see how glorious, as Bernard says, is "that
celestial city, that safe abode, that homeland ... that
contains all that is delightful."[376] See how luminous, how
splendid is that celestial city *which has no need for the
sun or the moon to shine on it,*[377] but the Lord himself,
the sun of justice,[378] *the refulgence of eternal light,*[379] is its
light, and *its lamp is the Lamb.*[380] *What glorious things
are said of you, O city of God.*[381] *O Israel, how vast is the
house of God, how broad the scope of his dominion.*[382] O
soul, even though you are here in body, be there in spirit,
because there "there is repose without labor, life without
death, youth without age, light without shadows,"[383] and
imperturbable peace. For *my people will sit in beautiful
peace, in secure dwellings, and in opulent rest.*[384]

---

[375] Cf. Matt 13:44.

[376] This is an abbreviation of Pseudo-Bernard, *Meditationes piissimae*, ch. IV, n. 11, (PL 184: 492D).

[377] Rev 21:23.

[378] Mal 3:20.

[379] Wis 7:26.

[380] Rev 21:23.

[381] Ps 87:3.

[382] Bar 3:24.

[383] There is a parallel in Pseudo-Augustine, *Liber unus Soliliquio-
rum animae ad Deum*, ch. XXXV (PL 40: 895): "There infinite happiness, joy without sorrow, health without pain, life without labor, light
without darkness, life without death, everything good without any
evil. There youth never grows old, there life knows no end...." See also
Augustine, *Sermo* 65 and *Sermo* 67, *Sermones ad fratres in eremo* (PL
40: 1350 and 1353).

[384] Isa 32:18.

11. And who might be our *food* unless it be that most
blessed Lamb, that pure and immaculate Jesus, Son of
God the Father and the Virgin Mary, that most savory of
delights[385] made from his dazzling humanity and most
excellent divinity and served to satiety by the saintly
spirits? O how *blessed are those who have been called to
the wedding feast of the Lamb!*[386] "In that place there will
always be both thirst and satiety; but, marvelous to say,
compulsion will be far removed from thirst, and boredom
far away from satiety."[387] For *they will be inebriated with
the plenty of the house of the Lord, and from the torrent of
his pleasure they will be made to drink.*[388]

12. *SOUL.* Tell me please, when will this happen?

INNERMOST SELF. Not before, in my opinion, that
handsome *cupbearer of the* High *King,*[389] *the brightness
of the Father's glory,*[390] *the splendor of eternal light,*[391] *the
image of divine goodness,*[392] *the spotless mirror,*[393] *of god-
like clarity, into which angels longed to look,*[394] at that
time when *he will gird himself, have them recline at table,*

---

[385] This is a rather free translation. The Latin has *fercula nobilis-
sima*, that is, most noble platter.

[386] See Rev 19:9: "Blessed those who have been called to the wedding feast of the Lamb."

[387] This is an adaptation of Gregory, *Moralia in Iob*, XVIII, ch. 54,
n. 91 (CCSL cxliii a, 954); *Morals*, II, 91.

[388] See Ps 35:9: *They will be inebriated with the plenty of your
house, and from the torrent of your pleasure you will make them
drink.*

[389] See Nehemiah 1:11: *I was the cupbearer of the king.*

[390] Hebr 1:3.

[391] See Wis 7:26

[392] See Hebr 1:3.

[393] See Wis 7:26

[394] 1 Peter 1:12.

and proceed personally *to wait on them.*[395] O soul, reflect on these things with a devout mind. Imagine what joy there will be for those blessed spirits arising from the unbelievable dignity of the Server, from the wonderful charity of each of the convivial companions, from the delicious opulence of the dishes served, from the frequent and numerous [visits to the table] of the servers, from the dulcet echoes of the musical instruments, and [the voices] singing psalms and praising the King of Glory, the Son of God! In this wonderful, great, and celestial gathering you will hear jubilant angels, apostles singing psalms, triumphant martyrs, confessors, and virgins singing songs of praise, joyful patriarchs and prophets, and all the saints and elect of God joined in praise of the Father, Son, and Holy Spirit saying with one voice: *Holy, holy, holy, Lord God of hosts! All the earth is filled with his glory!*[396] "O how glorious is that kingdom, where with Christ all the saints reign, *wearing white robes, follow the Lamb wherever he goes.*"[397] O soul, how could any good thing be lacking there, since there are so many different reasons for rejoicing?

13.   Look around you at the company of all the saints who by divine clemency have gathered to share your happiness, because, as Seneca says: "There is no happiness in the possession of a good that is not shared."[398] Thus Gregory says: "What tongue is capable of telling us or what intellect capable of grasping how joyful it is to be in

---

[395] See Luke 12:37. Cf. Bernard, *De Diligendo Deo,* ch. XI, n. 33 (SBOp 3: 146-47); *On Loving God* (Evans, 199-200).

[396] Isa 6:3.

[397] See the Magnificat Antiphon for Vespers of the Feast of All Saints in the Roman Breviary. The antiphon quotes Rev 7:9, *wearing white robes,* and Rev 14:4, *they follow the Lamb wherever he goes.*

[398] This is an exact citation from Seneca, *Epistola* 6 n. 4, LCL 27: "No good thing is pleasant to possess, without friends to share it."

that heavenly city, to be with the choirs of angels, and to participate with those most blessed spirits in the glory of the Creator;"[399] never to leave their most blessed society, but constantly to be with them and rejoice forever with them in their joy. Anselm: "There everything will be known about everyone, and everyone will be known by everyone else. Nothing will be ... hidden: country of origin, race, genealogy."[400] The charity of the just will be so blessed and perfect there that "each will love his neighbor as much as he loves himself."[401] From this follows the priceless good that "each will rejoice in another's joy as if it were his own."[402] Consequently, since the number of the elect cannot be counted, who, do you think, could possibly tell us about their joy?

14. As Jerome says:[403]

> How wonderful will be that day when Mary, the mother of the Lord accompanied by choirs of virgins will come to meet you ... when the Spouse himself comes with all the saints and says: *Arise, hasten, my beloved, come, my beautiful one, O my dove. For see, the winter is past, the rains are over and*

---

[399] See *Homilia* 37, n. 1 of GGHG (CCSL cxli, 348). The citation is virtually verbatim.

[400] This is a modification of Eadmer, *Liber de sancti Anselmi* 59 (PL 159: 635B).

[401] This is an adaptation of Alcher of Clairvaux, *De spiritu et anima*, ch. 57 (PL 40: 822).

[402] This, too, is an adaptation of Alcher of Clairvaux, *De spiritu et anima*, ch. 57 (PL 40: 822). See Anselm, *Proslogion* XXV (Schmitt I, 120): "In that perfect love of the countless blessed angels and humans no one will love another less than himself nor will anyone rejoice over others less than over himself." See also *Proslogion* (Davies and Evans, 102).

[403] This is a considerable adaptation of *Epistola* 22, n. 41 (PL 22: 424-25).

gone.[404] Then the angels will gaze in admiration at your splendor saying: *Who is this coming up from the desert, abundant in delights, leaning upon her lover?*[405] They will see you, daughter of Zion, and they will praise you.... There the one hundred and forty four thousand in the sight of the throne and the elders will take up their harps and sing a new song.[406] Then you will fly aloft, secure in the embrace of your Spouse and joyfully say: *I found him whom my heart loves. I took hold of him and would not let go.*[407]

Then each of *the seven sons* of that great man Job,[408] (there was no one on earth like him) who dwelt in that blessed land to the East, took will take turns giving feasts and will invite their sister, *you,* to be their companion. And each will say to you: "Drink now and lie down joyfully because you have found favor with the High Prince."[409] And then you will respond with joy saying: *I will drink* and become happier still, *because my life is magnified this day above all the days of my life.*[410] O truly unheard-of magnificence! O joyous and happy excellence, unheard-of in this world! I think that in comparison to it, all the pomp of this world would hardly come to a little *drop.*

---

[404] See Cant 2:13-14, 11.

[405] See Cant 8:5.

[406] See Rev 14:1, 3.

[407] See Cant 3:4.

[408] For background see Job 1:2, 4: *To Job were born seven sons and three daughters.... And his sons went and made a feast by houses every one in his day. And they sent and invited their three sisters to eat and drink with them.*

[409] See Judith 12:17: *And Holofernes said to Judith: Drink now and sit down and be merry, for you have found favor before me.*

[410] See Judith 12:18: *And Judith said: I will drink, my lord, because my life is magnified this day above all my days.*

15. *SOUL.* I have been silent long enough, because what you have proposed I have heard with delight and admiration. However, before you go further, please tell me more about that company of celestial spirits. You touched on it before,[411] but all too briefly.

INNERMOST SELF. Actually, O soul, I would prefer to pass over your request in silence, rather than to say even a little with "polluted" lips or even to think about that celestial mystery. Unfortunately, I have too often been implicated in worldly and rather useless matters, and with the other worldly ones, have eaten fodder for the pigs,[412] such that I am ashamed and confused in speaking about the normal activities of the divine spirits. However, because I do not wish to run contrary to your *pious* requests, I will briefly present what I, although *unworthy*, have sometimes thought about when moved by the Spirit. Now, although in that celestial palace where the plenitude of all goodness is perfect in one and all, and although in that place each receives in an excellent way according to the diversity of his merits,[413] nevertheless, according to Gregory, nothing in heaven is possessed exclusively by anyone because the divine goodness is so boundless.[414] All things are common to all, because of

---

[411] See nn. 11-13 above.

[412] See Luke 15:16.

[413] See John 14:2: *In my Father's house there are many mansions.*

[414] QuarEd refer (p. 61, n. 1) to four passages in Gregory's writings for parallels. See, *Moralia in Iob* IV, ch. 36, n 70 (CCSL cxliii, 214-15); *Morals* I, 237. The closest parallel, however, is Augustine, *Tractate* 67 n. 2 (CCSL xxxvi, 495-96). See FC 90, 59: "But the many dwelling-places signify the varied values of merits in the one eternal life.... But because of the one denarius (given to all the laborers) no one is separated from the kingdom; and so God will be all in all, so that, because God is love, it may come to pass through love that what each has may be common to all."

him who is *all in all*.[415] There the virgin will rejoice over the merits of a holy widow; there the widow will exult about the privilege of chaste virginity; there the confessor will be happy about the triumph of the martyrs; there the martyr will dance because of the prize [won by] the confessors; there the prophet will praise the pious life of the patriarchs; the patriarch will rejoice concerning the faith and the insights of the prophets; there the apostles and angels will find joy over the merits of those in the lower orders and there those in the lower orders will be happy about the glory and the crowns of those in the higher orders. From all of this issue the bonds of perfect and holy charity, where everyone enjoys in the other what he does not merit for himself.

16. *Soul.* These are still not enough to put my mind at rest. So please, lest you pass them over, explain to me singly and distinctly more about that company [of the blessed].

Innermost Self. O soul, you know well, "only by stammering can we echo the exalted things of God."[416] This should not be surprising because, since we are less capable of understanding, how can we be capable of speaking? Because after all, these high and celestial things upon which we gaze with bleary eyes, are more true in reality than when understood, and more truly understood than when expressed vocally. However, lest I run on too long, listen to what the intellect imagines, if but little savored by the affections. I think that the seven sons, of whom we have spoken above,[417] are all the holy and chosen spirits, heirs, and sons of the most high

---

[415] See 1 Cor 15:28.

[416] This is a modification of Gregory, *Moralia in Iob*, V, ch. 36, n. 66 (CCSL cxliii, 265); *Morals*, I, 292.

[417] See ch. 4, §III, n. 14 above, p. 325.

Father. They all take turns giving banquets, during which they feast on one another's celestial joys; here according to their talents and merits they serve most delicious dishes. Therefore, on the first day the firstborn – that is that number of celestial angels, who are rightfully called 'firstborn' because they came first in being created and in turning to God, from whom they never deviated by sin, but always with steadfast charity remained loyal to God the Father and were thus the first to possess that blessed inheritance of the heavenly kingdom – to you, O my soul, at their feast serve delicious and precious dishes, since each order serves up with special delight [the dish] for which it is especially talented.[418]

17.   Imagine, O soul, what dish will be offered you by the Seraphim, that highest order of spirits who "are so close to the eternal Father that no other spirits are found between them and [God],"[419] who are the closest in gazing upon him and more perfectly enjoy his eternal goods. Can you imagine what joys they serve from the nobility of their nature, from the clarity of their vision, from the sincerity of their love? Therefore, these who are called Seraphim, adorn the banquet with the ardor of divine charity, the Cherubim with the splendor of eternal clarity, the Thrones with the rightness of divine majesty, the Dominations with the excellence of rule over others,

---

[418] Cf. *Homilia* 34, n. 14 of GGHG (CCSL cxli, 313).

[419] This is a modification of *Homilia* 34, n. 10 of GGHG (CCSL cxli, 309): "Since they (the Seraphim) are so closely joined to God that no other spirits come between them, they burn more fiercely as they see him more closely." Cf. Bernard, *De Consideratione*, V, ch. 4, n. 8 (SBOp 3: 473); *On Consideration* (Anderson and Kennan, 149): "the Seraphim, Spirit totally enkindled with divine fire, enkindle all so that each citizen is a lamp burning and shining: burning with love, shining with knowledge." Also Book V, ch. 5, 11 (SBOp 3: 475; Anderson and Kennan, 152): "The Seraphim burn, but with the fire of God, or rather with the fire which is God. What is special with them is that they love, but not as much as God, nor in the same way."

the Principalities with the magnificence of presiding over inferiors, the Powers with the authority of coercing evil spirits, the Virtues with the power of working miracles, the Archangels with the dignity of announcing higher things, the Angels with the facility of revealing the secrets of divine knowledge. And so you see how the minds of the blessed feast on those things according to the special talents they have received from that high and heavenly palace. – It should not be surprising that the aforesaid and many more things have been offered us by these spirits to augment our joy, since they are so faithful in watching over us in *this vale of tears,*[420] while with all their strength they want to lead us to that homeland of eternal happiness. Bernard:

> O, if only one might know with what care and solicitude those blessed spirits assist those who sing, are present to those who pray, are involved in their meditations, hover above those who are at rest, and preside over those who administer![421]

O fasting and famished soul, if only you might with open mouth eat of but one scrap *that falls from the table of their masters,*[422] then I think you might more patiently bear with this pilgrimage and its trials. I believe that even if you could taste but a single drop of his wine, then you would be bored with all the sweetness of this world. As Gregory in his *Morals* says: "Were the heart to dwell but once among the things of heaven, it would

---

[420] See Ps 83:7.

[421] This is an adaptation of Pseudo-Bernard, *Meditationes piissimae,* ch. VI, n. 16 (PL 184: 495D-496A).

[422] Matt 15:27.

quickly understand how lowly are those things which had previously seemed so lofty."[423]

18. O beloved soul, what can I say about the banquet of the patriarchs, prophets, apostles, martyrs, confessors, and virgins who are rightfully prefigured by the six other sons [of Job]? Each of them in their banquets offers as many dishes as were matched in this life by their virtuous deeds. And who might be capable of telling us how much joy each soul will receive from the most perfect humility and simplicity of the patriarchs, from the most certain credibility and faithfulness of the prophets, from the charity and great diligence of the apostles, from the patience and steadfastness of the martyrs, from the piety and clemency of the confessors, and from the chastity and continence of the virgins? Gregory observes: "Truly neither tongue nor voice can speak, because the intellect cannot grasp what joy ... is to be found in the company of the angels, to participate with them in the glories of the Creator, to gaze at the face of God, to see the boundless [radiance] of light, to have no fear of death, but to rejoice at the gift of perpetual incorruptibility."[424]

19. O how happy will that day be for you when you shall return to the heritage of your ancestors and with all of them be raised up in unspeakable joy and happily introduced into the chambers of the Highest King! Now is the time to wake up, O my soul, and with that famous queen,[425] accompanied by the aromas of the virtues, the

---

[423] QuarEd offer (p. 62, n. 3) six possible sources for Gregory's opinion. See, e.g., *Moralia in Iob*, V, ch. I n. 1 (CCSL cxliii, 219); *Morals*, I, 242.

[424] See *Homilia* 37, n. 1 of GGHG (CCSL cxli, 348). The citation is almost verbatim.

[425] See 1 Kings 10:1-13 and 2 Chronicles 9:1-12 for the Queen of Sheba's visit to Solomon in Jerusalem.

treasures of good works, the entire repertoire of celestial desires, climb up to that heavenly Jerusalem where you can diligently contemplate everything and see that truth conquers fame, and glory surpasses all speech. Then you will begin to say with blessed Peter and with great jubilation in your heart: *Lord, it is good that we are here*,[426] here father, here mother, here sister, here brother, here homeland! O Lord, allow us to stay here and never depart! Ambrose: "O soul, let us flee to our true homeland, because there is the homeland for which we were created, there is the Father by whom we were created, there is our secure abode, 'the heavenly Jerusalem, our mother.'"[427] Thus, Anselm:

> O soul, in this life great should be your love and desire ... to attain what you were made for; and there should be sorrow that you are not yet there; and there should be fear that you may ... not get there. So that there is no cause for joy except concerning those things which provide you with help and hope of reaching your goal.[428]

§ IV: THIRD, THE BLESSED TURN THE RAYS OF THEIR CONTEMPLATION TOWARD WHAT IS WITHIN THEMSELVES AND DERIVE THEREFROM A THREEFOLD JOY

20. Our body, which is composed of the four elements, will be remunerated with four gifts. For then, the earth will have eternal immortality, water [will render it]

---

[426] Matt 17:4.

[427] This is an adaptation of *Isaac uel anima*, ch. 8, n. 78, in *Sancti Ambrosii Opera, Pars Secunda*, Karl Schenkl, ed., CSEL, xxxii (Prague: Tempsky, 1897), 698. The reference at the end is to Gal 4:26.

[428] This is a modification of *Cur Deus Homo*, I, ch. XX (Schmitt II, 87); translation by Brian Davies and G. R. Evans, "Why God Became Man," in *Anselm of Canterbury: Major Works* (Oxford: Oxford University Press, 1998), 303.

altogether immune to pain, air will give it speedy agility,
fire resplendent clarity.[429]

> – In the eternal homeland the hearts of the blessed
> will be to one another both brightly luminous and
> purely transparent.... There everyone's face is
> in full view and one's conscience patent.... There
> the body does not shield the mind of anyone from
> being viewed by another.[430]

As Augustine says: "There, wherever the mind decides
to be, the body will be there immediately."[431] For, just as
then the mind will most perfectly obey the Creator, so the
body will be most prompt in obeying its mover. – There all
the senses will act properly. There the eye will see most
beautiful decor, the sense of taste will savor the sweetest
of tastes, the touch will embrace the most delightful
object, the hearing will be refreshed with the most
pleasant of sounds. "O soul, let the love of this present
life go away ... and the love of the life to come draw near
... where no adversity disturbs, no dire needs hem us in,
no troubles disturb us, but where unending joy reigns."[432]
There "our existence will not change, our knowledge
will have no errors, our love will have no obstacles."[433]

---

[429] For a greater development of this theme, see Bernard, *Sermo 4
in festivitate omnium Sanctorum,* n. 6 (SBOp 5: 359-60); "Fourth Sermon for the Feast of All Saints" (SBSermons, III, 380).

[430] This is an adaptation of Gregory, *Moralia in Iob*, XVIII, ch. 48,
nn. 77-78, (CCSL cxliii a, 941); *Morals*, II, 377.

[431] This is a paraphrase of *De Civitate Dei*, XXII, ch. 30, n. 1 (CCSL
xlviii, 862); *The City of God* (Dods, 864).

[432] This is a modification of Pseudo-Augustine, *De conflictu vitio-
rum et virtutum,* ch. 26 (PL 40: 1103).

[433] See Augustine, *De Civitate Dei*, XI, ch. 28 (CCSL xlviii, 348);
The City of God (Dods, 539): "There our existence will not experience
death. There our knowledge will have no errors. There our love will
have no obstacles."

"That place will be devoid of all deformity, all infirmity, all slowness, all corruption. There will be *a new heaven and a new earth*.[434] There we will be like the angels of God,[435] although not in age, but certainly in happiness."[436] "There will be life without death, youth without age, joy without sadness, peace without discord, the [power of the] will without injury, light without shadows, an eternal kingdom immune from change."[437] "There, whatever you want will be, whatever you do not want will not be."[438]

21. You should also consider how elated your mind will be when again it takes on that body which, as you have heard, is not the one you bore with great pain and conquered after many battles, concerning which more often fearful and impatient, angry and yet patiently forgiving you said: *Who will deliver me from this mortal body?*[439] No, not that body, but one now perfectly obedient and spiritual; one which, I say, will bring solace in contemplation and an increase in eternal happiness. It is certain that the soul would never desire reassuming a body, no matter how glorious it might be, if it were to impede the contemplation of the divinity. Now, according to the opinion and doctrine of Augustine, the holy soul desires its [the body's] resumption and waits to be reunited to it, because without it happiness cannot be consummated or joy be complete; and hence their

---

[434] See Rev 21:1: *And I saw a new heaven and a new earth.*

[435] See Luke 20:36: *They are equal to the angels.*

[436] This is an adaptation of Augustine, *De Civitate Dei,* XXII, ch. 20 (CCSL xlviii, 841); *The City of God* (Dods, 845).

[437] For this sevenfold listing, see *Sermo* 49 of Pseudo-Augustine, *Sermones ad fratres in eremo* (PL 40: 1333). The citation is not verbatim.

[438] This is a paraphrase of Anselm, *Proslogion*, ch. XXV (Schmitt I, 1118); *Proslogion* (Davies and Evans, 102).

[439] Rom 7:24.

desire is so strong that in some way their contemplation is impeded and retarded.[440] Thus Bernard says:

O miserable flesh, putrid and loathsome! Whence comes this glory to you, such that the holy souls, whom God has signed with his image and redeemed with his own blood, should desire and hope for you, such that without you their happiness cannot be complete nor their joy fulfilled?[441]

Augustine:

When the soul shall have received, not this animal body, but a spiritual one ... it will have the perfect mode suited to its nature: obedient and yet in control, alive and life-giving. Then there will be ineffable happiness, so that what had been burden-some would now be glorious.[442]

22. O soul, think how glorious it will be for you, when you will be clothed with that new and splendid stole *adored with every precious stone*,[443] namely, your glorified body from which will shine so many precious gems corresponding to as many virtues now in your mind. Who is about to recount what great joy, what unbelievable glory, what incomprehensible praise you will have, because you

---

[440] See *Sancti Avreli Avgvstini De Genesi ad Litteram Libri Dvo-decim ...*, XII, ch. 35, Joseph Zycha, ed., CSEL xxviii [pars 1], 432 (Prague: Tempsky, 1894); trans. John Hammond Taylor, *The Literal Meaning of Genesis*, vol. 2 (NY: Paulist Press, 1982), 229.

[441] This is a modification of Bernard, *Sermo 3 in festivitate om-nium Sanctorum*, n. 2 (SBOp 5: 350); "Third Sermon for the Feast of All the Saints" (SBSermons, III, 365-66).

[442] See Augustine's *De Genesi ad Litteram* XII, ch. 35 (CSEL xxx-viii/1, 433); *Literal Meaning of Genesis* (Taylor II, 229). The citation is virtually verbatim and refers to 1 Cor 15:44.

[443] Sir 50:10.

have so bravely conquered your own body with the shield
of chastity and continence, because you have so strongly
battled against the world by fleeing from it and despising
it, because you have courageously resisted all inordinate
thoughts, affections, and individual movements [of
passion]? Consider, if you can, what praise you will have
from those whom you have encouraged to better things
by word and example! And what is more, you will receive
special and eternal praise for each and every virtuous
thought, word, and action.

§ V: Fourth, the Blessed Turn the Rays of Contemplation toward Those Things Which Are Above Them, and with the Three Powers of Their Soul Rejoice Perfectly in the Highest Good

23. *INNERMOST SELF.* Therefore, O soul, I advise you that,
after having practiced and been disposed and attracted
to the aforesaid, you now turn to your Author and to the
great joy that those blessed spirits have received from
God, so that you might diligently consider and realize
what Anselm says:

> how delightful is that Good which contains in
> itself the happiness of all goods, not such as we
> have experienced in created things, but which
> are as different as the Creator differs from the
> creature.... Whoever enjoys this Good ... will get
> whatever he wants, and whatever he does not
> want will not happen.[444]

The blessed life is easier to attain than to
describe; its course is without end, its use without

---

[444] This is an adaptation of Anselm, *Proslogion*, the end of ch.
XXIV and the beginning of ch. XXV (Schmitt I, 118); *Proslogion* (Davies and Evans, 101).

boredom, its nourishment without food ... a new happiness is always generated from previous and perpetual joys, continual felicity without fear of its being lost,[445] and where all error is absent from the mind, all pain from the will, all fear from the memory ... where there is marvelous serenity, abundant sweetness, and eternal security without boredom regarding all goods. Thus Bernard.[446]

24. O soul, how happy and joyful, do you think, are they who constantly contemplate that mirror of eternity, wherein all past, present, and future things which pertain to that highest happiness are observed? Augustine: "When we shall arrive at that heavenly light of the Father of lights,[447] then we shall understand whatever [there is to know] in creatures."[448] Anselm: "Then the just will know everything that God has made to be known."[449] And "what is there that cannot be known by him who sees the One who knows all?"[450] Fulgentius: "As in a mirror a threefold vision is shown us, namely because we see ourselves, the mirror itself, and whatever is present, so also in the

---

[445] This is a modification of Caesar of Arles, *Homilia* 9 (PL 67: 1067B).

[446] This is a modification of *Sermo* 11, in *Cantica,* n. 6 (SBOp 1: 58); *On the Song of Songs* (Walsh, I, 73-74).

[447] See James 1:17.

[448] See Pseudo-Augustine, *De mirabilibus sacrae Scripturae,* I, ch. 7 (PL 35: 2159): "But if we will come to that light of the Father of lights, there will be nothing in creatures that we do not know."

[449] See Eadmer, *Liber de sancti Anselmi* ch. 59 (PL 159: 635B): "For then the just will know all that God has made to be known."

[450] See Gregory, *Dialogues*, IV, ch. 33 (PL 77: 376B): "What is it that they may not know there, where they know the one who knows everything." See *Dialogues* (Zimmerman, p. 230). See also Gregory, *Moralia in Iob,* II, ch. 3, n. 3 (CCSL cxliii, 61): "For what of those things that are to be known do they not know, who know the one who knows everything." See also *Morals,* I, 69.

mirror of divine clarity we know God himself, ourselves, and other creatures."[451]

O soul, whatever you might naturally desire to know,[452] set yourself to look at that mirror and [fervently] desire to study and read in that mirror, because having seen it once is to have learned everything. There it will be seen how stupid will be considered the theories of Plato, the philosophy of Aristotle, the astronomy of Ptolemy, because whatever of truth we learn there, it is but the smallest part of all those things of which we are ignorant. *Then you will see and abound, and your heart will wonder and expand.*[453]

25. *SOUL.* And what will I see?

INNERMOST SELF. The King of heaven *in his splendor.*[454] Bede: "The splendor of eternal glory is of such beauty and sweetness that even the angels, who are incomparably brighter than the sun, can never get enough of it."[455] Then you will abound in the delights of that wonderful vision of divine brightness, you will marvel in a delightful view of it, you will grow in the perfect vision of all creatures. O wonderful and admirable contemplation! O joyful and ineffable view! It is all so rightfully said of you, O Lord my God: *One day in your courts is better than a thousand*

---

[451] This citation does not come from Fulgentius, but is a modification of Pseudo-Augustine, *De triplici habitaculo*, ch. 6 (PL 40: 996).

[452] See Aristotle, *Metaphysics*, book I, ch. 1, in *The Complete Works of Aristotle*, vol. 2, Jonathan Barnes, ed., Bollingen Series (Princeton, NJ: Princeton University Press, 1984), 1562.

[453] Isa 60:5.

[454] See Isa 33:17: "His eyes will see the king in his splendor."

[455] There is a slight parallel in Book III, section 1, *Homilia* 70, of Bede's *Homiliae subdititiae* (PL 94: 451A). This citation has more in common with Pseudo-Augustine, *De cognitione verae vitae*, ch. 8 (PL 40: 1012).

elsewhere,[456] *for a thousand years in your sight are as yesterday that is past.*[457] According to Augustine:

> Such is the beauty of heavenly glory, such the happiness of eternal light, that even if it were granted us to enjoy it for but an hour of one day, on this account alone the countless days of this life, filled as they might have been with delights and abounding in temporal goods, would rightly be despised.[458]

It is so beautiful and sweet, that once seen, nothing else is delightful; it conquers all [other] sweetness, rises above all disordered desire.

26. *Soul.* Is there still something else which delights our eyes, whose contemplation brings joy?

Innermost Self. O soul, although the aforesaid alone might suffice, even if there were no others, still there is one [vision] – passing over completely the happy sight of virtually innumerable others – which in a wonderful way brings joy to the minds of all the spirits and inebriates, as it were, every blessed creature with wonderful and unspeakable joy. It is to gaze upon the god-like clarity of that heavenly Queen and the glorified humanity of her most blessed Offspring. O soul, who can estimate the joy that stems from seeing that Mother of mercy, that Queen of piety and clemency, now no longer reclining with her little one crying in the manger, with whom as their lady all the choirs of angels associate, no longer worriedly fleeing with him from the face of Herod into Egypt,

---

[456] Ps 83:11.

[457] Ps 89:4.

[458] This is a modification of *De Libero Arbitrio*, III, ch. 25, n. 77 (CCSL xxix, 321); *On Free Will* (Burleigh, 217).

because he rose up to heaven and Herod descended into hell; no longer disturbed about all the things the Jews did to her Son, because *all things have been subjected to him*;[459] certainly no longer wailing, crying out and complaining: "Who will let me, my Son, die for you?"[460] – when she was standing near her only-begotten Son dying and hanging from the tree of the cross; now no longer lamenting tearfully as when she was given "the disciple for the master, the servant for the Lord,"[461] a stranger as it were for her only and most dear Son. But now she, who had been so miserable and full of sorrow on our account, is raised immeasurably above the choirs of angels and above every creature where she reigns with Christ her Son in the palace of the Trinity.

27. O soul, with a devout mind reflect how filled with sweetness will be your joy in seeing that Man the Creator of men, that Lady the mother of the Creator, Jesus our brother, once lost, abject and despised, but now found, returned, now reigning and ruling over all. *Oh, who would give me that I might see you as my brother nursing at my mother's breasts, so that I may find you outside and kiss you*[462] with lips of devotion, I would embrace you with arms of love, and *now no one would despise me,*[463] when I

---

[459] See 1 Cor 15:28: *And when all things have been made subject to him, then the Son himself will also be made subject to him who subjected all things to him, so that God may be all in all.*

[460] See 2 Sam 18:33: *And as he (David) went, he spoke in this manner: My son Absalom, Absalom, my son. Would to God that I might die for you, Absalom, my son, my son Absalom.*

[461] See Bernard, *Sermo in Dominica infra Octavam Assumptionis*, n. 15 (SBOp 5: 273): "John is given you for Jesus, the servant for the Lord, the disciple for the Master, the son of Zebedee for the Son of God, a mere human for the true God." See also "Sermon for the Sunday within the Octave of the Assumption" (SBSermons, III, 278).

[462] See Cant 8:1.

[463] Cant 8:1.

shall have led you into my chambers with the sweetness of most wonderful enjoyment! This is the vision that the devout Anselm desired when he said in his *Meditations*:

> O sweetest youth, when shall I look at you, when shall I appear before your face, when shall I be satiated with your beauty, when shall I gaze upon your desirable countenance at which *the angels longed to look*?[464]... Woe to the soul who does not love you, to the soul who does not seek you! If such a soul loves the world and is enslaved by sin, it will never be at rest, never secure. I beg you that nothing might please me without you, nothing be sweet, nothing pleasant, that nothing precious might "smile" at me unless it be you. Everything is vile except you. Whatever is contrary to you is annoying to me, and your pleasure is my undying desire. It is wearisome to be joyful without you, enjoyable to rejoice and weep with you.... O good Jesus, if it is so sweet to weep for you, how sweet will it be to rejoice with you.[465]

SOUL. I am now languishing with love to see my Lord God and Creator, the soul's desire. I am faint with love to gaze upon Jesus, my brother and redeemer. Wounded, I already groan with the desire to look upon the Virgin Mary. "Oh, when will I see my joy which I desire? When will the glory appear for which I thirst?[466] When will my consoler come for whom I wait? When shall I be inebriated

---

[464] See 1 Peter 1:12: *Into which the angels longed to look.*

[465] See Pseudo-Bernard, *Lamentatio in Passionem Christi*, n. 3 (PL 184: 770C, 184: 771AB) where the author has collected pieces of the following writings of Anselm: *Oratio* 19, *Meditatio* 14, n. 3, *Oratio* 2.

[466] See Ps 16:15: *I will be filled when your glory will appear.*

with the abundance of his house[467] to which I aspire?"[468] It is already painful for me to look at any creature, because [God's] beauty is incomparably greater from whom all else has proceeded.

INNERMOST SELF. O soul, wait with patience so that your desires might grow, because it is written: *A little while and you will not see me, and again a little while later and you will see me.*[469]

SOUL. What a long and drawn out "little while"! Although my merits might be "short," nevertheless my desires are "long."[470]

INNERMOST SELF. O soul, if indeed your desires seem to you "long" and great whereby you "burn" to contemplate the eternal brightness, with what great desire ought you to be aflame, do you think, at the prospect of perfectly loving the eternal Goodness and eternally possessing the supreme Majesty? If you do not love to the highest degree, how can you rejoice in seeing [God]? And if you should indeed see and love, and not possess with peace of mind, how would you remain happy?

---

[467] See Ps 35:9: *They will be inebriated from the abundance of your house.*

[468] This is a modification of Anselm, *Oratio* 2 (Schmitt, III, 9): "When will you, my consoler, come whom I await? Oh, when will I see my joy that I desire? Oh, that I may be filled when your glory appears, for which I thirst. Oh, that I might be inebriated from the abundance of your house, to which I aspire."

[469] See John 16:16. The Vulgate reads *iam non* ("no longer") while Bonaventure has *non* ("not").

[470] This is a paraphrase of Bernard, *Sermo 74* in *Cantica* n. 4, (SBOp 2: 242): "Let the word of my Lord be kept: it (the little while) is long and very, greatly, exceedingly long. Nevertheless, both things are true: both a short while for merits and a long while for promises." See also *On the Song of Songs* (Walsh, IV, 89).

There [in heaven] we will be at ease and we will
see; we will see and we will love; we will love
and we will possess.[471] He is the completion of
our desires, who will be seen without end, loved
without boredom, praised forever in perfect
happiness without weariness.[472]

Listen to what the devout Anselm has to say about all the
celestial joys at the end of his *Proslogion*. Pay attention
[carefully]:

How delightful that Good which contains the
happiness of all goods.... If created life is pleasant,
how pleasant is the Creative Essence! If the salvific
deed is pleasant, how pleasant the Salvation which
made everything! If wisdom concerning creatures
is lovable ... how delightful is that [wisdom]
regarding uncreated things![473]

Why do you wander about looking for created
goods? Love one Good as the source of all others....
If beauty delights you, *the just will shine like
the sun.*[474] If ... liberty or power, then you will be
like angels of God in heaven[475].... If a long and
healthy life, you have eternal health.... If satiety
or inebriation, you will be filled by the glory of the

---

[471] See Augustine, *De Civitate Dei*, XXII, ch. 30, n. 5 (CCSL xlviii,
866): "There we will be at ease and we will see; we will see and we will
love; we will love and we will praise." Also, *City of God* (Dods, 867).

[472] See Augustine, *De Civitate Dei*, XXII, ch. 30, n. 1 (CCSL xlviii,
863): "He is the completion of our desires, who will be seen without
end, loved without boredom, praised without weariness." Also, *City of
God* (Dods, 864).

[473] This is an adaptation of *Proslogion*, ch. XXIV (Schmitt I, 118);
Proslogion (Davies and Evans, 103-104).

[474] See Matt 13:43: *Then the just will shine like the sun in the
kingdom of their Father.*

[475] See Luke 20:36: *They will be equal to the angels.*

Lord and *they will be inebriated from the abundance of your house.*[476] If music, the angels sing there....
If company and friendship ... there is the society
of the blessed united in one will for all. If honors
and wealth, *glory and riches in his house*[477].... If
security and certainty, there you will have eternal
duration of all times.... O human heart, indigent
heart, heart laden with tribulations, nay more
buried with tribulations, how joyful would you be
if you were flooded with all these things! Examine
your inmost being to see if you can grasp such joy
as stems from such happiness.[478]

But if human beings are scarcely capable of
grasping their own joy from such happiness, how
will they be capable of the manifold and great joys
such as are possessed by the number of the elect
where each loves his neighbor as much as himself
and rejoices in his own joy as much as he loves [the
joys of his neighbors]! And so without counting, as
it were, he rejoices more over the happiness of God
than of his own or that of all the elect, because,
just as he loves God *with all his heart, with all
his soul and with all his mind,*[479] so one's whole
heart and soul and mind can never exhaust the
plenitude of that joy, because we will rejoice to the
extent we love and we will love to the extent we
know. Surely, *eye has not seen nor has ear heard*

---

[476] Ps 35:9.

[477] Ps 111:3.

[478] This is a modification of *Proslogion*, ch. XXV (Schmitt I, 118-20); *Proslogion* (Davies and Evans, 102).

[479] See Matt 22:37.

nor has it entered into the human heart[480] how much the saints of God will love and know you.[481]

I pray, O my God, that I might know you and that I might love you, so that I might rejoice over you for all eternity. And if I cannot fully do so in this life ... at least may my knowledge and love of you grow, so that there [in heaven], there will be the fullness of joy, for which now I hope and which there will be real. Lord Father, through your Son you advised us, nay you ordered us to ask and you promised to listen, so that our *joy may be complete.*[482] I ask you, O Lord, because of your admirable counsel whereby you advise us to seek and promise to listen – so that our joy may be complete – that my mind may reflect on it [this joy], that my tongue might speak of it, that my heart might love it, that my mouth might preach it, my soul hunger for it, my body thirst for it and my whole being desire it, until I might *enter into the joy*[483] of my God, who is three and one, *who is blessed forever.*[484] Amen.[485]

---

[480] 1 Cor 2:9.

[481] This is a modification of *Proslogion*, ch. XXV and the first paragraph of ch. XXVI (Schmitt I, 120-21); *Proslogion* (Davies and Evans, 103).

[482] See John 16:24: *Your joy may be complete.*

[483] See Matt 25:21: *Enter into the joy of your master.*

[484] See Rom 1:25.

[485] This is an adaptation of *Proslogion*, ch. XXVI (Schmitt I, 121-22); *Proslogion* (Davies and Evans, 103-104). Bonaventure concludes both *On the Perfection of Life* and the *Breviloquium* with quotations from the last chapters of the *Proslogion*.

Prologue
Commentary on Book II of
The Sentences

Commentarius in II Librum Sententiarum

COMMENTARY ON BOOK II OF THE SENTENCES[1]

PROLOGUE

Only this have I found out: God made humankind[2] straight, and human beings have entangled themselves in endless questioning.[3]

INTRODUCTION

1. To anyone who carefully considers this passage from Ecclesiastes, it will become apparent that the whole import and ambit of the present book is directed toward what the Wise Man proposes in the aforesaid passage. Since he had tried all manner of things to reach wisdom and had more often failed than succeeded, he finally admitted that he had found out that *God had made humankind straight* and so forth.

This text contains two elements, namely that humankind's right formation and uprightness is from God,[4] and this is alluded to when it is said that God made humankind straight. The other element is the fact that humankind's miserable deviation comes from itself,

---

[1] The Latin text is Bonaventure's Prooemium, *Commentarius in II librum Sententiarum,* Opera Omnia II, 3-6.

[2] The Latin word *homo* is a common noun referring to any human person. The word is frequently used in this tightly argued text and is translated humankind or some variant.

[3] See Ecclesiastes 7:30. The Vulgate reads *miscuerit* ("mixed up") while Bonaventure has *immiscuit* ("entangled").

[4] The Latin *recta formatio et rectitudo* indicates not only a play on words but also articulates an important word image which seeks to convey a depth of meaning. See below n. 4 and n. 5; *On the Reduction of the Arts,* nn. 23-25 (Hayes, 59-61)

and this is alluded to when it is said that humankind is entangled in endless questioning.[5]

In these two elements are included the goal of all human comprehension, namely that humankind should know the origin of good so that humanity might seek this origin until it is reached and find rest therein; at the same time, humankind ought to know the origin and source of evil in order to avoid it. In these two elements are likewise contained the purpose of the present book which deals with two things, namely the creation of humankind and how it has gone astray.

2. HUMANKIND WAS CREATED UPRIGHT

Humanity's creation is touched upon when it is said that God made humankind straight. This is explained in Ecclesiasticus 17: *The Lord from the earth created humankind* – which refers to the body – *and made them in the image of God* – and this refers to the nature of the soul; *and turned humankind into it again,* which refers to the gratuitous gift that turns the soul toward God by virtuous habits.[6] This text shows that not only did God make rectitude possible for humankind by endowing it with God's own image, but God also actually made humankind upright by turning (*conversus*)[7] humanity toward God.

---

[5] The Latin is *et ipse se infinitis immiscuit questionibus* and is rendered "endless questioning" to emphasize humankind's failure to understand – to use "rightly" – the capacity to know and to love God their Creator, Source, and End.

[6] See Ecclesiasticus 17:1-2.

[7] The Latin *conversus* is rendered "turning toward" (conversion) to image and emphasizes humanity's fundamental relationship with God as well as to indicate the basic nature of sin itself ("a turning away from God" and "a turning toward" lesser goods as indicated in nn. 11-17).

Thus it is that humankind is upright when intelligence is consonant with the highest truth in knowing, when the will is in conformity with the highest goodness in loving, and the powers conjoined with the supreme power in acting. This happens when a human person turns totally toward God.

3. THE RECTIFICATION OF THE HUMAN INTELLECT

Consequently, humankind is first of all upright when intelligence is consonant with the highest truth. By "consonant" I do not mean that the mind is thereby completely filled [or all-knowing], but only by way of a certain imitation. If as Anselm says: "Truth is rectitude perceptible only by the mind,"[8] and only what is upright is consonant with rectitude, then when our intellect is consonant with truth, it is necessarily rectified. It is rendered consonant with the truth only when it actually turns toward the truth. Actual truth is defined as "an agreement between a thing and the intellect."[9] Once our intelligence is turned to the truth, it is "made true" and consequently consonant with the truth, and when consonant with rectitude, it is rectified. Thus, "without truth no one judges correctly," as is said in the book *De vera religione*,[10] and the person who looks to the truth judges rightly, as the Lord said to Simon in Luke 7: *You have judged rightly*,[11] that is, you have decreed rightly.

---

[8] See *De Veritate*, ch. 11 (Schmitt, I, 191); *On Truth*, ch. 11 (Davies and Evans, 166). The citation is verbatim.

[9] This definition, although often attributed to Aristotle, is from Averroes. See Opera Omnia (I:707, n. 5).

[10] This is a modification of Augustine; see *De Vera Religione*, XXXI, n. 57 (CCSL xxxii, 224); *Of True Religion*, book XXXI, n. 57 in *Augustine: Earlier Writings*, John H.S. Burleigh, trans., LChC, vol. VI (Philadelphia: Westminster Press, 1953), 254.

[11] Luke 7:43.

4. THE RECTIFICATION OF THE HUMAN WILL

Similarly, humankind is rectified when the will is in conformity with the highest goodness. Highest goodness is the highest equity or justice. A human person is better to the extent that the person is more just. As Anselm says: "Justice is the rectitude of the will."[12] However, only what is upright is in conformity with rectitude. As long as the will is in conformity with the highest goodness and equity, it is necessarily made upright. Thus Hugh of St. Victor wrote: "Know, O my soul, that somehow by the association of love you are transformed to the likeness of the very one to whom you are joined by affection."[13] The person who loves goodness is made upright. And this is what is said in the book of the Song of Songs: *The upright love you.*[14] The upright are turned to your goodness and your goodness bends down to them. The soul experiencing this exclaims and says: *How good the God of Israel is to those who are upright in heart.*[15] And because only the upright experience this, therefore: *Praise from the upright is fitting.*[16]

5. THE RECTIFICATION OF HUMAN POWER

Moreover, humankind is made upright when its powers are conjoined to the highest power.[17] The upright

---

[12] See *De Veritate*, ch. 12 (Schmitt, I,196); *On Truth*, ch. 12 (Davies and Evans, 167). See also *On Free Will*, ch. 3 (Davies and Evans, 179).

[13] QuarEd indicate (p. 4, n 8) that this citation comes from *Soliloquium de arrha animae,* but give no specific reference. See PL 176: 951-70; *Earnest Money* (Herbert, 16).

[14] Cant 1:3.

[15] Ps 72:1.

[16] Ps 32:1.

[17] The primary meaning of the Latin *virtus* is power, the strength or ability to act. The person who acts rightly (virtuously) is understood

is a mean between extremes.[18] The extremes are the first and the last, the alpha and the omega, the beginning and end.[19] The mean between these is action whereby the agent attains his goal. Hence, a virtue is upright whose action comes from the first principle and tends toward the final goal. Since therefore divine power does everything and does so on account of God, this is why the divine power is most righteous in acting. Nothing is conjoined to the upright except the upright. Consequently, when our powers are conjoined to the highest power, they are undoubtedly rectified. This is why a humankind is not only upright, but ruler and king,[20] as is intimated in Deuteronomy: *And he will be king with the most upright, the princes of the people having been assembled with the tribes of Israel.*[21] This will happen in heaven when our powers will be conjoined to the divine power. Then we will be in full control of our powers, as God is of his. And thus all are kings and all are promised the kingdom of heaven.

6. THE RECTITUDE OF HUMANKIND IS IN ITS TURNING

Thus God made humanity upright when God made it to be turned toward God. In humanity's turning to

---

to be developing those strengths of character which reflect a right relationship with God, the source of all power.

[18] Plato, Parmenides, 137 in *Parmenides: Lessons, Translation and Explanation of Plato's Parmenides*, trans. Kenneth Sayre (Notre Dame, IN: University of Notre Dame Press, 1996), 140-41. The Latin *medium* (mean) or *medio* (middle) in the next section has important neo-Platonic and metaphysical meaning for Bonaventure. It implies much more than an arithmetic mean or a fixed point as the English words "mean" and "middle" more typically convey.

[19] See Rev 22:13: "I am the alpha and the omega, the first and the last, the beginning and the end."

[20] Bonaventure employs a play on words: *rectus* ("upright"), *rector* ("ruler"), *rex* ("king").

[21] Deut 33:5.

God, human beings were not only made rectified with respect to what is above, but also with respect to what is below. Humankind stands in the middle, and as long as humanity is turned toward and subject to God, then all other things are subject to humankind. Thus God subjected every created truth to be judged by the human intellect, every good to human affections to be used, and every power to humanity's power to be governed.

7. THE TURNING OF THE HUMAN INTELLECT

Thus it is that from the fact that the intelligence is turned toward divine truth that it can lay claim to wisdom whereby everything is judged, as we read in Wisdom: *He has given me knowledge of all existing things, that I might know the organization of the universe and the force of its elements. The beginning and the end and the midpoint of times, the alterations of their courses and the changes of the seasons. Cycles of years, positions of the stars, natures of animals, tempers of beasts. Powers of the winds and thoughts of men, the uses of plants and the powers of roots, and whatever things are hidden and unforeseen.* [22] This is why Adam gave all things their names. [23]

8. THE TURNING OF THE HUMAN WILL

God subjected all things to the will of a human being to be used, so that humankind might turn everything to its use and utility. The Psalmist says: *You have subjected all things under his feet.* [24] The Apostle said to those who had converted and turned to God: *All things are yours.* [25]

---

[22] This is an adaptation of Wis 7:17-21.

[23] See Gen 2:20.

[24] Ps 8:8.

[25] 1 Cor 3:21.

9. THE TURNING OF HUMAN POWER

God also subjected everything to humankind's govern-
ance. Genesis reads: *Subdue the earth, and have dominion
over the fish of the sea and the birds of the air.*[26]

10. SUMMATION: HUMANKIND WAS CREATED UPRIGHT

The fact that the human person was created upright,
both with regard to what is above and what is below, is
alluded to in the passage: *Let us make humankind in
our image and likeness. Let them have dominion, etc.*[27]
Therefore, God made humankind upright, and as long
as human beings turned toward God, the human person
became like God, and thereby humankind was given ruler-
ship over all things. Thus humanity's upright condition is
obvious.

11. THE MISERABLE DEVIATION OF HUMANKIND: MANNER OF FALLING AND FALLEN STATE

The Scripture passage that follows shows humankind's
miserable deviation: *And human beings have entangled
themselves in endless questioning.*[28] In this text, we can
see the manner in which humanity fell and the state into
which it fell.

12. THE MANNER OF FALLING

The manner of the fall is to be found in the three things
expressed in the passage, which three things are likewise
to be found in sin. For in sin, there is a certain aversion or
"turning away," a certain conversion or "turning toward,"

---

[26] See Gen 1:28.

[27] Gen 1:26.

[28] Ecclesiastes 7:30.

and finally a loss or deprivation of the good. Conversion is expressed by "being entangled," aversion by "losing sight of the final goal," and deprivation by "questioning." The conversion makes one impure, the aversion makes one weak, and the deprivation makes one a beggar. All of this is expressed in the text: *Human beings have entangled themselves in endless questionings.*

13. HUMANKIND'S FALLEN STATE

We can also see the state into which humankind has fallen. Humankind fell from rectitude such that rectitude was lost, but not the tendency to rectitude; lost the habit but not the appetite for rectitude. Thus humankind lost its "likeness," but retained its image.[29] And because the appetite without the corresponding habit was retained, humans became worrisome seekers. Since no creaturely thing can make up for a lost good that is infinite, humankind desires, seeks, and is never at rest. Hence, turning away from rectitude, *human beings have entangled themselves in endless questioning*.

14. HUMANKIND'S INTELLECT IN ITS FALLEN CONDITION

Therefore, by turning away from the highest truth, intelligence has become ignorant and mixed up in an infinite number of questions by curiosity, as we read in Ecclesiastes: *There are people who day and night take no sleep with their eyes. And I understood that human beings could find no reason for all the works of God,*[30] meaning a rest that would satisfy its appetite and searching. Rather one question generates another and gives birth to a new contention, and so humanity ends up by getting bogged down in inextricable doubts. This is why Proverbs

---

[29] See Ps 38:7.

[30] Ecclesiastes 8:17.

says: *It is honorable for a person to distance himself from quarrels. But all fools are entangled in reproaches.*[31] Such are miserable human beings who, as we read in 1 Timothy, *study fables and endless genealogies,* etc.[32] They get involved in charges and countercharges because, as 2 Timothy says, *they are*[33] *always learning,* "but never attaining knowledge of the truth."[34]

15. THE FALLEN STATE OF THE HUMAN WILL

By its lack of harmony with the highest goodness, the will is rendered needy and becomes involved in an infinite quest through disordered desire (*concupiscentia*)[35] and cupidity, as is related in Proverbs: *Fire never says "enough."*[36] *The covetous person will not be filled with money,* as we read in Ecclesiastes.[37] Thus humankind is always seeking and begging. Likewise, disordered desire is never satisfied; rather it becomes involved in an unending search for pleasure. Wisdom says: *And all is confusion – blood, murder, theft ... guile, corruption, faithlessness, turmoil ... perjury, disturbance, forgetfulness of the good things of the Lord, besmirching of souls, changing of the birth process, instability in marriage, the disorder of adultery and impurity.*[38] These are the endless quests in which humankind becomes involved when the will was deformed by turning away from the highest good.

---

[31] Prov 20:3.

[32] See 1 Tim 1:3.

[33] The QuarEd note rightly (p. 5, n. 13) that the Vulgate does not read *sunt* ("they are").

[34] 2 Tim 3:7.

[35] As indicated above, the Latin *concupiscentia* is rendered "disordered desire." See the Introduction, p. 11 and pp. 33-34, and *Threefold Way,* ch. I, n. 4, note 17.

[36] Prov 30:16.

[37] Ecclesiastes 5:9.

[38] This is a modification of Wis 14:25-26.

16. THE FALLEN CONDITION OF HUMAN POWER

Likewise, by cutting itself off from the highest power, humankind's powers were made weak. Because of its instability, it became involved in an endless search. Thus humankind always seeks rest and never finds it. So Isaiah says: *The Lord has entangled*[39] *a spirit of dizziness within Egypt.*[40] This is the spirit of instability because there is nothing left to give humankind stability. Thus the sinful person will be "like the dust that the wind blows away from the face of the earth."[41] Therefore, the Psalm states: *If you turn away your face, they will be troubled. You will take away their spirit,* etc.[42] And so he will be *like dust that the wind blows away from the face of the earth.* Hence, just as dust cannot rest as long as it is in the whirlwind, so neither can our powers remain stable. Therefore humankind roams endlessly about, is constantly changing, and begging for relief.

17. CONCLUSION

Thus humankind has become entangled in endless questioning by curiosity when humanity fell from truth into ignorance; by cupidity when humanity fell from goodness into malice; by instability when humanity fell from power into impotency. And so, as we have noted from the passage in Scripture, we see humankind's creation and fall. And this is what I really see as being determined in this book.

---

[39] QuarEd indicate accurately (p. 3, n. 3) that the Vulgate reads miscuit ("mixed") while Bonaventure has *immiscuit* ("entangled"). Also, the Vulgate reads in medio eius ("in its midst") but Bonaventure has *in medio Aegypti* ("within Egypt"). Bonaventure modifies Isa 19:14 to make it correspond to his opening citation from Ecclesiastes 7:30.

[40] See Isa 19:14.

[41] See Ps 1:4.

[42] See Ps 103:29 which concludes: "... and they will fail and will return to their dust."

"On The Way of Life"

De Modo Vivendi

"ON THE WAY OF LIFE"[1]*

Whoever you are that wish to attain salvation through faith, hope, and love, you must submit yourself to three occupations: namely, to devout prayer, to an honest way of life, and to satisfactory confession, according to what [is written] in Micah: *I will show you, O human, what good is, and what God requires*[2] *of you: Namely, to make judgment, by* confessing truthfully, "and *to love mercy,*" dealing with everyone in a holy manner, "and *to walk solicitously with your God,*"[3] vigilantly persisting in your prayers.

1.   First of all, and before anything else, since we can do no good on our own, *we must pray to God*, according to what he himself said in Matthew: *Seek first the kingdom of God and his righteousness.*[4] But this prayer must be offered to God in a twofold manner, namely, in your words and in your thoughts, in accordance with the twofold division within humankind, according to this prophetic word: *My heart and my flesh have rejoiced in the living God;*[5] and according to this apostolic word: *Singing and chanting to the Lord in your hearts.*[6] For this prayer in words must be offered distinctly, attentively, and devoutly: distinctly, lest the words be mixed up; attentively, lest the mind might wander on to other things; devoutly, in order that the

---

[1] Bonaventure, *Sermones de diversis*, Sermo 1: *De Modo Vivendi*, Opera Omnia, IX: 723-25. This text has been translated by Oleg Bychkov, Ph.D. This is a tractate rather than a sermon. See also Saint Bonaventure, *Sermons De Diversis*, I, 50.

[2] The Vulgate reads *quaerat* ("asks") while Bonaventure has *requirat* ("requires").

[3] See Micah 6:8.

[4] See Matt 6:33: "But seek first his kingdom and righteousness."

[5] Ps 83:3.

[6] Eph 5:19.

mind might delight in praising God. And this [you should do] seven times a day according to the statutes of the Church and the testimony of David who says: *Seven times a day I have given praise to you*;[7] and this [you should do] in order to deserve the sevenfold grace of the Holy Spirit. At the same time, prayer in your thoughts must also be offered to God, of which the Apostle speaks to Timothy: *It is my wish that the men pray in every place, lifting up blameless hands, without wrath and contention,*[8] to God, for in any of our needs our mind must find refuge in God, as in a unique and foremost helper. This certainly happens by way of pure and affectionate moaning of the heart to God, according to what Gregory says: "To pray in a true manner is to resound in bitter sighs of compunction and not in words that are artfully arranged."[9] And, although this prayer must be offered to God most frequently, it must especially be offered on solemn and feast days established for this purpose, as well as on other days at established times, and especially in the morning and late at night, so that the "rain, both timely and late,"[10] might be absorbed, and the morning prayer would bring about directing grace, but the late evening prayer – correcting and cleansing grace.

However, this prayer must have two companions, one preceding and one following. For it must be preceded by meditation, according to what the Wise Man says in Sirach: *Before prayer prepare your soul*;[11] and this happens through meditation, of which the Prophet speaks in the

---

[7] Ps 118:164.

[8] 1 Tim 2:8.

[9] *Moralia in Iob,* Book XXXIII, ch. 23, n. 43, CCSL cxliii b, 1712: "For to pray in a true manner is to resound in bitter sighs with compunction and not in words that are artfully arranged." See also *Morals,* III.2, 507.

[10] See Hosea 6:3.

[11] Sir 18:23.

Psalm: *In my meditation a fire will be kindled*,[12] that is, the fervor of desire, without which no sacrifice of devout prayer can, nor should, be offered. A thanksgiving must follow, and to signify this every prayer of the Church is ended in the following words: "Thanks be to God." The Apostle exhorts the Colossians to this, saying: *Be earnest in prayer, be watchful in it with thanksgiving*,[13] for thanksgiving – which must be not so much verbose as affectionate – must make up the greatest part of the prayer. For this expression of affection arises – both in prayer and in thanksgiving – from an intent and concentrated meditation on our miseries and the mercy of God, both general and specific, common and particular. For no one asks ardently, unless one believes, [first,] that one is in need of the thing that is asked for, and, [second,] that one can be certain of being heard. Nor does anyone devoutly give thanks to God, unless one perceives the greatness of the divine gift as well as the lack of merit on one's own part. And this sacrifice of mental prayer is most pleasing and most acceptable to God, according to these words of the Lord from John: *The Father seeks such as those who worship him in spirit and truth*.[14]

2. And, since the ladder of Jacob is not the place to stand, but to ascend or descend,[15] therefore one must find time not only for a devout prayer, but also for an honest and holy way of life. And the holiness of the way of life consists in two things, namely, in the straightening of justice and the restrictions of discipline. And the straight

---

[12] Ps 39:4.

[13] Col 4:2. See *Threefold Way*, ch. II: On Prayers, esp., nn. 4-8.

[14] Bonaventure has inverted parts of John 4:23: *But the hour is coming and is now here, when the true worshippers will worship the Father in spirit and in truth. For the Father also seeks such to worship him.*

[15] See Gen 28:12.

way of justice consists in that the will is made straight in rendering to each one what is due them, such as reverence and subjection to your superiors, benevolence and mutual respect[16] to your equals, and care and compassion to your inferiors. For *each one must administer grace to each other,* in proportion to receiving [it], *as good stewards of the manifold graces of God,* according to the teaching of Peter the Apostle.[17] The same happens when the needy receive help, the ignorant education, the wayward correction, the wicked guidance, the afflicted comforting, the falling elevation, all the other wretched ones compassion, and all people peace and love, in which is contained the summit of all law and justice, according to the testimony of the Apostle who says: *The person who loves his neighbor has fulfilled the law.*[18] And for this reason he especially exhorts people to repay this debt, saying: *Owe no one anything except to love one another.*[19] For in paying this debt all debts are paid, especially when we love our neighbors "not only in words or speech," but also "in deeds and truth,"[20] when there is an opportunity. For when there is none, the will itself counts for the deed, according to Gregory, who writes: "The hand never lacks a gift when the enclosure of the heart is full of good will."[21] And he adds: "For good will means to fear someone else's adversities just as [you would] your own; and to rejoice at the prosperity of your neighbor, just as [you would] at your own progress; to believe that someone else's injury is your own; to consider someone else's gains as your own; to love a friend not for

---

[16] It is difficult to render the Latin *conformatio*, agreement, in this context.

[17] See 1 Peter 4:10.

[18] Rom 13:8b.

[19] Rom 13:8a.

[20] See 1 John 3:18.

[21] See *Homilia* 5, n. 3 of GGHG (CCSL cxli, 35). The citation is verbatim.

the sake of the world, but for the sake of God; and even to tolerate your enemy lovingly; to do to no one what you do not wish to suffer yourself; to deny to no one what you wish to be justly rendered to yourself; not only to assist the need of your neighbor according to your capacities, but to wish to render him help [that is] beyond your capacities."[22] And this is a correct description of good will, in which lies the rightness of justice that cannot exist without the sweetness of compassion.

But, in order to acquire, increase, and preserve this good will, the restrictions of discipline are necessary,[23] whose role is to adjust the spirit of our mind to a norm and rule according to our outer and inner [states]. For the outer discipline is achieved through the regulation of the senses and the things adjacent to them, but the inner discipline in the regulation of affections and thoughts.

So, first of all, anyone desiring to restrict oneself under the rule of discipline must restrain the sense of touch by the tightest girdle of chastity; the sense of taste through the moderation of sobriety; in equal measure the sense of smell through fleeing that which inflames the flesh by adding fuel to gluttony or lust; the sense of hearing through fleeing the delight of songs and sounds, as well as all useless words, and especially, those of slander and flattery; but the sense of sight must be restricted from seeing the desirable things, for, as Gregory says, "it is inappropriate for a person to gaze at that which he is not allowed to desire."[24] This is the first rule of discipline in restraining the five senses, which are like five windows

---

[22] See *Homilia* 5, n. 3 of GGHG (CCSL cxli, 35). The quotation is virtually verbatim.

[23] See above n. 2, pp. 361-62.

[24] See *Moralia in Iob*, Book XXI, ch. 2, n. 4 CCSL cxliii a, 1066: "Because a person should not gaze at that which should not be desired." See also *Morals*, II, 548-49.

"through which death enters," as the Prophet Jeremiah says,[25] unless vigilant discipline puts up resistance.

In conjunction with such guarding against the
senses, discipline must be observed also regarding those
things that are related to the external senses:[26] first,
that pronouncements or elocutions should be restrained
from any undisciplined word, be it slander, or flattery, or
gossiping, or buffooning, or obscenity, or cursing, or insult,
or swearing, or lies, or any "vain word of which" you must
"render account on the judgment day."[27] And this refers
not only to conversation, but also to signs and gestures.
The clothing of the body must be equally restricted, lest
it be superfluous, or too refined, or expensive, or with too
much ornament. Equally restricted must be laughter and
especially giggling. Also, it is most important that your
gait be restrained, lest it become loose and dissolute. Any
bodily gesticulation and vulgarity must also be avoided,
insofar as it can offend you or anyone else, according to
the teaching of the Apostle who says: *Keep yourselves from
every kind of evil.*[28] In addition one must preserve also the
control of discipline in regulating affections: especially in
order to avoid the affection of lust, lest the spirit desire
the delights of the flesh or embrace the transitory goods
or human praise: the threefold worldly lust. One must
also avoid the affection of anger, lest the spirit be stirred
up against someone: so that even if anger is appropriate,
it should be directed against vice so as to avoid animosity
toward a person. One must also avoid the affection of
sloth or sadness which usually results from worldly fear
and the weariness of [doing] good; and this no one can

---

[25] See Jer 9:21. Gregory also cites Jer 9:21. See CCSL cxliii a,
1065.

[26] See also *On Governing the Soul*, n. 8, p. 206-07.

[27] See Matt 12:36: *But I tell you that for every idle word that people
speak they will give an account on the judgment day.*

[28] 1 Thes 5:22.

avoid perfectly among the evils of our present life, unless one rejoices in the Holy Spirit. Afterwards, under the rule of this discipline, one must restrain even thoughts, so that the mind might be prevented from vain, filthy, and wicked thoughts. I call "vain" the thoughts about human activities; "filthy," the thoughts of carnal pleasures; "wicked," suspicious thoughts, and [the thoughts] of all sorts of harmful schemes.

However, we cannot maintain this fourfold discipline, unless our body is weakened by fasting, vigils, and work; our hand is exerted in [hard] labors or humble and fruitful activities; our tongue in praising God, our ear in hearing divine words; our eyes in holy and worthy reading; but our heart in holy and worthy meditations. But since it is most difficult to focus the heart on one object, God provided for it, that there be [some] good [objects] on every side for it to think of: above, the celestial things, that is, the heavenly homeland; below, eternal punishment; in front of it, the examples of the Saints; behind, its own committed sins; to the right, divine beneficence; to the left, divine judgment, and on all sides divine precepts that regulate us in all aspects,[29] and to which our mind must look wherever it turns, according to what the Prophet says about the just person: "the just one must *meditate on the divine law day and night.*"[30] And the Wise Man says: *What God has commanded you, think about always.*[31]

3. However, since there is no one who can preserve discipline and justice in such a way as not to neglect or omit anything, it is necessary to turn to satisfactory confession in which the confessing person must unravel

---

[29] Bonaventure, *Collations ... Six Days*, col. 17, n. 9ff. and col. 18, n. 17ff (de Vinck, 256 ff. and 275 ff.).

[30] See Ps 1:2: *And he will meditate on his (the Lord's) law day and night.*

[31] Sir 3:22.

all defects wholly, truthfully, and openly, without any veil of excuse, or secretiveness or obscurity; and, first of all, by retelling omissions that one made in respect to the things pertaining to God, primarily regarding prayer, as far as its double nature is concerned, that is, mental and vocal; then the defects in preserving justice in respect to one's neighbor; after that the omissions that proceed from the lack of restraint of the senses and the affections and thoughts adjacent to the senses, according to the fourfold description of the discipline explained above. And this confession must have two companions, namely, contrition and satisfaction. And let the confessing person grieve over all his offenses, not only the great ones, but also the small ones, for the Wise Man says: *The person who contemns small things will fall little by little.*[32] But let him beware of repeating his crime, even though [he be] grieving, but let him rather try to cut off the cause of, and the occasion for sin, insofar as it seems to be connected to himself through desire. For, according to the pronouncement of the Savior, *the eye that is an occasion of sin is to be plucked out,*[33] which should not be understood as referring to our bodily member, but to the occasion for sin, even though the cause of sin may seem precious to the sinner, just as the eye is a member that is precious to the whole body.

And the truthfulness of pure confession depends on the purity of prayer, and the reverse, for the closer someone approaches light, the clearer one sees whatever is deformed; and the better one wipes away deformities from one's sight, the sweeter [this] light tastes. Whence pure confession leads to prayer, just as the morning follows the evening. But prayer [is oriented] towards the light of contemplation as towards the [sun at] noon time, where every holy soul desires to rest with

---

[32] Sir 19:1.

[33] See Matt 5:29: *So if your right eye is an occasion of sin to you, pluck it out and throw it away from you.*

Christ, its bridegroom, through grace in the present life, until God appears in his glory, to which God may lead us, who lives and reigns forever and ever. Amen.

"ON HOLY SATURDAY"
Sabbato Sancto

"ON HOLY SATURDAY"[1]

Come to me, all you who labor, etc.[2]

1. At the beginning I say that through these words we are invited to the banquet, to the cross, and to the rest. We are invited to the banquet on Holy Thursday, to the cross on Good Friday. Now we are invited to the rest on this Sabbath of Sabbaths. For whatever was said at the beginning of the world about the observance of the Sabbath was said for the sake of rest. For after the completion of all his works the Lord rested on the seventh day. Psalm 15:9 proclaims: *Therefore,[3] my heart has rejoiced, and my tongue has exulted, and ... my flesh will rest in peace.* And in another place in the Psalms it says: *In peace in the Lord himself I will sleep and I will rest.*[4] Another place states: *Because you, O Lord, have specially established me in hope.*[5] And yet another scripture says: *Because you have not abandoned my soul ... at the end.*[6] Because the rest of this Sabbath is like that at creation it is said: *The Lord rested on the seventh day.... So he blessed ... and sanctified it.*[7] Although it is true that in creating things the Lord worked for six days and rested on the seventh, it is even more true with regard to the works of re-creation,

---

[1] See Sermon 21, "Sabbato Sancto," in *Saint Bonaventure, Sermons de diversis*, I, (Paris: Les Editions Franciscaines, 1993), 307-16. See also Opera Omnia IX: 267-70. The translation is by Robert J. Karris, OFM.

[2] Matt 11:28 concludes: *... and are burdened, and I will give you rest.*

[3] The Vulgate reads *Propter hoc* ("Therefore") while Bonaventure has *Propterea* ("Therefore").

[4] See Ps 4:9.

[5] Ps 4:10.

[6] This is an adaptation of Ps 16:10-11: *Because you will not abandon my soul ... at the end.*

[7] See Gen 2:2-3.

for the Lord worked for six periods of time[8] and then rested on the seventh. At the beginning of his Incarnation Christ was poor and in labors from his youth.[9] But he was especially in labors during the six days before his passion when he exposed himself to suffering and came to Bethany and preached. But on the seventh day, after he had suffered, he was placed in the tomb and rested. Today the most blessed soul of Christ made it happen that all the holy souls might be with him in the delight of eternal joy and the rest of the beatific vision. To this rest we are invited, and we should find it during our life. For every labor is for the sake of rest, and every activity is for the sake of eternal rest. Now there are four things by which human beings come to that rest. First, through exercise.[10] Second, through the groans of bitter compunction. Third, through the leisure of contemplation. Fourth, through the prize of eternal recompense. In the first rest begins. In the second it makes progress. In the third it is perfected. In the fourth it is perpetuated.

2. So first we must seek rest through the exercise of virtuous activity. For it is said in Exodus: *For six days you shall do all your works. On the seventh day you shall celebrate the Sabbath of the Lord your God.*[11] On six days you shall labor, that is, through the six exercises of the virtues. About these the Psalmist says: *Lord, who will dwell in your tabernacle? Or who will rest on your holy mountain? The person who enters without blemish and does justice. The person who speaks the truth in his*

---

[8] Literally: "The Lord worked for six five-year periods."

[9] See Ps 87:16: *I am poor and in labors from my youth.*

[10] Bonaventure will specifies this as "the exercise of virtuous activity" in the next section, n. 2 below.

[11] See Ex 20:9-10: *For six days you shall work and you shall perform all your works. But on the seventh day of the Sabbath of the Lord your God, you shall do no work.*

heart, who has not wrought deceit through his tongue. That person has not done evil to his neighbor and has not taken up a reproach against his neighbors. In his sight the malignant has been brought to nothing while he glorifies those who fear the Lord.[12] – This text sets forth the six things in which the soul must exercise itself to attain justice, namely, under the form of virtue, under the form of holiness, under the form of justice, under the form of truth. On these matters the Psalm speaks when it says: *The person who enters without blemish and does justice. The person who speaks the truth in his heart,"* etc. These are the things that purify human beings taken by themselves. But in addition, men and women must extend themselves to their neighbor through justice, since truth disposes a person to the light of truth. Now it is characteristic of this truth that it extend itself to the neighbor, so that it does not want to harm the neighbor and does not take delight in harming his neighbor. Therefore, it follows: He *is innocent with his hands*, etc.[13] That is, the person exercises himself innocently and attends to neighborly matters. Wherefore, the text states: *That person has not done evil to his neighbor and has not taken up a reproach against his neighbors.* After this the only thing that remains is to have love. And so the text concludes: *In his sight the malignant has been brought to nothing while he glorifies those who fear the Lord.* The person who fears the Lord is the one who *does not rejoice in the iniquity of another person, but rejoices in the truth.*[14] Sixth, the person must exercise himself with complete mercy, so

---

[12] Bonaventure cites Ps 14:1-4a verbatim.

[13] Bonaventure alludes to Ps 23:4, which, like Ps 14:1-4, deals with those who are worthy to be on the Lord's holy mountain. Ps 23:3-4 reads: "Who will ascend to the mountain of the Lord? Or who will stand in the Lord's holy place? The person who is innocent with his hands and clean of heart...."

[14] See 1 Cor 13:6: Love "does not rejoice over iniquity; rather it rejoices in the truth."

that he does not deceive in any way. And therefore, the Psalm text adds: *The person who swears to his neighbor and does not deceive, who does not put out his money for usury, and has not taken bribes against the innocent. The person who does these things will not be moved forever.*[15] This is the Psalm of rest, and about such Proverbs says: *The person who hears me will rest without terror and will enjoy abundance without fear of evils.*[16] But the person who does not want to obey the Lord will not have peace within himself. And for this reason the Psalm states: *Today if you hear the voice . . . they will enter into my rest,*[17] that is, the voice of virtue, holiness, justice and truth, innocence and love. Through these we arrive at the rest to which the apostle invites us when he says: *Let us hasten to enter into that rest,*[18] namely, through the works of the virtues. And on account of this Eccesiastes says: *Whatsoever your hand is able, do it earnestly.*[19] And about these paths of virtue the Psalm says: *You have made known to me the paths of life,* etc.[20] The children of Israel did not enter the promised land because they did not exercise themselves in the paths of the virtues. – Now it is evident how we will arrive at rest through the exercise of virtuous activity.

3. But since men and women sometimes stumble or lose their way, it is necessary that there be a second way which arrives at rest through the groans of bitter compunction. For *all our justices are like the rag of a*

---

[15] Bonaventure quotes Ps 15:4b-5 verbatim.

[16] Prov 1:33.

[17] Bonaventure adapts Ps 94:8-11 by quoting their first and last lines.

[18] See Hebr 4:11.

[19] See Ecclesiastes 9:10: "Whatsoever your hand is able to do, do it earnestly."

[20] Ps 16:11.

menstruous woman.[21] There is hardly anyone who does not have sufficient reason to weep for his sins, and so the Psalm says: *Who will give me wings like a dove, and I will fly and I will be at rest.*[22] The song of the dove is a groan and signifies persons who exercise themselves with the groans of compunction, about which the prophet Isaiah states: *I will cry like a young swallow. I will meditate like a dove.*[23] When the dove found the olive branch, it returned to the ark,[24] that is, to its home, because rest is found in it. For Matthew states: *In the world you will find affliction, but you will have peace in me.*[25] The soul is the dove that does not experience rest away from the ark, and because of this the Psalm says to those who must fixate on an earthly occupation: *Who will give me wings like a dove, and I will fly and I will be at rest.* If you desire to come to the rest, you ought to have six wings. They are: shame, fear, sorrow, clamor, rigor, ardor.[26] – Shame should result from acknowledgment of sin, fear in advance meditation on final judgment, sorrow in considering damnation, clamor in imploring for relief, rigor in afflicting oneself, ardor in deepening one's desire. Upon these follow sleep and rest. – Wherefore, I maintain that the first wing that we ought to have is shame in acknowledgment of sin, so that men and women may blush on account of their sin. But there are some who do not blush. About them Jeremiah says: *You had the forehead of a … prostitute,*

---

[21] See Isa 64:6.

[22] Ps. 54:7

[23] Isa 38:14.

[24] See Gen 8:11.

[25] This quotation does not come from Matthew. See John 16:33: *These things I have spoken to you, so that you may have peace in me. In the world you have affliction.*

[26] With the last three words I have been able to duplicate Bonaventure's word play: pud*or*, tim*or*, dol*or*, clam*or*, rig*or*, ard*or*.

yet you would not blush.[27] Against such people it is said: "I am confounded and I did not blush,[28] because I have borne the reproach of my youth."[29] – The second wing is fear in pre-meditation on final judgment. This occurs when people consider that everyone will have to render an account and further that it is written: *A just person will scarcely be saved.*[30] Job observes: *I feared for all my works, knowing that you will not spare the offender.*[31] – The third wing is sorrow in considering damnation when men and women realize that they have squandered their time and the grace of the Holy Spirit and have offended God. Should there not be great sorrow then? For this reason it is said: *Be troubled with sorrow, O daughter of Zion.*[32] – The fourth wing is the clamor of prayer in imploring for relief. The Psalmist prays: *I cried aloud with the groaning of my heart.*[33] In another place the Psalmist pleads: *O Lord ... during the day I cried out to you,* etc.[34] And then men and women should beat their breasts. – The fifth wing is rigor in afflicting oneself. The Psalm says: *Since I am ready for scourges,* etc.[35] – The sixth wing is the ardor of desire to obtain the gift of the Holy Spirit. The Holy Spirit appeared in the form of a dove,[36] and the Holy Spirit is fire.[37] When men and women have these six wings, then

---

[27] See Jer 3:3.

[28] The Vulgate reads *erubui* ("I blushed"), Bonaventure has *non erubui* ("I did not blush").

[29] See Jer 31:19.

[30] See 1 Peter 4:18: *And if a just person will scarcely be saved, where will the impious and sinner appear?*

[31] Job 9:28.

[32] See Micah 4:10: *Be sorrowful and troubled, O daughter of Zion.*

[33] Ps 37:9

[34] See Ps 88:2.

[35] See Ps 37:18.

[36] See Matt 3:16.

[37] See Luke 3:16 and Acts 2:3-4.

the Holy Spirit overshadows[38] them to protect them against the heat of sins, so that they can say: *Under his shadow . . . I desired to sit, and his fruit was sweet to my palate.*[39] When human beings flee from the heat of sins and come to God, then they are at rest when they hear: *Your sins are forgiven you.*[40] And this is the second way of arriving at rest. Men and women travel along this way, even though it is sometimes rough,[41] because of a good bed. The bed is one's conscience. Some people lie on a good bed over the thorns of the cares and worries of earthly concerns.

4. The third way of arriving at the rest is through the leisure of devout contemplation. For Deuteronomy says: *Benjamin, most beloved of the Lord, will dwell confidently .... As in a bride chamber he will dwell all day long and will rest upon his shoulders.*[42] Benjamin, son of the right hand, at whose birth his mother Rachel died,[43] is a figure of the person who is in ecstasy of mind through contemplation. This person will dwell confidently and will rest on account of the contemplation of wisdom. You must imitate this person by contemplating eternal wisdom, so that we may find rest. The wise person in Sirach compares wisdom to silver, because she is near

---

[38] See Luke 1:35.

[39] See Cant 2:3.

[40] Matt 9:2.

[41] See Ps 16:4: *For the sake of the words that came from your lips, I have kept moving along rough ways.*

[42] This is an adaptation of Deut 33:12: *And to Benjamin he said: The most beloved of the Lord will dwell confidently in him. As in a bride chamber he will dwell all day long, and between his shoulders he will rest.*

[43] See Gen 35:18: *And when Rachel's soul was departing for pain and death was now at hand, she called the name of her son Benoni, that is, the son of my pain. But his father called him Benjamin, that is, the son of the right hand.*

at hand to be found: *Behold with your eyes that I have labored a little, and have found ... rest for myself.*[44] It is said of Jacob in Genesis that he served seven years for Rachel, and the years seemed few to him because of the greatness of his love.[45] For this reason it is said in the Song of Songs: *If a person should give all his substance ... for love, he will regard it as nothing.*[46] It is necessary for a person to labor seven years to have rest. These seven years are the seven stages of contemplation that blessed Bernard expressed in one way,[47] Richard of Saint Victor in another,[48] and other holy men in still other ways. But a certain lay brother, who for thirty years had the grace of ecstasy of mind and who was most pure and a virgin and the third brother to follow after blessed Francis, said that the seven stages of devout contemplation are these: fire, unction, ecstasy, contemplation, taste, consolation, rest, and that glory follows as the eighth stage.[49] – I understand

---

[44] Although Bonaventure cites Sir 51:35, he also has 51:33-34 in mind: *I have opened my mouth and have spoken: buy wisdom for yourselves without silver ... for she is near at hand to be found.*

[45] See Gen 29:20: *So Jacob served seven years for Rachel, and they seemed but a few days, because of the greatness of his love.*

[46] See Cant 8:7: *If a person should give all the substance of his house for love, he will despise it as nothing.*

[47] See *De Consideratione,* V, ch. 14, n. 32 (SBOp 3: 493); *On Consideration* (Anderson and Kennan, 178-79) where Bernard has four stages: to wonder at God's majesty; to behold God's judgments; to recall God's beneficence; to await fulfillment of God's promises.

[48] See *Benjamin maior,* Book I, c. 6 (PL 196:70B). See Zinn, "The Mystical Ark", p. 161: "There are six kinds of contemplation in themselves, and within each there are many divisions. The first is in imagination and according to imagination only. The second is in imagination and according to reason. The third is in reason and according to imagination. The fourth is in reason and according to reason. The fifth is above but not beyond reason. The sixth is above reason and seems to be beyond reason. And so, there are two in imagination, two in reason and two in understanding."

[49] See *Dicta Beati Aegidii Assisiensis,* ch. 13, *Bibliotheca Franciscana Ascetica Medii Aevi* 3 (Quaracchi: Collegium S. Bonaventurae,

that the contemplative soul, that exercises itself so that it might come to rest, must pass through these ways. First let it burn and pass through the flaming and revolving sword and do this through a most ardent desire for the love of God and forgetfulness of self. And by this sword let it separate itself from earthly things. And this is the principle and the beginning that embraces all the others and is the strongest.[50] – The second stage occurs when the Holy Spirit flows upon the soul, and this is unction. And this unction is the sense of the consolation of the Holy Spirit descending into the fervent soul. – The third stage occurs when men and women feel themselves filled with the unction of the Holy Spirit to their inner depths. And then they are separated. And this is called ecstasy which is a separation from the senses, and the soul is separated from everything that is outside itself and within itself.

1905), 48: "There are seven stages in contemplation: fire, unction, ecstasy, contemplation, taste, rest, glory." See also *Golden Words: The Sayings of Brother Giles of Assisi With a Biography* by Nello Vian, translated by Ivo O'Sullivan (Chicago: Franciscan Herald Press, 1990), 83. In ch. 13 (pp. 48-49) Giles of Assisi gives his own explanation of the stages of contemplation: "Fire, that is, a certain light that precedes to illumine the soul. Then the unction of ointments. Thus, a certain wonderful fragrance arises and follows upon that light. About this the Song of Songs (1:3) says: In the fragrance of your ointments, etc. Afterwards, there is ecstasy, for after experiencing the fragrance, the soul is seized and taken away from bodily sensation. From this follows contemplation. For after the soul is thus separated from bodily senses, it wondrously contemplates God. Afterwards follows taste. For in that contemplation the soul experiences a wondrous sweetness. About this the Psalm says: Taste and see, etc. Then there is rest, because once the spiritual palate has experienced this sweetness, the soul rests in it. Finally, glory follows, since the soul glories in so great a rest and is refreshed with immense joy. Therefore, the Psalm states: I will be satiated when your glory appears." See also McGinn, *Flowering of Mysticism*, 75-78.

[50] Behind this interpretation of the first stage is Gen 3:24: "And God cast out Adam and placed before the paradise of pleasure Cherubim and a flaming and revolving sword to guard the way of the tree of life."

– The fourth stage occurs when the soul, having been separated in this way, returns to itself. Then it is apt for contuition of eternal light, when it has been separated from phantasms. – The fifth stage occurs when the soul has experienced a contuition of eternal light and then tastes its consolation. For Exodus states: *They saw the Lord God of Israel and ate*[51] and were refreshed. – The sixth stage is the embrace. After the soul sees how *good his business is,*[52] it strives to hold on and to be embraced and says: *I held him and would not let him go.*[53] And the soul can then say: *His left hand is under my head, and his right hand will embrace me.*[54] *The king brought me into the wine cellar and ordained love in me.*[55] *Prop me up with flowers. Surround me with apples, because I languish with love.*[56] Then rest is given to the soul, and it sleeps. Then the text continues: *I adjure you, daughters of Jerusalem, by the roes and the stags of the field, that you not stir or wake up my beloved, until she herself wants to.*[57] *The roes* are said to be the inferior powers of the soul that are controlled according to the rule of eternal light through the mediation of the superior powers. A roe has keen vision, but the stag leaps high and is very thirsty. This signifies that the contemplative soul must ardently desire the heavenly spouse and look for him with keen eye. Now you simple ones should not despair when you hear these matters, because you cannot have them, but it will be possible for you to have them later. We need

---

[51] Ex 24:11 reads: *And they saw God and ate and drank.*

[52] See Prov 31:18. Obviously, "business" is to be taken in a figurative sense.

[53] See Cant 3:4.

[54] Cant 2:6.

[55] See Cant 2:4: *He brought me into the wine cellar and ordained love in me.*

[56] Cant 2:5.

[57] Cant 2:7.

say nothing more except that when the soul has these six, then it is disposed to see glory. This is the rest that we should seek. And eternal wisdom says: *In all ... things I have sought rest, and I will abide in the inheritance of the Lord.*[58] If you want to be a tabernacle of the Lord of wisdom, yearn to have these dispositions. And if men and women do not want to attain this perfection, nevertheless it is a great thing that the Christian dispensation has those who do. All others who are not Christians are thirsty for this grace. So this is the third way of arriving at rest: through the endeavor of devout contemplation.

5. Fourth, the soul attains to rest through the prize of eternal recompense, and that rest begins now when the soul is separated from the body. About this rest it is said in Revelation: *I heard a voice from heaven saying to me: Write: Blessed are the dead who die in the Lord henceforth. Yes, says the Spirit, so that they may rest from their labors. For their works follow them.*[59] And this rest is consummated in the resurrection. For the soul desires the body, and the soul is held back until it is joined to the body, and then as a totality it is brought to heaven.[60] The Arab philosophers doubted whether the soul was the true perfection of the body.[61] But in reality, the soul and the body are one species, and the soul is the proper form

---

[58] See Sir 24:11: *And in all these things I sought rest, and I will abide in his inheritance.*

[59] Rev 14:13.

[60] See Augustine, *De Genesi ad Litteram*, XII, ch. 35, n. 68 (PL 34: 183); *The Literal Meaning of Genesis*, (Taylor, II, 229) where he argues that the resurrection of the body is necessary for the perfect beatitude of the soul because the mind (*mens*) is in "possession of a natural appetite for managing the body. By reason of this appetite it is somehow hindered from going on with all its force to the highest heaven, as long as it is not joined with the body, for it is in managing the body that this appetite is satisfied."

[61] The critical edition refers to Averroes, *De anima*, III, Text. 5.

of the body and is essentially drawn to the body like a proper act towards the proper material, since the soul is the proper act of the body.[62] Therefore, it is necessary that in whatever body the soul is as its proper form, it is drawn to the body and individualized according to the individuation of the body. And so the soul is not blessed with perfect blessedness except with its body. And this will occur in the general resurrection, and of this blessedness Jeremiah says: *My people will sit in the beauty of peace,*[63] for so great will the peace and beauty be that there will be nothing there that is not beautiful. *In the tabernacles of confidence,*[64] since no one will falter there. *And in rich rest,*[65] because the soul will experience such a fullness of delights when it is consummated in the resurrection. This is the blessedness. Behold the Holy Spirit ordained that Sunday would always be celebrated in place of the Sabbath. But the Jews, taking into account the works of creation and not of re-creation, and since Saturday or the Sabbath was the seventh day from the day of the creation of things, sanctify the Sabbath. Let us beseech the Lord that he may lead us to this peace. Amen.

---

[62] See IV *Sent*, d. 43. a. 1. q. 5. ad 6 (IV: 893-94).

[63] The citation actually comes from Isa 32:18.

[64] Isa 32:18.

[65] Isa 32:18.

"THE MONDAY AFTER PALM SUNDAY"
FERIA SECUNDA POST DOMINICAM IN PALMIS

"The Monday after Palm Sunday"[1]

Six days before Passover Jesus came to Bethany.[2]

1. In this passage the way of our salvation is morally designed for us by three points, that is, with regard to the righteousness of the journey where the text reads: *Six days before.* With regard to the benefit of the goal where the text says: *Passover.* With regard to the wisdom of the one directing the journey where the text has: *Jesus.*

2. Relative to the first point it should be noted that the six days mean the spiritual exercise of the six illuminations that the spiritual sun shines in the soul through the presence of grace. – The first is shame in remembering one's iniquity. The Psalm says: *All day long my shame is before me*, etc.[3] And this on account of the purification of contrition, confession, and deeds or on account of the magnitude of the sins because they are as great as the one offended is great. Or on account of the multitude of the sins since the sinner abused everything. Or on account of the turpitude of the sins, for the soul, although it had been very beautiful, has now become very ugly through sin. This day corresponds to the first day of creation, during which light was made.[4] For just as men and women do not blush at night, but during the day, the same holds true for the sinner. – The second is fear in consideration of the final judgment. The Psalm states: *From the height of the day I will fear*, etc.[5] That is, from the profundity of abysmal judgment, because it will

---

[1] See *Sermons de diversis,* I, *Feria Secunda Post Dominicam in Palmis,* 256-59; this translation has been done by Robert J. Karris, OFM.

[2] See John 12:1.

[3] Ps 43:16.

[4] See Gen 1:3.

[5] Ps 55:4.

be infallible, inflexible, inescapable. For nothing can be hidden from the judge. No one can revoke the sentence. No one whosoever can escape. This day corresponds to the second day in which the firmament was made that separates the heavenly waters from those below.[6] So through fear of the judgment men and women will be set in the firm foundation of the good and be preserved from earthly fluctuation. – The third is sorrow because of a consideration of damnation. The Psalm states: *All the day long I walked about in sorrow*.[7] And this on account of the loss of divine grace or friendship, on account of a wounded nature, on account of the loss of a former life. And this corresponds to the third day during which the dry land appeared, bearing green herbs and producing fruit.[8] For the human heart, as long as it is covered by the waters of carnal affections, can have no purity and cannot produce the fruits of good deeds. – The fourth is clamor in pleading for help. The Psalmist says: *Since I have cried to you all the day long,* etc.[9] One should cry out and invoke the help of the Trinity now. At another time the patronage of the Blessed Virgin. At yet another time the assistance of the entire Church Triumphant. And this corresponds to the fourth day during which the lights of the heaven were made,[10] because then the charisms of graces are being sought. And these are the charisms of wisdom with regard to devotion, discretion with respect to governing one's life, vigor relative to virtuous activity. These things are understood to be the sun, moon, and stars. – The fifth is rigor in extinguishing incentives to evil. The Psalm states: *For your sake we are killed all*

---

[6] See Gen 1:6-7.

[7] Ps 37:7.

[8] See Gen 1:11-12.

[9] Ps 85:3.

[10] See Gen 1:16-17.

the day long, etc.[11] And this by excluding and mortifying spiritual vanities, carnal desires, and temporal greed. And this corresponds to the fifth day, on which the fish in the waters were produced. If taken out of the water, they die. In like manner a religious, situated outside of the rigor of discipline, is immediately killed. – The sixth is ardor in desiring the spouse. The Song of Songs 2 has: *My beloved to me, and I to him who feeds among the lilies, till the day dawns and the shadows retire.*[12] This is the sixth day and the sixth hour, during which the spouse not only is loved, but also loves and shows his love in a wondrous manner. For during the sixth hour he suffered.[13] The Song of Songs 1 states: *Show me, O you whom my soul loves*, etc.[14] And this corresponds to the sixth day, on which humanity was made in the image of God and was set over the beasts of the earth and other creatures.[15] For through ardor and desire for God the soul is rendered godlike, and mind and reason, in as far as it is possible, dominate over all bestial movements of sensuality. – The seventh day follows afterwards, namely, the paschal day that can be called sleep, which is quietude in God that comes from contemplation and tasting divine sweetness. The Psalmist exclaims: *A day is better,* etc.[16]

3. Now it should be recognized that this occurred in Bethany, which is interpreted as the house of obedience, the house of affliction, the house of the gift of God, the

---

[11] See Ps 43:22. The Vulgate reads *omni die* ("every day") while Bonaventure has *tota die* ("all the day long"). Bonaventure's reading agrees with Ps 43:22 when it is quoted in Rom 8:36.

[12] Cant 2:16-17.

[13] See Luke 23:44: *It was now about the sixth hour, and there was darkness over the whole land until the ninth hour.*

[14] See Cant 1:6.

[15] See Gen 1:26-27.

[16] See Ps 83:11: *For one day in your courts is better than a thousand elsewhere.*

house that the Lord has showered with favors. Through this is fittingly understood the religious order of blessed Francis. It is a house of obedience, and in it there should be obedience without contrary wills, without murmuring in speech, without a delay in compliance. – Likewise, it is a house of abstinence. There chastity is offered to God, by which is understood something with substance, such as the avoidance of every carnal corruption both in deed and in will. There aids to chastity are offered such as multiple and harsh practices. There medicinal antidotes to chastity are offered such as flight from suspicious company. – But the house has been showered with favors by God through poverty. But when avarice or ownership dwells within a religious, he is not worshipping God, but an idol. Religious are obligated to true and perfect poverty. They should appropriate nothing to themselves, should possess or retain nothing, and should give or receive nothing without the permission of the superior. Let us pray, etc.

INDICES

SELECTED BIBLIOGRAPHY

Bonaventure of Bagnoregio
Latin Texts

Doctoris Seraphici S. Bonaventurae opera omnia. 10 vols. Quaracchi, 1882–1902.

S. Bonaventurae, *Decem Opuscula.* Quaracchi: Collegium S. Bonaventurae, 1965.

—. *Sermons De Diversis.* Volume I. Edited by Jacques Guy Bougerol. Paris: Les Editions Franciscaines, 1993.

Bonaventure of Bagnoregio
Texts in Translation

*Breviloquium.*WSB IX. Translation and introduction by Dominic V. Monti. St. Bonaventure, NY: Franciscan Institute Publications, 2005.

"Christ, the One Teacher of All." *What Manner of Man?* Translated and edited by Zachary Hayes. Chicago, IL: Franciscan Herald Press, 1974, 21-56.

Collations on the Seven Gifts of the Holy Spirit. Translation with Introduction and Notes by Marcian Schneider. MA Thesis. The Franciscan Institute, St. Bonaventure University, St. Bonaventure, NY, 1950.

Collations on the Six Days. The Works of Bonaventure V. Translation and introduction by José de Vinck. Paterson, NJ: St. Anthony Guild, 1970.

Collations on the Ten Commandments. WSB VI. Translation and introduction by Paul Spaeth. St. Bonaventure, NY: The Franciscan Institute, 1995.

Commentary on Ecclesiastes. WSB VII. Translation and notes by Campion Murray and Robert J. Karris. Introduction by Robert J. Karris. St. Bonaventure, NY: Franciscan Institute Publications, 2005.

Commentary on the Gospel of Luke. WSB VIII/1-3. With an introduction, translation and notes by Robert J. Karris. St. Bonaventure, NY: Franciscan Institute Publications, 2001, 2003, 2004.

"Constitutions of Narbonne." WSB V. Introduction and translation by Dominic V. Monti. St. Bonaventure, NY: The Franciscan Institute, 1994, 71-135.

Defense of the Mendicants. The Works of Bonaventure, II. Translated and edited by José de Vinck. Paterson, NJ: St. Anthony Guild, 1963.

Disputed Questions on the Knowledge of Christ. WSB IV. Introduction, translation and notes by Zachary Hayes. St. Bonaventure, NY: The Franciscan Institute, 1992, 2005.

Disputed Questions on the Mystery of the Trinity. WSB III. Introduction and translation by Zachary Hayes. St. Bonaventure, NY: The Franciscan Institute, 1979.

"Instruction for Novices." WSB V, 145-175.

Itinerarium Mentis in Deum. WSB II, Revised and Expanded. Introduction and commentary by Philotheus Boehner. Translated by Zachary Hayes. St. Bonaventure, NY: Franciscan Institute Publications, 2002.

"Letter in Response to Three Questions of an Unknown Master." WSB V, 39-56.

"Letter to the Abbess and the Sisters of the Monastery of St. Clare in Assisi (1259)." WSB V, 67-70.

On the Reduction of the Arts to Theology. WSB I. Introduction, commentary and translation by Zachary

Hayes. St. Bonaventure, NY: The Franciscan Institute, 1996.

—. St. Bonaventure's *De Reductione Artium Ad Theologiam*. WSB I. Translation and commentary by Emma Thérèse Healy. St. Bonaventure, NY: The Franciscan Institute, 1955. Original Edition.

"Sermon II, The Third Sunday of Advent." *What Manner of Man?*, 95-124.

"Sermon on St. Anthony." Translated by Brad Miluski. *The Cord* 36 (1986): 182-191.

Sermons on St. Francis. FA:ED 3. The Morning Sermon on St. Francis (1255), 508-516. The Evening Sermon on St. Francis (1255), 517-524. The Evening Sermon on St. Francis (1262), 718-730. Sermon on St. Francis (1266), 731-736. The Morning Sermon on St. Francis (1267), 747-758. The Evening Sermon on St. Francis (1267), 759-765.

The Major Legend of St. Francis. FA:ED 1, 525-683.

Other Primary Sources
In English Language Translation

Ambrose, Saint. *Hexameron, Paradise, and Cain and Abel*. Translated by John J. Savage. FC 42. New York: Fathers of the Church, 1961.

Anselm, Saint. "On Free Will." *Anselm of Canterbury; Major Works*. Edited by Brian Davies and G. R. Evans. Oxford University Press, 1998, 175-192.

—. "On Truth." *Anselm of Canterbury; Major Works*, 151-174.

—. *Proslogion*. Translated by M. J. Charlesworth. Notre Dame: University of Notre Dame Press, 1965.

—. *Why God Became Man and The Virgin Conception and Original Sin*. Translated by Joseph M. Colleran. Albany: Magic Books, 1969.

Aristotle. "Metaphysics." *The Complete Works of Aristotle.* Translated and edited by Jonathan Barnes. Vol. 2. Bollingen Series LXXI. Princeton, NJ: Princeton University Press, 1984, 1729-1867.

—. "Nicomachean Ethics." *The Complete Works of Aristotle.* Vol. 2, 1729-1867.

—. "Posterior Analytics." *The Complete Works of Aristotle.* Vol. 1, 114-166.

Augustine, Saint. "Of True Religion." *Augustine: Earlier Writings.* Translated by John H.S. Buleigh. LChC 6. Philadelphia: Westminster Press, 1953, 222-283.

—. *De Doctrina Christiana.* Translated by R. Green. Oxford: Clarenden Press, 1955.

—. "On Free Will" (*De libero arbitrio*). *Augustine: Earlier Writings.* Vol. VI, 106-217.

—. "On Music." *Writings of Saint Augustine.* Translated by Robert C. Taliaferro. FC 2. New York: CIMA, 1947, 153-379.

—. *St. Augustine On the Psalms* (*Enarrationes in Psalmos*). Translated by Scholastica Hebgin and Felicitas Corrigan. ACW 29-30. Westminster, MD: Newman Press, 1960 and 1961.

—. *Sermons.* 10 Vols. Translated and edited by John E. Roselle. Hyde Park, NY: New City Press, 1990-1995.

—. *The City of God.* Translated by Marcus Dods, New York: The Modern Library, 2000.

—. *The Confessions.* Translated by Maria Bouling. New York: Vintage Books, 1997.

—. *The First Catechetical Instruction* (*De Catechizandis Rudibus*). Translated and annotated by Joseph P. Christopher. ACW 2. Washington: CUA Press, 1968.

—. "The Happy Life." *Augustine of Hippo: Selected Writings.* Translated by Mary T. Clark. Ramsey, NJ: Paulist Press, 1984, 163-193.

—. *The Literal Meaning of Genesis*. Two volumes. Translated by John M. Taylor. New York: Paulist Press, 1982.

—. "The Nature of the Good" (*De Natura Boni*). *Augustine: Earlier Writings*. LChC 6, 324-352.

—. *The Teacher. The Free Choice of the Will. Grace and Free Will*. Translated by Robert P. Russell. Washington: CUA Press, 1968.

—. *The Trinity*. Translated by Edmund Hill. Brooklyn: New City Press, 1991.

Benedict, Saint. *The Rule of St. Benedict: Latin and English*. Translated by Luke Dysinger. Trabuco Canyon, CA: Source Books, 1997.

Bernard of Clairvaux, Saint. *An Apologia to Abbot William*. WBC 1, Treatises I. Translated by Michael Casey. Spencer: Cistercian Publications, 1970, 3-69.

—. *Five Books on Consideration. Advice to a Pope*. Translated by John D. Anderson and Elizabeth T. Kennan. Kalamazoo: Cistercian Publications, 1976.

—. "*In Praise of the New Knighthood*." WBC 7, Treatises III. Translated by Conrad Greenia. Kalamazoo: Cistercian Publications, 1977, 115-167.

—. "On Humility and Pride." *Bernard of Clairvaux: Selected Works*. Translated by G. R. Evans. Mahwah, NJ: Paulist Press, 1987, 173-205.

—. "On Loving God." *Bernard of Clairvaux; Selected Works*, 173-205.

—. "On Precept and Dispensation." WBC 1, Treatises I, CFS I. Translated by Conrad Greenia. Spencer: Cistercian Publications, 1970, 73-150.

—. *On the Song of Songs*. Four Volumes. Translated by Kilian Walsh. Kalamazoo: Cistercian Publications, 1976, 1979, 1980, 1981.

—. *St. Bernard's Sermons for the Seasons and Principal Festivals of the Year*. Three Volumes. Translated by

A Priest of Mount Melleray. Westminster, MD: The Carroll Press, 1950.

—. *St. Bernard's Sermons on the Blessed Virgin Mary.* Translated by A Priest of Mount Melleray. Chulmleigh, Devon: Augustine Publications, 1984.

—. *St. Bernard's Sermons on the Nativity.* Translated by A Priest of Mount Melleray. Chulmleigh, Devon: Augustine Publications, 1985.

—. *Sermons on Conversion.* Translated by Marie Bernard Saïd. Kalamazoo: Cistercian Publications, 1981.

—. *Sermons for the Summer Season.* Translated by Beverly Mayne Kienzle. CFS 53. Kalamazoo: Cistercian Publications, 1991.

—. *Sermons of St. Bernard On Advent and Christmas.* Translated by St. Mary's Convent, York. Manchester: R. and T. Washbourne, 1909.

Caesarius of Arles, Saint. *Sermons.* 3 vols. Translated by Sister Mary Magdeleine Mueller. FC 1. New York: 1956; Washington: CUA Press, Vol. II, 1964; Vol. III, 1973.

Clare of Assisi, *The Rule, The Letters to Agnes of Prague.* CA:ED.

Francis of Assisi. *The Writings of St. Francis.* FA:ED 1, 35-166.

Francisco de Osuna, *The Third Spiritual Alphabet.* Translated by Mary E. Giles. New York: Paulist Press, 1981.

Giles of Assisi, *Golden Words: The Sayings of Brother Giles of Assisi.* Translated by Ivo William. Chicago: Franciscan Herald Press, 1966.

Gregory the Great, Saint. *Dialogues.* Translated by Odo John Zimmerman. FC 39. New York: Fathers of the Church, 1959.

—. *Forty Gospel Homilies.* Translated by Dom David Hurst. Kalamazoo: Cistercian Publications, 1990.

—. *Morals on the Book of Job*. Library of Fathers of the Holy Catholic Church, Vols. 18, 21, 23, 31. Oxford: J.H. Parker, 1844-1850

—. Gregory the Great, Ephraim Syrus, Aphrahat. NPNF 2/13.

—. *Pastoral Care*. Translated and annotated by Henry Davis. ACW 11. Westminster, MD: Newman Press, 1950.

Gregory Nazianzen, Saint. Cyril of Jerusalem, Gregory Nazianzen. NPNF 2/7.

Hugh of Saint Victor. *Didascalicon; A Medieval Guide to the Arts*. Translated by Jerome Taylor. New York: Columbia University Press, 1961.

—. "Of the Nature of Love." *Hugh of Saint-Victor Selected Spiritual Writings*. Translated by a Religious of C. S. M. V. New York: Harper & Row, undated.

—. *Soliloquy on the Earnest Money of the Soul*. Translated by Kevin Herbert. Milwaukee: Marquette University Press, 1956.

Jerome, Saint. *Jerome: Letters and Select Works*. NPNF 2/6.

John Chrysostom, Saint. *Homilies on the Gospel of Saint Matthew*. NPNF 1/10.

Leo the Great, Saint. *St. Leo the Great Sermons*. Translated by Jane Patrick Freeland and Agnes Josephine Conway. Washington: CUA Press, 1996.

Leo the Great, Gregory the Great. NPNF 2/12.

Lothario Dei Segni (Pope Innocent III). *The Misery of the Human Condition: De Miseria Humana Conditionis*. Edited by Donald Howard. Indianapolis: The Bobbs-Merrill Co. Inc., 1969.

Plato, *Parmenides*. Translated by Kenneth M. Sayre. Notre Dame: University of Notre Dame Press, 1996.

Pomerius, Julius. *The Contemplative Life*. Translated and annotated by Mary Josephine Suelzer. ACW 4. Westminster, MD: Newman Bookshop, 1947.

Pseudo-Dionysius. "The Celestial Hierarchy." *Pseudo-Dionysius, The Complete Works*. Translated by Colm Luibheild. New York/Mahwah, NJ: Paulist Press, 1987, 143-192.

—. "The Ecclesial Hierarchy." *Pseudo-Dionysius, The Complete Works,* 193-259.

—. "The Mystical Theology." *Pseudo-Dionysius, The Complete Works*, 133-141.

Richard of St. Victor. *On the Four Degrees of Passionate Love. The Catholic Tradition*. Edited by Charles Dollen et al. Wilmington, NC: McGrath, 1979, 235-254.

—. "The Mystical Ark (Benjamin Major)." *Richard of St. Victor, The Twelve Patriarchs, The Mystical Ark, Book Three of the Trinity*. Translation and introduction by Grover Zinn. New York: Paulist Press, 1979, 149-370.

Seneca. *Seneca Ad Lucilium Epistulae Morales*. Translated by Richard M. Gummere. LCL; London: Heinemann, 1934.

—. "On Clemency." *Seneca, Moral Essays* I. Translated by John W. Basore. LCL, New York: Putnam's Sons, 1928.

William of St. Thierry. *The Golden Epistle, A Letter to the Brethren at Mont Dieu*. Translated by Theodore Berkeley. CFS 12. Kalamazoo: Cistercian Publications, 1976.

Secondary Sources and Studies

Bougerol, Jacques Guy. *Introduction to the Works of Bonaventure*, Translated by Jose de Vinck. Paterson: St. Anthony's Guild, 1964, 171-177.

—. *Saint Bonaventure: La Triple Voie, traduction française, commentaries et notes*. Paris: Les Éditions Franciscaines, 1998.

Cousins, Ewert. "Bonaventure's Mysticism of Language." *Mysticism and Language*. Edited by Steven Katz. New York: Oxford University Press, 1992, 236-257.

—. *Bonaventure and the Coincidence of Opposites*. Chicago: Franciscan Herald Press, 1978.

—. *Bonaventure: The Soul's Journey into God, The Tree of Life and the Life of St. Francis*. The Classics of Western Spirituality. Mahwah, NJ: Paulist Press, 1978.

Crowe, M. B. "The term Synderesis and the Scholastics." *The Irish Theological Quarterly* 23 (1956): 151-164.

Dreyer, Elizabeth A. "Affectus in St. Bonaventure's Theology." *Franciscan Studies* 42 (1982): 5-20.

Hayes, Zachary. "Bonaventure: Mystery of the Triune God." *The History of Franciscan Theology*. Edited by Kenan Osborne. St. Bonaventure, NY: The Franciscan Institute, 1994, 39-125.

—. *The Hidden Center: Spirituality and Speculative Christology in St. Bonaventure*. St. Bonaventure, NY: The Franciscan Institute, 1992, reprint 2000.

—. *What Manner of Man? Sermons on Christ by St. Bonaventure*. Chicago, IL: Franciscan Herald Press, 1974.

Hellmann, Wayne. *Divine and Created Order in Bonaventure's Theology*. Translated by J.A. Hammond. St. Bonaventure, NY: The Franciscan Institute, 2001.

Johnson, Timothy. *The Soul in Ascent: Bonaventure on Poverty, Prayer, and Union With God*. Quincy, IL: Franciscan Press, 2000.

Langston, Douglas. "The Spark of Conscience: Bonaventure's View of Conscience and Synderesis." *Franciscan Studies*, 53 (1993): 79-96.

McGinn, Bernard. *The Flowering of Mysticism*, Vol. III of The Presence of God: A History of Western Mysticism Series. New York: Crossroad, 1998.

Prentice, Robert. *The Psychology of Love According to St. Bonaventure*. St. Bonaventure, NY: The Franciscan Institute, 1949, 1992.

Schlosser, Marianne. *"Bonaventura, De perfectione vitae." Wissenschaft und Weisheit* 57.1 (1994): 21-36.

INDEX OF SCRIPTURE PASSAGES

Index of Ecclesiastical Authors

Index of Philosophers, Mathematicians, Rhetoricians